A Fan's Notes On Post-War American Roots Music

Bill Millar

MUSIC MENTOR BOOKS
York, England

© 1971-2004, Bill Millar. All rights reserved. First edition.

The right of Bill Millar to be identified as Author of this Work has been asserted in accordance with the UK *Copyright, Designs and Patents Act 1988*.

Every effort has been made to trace the copyright holders of material used in this volume. Should there be any omissions in this respect, we apologise and shall be pleased to make the appropriate acknowledgments in future printings.

Any references within this book to unauthorised (bootleg) recordings and illegal reissues of copyright material are included solely for the purpose of review and historical record, and should not be construed or interpreted as an endorsement of the practice of record piracy either by the author or the publisher.

All rights reserved. No part of this publication may be reproduced, stored in a retrieval system or transmitted in any form by any means, electronic, mechanical, reprographic, recording or otherwise without prior written permission from the publisher.

This book is sold subject to the conditions that it shall not, by way of trade or otherwise, be lent, resold, hired out or otherwise circulated without the publisher's prior consent in any form of binding or cover other than that in which it is published and without a similar condition including this condition being imposed on the subsequent purchaser.

Whilst every effort has been made to ensure the correctness of information included in this book, the publisher makes no representation — either express or implied — as to its accuracy and cannot accept any legal responsibility for any errors or omissions or consequences arising therefrom.

British Library Cataloguing-in-Publication Data
A catalogue record for this book is available from the British Library.

ISBN 0 9519888 8 3

Published worldwide by Music Mentor Books *(Proprietor: G.R. Groom-White)*
69 Station Road, Upper Poppleton, York YO26 6PZ, North Yorkshire, England.
Telephone/Fax: +44 (0)1904 330308   *email:* music.mentor@ntlworld.com

Cover by It's Great To Be Rich, York.

Printed and bound in Great Britain by Antony Rowe Ltd, Eastbourne, East Sussex

Foreword by Peter Guralnick

I'm still waiting to graduate from the University of Bill Millar. But I don't think it's going to happen anytime soon.

We have all been the beneficiaries of Bill's critical acuity, his passionate advocacy, his encyclopedic knowledge, and his clear-eyed disdain for sentimental bullshit, the basis for any true historian's considered methodology.

Who else can write with greater accuracy, precision, insight and wit — and cram it all into a concise package, replete with both eloquence and irrefutable logic?

No-one that I know.

The range of material presented in this book, the broad spectrum of music that is illuminated here, is staggering enough in the present day. But try to cast yourself back ten or fifteen or twenty years, to a time when Eddie Noack and Jerry Jaye and Jimmy Murphy were not household names, when Sonny Knight and Roy C were not celebrated in the pages of the popular press — I'm kidding. But my point is that Bill has been exploring the highways and byways, digging up information, and pointing us to the music of absolutely seminal (if often unknown) figures on the American musical scene for nearly forty years now. And it's time to admit that I didn't really know all about Lattie Moore before Bill introduced me to him in the pages of *Let It Rock* in 1973.

Bill introduced me to Sonny Knight, too, in person — along with all his rock'n'roll-loving pals at their regular Monday-night get-together at a London pub in 1982. He had already been helping me out at that point for quite some time — well, I like to think we had been helping each other out, but I'm not sure that I had anything to offer like his all-encompassing knowledge or librarian's gift for instant recall. In any case, meeting him and his friends in person was like being let in on a discussion that never stopped. And Sonny Knight (*né* Joseph Smith), on a visit from Hawaii to promote his novel, *The Day The Music Died*, was only the frosting on the cake.

I don't want to say too much here, because Bill will just object. He has never encouraged emotional self-indulgence either in his writing or in real life. But I can't let the opportunity pass without mentioning his unstinting generosity toward friend and (sometimes) foe alike. I know a lot of hoarders. I'm sure most of you do. It's the endemic collector's disease: if I possess it, do I really need to share it with anyone else? Well, Bill *does*. He may grumble a bit, he may question whether this is really all in a good cause (sometimes it's not) — but he is *always* prepared to share, whether it's knowledge, clippings, illustrations or — most valuable of all — his own thoughtful consideration and reconsideration of 'the truth'.

There is, of course, no such thing. But what is so extraordinary about Bill's writing, especially in this collection, is that he never gives up on the possibility of finding it. When you read Bill, you always know you are in good hands. Because he never communicates a conclusion lightly; he never takes a fact for granted; and he will never present raw, unexamined data. But even after he's finished with the writing, he's still not done — he will continue to worry the subject, he will continue to explore it, he will continue to offer up those same 'decisions and revisions' that T.S. Eliot once said 'a minute' might revise, but in Bill's case there is a lifetime on the line, and he is not prepared to give up until he has unearthed every last element of — the truth?

I worry that I may be making this all sound too hard: reading Bill Millar, I mean. Nothing could be further from the actual experience. Reading Bill is an unalloyed pleasure. He writes in a direct but elegantly aphoristic style, with all kinds of sly little digs and asides running through the otherwise placid surface. Bill's writing operates on so many different levels, but it is above all entertaining and informative. If I were looking for anyone to write a comprehensive history of early rock'n'roll, it would be Bill I would turn to first.

Not that he would accept. As you'll see in his introduction, he has long since announced his retirement from the fray. And perhaps he's right. But don't believe him for a moment when he protests that he no longer writes. The 'Millar's Tale' argues otherwise. And this book is living proof of how one person's idiosyncratic love affair with a subject, an improbable passion fuelled by a disaffected youth, can in its own way change the world. Or at least establish a university at which we can all profitably enrol.

Acknowledgments

I would like to thank the trusting folk who commissioned these bits and pieces in the first instance: John Beecher (Rollercoaster Records), Jonas Bernholm (Route 66 Records), John Broven, Carol Fawcett and Tony Rounce (Ace Records Ltd), Ashley Brown (*The History Of Rock*), Trevor Cajiao (*Now Dig This*), Bob Fisher (Sequel Records), Charlie Gillett (*Record Mirror*), Phil Hardy and Dave Laing (*Let It Rock*), Tony Rounce (then at Demon Music Group Ltd), Richard Williams (*Melody Maker*) and Richard Weize of Bear Family — the only record company on the planet which habitually puts documentation before profit.

Three names crop up in the acknowledgments to most of my liner notes: Colin Escott deserves co-authorship credit for rewriting some of my woolly opening paragraphs, and I couldn't have functioned without drawing on the phenomenal knowledge of Wayne Russell and Ray Topping. If you've written about rock'n'roll without consulting either you're likely to have been ill-informed.

Thanks go as well to the many writers, researchers, promoters and friends who supplied fax'n'info without a quibble: the late John Mal Anderson, David Barnes (British Archive Of Country Music), Paul Barrett, Bruce Bastin, John Berg, Bettye Berger, Dave Booth (Showtime Music Archives), John Broven, Kevin Coffey, Jim Dawson, Bob Embrey, Eric Dunsdon, Adam Finn, Rob Finnis, Derek Glenister, Peter Gregory, Peter Guralnick, Paul Harris, Martin Hawkins, Norbert Hess, Barney Hoskyns (rocksbackpages.com), Willie Jeffery, Peter B. Lowry, Dave Luxton, Ken Major, Seamus McGarvey, Steve Richards, Brian Smith, Chris Smith, Brian Taylor, Dave Travis, Ian Wallis, Valerie Wilmer, Cliff White, Richard Wootton and David Yeats.

I am especially indebted to Michael Lydon for suggesting that Music Mentor Books might like to publish 'A Bill Millar Reader' and to my son, Carl, who typed all those yellowing pieces which had faded beyond the scope of optical recognition software.

Finally, for technical support, proofreading skills, photographic research — in fact, duty above, beyond and every which way — utmost appreciation to my editor, George White, a man who strives for perfection in a corner-cutting world.

Contents

A Millar's Tale 13

1   HILLBILLY HEROES

1.1   **Eddie Noack:** *Right Place, Wrong Time* 17

1.2   **Roy Clark:** *Country Pickin' Good* 21

1.3   **Bob Montgomery:** *Bob And His Buddies* 27

1.4   **Marvin Rainwater:** *Back On The Warpath* 31

1.5   **Lattie Moore:** *I'm Not Broke, But I'm Badly Bent* 37

1.6   **Jimmy Murphy:** *Southern Roots* 45

2   ROCKABILLY RULES

2.1   **Carl Perkins:** *The Decca Years* 53

2.2   **Jerry Jaye:** *The Last Of The Rockabillies* 59

2.3   **Benny Joy:** *Rockabilly Party Crasher* 63

2.4   **Mac Curtis:** *Bluejean Heart* 75

2.5   **Johnny Carroll:** *Rock, Baby, Rock It* 81

2.6   **Bob Bertram:** *Hawaiian Hillbilly* 89

2.7   **Big Al Downing:** *The Story Behind The Story* 93

2.8   **Ray Campi:** *Eager Beaver Boy* 101

3 A SHOT OF RHYTHM & BLUES

3.1	**Etta James:** *Payin' The Cost*	107
3.2	**Albert Collins:** *Albert Collins Keeps His Cool*	113
3.3	**Herb Hardesty:** *The Sax That Rocked The World*	117
3.4	**Gatemouth Brown:** *The Country-Style Blues*	121
3.5	**Ivory Joe Hunter:** *Blues, Ballads And Rock'n'Roll*	127
3.6	**Stick McGhee:** *Drinkin' Wine Spo-Dee-O-Dee*	133
3.7	**Big Jay McNeely:** *Roadhouse Boogie*	139
3.8	**Young Jessie:** *Shuffle In The Gravel*	153
3.9	**Screamin' Jay Hawkins:** *A Most Singular Man*	161
3.10	**Big Jim Wynn:** *Saxman*	165
3.11	**Bull Moose Jackson:** *Handsome Is As Handsome Does*	169
3.12	**Sonny Knight:** *Confidential*	175

4 COTTON PICKIN' ROCK

4.1	**Jerry Lee Lewis:** *Rock's Greatest Entertainer*	185
4.2	**Major Bill Smith:** *Fort Worth Boogie*	189
4.3	**Charlie Gracie:** *Back From The Cold*	195
4.4	**Johnny & The Hurricanes:** *Blowing Up A Storm*	201
4.5	**Link Wray:** *A Link With The Past*	205
4.6	**Baker Knight:** *Good Knight*	211
4.7	**Roy Buchanan:** *Before And After*	215
4.8	**Dale Hawkins:** *The Shreveport Tornado*	225
4.9	**Mike Pedicin:** *Jive Medicin*	235
4.10	**Tommy Sands:** *The Worryin' Kind*	243

5	**DOO-WOP DAYS**	
5.1	*Acappella: Voices In The Night*	255
5.2	**The Platters:** *The Birth Of The Platters*	261
5.3	*Bring Back Those Doo-Wops*	269
5.4	**Cecil Holmes:** *Doo-Wop Survivor*	273
5.5	**The Velvets:** *The Complete Velvets*	279
6	**SOUNDS OF THE SWAMPS**	
6.1	*Rockin' On The Bayou*	287
6.2	**Rod Bernard:** *Hot Rod*	291
6.3	**Johnnie Allan:** *Cajun And Proud Of It*	297
7	**SOULED OUT**	
7.1	**John Richbourg:** *Southern Soul Man*	305
7.2	*Blue-Eyed Soul*	311
7.3	**Tony Orlando:** *The Last Of The Teenage Idols*	317
7.4	**Lonnie Mack:** *Memphis Wham*	321
7.5	**Roy C:** *That Shotgun Wedding Man*	327
	Index of People's Names	333
	Index of Songs & Album Titles	345
	Index of Films & Shows	357
	Illustrations & Photo Credits	358

A Millar's Tale

If I told you I grew up with rock'n'roll I'd be lying. I was placed in care in 1954 and remained there until 1963. I can barely remember hearing any music at all during the first five years. I was told that older boys had climbed out of a dormitory window to see a film called *Rock Around The Clock* but, if they did, they weren't going to discuss it with an eleven year old.

At some point my adoptive father's second wife told me to buy a record by Charlie Gracie. I'm skipping the Dave Pelzer-ish stuff here; I know it sells books by the shed-load, but rock'n'roll is a lot more interesting. Besides, I got to hear Charlie Gracie, so it can't have been all bad.

I definitely heard Larry Williams's 'She Said Yeah' on *Saturday Club*. As to how this epiphany occurred I'm not too sure — Saturday mornings were reserved for compulsory woodwork — but then nothing I say on a page could possibly explain my immediate and full-blown predisposition to music like that. The Caldecott Community was (and still is) a progressive-minded establishment always keen to nurture a child's grand passion in life. By 1960, Simon Rodway, the residential social worker (and life-long friend) had taken me to see Vince Taylor at Soho's 2i's coffee bar. Taylor couldn't carry a tune on a tray but he looked the part. (Incidentally, don't believe all you read; the 2i's was full of bohemians in beards and sandals.) After that, we saw every rock'n'roll package show within sixty miles of Ashford, Kent starting with Bobby Darin, Clyde McPhatter and Duane Eddy.

The Civil Service beckoned in 1964. I spent the first fifteen years in Immigration and Criminal Justice. I let in Bob Guccione, the founder of *Penthouse*, and trumpet-player Howard McGhee (his mid-40's recordings feature the first bebop solo by a tenor saxophonist). Efforts to deport the one Australian-born member of the Bee Gees were doomed when they reached No. 1. The Minister decided he could stay as he'd reached the peak of his profession. In truth, official work took up, maybe, four or five hours a day. The rest of the time I wrote articles for soul music fanzines, eventually graduating to *Record Mirror, Let It Rock* and *Melody Maker*. Tax-paying friends were not best pleased.

It all went pear-shaped in 1981. I was promoted to Senior Executive Officer (not as grand as it sounds) and posted to a mismanaged section which processed Parole Board dossiers. I was suddenly in charge of colleagues whose attitude to work was even more relaxed than mine. But the arrears reached vertiginous heights and I tried to shift them by getting in early, sharpening a clutch of pencils, chanting a psych-up mantra of obscenities and then scribbling frantically for nine to ten hours non-stop (longer at weekends).

The first heart attack was tolerable. The second, after a week in intensive care, was worse. Cue medical convention around the bed, shouts of 'Atrial flutter' and several shots of morphine. Nowadays, we know all about the debilitating effects of bypass surgery which leave 79% of British patients with some degree of negative brain function. Mine turned to blancmange. Confidence evaporated along with concentration. Reading for pleasure became impossible. One minute, I've got aspirations to become the Max Jones* of rock'n'roll. Next minute I'm fucked; the curtain had dropped on my alternative career as columnar rock journalist. No wonder they call it 'cabbaged' (Coronary Artery Bypass Grafts).

I asked for early retirement and the Treasury Medical Adviser told me to pull myself together. I turned down further promotion boards, demoted myself and returned to Criminal Justice where going to work had been such a leisurely treat. These moves, intended to assist recuperation, could not have been more bilious. I inherited the case of the four men eventually acquitted of killing a thirteen year old newspaper boy. There was scarcely a day between 1990 and 1995 when I wasn't thinking about the murder of Carl Bridgewater. Five long years beavering away with all the devotion of a monk. It wasn't healthy, but there was an unexpected bonus. I was so focused on that case I'd no time to consider representations on behalf of the notorious killer and rapist, James Hanratty. His papers lay festering in a cupboard until DNA techniques were sufficiently advanced to establish his guilt beyond any scintilla of doubt.

I finally got early retirement in 1995. If I couldn't cope with a column, I could still write liner notes providing I spent a few months on each one — longer on the more substantial Bear Family booklets we didn't have room for here. Even then, I was never without a fat pile of clippings for 'inspiration', so big nods of gratitude to such admirable writers as Jack Massarik (*Evening Standard*), Tony Russell (*Mojo, Jazz Express*, etc) and Richard Williams (*Melody Maker, The Times et al*).

---

* Melody Maker's respected jazz critic 1944-82.

1

HILLBILLY HEROES

1.1
EDDIE NOACK
Right Place, Wrong Time

There's an awkward feeling, common to rock historians, that life's too short and we don't have enough of it left. Too much credit has been unfairly distributed and a lot of stories haven't been widely told. It gets worse when you talk to performers in their declining years, to artists who evidently don't have long to go themselves. That's how I felt when I spoke to Eddie Noack who died in 1978 not long after a tour of this country. He was ill before he arrived and his performances were not well-received. The tour, which had taken him to far-flung corners, left him pretty weak and when I called the curtains were drawn (it was 4.00 pm) and there was no sign of life. Long before he answered the door of his pre-fab — somewhere South of Barking by-pass with nothing but gasworks and scrap-metal yards for company — I was wondering what sort of problems had brought this talented artist to such a lamentable state. There was a lot of sadness in the air.

DeArmand A. Noack was born of German-Welsh stock in Houston, Texas on 29 April 1930. He gained impressive credentials as a writer during the Fifties when he penned songs for Hank Snow, George Jones, Hank Locklin and himself. He'd dabbled in rockabilly with the air of someone who was embarrassed by a fad which he didn't think would last and, although he enjoyed a Top Twenty C&W hit with 'Have Blues Will Travel' (issued here on Top Rank), he spent the next decade and a half recording a form of music which had already died at the hands of both rock'n'roll and Nashville crossover pap. It was a death in spirit as well as form since — unlike rockabilly, blues or Cajun — very few still play or re-create hillbilly music today. It's a beautiful but misunderstood heritage abused in silly television serials and misappropriated by commercial 'outlaws'. Much has been written about the transition from black blues to white rock'n'roll and very little about the quality of hillbilly artists like Jimmie Skinner, Lonnie Glosson or Eddie Noack, whose music did just as much to suggest the vitality of a new movement long before Elvis and other star performers gave it dimension.

Whites and blacks in the Texas of Noack's youth were neatly divided in a society where everyone knew his place. The only blues he heard were filtered through the performances of Bob Wills and his own music was an extension of western swing. Pyjama'd and complaining of dysentery, he sat on the edge of his bed and recalled those years in a non-aggressive soft-spoken manner which probably contributed to his anonymity: 'My father took me out to hear Bob Wills at the Old Hitching Rack in Attucks, Texas. He'd drive a hundred miles to see Bob, who had twenty-three musicians with brass and reeds and a pianist who wore pieces of wood on his fingers to pound the piano. You've heard Bob call out: "The old piano pounder now!" — well, it's a literal.'

In 1949, Noack recorded for Bill Quinn's Goldstar, the first independent record company in Houston. His already inventive songs included 'Pyramid Club', about the get-rich-quick selling craze then rife in California, and 'Raindrops In A River', recorded much later by Wills himself. In 1951, he joined R.D. Hendon's Western Jamboree Cowboys and cut several sides for Bill McCall's 4-Star label. 'Too Hot To Handle', which brought Noack to the fore as a writer, was cut for 4-Star but leased to TNT after Sonny Burns covered it. Other versions of this — probably my all-time favourite hillbilly tune — included Jimmie Skinner, Gene O'Quin, Lattie Moore, a polka band and Frankie Miller, another neglected singer who's now selling cars in Fort Worth.

Noack joined Starday at the behest of Pappy Daily in 1953. The two men were very close but Daily's partner, Jack Starnes, onetime manager of Lefty Frizzell, had bought into Starday when Frizzell gave him $28,000 to get out of his life. Starnes saw hillbilly as a businessman's music and his palm-greasing attitude led to many battles over music publishing. He'd draw up contracts which had Noack and Sonny Burns as co-writers when Burns hadn't contributed so much as a comma. 'Well,' he'd say when Noack protested, 'I wouldn't put the damn thing out unless Sonny gave me his half.'

The records that did emerge — eighteen sides — are probably the finest examples of downhome ear-to-ear-grinning hillbilly outside Hank Williams's 'Rootie Tootie' and 'Move It On Over'. Cut at Bill Quinn's studio, the first featured the Western Cherokees, whose terrific but unknown pianist can be heard on 'Don't Trade Your Love For Gold' and 'Take It Away Lucky'. The accompaniment for later singles was provided by Buddy Doyle (steel), Ernie Hunter (fiddle), Ira Doyle (bass), Gene Doyle (drums) and ex-barber 'Doc' Lewis, another two-fisted pianist who'd played with Bob Wills and contributed honky-tonk sounds to a great many Starday records. His rippling interventions should be heard by those who wouldn't normally listen to Hank Williams, whose records featured little or no piano. Noack's songs — which were covered by George Jones, Jimmie Dolan, Phil Sullivan, Ernest Tubb and others — are fine too; that's to say they tell stories in the self-pitying whine detested by rock critics but much loved by followers of sincere, unvarnished Fifties C&W. It isn't rockabilly but, again, the bite and verve of these performances should appeal to the less rabid rockabilly fan.

On leaving Starday, Pappy Daily formed the D label and took

Noack with him. Much to Eddie's reluctance, Daily persuaded him to cut rockabilly under the pseudonym of Tommy Wood: 'Some of the English publications call my stuff rockabilly,' said Eddie, 'but they're really country songs with an uptempo beat. I'd gotten *Billboard* Spotlights on records that sold 185 copies and Pappy said: "We're gonna have to try something else." I thought: "That's fine by me, but you're not gonna use my name on it." I'm not hostile to rock'n'roll though... Y'see, I first heard Presley before I was drafted in the summer of '54 and I really liked him. A deejay named Smokey Stover got hold of 'That's All Right' and I bet you he played it fifteen times a day. At that time we were still in the golden era of country music — you don't have the fingers and toes to count the really huge artists — my band and every band had full houses. What Presley and Perkins were doing wasn't radically different. We'd been doing 'Blue Moon Of Kentucky' and 'Milk Cow Blues' for years, but I'd never heard them by a black artist — I'd only ever heard 'Milk Cow Blues' by Johnnie Lee Wills. Then RCA bought Presley and, of course, they changed him entirely. When I came out of the army you could scarcely make a living playing country music any longer.'

Noack was a stubborn man ('It dates back to my grandfather, who stuck to selling horses and mules long after automobiles came out') and he continued to record country songs with an uptempo beat for the rest of his life. After a spell on Mercury, he spent the Sixties label-hopping from one small company to another, never losing his ability to get a deal and always coming up with new but outdated material which dealt with subjects alien to crossover country: prisons, religion, strikes, depressions and tributes to Jimmie Rodgers. These themes were common enough in the hillbilly era when country music reflected the life of the poor farm-worker — Noack's beautiful song 'These Hands', a 1953 C&W hit for Hank Snow, is another tear-jerking example — but C&W had now moved uptown and the prevailing forces failed to accommodate his anachronistic approach. Some of his songs would have fared better in the Twenties when horrible ballads of death and murder were all the rage. 'Dolores', on the flip of 'Beer Drinkin' Blues' (K-Ark), has Noack warning his girlfriend not to go out alone because there's a maniac about. The singer then kills her by mistake in the dark. 'Psycho' explores similar territory. No-one covered those, but Eddie had better luck with 'Snowbird', about hobos who travel North during the summer. 'I didn't stop to listen to Hank Snow's version — I thought he'd covered Anne Murray's song. Since then we've gotten about ten licences for it with different companies, K-Tel, Pickwick and so on. I figure they want to do Anne Murray's 'Snowbird', have the sleeves made up and then find out that the publisher won't give 'em a low enough rate, so they have to turn to my song.'

To coincide with Eddie's tour, Look Records of Huddersfield released an album of new re-recordings (Look LP-6041). It contains all his most successful songs — and to that extent it's worth hearing — but too many musicians are present and it would have been so much the better for coming out twenty years before. Typically, Noack devoted his own liner note to Pappy Daily who'd produced all his finest records: *'All Pappy asked was honest effort and loyalty, and while I never quite made it as a big artist, I like to think I gave him those. I know he gave them to me in abundance.'*

Before the evening was over, we sat amidst the debris — the overflowing ashtrays, loose change, cowboy boots, pills and bottles — and listened carefully while Eddie free-associated on other people whose lives had touched his: Slim Whitman, who used to stutter so bad he wouldn't talk to anybody; George Jones who overdubbed his own voice on 'Why Baby Why' when Sonny Burns failed to show up ('Until then, Starday were putting Jones on Sonny's records to try and get *George* off the ground'); bald Bennie Hess who peddled hair-restorer and bootlegged his own Mercury records until the company found out ('Bennie has been a hustler, but not to his best advantage') and Pappy Daily's rock'n'roll star, J.P. Richardson ('I don't know,' said J.P. 'I've been doing some commercials for a lawnmower and I think I'll call myself "The Big Yazoo". 'I think,' said Daily, 'that "The Big Bopper" would be better.')

Back in Nashville, Eddie wrote to me about plans for a bootleg album of his own. He'd found a good engineer who'd make his old records sound like true stereo and he was more than happy to supply 'good liner notes with young pictures of myself'. Three months later — on 5 February 1978 — he died of cirrhosis. Ted Carroll and Ray Topping have now compiled the ultimate (and entirely legitimate) collection of Noack's brilliant Starday sides and the album should be available early next year. Until then, take my word for it: songs like 'Take It Away Lucky' and 'If It Ain't On The Menu' are as melodic and as lyrically compelling as any Nashville can offer today. Hear them once or twice and they'll dance in your head for years.

Originally published in *Melody Maker* (17 November 1979).

1.2

ROY CLARK
Country Pickin' Good

They'll tell you that Roy Clark is the highest paid performer in country music; a walking conglomerate with interests in real estate, cattle ranching, racehorses, broadcasting and advertising. He pilots one of his own planes to concert dates and grosses around $7.5 million a year. That much is true.

They'll also tell you that Clark has changed the definition of 'country singer' from an association with grass-chewing sub-normals to one of slick, professional, calculated wholesomeness; that he's a totally inoffensive, all-round, family-oriented entertainer who takes the country out of country music and carries what's left around the world, including a recent tour of the Soviet Union. This time, the reality is different.

The man *The Observer* compared to Val Doonican and Roy Castle isn't always that bland. *Makin' Music*, his new album with Gatemouth Brown (MCA MCF-3009) is simply unreal. He wails the blues like Lonnie Mack and it's full of superlative songs from the dawning of rock: 'Caldonia', Gate's 'Justice Blues', 'Talk About A Party' and 'J.H. *[Jim Halsey]* Boogie', which sounds like 'Guitar Boogie Shuffle' to me.

It's been a while since Roy Clark turned on the heat, but no-one should be surprised. Some of his early sides are wild enough to strip the enamel from your teeth and the kids down at Southgate's Royalty — London's foremost rockabilly venue — bop to his guitar solos without realising who's playing them.

Clark started out in the rock'n'roll of the Fifties; although that normally unshakeable influence no longer dominates his music, he certainly hasn't left it behind. We played him some of his old records and had a party ourselves:

'Hey Vernon, come here!' (Vernon Sandusky, Roy's rhythm guitarist: he played lead on Wanda Jackson's 'Mean Mean Man' and most of Big Al Downing's records, including 'Down On The Farm'.) 'Vernon, come and listen to this, man. This is me in 1958, can you believe it?'

'Hey Rodney.' (Rodney Lay, Roy's bass guitarist: he led Rodney & The Blazers — silver-sprayed hair, red jackets and sunglasses — who accompanied Don Downing on his Chan records). 'You gotta hear this, Rodney. Jeezus, this is so exciting!'

Roy loses all composure; he twangs an imaginary guitar and shouts the lyrics to 'Please Mr. Mayor' *[don't ban rock'n'roll]* with an ear-to-ear grin and total recall. Kathy Gangwisch, Roy's publicist, leans forward; she looks as if someone has dropped an ice-cube down the back of her dress: '*That* is Roy Clark?'

The centre of this commotion was born in the foothills of the Blue Ridge Mountains in Meherrin, Virginia, in 1933. His father raised five children during the Depression, but they moved where the work was and nobody starved.

'It's true,' says Roy. 'I don't have the background to be in this business, but I've heard blues and country all my life and something somewhere in all of that, I thought: "That's me." My family, who've now made two albums and appeared on *Hee Haw*, include my dad, Hestor Clark, who plays one of the finest old-time guitars in the world, and his brothers - my Uncle Paul on fiddle and my Uncle Dudley who plays rhythm mandolin with a beat that's unbelievable.

'They played the earliest music I heard because we didn't have radios or electricity. I was about eight when I first heard a radio and then it dawned on me: "Hey, somebody else in the world plays music." Bill Monroe became a great favourite, then Grandpa Jones and Hank Williams. Blues — I liked all of 'em, especially B.B. King and Ruth Brown.'

Gatemouth Brown passes by our table and Roy turns his head: 'Look, man, we're talking about black blues — you hillbillies can go in the back room.' They slap hands.

'Gatemouth is so hillbilly, he would sit around on the porch with his white friends playing fiddle while I was sitting around with my black friends playing blues. I moved to Washington when I was eleven, and by the time I was seventeen I worked the illegal, after-hours strip clubs among black musicians.

'No other town offered opportunities like Washington; it was a military town and a Government town with a lot of single girls, so you had a great deal of entertainment, maybe a thousand clubs with some of the best country musicians and some of the greatest blues singers. Every night was Saturday night.'

Washington was probably the biggest country market outside Nashville with numerous radio and TV stations promoting local artists. It was also home to Connie B. Gay, the country music entrepreneur who co-founded the Country Music Association, hosted radio WARL's widely-syndicated *Town And Country Time* and brought several important country stars to the city including Jimmy Dean and Patsy Cline. Roy Clark spent two years as a sideman with Jimmy Dean & His Texas Wildcats, who were managed by Gay.

In 1951, Clark made his first recordings for the late Ben Adelman, a concert violinist whose wife inherited enough money for him to buy some cheap equipment, which he installed in a building on New York Avenue. He recorded a great many local country acts including the Wray family, Jimmy Dean and Marvin Rainwater, but relatively few records emerged at the time.

Roy Clark & The Wranglers — Jimmy Dean (piano), Buck Ryan (fiddle) and Marvin Carrol (steel) — had a couple of basic hillbilly tunes on 4-Star and Coral, but most of their work surfaced on the kind of cheapo album that rots away in bargain bins and does nobody much credit: 'We recorded everyday forever — I did the second version of 'Release Me' in 1954 — but Ben was a pawn who wasn't that sharp. He leased the tapes to 4-Star owned by Bill McCall who — may he rest in peace — was a very cold, crooked man for whom music was a plaything, 'cos he also owned a clay mine that went into women's make-up. I thought Ben had destroyed all the stuff with Jimmy Dean and Link but all of a sudden... pow! ...it comes out on the worst kind of budget album.'

I mention 'Mr. Blues' and 'Hot And Cold', two of Marvin

Rainwater's finest rockabilly recordings on which Roy is reputed to have played the grainy lead guitar licks. He looks nonplussed for a second... 'Jesus, that *was* me. You guys are altering my mind.

'Marvin had a tree-trimming service; he bought a bent-in 1936 Ford pickup from a police sale and wrote on the side: *'Marvin Rainwater. Tree Surgeon — Let Me Work On Your Family Tree.'* He began coming into the bars around 1952 and I played on the first record he made. It was the night Hank Williams died. Marvin was utterly consumed by Hank and at 2.00 am, six hours after Hank died, he went into a Washington studio with my band and cut a tribute which was released through the Bluebird Friendship Club.'

In 1956, the year of 'Mr. Blues' (and Rainwater's 'Sticks And Stones' and 'Albino Stallion', on which our avuncular guitar hero also played), Clark formed his first rock'n'roll combo with Carl Nelson (piano), Marvin West (saxophone), Marvin Carrol (bass), and Flip Bacher (drums). Since the group played western swing and what Clark calls semi-heavy rock, they dubbed themselves the Versatiles and recorded 'Rock, Maggie, Rock' for Don Owens, a local deejay who owned the Blue Ridge and Owens labels. 'Rock, Maggie, Rock' (on Owens) was a hopped-up folk song ('Fats Domino was taking all the old songs and making hits out of 'em'), but it wasn't a hit for Roy.

His next recording ('Please Mr. Mayor' on Debbie) fared no better, although it was issued on HMV in 1958 and most rock'n'roll enthusiasts can hum the guitar solo — two parts Chuck Berry plus a seemingly original lick which Clark pinched from an old steel-player; Link Wray borrowed the same riff for 'Fatback' and 'Ace Of Spades'. Debbie was owned by Marvin Rainwater and his brother Ray ('it had a little circle on the label where you could stick a photo of the artist; we sold the record for fifty cents and charged a dollar for the photograph'), while 'Please Mr. Mayor', inspired by a riot at an Alan Freed concert in Boston, was written by Bobby Stevenson ('a very crude, semi-white guy: first time I met him I walked into a club and he was singing "Splish sploosh, I was taking a douche" ').

Records like 'Please Mr. Mayor' were said to have brought outraged howls of anguish from hardcore country singers who believed they represented a febrile threat to the Nashville establishment. Ironically, some of the best rock'n'roll records were made by the very artists whose over-produced and denatured MOR now disturbs the mainline C&W fan. Does Roy Clark, whose repertoire has ranged from 'Rock, Maggie, Rock' to Charles Aznavour's romantic ballads, have any patience with the country music traditionalist?

'Every bit... country has come a long way, but if you run too fast you're gonna forget where you come from. When a young kid says to me: "I haven't heard of Ernest Tubb", then I boil, I really want to preach. If it wasn't for him and those like him there would be none of us... I really hope I haven't lost my roots.'

By 1959, Roy was playing teenage hops from Washington to New

Jersey, but his reputation as a country picker was growing quickly and when Wanda Jackson wanted to put a band together for Las Vegas she chose Clark to front the Party-Timers, with whom he stayed for two years. He also played on Wanda's first Nashville session along with Dave Ronson *aka* Lyles (guitar), 'some curly-haired kid from Houston' (bass) and Tom Morgan (drums). These records — notably the album, *There's A Party Goin' On* — led to a solo contract with Capitol and a hook-up with the Tulsa management company of Jim Halsey, the man who secured prime TV slots for Tammy Wynette, Don Williams, the Oak Ridge Boys and Hank Thompson. Halsey began booking Clark in 1960 and, although chat show spots brought his client to wider attention, it was a residency on *Hee Haw*, the Number One syndicated programme in the US, which made Roy a national star in 1969. As co-host of the only nationwide TV show to feature country music, Clark exerts a powerful influence, which he's used to help both old-time pickers and the more purist newcomer like banjo-player, Buck Trent.

Clark's earliest Capitol discs are listenable items; they include a mess of slightly wild twist instrumentals and the tune he's now re-recorded, 'Talk About A Party', from the pen of Kent Harris who wrote 'Cops And Robbers' and 'Clothes Line' (*aka* 'Shoppin' For Clothes'). What he's done since then hasn't wound up in my household, but plenty of other people bought 'Tips Of My Fingers' (Top Ten C&W in 1963), 'Yesterday When I Was Young' (Top Ten C&W in 1969), 'I Never Picked Cotton' (Top Five C&W in 1970) and twenty or more hits of lesser magnitude. The 1976 Soviet tour (Riga, Leningrad, Moscow) was a sellout and *Pravda* linked the sounds of Clark's banjo with the spirit of the industrious but oppressed American worker. Commie-bashing is a popular sport among country singers, but Roy pushed songs and not ideologies: 'People are people and I don't go in for politics; if one person stands up and says "I like you, I believe," then it's worthwhile.' In fact, it's nigh on impossible not to like Roy Clark, whose mischievous grin and outgoing country friendliness would force a smile from the lips of the most hardened member of the Politburo. And even those who despise *Hee Haw* stayed tuned for Clark's instrumental skills — be they electric guitar, 12-string acoustic, fiddle, banjo or mandolin. Brimming with sparkle and enthusiasm, these retain a pleasing old-timey quality which stands out amongst the rest of the standard lounge fare. One thing's for sure; he's still a better picker than Val Doonican.

Note 1   This article originally appeared in *Melody Maker* (1 September 1979), but I've restored the sub-editor's cuts.

Note 2   Roy Clark's autobiography with Marc Eliot, *My Life In Spite Of Myself* (Simon & Schuster, 1994) doesn't mention his rock'n'roll records at all, but it's very readable and there are some wonderful early photos and newspaper clippings. 'I've never been ashamed of or embarrassed by saying I'm a hillbilly singer,' he declares. 'On the contrary, to me hillbilly is authentic American music and I've always been extremely proud to play it.'

1.3

BOB MONTGOMERY
Bob And His Buddies

'They're real collector's items. They were made when Buddy was only fifteen, when he was singing with Bob Montgomery. I taped them from the original discs and provided new modern backings by Jimmy Gilmer & The Fireballs. These recordings sound really good and should be available in Britain as an album with four more Buddy Holly tracks in the New Year. Most of them are Bob Montgomery songs, so these will be entirely new to Buddy's millions of admirers.' — Norman Petty, talking to Disc, 1964.

'Well, what can you say? It's not good at all... it's simply what we were when we were kids.' — Bob Montgomery, talking to me, April 1974.

Most rock'n'roll fans are aware of Montgomery through his connections with Buddy Holly, but his name is also tacked on to a number of giant pop and country hits, particularly in the Sixties. He's now a wealthy music publisher, a songwriter of some distinction and a pop producer's producer; a sort of de-urbanised Shadow Morton who makes the kind of silky, sugary — some say beautiful — productions that I don't usually find room for around the house. Now and again some rock'n'roll creeps in — *'Take me back to my rockin' days'* sang the Crickets on their last Montgomery-produced album — but, as far as Bob is concerned, that just ain't where it's at anymore.

The only son of a construction worker, Montgomery was born in Lampasas, Texas about 280 miles south-east of Lubbock, to which he moved in 1949. There, at Hutchinson Junior High he met Buddy Holly. Bob was twelve, Buddy nine months older. While Buddy Knox (from Dumas, 160 miles to the North) may not have heard any R&B before moving to New York after 'Party Doll' in 1957, Buddy and Bob tuned in to Shreveport's 50,000-watt R&B station: 'We heard a lot of pop and country but we also used to listen to Gatemouth in Shreveport, who played nothing but R&B. In fact, we were listening to R&B before it was ever hip to be into it — the real old true rhythm and blues: Lightnin' Hopkins, Louis Jordan, John Lee Hooker, Tiny Bradshaw and the Dominoes. There were black communities in Lampasas and Lubbock but they were too small to bring in any black performers. Lubbock had a Saturday night jamboree which would have local white musicians and usually one big star — Lefty Frizzell, the Wilburn Brothers or Webb Pierce. Hank Williams was popular with everyone — he came to town and my folks wouldn't let me go and he died after that, something I've always regretted — but our strongest influence was Lester Flatt & Earl Scruggs.'

Buddy and Bob began playing guitar together at school talent shows around 1951, and by '53 (the year Hank Williams died) they had secured a radio slot on station KDAV-Lubbock. Bob would spend a lot of time around Buddy's house — 'Baby It's Love' on *Holly In The Hills* was written with Buddy's mother — and when they could scrape together sufficient money they travelled two hundred miles to Nesman's studios in Wichita Falls where they made the demonstration tapes which comprised the bulk of that album. The personnel has, for obvious reasons, been more contentious than these lacklustre bluegrass sides (the absence of a mandolin is perhaps the only characteristic they share with Flatt & Scruggs) would normally demand. Here's Bob's version: 'Well, some of the instruments were added later and I don't recollect an organ or a third guitar, they must have been dubbed. I was rhythm, Buddy played lead and the bass-player was Larry Welborn, a kid from Lubbock who was even younger than us, about thirteen when we cut these in '54–'55. Later on, Larry played with Gene Evans and Niki Sullivan in the Hollyhawks who were managed by Buddy's father. The fiddle was Sonny Curtis, who we met on one of the jamboree shows where he was playing with his two brothers. Don Guess, who sometimes played steel guitar or bass with us, wasn't actually on those things.' *[Foremost Holly experts and researchers maintain that Guess probably played steel guitar on a couple and bass on others.]*

On 15 October 1955, Buddy and Bob opened the famed Presley show in Lubbock: 'We were doing KDAV shows every Sunday afternoon and Pappy Dave Stone, who owned the station, was also responsible for bringing shows to town, so we were a natural for opening the bill. Colonel Tom Parker was there looking over Presley but he put Buddy in contact with Jim Denny who, I think, managed Marty Robbins, who was also on the show. *[According to Bill Griggs, Marty Robbins was not on that show, but on another on the 28th of that month, which is where Eddie Crandall saw Buddy and informed Decca Records of Buddy's talent.]*

In January 1956, Buddy, Sonny Curtis and Don Guess went off to Nashville to record for Decca. Although Bob went too, the contract specified Buddy only and Bob didn't record. For a short while, he quit music for a day gig in a TV repair shop. A year later, Buddy travelled to Clovis with Niki Sullivan, Jerry Allison and Larry Welborn for the session that produced 'That'll Be The Day', which Norman Petty placed with Brunswick.

Bob followed Buddy to Clovis, where he helped Petty with the engineering ('We were converting the studio to three-track, heh') but also wrote some more songs including 'Wishing', 'Love's Made A Fool Of You' and 'Heartbeat' which, of course, Holly recorded. 'I was in the studio when some of these were cut. I remember 'Think It Over', 'Heartbeat' and 'It's So Easy'. There was a vocal group, the Roses, including Ray Rush, whose voices were recorded separately and then added on later by Petty, but otherwise there was nothing really spectacular about it. Maybe funny things went on that I didn't know about, but the studio was always very serious business to Buddy.'

During Bob's tenure, Petty also recorded the Fireballs' big hit instrumentals of 1959, 'Torquay' (Top Rank 2008) — titled after the English resort because lead guitarist, George Tomsco, liked the sound of the name, 'Bulldog' (Top Rank 2026) and several more on which Bob played rhythm guitar. 'Everything in Petty's studio was cut as a demo, just about. People were coming in, recording there and then submitting their stuff to a label. If Norman liked them, he would go all-out to interest a label in the demos. Same with me, I gave the songs I wrote to Norman and he would place them for me.' Jim Reeves cut 'After A While' and Buddy Knox did 'A Taste Of The Blues', which Bob also recorded himself (Brunswick 55157) — it seems to have been his only solo item: those by Bob Montgomery on Vault are not by him.

Late in '59, Bob and his wife moved to Nashville, where he continued to hustle his songs. 'Just before Buddy went to New York he tried to get me to go with him 'cause he was fixin' to start a publishing company and wanted me to run it for him. Buddy had tremendous drive, and if he wasn't active as a singer, he would have been into publishing or production by now. I knew nothing about publishing then and I didn't like the idea.'

The seed, however, was sown; after a number of successful compositions for Acuff–Rose (album cuts for the Everly Brothers and Bob Luman plus a Top Forty hit with Sue Thompson's 'Two Of A Kind'), Bob went out on his own as a publisher and independent producer. The first efforts included David Houston's 'Sherry's Lips' (Phillips International 3583) — Bob, who wrote the song, produced the disc with Fred Carter, who leased the master to Sam Phillips — and Mel Tillis, whose version of 'Wine' (Ric 158) was a Top Twenty country hit in 1965.

Bob also set up Talmont Music with erstwhile rockabilly John Talley and scored immediately with a number of his own compositions, particularly 'Misty Blue', a Top Five country hit for Wilma Burgess in 1966. A country soul standard, it has since been revived by Eddy Arnold (who took it to No. 3 on the Hot 100 in 1967), Ella Fitzgerald and, more recently, Joe Simon. Other big ones included Patsy Cline's 'Back In Baby's Arms' and 'Wind Me Up', a No. 2 in Britain for Cliff Richard in 1965.

After failing to interest Atlantic in country music, Bob went to United Artists as a staff producer in 1966. His productions helped change the face of country music from, in fact, country music to country pop; he constantly attempts to come up with a product (his word) that'll sell beyond the boundaries of the country charts: 'C&W is becoming indistinguishable from pop music and I've always tried to move it in that direction. I'm no longer country-oriented and I don't listen to R&B either. The R&B that we used to like is gone and I don't regret it. It wouldn't be interesting now, and that goes for country as well. We have to move country into the Top Forty. It's a business and you have to grow.' Efforts like these mirror exactly what Bill C. Malone envisaged when he wrote in *Country Music USA: 'Every change, every modification, every surrender to the 'popular' audience, and even the destruction of country music itself, will be rationalised under the general heading of 'progress'.*

It's not a rationale which readers will find totally attractive and, in all the glossy sophistication of Montgomery-style country pop, there is very little that appeals to me. But then Montgomery's productions simply burned up the charts. There was a long bunch of smash hits for Johnny Darrell, including the original recordings of 'Ruby, Don't Take Your Love To Town' and 'The Son Of Hickory Holler's Tramp', as well as 'With Pen In Hand.' Del Reeves did just as well and Bobby Goldsboro had a Number One pop and country hit with 'Honey'. The return of Buddy Knox with 'Gypsy Man' qualifies as one of the nicer moments, but the album of the same name with all the old friends — Sonny Curtis and Fred Carter (guitars), Jerry Allison and Jerry Carrigan (drums) — was pretty dull Nashville muzak full of soporific twin guitar sounds.

The nearest thing to rock'n'roll, and really as fine as you could expect of 1969, was Bob's production of Earl Richards's revival of 'House Of Blue Lights', a deep-voiced hunk of uncluttered boogie which made the Top Forty country charts. The ex-Cricket (alias Earl Sinks) had also recorded under other pseudonyms — Earl Henry (Dot) and Sinx Mitchell (Hickory) — but he kept with 'Richards' for half a dozen singles on United Artists, including two lesser hits with 'Corrine, Corrina' and 'Sunshine'.

In 1969, Montgomery formed two fresh publishing companies, House Of Gold with Bobby Goldsboro (they have 'Behind Closed Doors') and Passkey Music with Jerry Chesnut ('Another Place, Another Time', 'It's Four In The Morning' and others). Once again, he's an independent producer working with Bobby Goldsboro for UA.

Richard Williams recently panegyrised the sweet'n'icky Montgomery production of 'Summer (The First Time)'. And Bob is returning to Britain to size up the possibility of giving Peters & Lee ('Welcome Home' made the US country charts!) a 'completely new sound'. If you can't wait for that, there's better news in another Crickets album which should be out before the end of the year.

Note   This piece originally appeared in *Let It Rock* (December 1974), but it incorporates corrections which Bill Griggs of the Buddy Holly Memorial Society made to a reprinting in *Goldmine* in May 1981.

1.4

MARVIN RAINWATER
Back On The Warpath

'I could never get on with young people at all, not even my own children. To get them to accept me seemed impossible and now, after twenty-five years, little kids want me to sing 'Mr. Blues' or 'Boo Hoo'. I thought they wuz joking me.' Marvin Rainwater, 54 year old part-Indian and first-generation rockabilly, shrugs his burly shoulders and laughs at the ironies of the rockabilly renaissance: 'Y'know 'Boo Hoo' was cut in Ray Vernon's toilet when I was already a has-been. My voice was so bad, the record people from Warwick were making fun of me, treating me like a rag-doll and letting the dogs chew me up. They threw that record out the window and told me nobody would touch it. And now these young boys — they call themselves 'cats' — they come up and tell me to do it. They insist — sing 'Boo Hoo'. Once I get the beat going — *bonka chicka, bonka chicka, bonka chicka, bonk* — they're jumping up'n'down teaching me something I didn't know when I wrote the song. All of a sudden I can communicate with young kids. It's very strange.'

Marvin Rainwater may imply that he lacks the *gravitas* to be truly heroic but his admirers, long used to prising nuggets from obscurity, know differently. Although he's best remembered for 'Whole Lotta Woman' — a UK chart-topper in 1958 — rockabilly fans will point (with, I think, ample justification) to at least ten or fifteen classics. Blues like 'Why Did You Have To Go And Leave Me', on which Grady Martin contributes the bitter John Lee Hooker guitar riff; Indian folk ballads which are so believable you half-expect a feather or two to float out of the sleeve and, not least, a consistently fine legacy of rockabilly-cum-rock'n'roll stalwarts: 'Mr. Blues', 'Gamblin' Man', 'Hot And Cold', 'She's Gone', 'My Brand Of Blues', 'Dance Me Daddy' and more.

Until the appearance of MGM's *Rockabilly Collection (Volume Two)*, his finest records could be found only on expensive auction lists or hard-to-get bootlegs like CCL's four-volume set of *Rockin' Rollin' Rainwater*. This is no more than Marvin expects (he's an expert at self-disparagement) and it's time someone gave his flea-sized ego a boost.

Born 2 July 1925 in Wichita, Kansas, Marvin Karlton Rainwater played classical piano until a garage accident sliced off his right thumb. He took a mathematics course at Washington State University and then joined his father's logging crew in Oregon. He spent two years in the US Navy as a pharmacist's mate and, after the war, he worked as a tree surgeon until he nearly killed himself: 'I was trying to write a song while cutting out the top of a tree. I'd cut it off before I woke up and realised what I was doing. For the best part of a day, I was hanging upside-down by my safety-belt over 75 feet of concrete. That's when I quit tree surgery.' Moving right across the USA, Rainwater played the 'little bitty clubs' in Washington, DC alongside Roy Clark, Jimmy Dean, Billy Grammer and other country performers who were tied up with local studio-owner, Ben Adelman.

Rainwater cut over fifty songs in Adelman's studio and the first, a tribute to Hank Williams, was heard by Red Foley, which led to guest spots on the *Ozark Jubilee*. Most of the others were demos but Adelman sold them to 4-Star's Bill McCall, who leased them to a large number of budget labels. What I've heard I've liked, but Marvin is distressed by it all. 'That was really sick', he tells me. 'Ben had no right to sell them to McCall who was responsible for all my fifty or so bits of trash that came out on 99¢ albums like Premier, Crown, Pickwick, Spin-O-Rama... The public buys a record like that and then they hate me 'cos it sounds so terrible. I got a judgment against McCall for $50,000 and I never could collect a penny.'

One of Adelman's few legitimate sessions produced 'I Gotta Go Get My Baby' on which Mickey Woodward played steel, Wade Holmes picked lead guitar and Roy Clark doubled on rhythm and bass. Bill McCall released it on Rainwater Records in California and when it began to move he sold it to Coral in New York. Teresa Brewer racked up a million sales with a pop cover version and Justin Tubb outsold the original in the C&W field; as a songwriter, Marvin was now established in both markets. He was singing 'Gotta Go Get My Baby' on the *Arthur Godfrey's Talent Scouts* TV show when Frank Walker, President of MGM, tuned in and offered him a long-term contract. Walker, who'd helped develop the career of Hank Williams, thought Rainwater was the logical successor, but the music changed drastically and, instead of making the Country Music Hall of Fame, Rainwater acquired a cult following among those who like their hillbilly to be laced with rock'n'roll: 'Walker enjoyed cutting who he liked and what he liked,' says Marvin. 'He thought selling records was somebody else's problem. 'Tennessee Houn' Dog Yodel' was nothing more than a series of vocal exercises but the old man heard it and thought "I'll put that out!" He was a little senile I guess but he was a great person to work for as long as you didn't want to make any money.'

While the reference books (eg Joseph Murrells) list no fewer than five MGM million-sellers — 'Gonna Find Me A Bluebird', 'The Majesty Of Love', 'My Love Is Real', 'My Brand Of Blues' and 'Half-Breed' — Marvin refutes these statistics with a self-deprecatory grimace. He points out that, apart from 'Bluebird' (No. 22 in 1957), none of his records so much as dented the Top Fifty, and he doubts if they sold more than 300,000 copies

MARVIN RAINWATER

each. No-one gave him any gold records. Even 'Whole Lotta Woman' was a relative failure in the USA, where it was widely banned on account of the line 'I know I've been had'. Recorded in Nashville with Hank Garland (lead guitar), Floyd Cramer (piano), Grady Martin (six-string walking bass) and Buddy Harman (drums), it was one of the few authentic rock'n'roll records to feature a double-tracked voice: 'I went flat on it. In those days you couldn't overdub a part so instead of doing it all over again, I thought I'd sing along on top of my other singing to cover up my own mistakes. Some disc-jockey in Boston said the song was dirty and it didn't get played in the States. When it sold over here, MGM tried again but it was too late. It'd been off the airwaves for four months and that killed it.'

With 'Whole Lotta Woman' at No. 1, Rainwater toured the UK with Tennessee-born skiffler Johnny Duncan, who'd played 'Mr. Blues' on his BBC radio programme, *Tennessee Song Bag*. Duncan was a fervent admirer with an understanding of rockabilly which domestic groups lacked. The music went down well, but Rainwater appeared in a headband and buckskins, a publicity ploy from which it was hard to escape. Most of his 'Indian' songs — 'Indian Burial Ground', 'Valley Of The Moon', 'The Paleface Indian' (an international hit for Don Fardon in 1970 under the title of 'Indian Reservation'), 'Oklahoma Hills' and the rest — came from other songwriters including John D. Loudermilk who penned 'Half-Breed' after watching Rainwater on television. Marvin deliberately sought material of this kind and his performance of it shines with real conviction: 'I'm a quarter Cherokee but my parents weren't happy with their Indian heritage and used to deny it. The Indians were segregated and if you were part-Indian you were worse than being full-blooded. I wanted to declare I am what I am, but I finally dropped it when the Indians themselves objected. Over-zealous promoters thought they could sell more tickets by describing me as a full-blooded chief and they made a

bad thing out of it. I didn't want to be arguing with Indians all the time. I was trying to stand up for 'em but it got to be such a hassle...'

While he was here, Rainwater cut four titles at EMI including 'I Dig You Baby' and 'Dance Me Daddy', which was based on 'Gotta Rock', an old Dale Davis rockabilly tune. 'I'd got wise by now,' he says. 'Apart from 'Whole Lotta Woman', people had asked me if I was singing "Go fuck my baby" instead of "Go bug my baby" on 'Mr. Blues'. So I changed the words from *'Rock me'* to *'Dance me'* 'cos I was afraid people would think I'm singing dirty songs again. You should bring Dale's name into this 'cos his music has been intermingled with mine since the *Ozark Jubilee*; he had a terrific blues piano sound and he wrote 'Why Did You Have To Go And Leave Me Lonesome Blues'.'

By 1959, Marvin and his brother-cum-manager, Ray, are reasonably wealthy men with half a dozen publishing companies and no reason to suppose that Marvin won't continue to turn out songs which MGM can call million-sellers. Ray decides to publish a C&W magazine with all the glossiness of *Time* or *Look*. It's called *Trail*. They rent a suite of offices in the Rockefeller Center, hire a dozen staff and pump out 300,000 copies. The monthly print bill, $17,000, is coming out of Marvin's royalties while brother Ray is keeping the accounts in his head. The magazine lasts about a year and the whole fiasco is bleeding them dry. At this point, the story gets really pitiful: 'My voice gave out on me. I didn't know it then, but I had calluses on my vocal cords and should have quit for months. Instead, we'd spend hours and hours in the studio without ever getting anything decent. I felt bad for Jim Vienneau, the producer, 'cos he was really patient. One day I followed him out and he was setting light to a $20 bill. That gave me the message — he needed to spend his time with Connie Francis while MGM was burning money trying to cut a record on me. In Oklahoma, the mules would go blind from pulling and, when a mule's stone-blind, they'd dump him in a field full of rocks and stumps 'cos he's no use to anyone. That's what the business will do to a singer whose voice goes wrong.'

Leaving MGM in 1960, Marvin stumbled around amongst a number of independent labels including Warwick, where he was grossly humiliated, and Brave, which started 'years of trash and semi-trash'. Eventually, he underwent effective surgery and began cutting better records for Wesco, United Artists and Warner Bros. British tours in 1972 and 1975 yielded albums for Philips and Westwood including *Especially For You* (WRS 101). Its unique mix of re-recorded hits, Indian songs and unvarnished hillbilly is recommended.

His present tour is the first to coincide with the rockabilly revival and he's making the most of it, incorporating a Creedence Clearwater Revival medley and dusting off his originals. When the *Melody Maker* was first introduced to Marvin (April 1958), the reviewer thought it *'ludicrous to see a man of 34 giving out with rock'n'rollers like 'Good Golly Miss Molly' and 'Whole Lotta Woman'.'* Today, Marvin's twenty years older but nothing else has changed: 'I think rock'n'roll makes you look younger and stay younger. I'm certainly not gonna stop. I'll be doing it 'til I'm bald-headed and lose all my teeth.'

Originally published in *Melody Maker* (15 December 1979).

What's Doing in NASHVILLE...

FREE

Vol. 2 No. 41   October 16-22, 1972

Lattie Moore
Now Appearing
At Hillbilly Haven

WHERE TO GO .... WHAT TO DO
WHERE TO DINE .... WHAT TO SEE

1.5
LATTIE MOORE
I'm Not Broke, But I'm Badly Bent

Though highly revered within hillbilly and rockabilly circles, the name of Lattie Moore is practically unknown outside auction lists. Even there it's a tad mysterious. Eddie Bond's 'Juke Joint Johnnie', Jerry Reed's 'If The Good Lord's Willing' and George Jones's 'Out Of Control' have been reissued on CD but they were probably more familiar than Lattie's versions even before they were readily available. Yet, arguably, Lattie's records are more rewarding. His experience-laced vocals have far more expression than Jerry Reed's or the affectless Eddie Bond, and the countrypolitan elements which often diluted George Jones's Sixties music are almost entirely absent.

Lattie's voice is absolutely perfect in a coarse, grainy, ragged sort of way and there's the odd device like a half-yodel when he sings about the doleful effects of drink. Country traditionalists go for the light, twangy vocals on hillbilly songs like 'Don't Trade The Old For A New'. Conway Twitty fans might well prefer the ponderous beat of 'Mine Again'. Rockabilly enthusiasts bid big bucks for Lattie's very scarce records on Arc and Starday. Lattie, however, admits to singing about drink more than anything else. '(Here I Am) Drunk Again', 'Out Of Control', 'Bottle By Bottle', 'Juke Joint Johnny', 'Honky Tonk Heaven', 'Drivin' Nails In My Coffin' *[every time I drink a bottle of booze]*; in *Cash Box* vernacular these are 'booze-hound specials', performed by a man who must surely have seen a few demons in his time. 'I done my job,' he told me recently, 'but I drank a lot to keep doing it. In fact, I drank pretty good. I was doing radio shows and TV shows and working nightclubs and staying up to record after midnight and I drank heavily to keep going. But I was never an alcoholic and when I quit, I just quit.'

Lattie Harrison Moore was born in Scottsville, Kentucky on 17 October 1924. He was named after Lattie Graves, the family doctor who delivered him. His father, Homer Leo Moore, was a tobacco farmer-turned-minister who preached at Scottsville's Church Of God where Lattie and his five siblings sang the sacred hymns of the day. His mother, Dora, who came from Indian stock, joined in the worship.

Lattie grew up in Scottsville, where he went to school and learned to play guitar, mandolin and bass. On leaving school, he took a job as a projectionist at the Lyric Theatre in Scottsville and greatly enjoyed the performances of Gene Autry, the cowboy icon whose formulaic films depicted the West of the 1930s, featuring V-8 Fords as well as horses and six-guns. Only 65 miles from Nashville, Lattie also listened to the *Grand Ole Opry*. He was impressed by Roy Acuff and, later, Ernest Tubb and Hank Williams. Asked to fill in the names of his favourite artists on King Records' Biographical Information Form, Lattie also included Hank Snow and Kay Starr. But Hank Williams came first.

In 1944, Lattie hitchhiked two hundred miles North to Indianapolis, a city of greater opportunity for the professionally-minded musician. A brief stint in the navy interrupted his intentions, but on discharge he worked nightclubs and some of Indiana's large jamboree parks. In December 1944, he married Maxine Frost and the couple moved into Maplehurst Trailer Court on Washington Street. They raised four children and recently celebrated 55 years' togetherness. Lattie also hustled up a thirty-minute radio show over WISH and joined 'Cowboy' Lash LaRue's roadshow singing a couple of songs before accompanying LaRue, a fading film star who performed tricks with a whip.

If ever a record disappeared into collector holy graildom, it was Lattie Moore's first. He says it was made for an Indianapolis label called Arrow, though King's publicity referred to 'Ara' Records. Either way, no-one I know has seen a copy. It was called 'Hideaway Heart' c/w 'Married Troubles' and it was cut in 1951 at the home-built studio of Tate Boland, the label's owner. According to Lattie, the top side was a ballad and 'it didn't do much'.

That same year, Lattie joined the *Mid-Western Jamboree* held at Turner's Hall and broadcast over WIBC from the Indiana capital. He emceed the show and hired guests including Jimmie Skinner and Jimmy Osborne, the Kentucky folk-singer who built a career around 'death' discs and killed himself in 1957. A TV station in Bloomington, Indiana subsequently broadcast Lattie's show from an Indianapolis fairground.

In 1952, Moore travelled to Nashville with a view to recording for Bullet, the local granddaddy of independent labels. He discovered that Bullet wasn't signing anyone new but John Dunn, who handled Bullet's pressing plant, pointed him in the direction of the Speed label, a smaller company in which Dunn also had an interest. Nashville music scholar Martin Hawkins got the story of Lattie's Nashville debut from Dunn's partner, Frank Innocenti: 'In the summer of 1952, I met Lattie Moore as I came out of the Ernest Tubb Record Shop on Lower Broadway. Lattie was a writer and guitarist who wanted to make a record and he sung right there in the busy sidewalk for me to listen. The song was called 'Juke Joint Johnny'. I thought it was so good, I gave him a song contract and recording contract and cut it that very afternoon. In a hurried moment, I quickly found Noel Ball, a deejay who did some engineering for records, and three musicians, piano, bass, and drums. Lattie played guitar and had another guitarist with him. We went to a makeshift studio on Union Street above the Buckley Record Shop that Noel Ball sometimes used for WMAK. No-one in the band knew the song except Lattie and his lead player, so to fill out the sound I told the engineer to bring the drums in as loud as possible to fill out the sound of the piano. The song hit the jukeboxes fast and good. I think this was about the first rock'n'roll record out of Nashville, and in those early days we didn't know it.'

Short essays have been written about 'Juke Joint Johnny', an unconsciously new attempt to transform country boogie into rockabilly. Lattie claims to have been singing country with a beat since he was knee-high. 'But the first time I heard it by someone else was when Elvis's first one came in the record shop in Indianapolis. 'That's all right mama...' — gee, I thought it was a coloured singer trying to do hillbilly.'

'Juke Joint Johnny' had elements beyond the reach of Lattie's peers as evidenced by lacklustre versions from Red Sovine, and Jim Atkins & The Pinetoppers. 'Watch me go' he sang to a pounding departure from the plodding rhythms of conventional hillbilly. If it wasn't quite rockabilly, it was still a pioneering record on the leading edge of pre-rock rock.

Speed, a name inspired by the changeover from 78 to 45 rpm, issued a second single, 'Baby, I'll Soon Be Gone'. Written with Bluebird and Bullet artist Pete Pyle, this echoed Hank Williams's honky-tonk singing, a sound which would come to dominate Lattie's vocal style. Bobby Phillips, an overweight guitarist from Indianapolis, played steel on both Speed singles.

Dunn and Innocenti were keen on keeping Lattie on Speed, even offering him an interest in the company. But Sydney Nathan, the myopic, asthmatic, cigar-chewing tzar of King Records, soon came a-calling.

Lattie Moore cut twenty-five tracks for King, one of the nation's leading independents, over two periods: 1953-56 and 1959-63. The musicians on the earliest recordings, made at the label's own studio on Brewster Avenue in Cincinnati, included Zeke Turner, Zeb's younger brother (electric lead guitar), Don Helms, veteran member of Hank Williams's Drifting Cowboys (steel), Tommy Jackson (fiddle) and Louis Innis, the writer of 'Good Morning Judge' (rhythm guitar). They had as firm a grasp on the essentials of the honky-tonk genre as any musicians in Texas. All the requisite elements are here in spades; warm and vigorous passages from the lead instruments and a slick, danceable beat from the rhythm section to which Lattie, who also played rhythm guitar, often contributed. What's more, alcohol never impaired his singing. Apart from the deliberately twee inflections on 'A Brand New Case Of Love', the vocals are tensile, bluesy and often very emotional in a grimly-contained sort of way. If Lattie's natural baritone is pitched higher on some than others, he suspects Nathan may have speeded up the tape a fraction.

Lattie wrote many of the songs, including the supremely melodic 'Brand New Case Of Love', but his name didn't always end up in the credits. This was an era in which company bosses swapped songwriting credits for various favours and contracts included co-writers who hadn't contributed so much as a comma. 'Syd was a character,' Lattie recalled. 'There was only one like him. If it was the greatest song in the world, Syd would have to alter it a little 'cos then he would make money on it. He really got a kick out of doing that.'

Lattie thinks he contributed to 'I'm Not Broke But I'm Badly Bent', though sole credit goes to one Martha Ellis (check out, by the way, that proto-rockabilly guitar solo). He's adamant too that Charlie Gore had nothing to do with his first King single, the hardcore honky-tonk 'I'm Gonna Tell You Something'. 'I wrote that with Don Helms. We would often write a song and record it five minutes later. The band would have a beer while I learned the words. We recorded 'I'm Gonna Tell You Something' a few minutes after we wrote it. Charlie Gore wasn't even there. That was one of Syd's ideas. And I wrote 'Don't Trade The Old For A New' with Jack Howard, a singer from Indianapolis who kept me company on the road.'

Ray Scott, the Indiana-born rockabilly singer famed for writing 'Flyin' Saucers Rock & Roll', submitted one of his earliest compositions, '100,000 Women Can't Be Wrong', to Lattie Moore in 1956. Scott told Al Turner of the *Hillbilly Researcher* that Lattie agreed to record the song providing he was given half the songwriting credits. It was a common practice at the time and one to which Scott readily agreed.

As far as we know, Jimmie Logsdon *aka* Jimmie Lloyd deserved his co-writer credit on 'Lonesome Man Blues' (a very close relative of Hank Williams's 'Honky Tonk Blues'). 'Me and Jimmie were real good buddies for a long time. He became a deejay over WCKY in Cincinnati.' Other songs, like 'Pull Down The Blinds' and the jaunty 'Under A Mexico Moon', were brought in by Louis Innis or Cowboy Copas. 'They're Not Worth The Paper' had been recorded by Eddie Wilson on the Intro label in June 1953. Lattie's version was a big improvement.

King dropped Lattie after six singles. He cut a flat-out rock'n'roll version of 'Juke Joint Johnny' (as 'Juke Box Johnnie') for Arc Records in December 1956. Onstage, however, he mined the motherlode; Elvis and Little Richard were as important to his repertoire as Hank Williams and Ernest Tubb. I mentioned 'Skinny Minnie Shimmy', a $100 record by Lattie Moore on the Olympic label, but he denied all knowledge and, for what it's worth, this weedy mix of Larry Williams and Bill Haley sounds nothing like Lattie Harrison Moore. 'Well,' he offered, 'there was a guy in Cincinnati that used my name and tried to imitate me. Copied everything I done.' Lattie *does* own up to a rare EP on the Indianapolis-based Saga label. Recorded in the late Fifties, the four tracks included two songs associated with Hank Williams: Bonnie Dodd's 'Be Careful Of Stones That You Throw' and Fred Rose's 'I Dreamed About Mama Last Night'.

In 1958, Lattie joined Starday which had moved its HQ from Beaumont, Texas to a suburb of Nashville the previous year. Owner Don

Pierce began to expand the catalogue, embracing artists who'd been pruned in label roster cutbacks. 'Don Pierce looked me up in Indianapolis,' said Lattie. 'He really wanted me on Starday. We cut 'Why Did You Lie To Me' in Nashville at a studio which Floyd Robinson had in part of his house. Floyd played electric guitar and Benny Martin wrote it and played the acoustic flat-top guitar on it.'

'Too Hot To Handle', Lattie's second and last Starday single, was his take on Eddie Noack's enduring and much-loved song. Noack, who'd taken degrees in English and Journalism, was the most literate of hillbilly singer-songwriters and 'Too Hot To Handle' is a five-star classic covered by, among others, Sonny Burns, Jimmie Skinner, Gene O'Quin and Frankie Miller (whose version probably wins most applause).

Country superstar Webb Pierce persuaded Syd Nathan to re-sign Moore in 1959. 'Me and Webb were real good friends. He was always doing something for me. In fact, he brought me contracts with other companies which I couldn't sign. Of course, Webb wanted me to record songs on which he and Jim Denny had the publishing.' Another six King singles combined A-team pickers and brilliant songs. The echo-laden 'Cajun Doll', written by late vocalist Mark Webb, was recorded at a session on which Lattie produced himself. 'Out Of Control', from the same date, is the most melancholic description of alcoholic derangement on vinyl. Lattie wrote the song with George Jones after a show in Steubenville, Ohio: 'George stayed with me a lot when he came through Indianapolis. His problem *[George's binges were the stuff of straitjacket and padded cell]* was far worse than mine. He got on my nerves around me, boy!'

Jones's Mercury version of 'Out Of Control', which credits other drinking pals as co-writers, reached No. 25 on the *Billboard* C&W chart in August 1960, probably selling more than Lattie's version, which was popular around Cincinnati in 1963. 'Jimmie Logsdon played mine on the 50,000-watt WCKY and it started becoming a hit. George got aggravated about it. He'd told me to go ahead and record it 'cos he wasn't gonna do it. So I did it first and then, after he cut it, Syd released my version.'

Webb Pierce pitched 'Drunk Again', a Jack Kay–Autry Inman song, to Lattie in 1960 (Kay played fiddle on Pierce's Decca sessions). It was recorded in Nashville with Pete Drake (steel), Mel 'Pig' Robbins (piano) and a catchy arrangement built around harmony vocals by Wayne Walker and Marijohn Wilkin. Coupled with Jerry Irby's 'Drivin' Nails In My Coffin' (the only other song from this September 1960 session), 'Drunk Again' reached No. 25 C&W in January 1961. A minor hit didn't make a lot of difference to Lattie's career, but for a while he played classier joints supporting Johnny Cash. (A version by Clyde Beavers on Decca packed a bigger sales wallop peaking at No. 13 and staying on the chart for almost four months).

Follow-ups included a tough version of Jerry Reed's 'If The Good Lord's Willing And The Creek Don't Rise' (coupled with 'Sundown And Sorrow', which Hank Williams had recorded in 1949) and a quartet of songs from Ray Pennington *aka* Ray Starr, the Kentucky-born rockabilly singer who wrote 'Three Hearts In A Tangle' and cross-fertilised country and soul. In the Forties and Fifties, black King producer Henry Glover had looked for R&B elements to use in C&W records. In the Sixties, Ray Pennington admitted the harmonic structures of doo-wop and early soul to honky-tonk. For once, Lattie's voice wasn't able to transcend these effects. 'Heaven All Around Me' and 'I Told You So', mawkish songs best suited to smoother singers like Johnny Tillotson or Bobby Bare, featured a black girl trio whose cooing was a long way from hardcore country.

Whites and blacks in the Kentucky of Lattie's childhood were obviously divided. He'd heard next to nothing of blues in his youth, but at King Records he soon developed an affection for two of the label's greatest

R&B singers: 'I used to go in and watch a lot of rhythm and blues recording, and that was something else again. Syd would try and give 'em hell, but they'd be drunk and they'd throw bottles and instruments at him. I used to like Little Willie John and Otis Williams. They really dug country music. In fact, they'd both come in and watch me record. Otis, in particular, sang on a lot of country sessions. I liked Willie, not for a musician, but him being a bigger fan of country music more'n most country fans, it meant I could talk to him.' (Otis Williams, who made some sparkling C&W sides for Nashville's Stop Records, appeared at the *Hemsby Rock'n'Roll Festival* in 1998. Little Willie John cut several country songs including 'She Thinks I Still Care'. He died in prison in 1968.)

Leaving King for a second time, Lattie cut an album and a single for Derbytown and a single for WPL. In October 1972, I found him hosting a honky-tonk off Lower Broadway in Nashville. Around 9.00 pm he picked up his guitar and sat on a stool in the middle of the kiosk-sized stage. Pee Wee Mathis of the Newbeats tucked himself under an out-of-tune upright and Rocky Stone, a prison warder from Knoxville, joined in on spoons. That was it. His short set was magnificently resistant to any kind of countrypolitan schmaltz. No-one flocking towards the Municipal Auditorium for the *United Artists Dance Party* can have been as exhilarated or as deeply moved by anything they heard there.

Eventually, Lattie returned to Scottsville and worked in law enforcement for four years. He underwent laser surgery for throat cancer in 1986 and recovered from a quadruple heart bypass operation in 1999. Now, he says he's fine and keeps fit by walking thirty minutes every evening.

Lattie Moore never really got over his Hank Williams phase and, as wonderful as his records are, they often loomed too close to Hank's to have any truly independent influence of their own. But a couple have enjoyed an unexpected afterlife on celluloid. 'Juke Joint Johnny' cropped up in a Matt Dillon film, *The Big Town* (1987) and bluegrass connoisseur Ricky Skaggs sang 'I'm Not Broke But I'm Badly Bent' on the soundtrack of *For Richer Or Poorer*, an Amish-based comedy made for Universal Pictures in 1997. The Tractors have also recorded that one (as 'Badly Bent').

Lattie Moore cut a handful of tremendous songs: harrowing soliloquies to the bottle, amiable hillbilly novelties and evocations of a hardscrabble life observed by one of honky-tonk's most expressive if underrated singers.

Liner note to CD *I'm Not Broke But I'm Badly Bent* (Westside WESF-109) 2000.

Jimmy Murphy *(centre)* shares a joke with Carl Story & The Rambling Mountaineers.

1.6
JIMMY MURPHY
Southern Roots

Sad but true. Jimmy Murphy, a hard-country singer inspired by the folk-country and thriving white gospel traditions of the 1930s and 40s, had no real impact on the course of American music. His best records — a baker's dozen spread over twenty years — sold poorly and the tapes then languished in the darkest vaults of Columbia and RCA, never legally anthologised until CBS's *Rockabilly Classics* in 1977 and Bear Family's collection, *Sixteen Tons Rock'n'Roll*, in 1989.

But Murphy, who died in 1981 at the age of 55, deserves to be remembered as a glowing footnote in the history of C&W, country gospel and rockabilly. He was an outstanding guitarist by any measure; he was also a writer of memorable songs and hymns with downhome, bluesy qualities appreciated even by those with no patience for religious ritual.

The records he made in the Sixties drew ever more heavily upon a now much-neglected white gospel dimension. Murphy never really 'progressed' and his stubborn refusal to conform to the Nashville norm probably reinforced his lack of celebrity. There have been statelier white gospellers (Tennessee Ernie Ford) and ferocious preacher-shouters (Brother Claude Ely), but few besides Murphy continued making commercial recordings in such a raw, folksy and decidedly non-Nashville form well into the Sixties and Seventies.

In 1978, Sugar Hill Records of Durham, North Carolina, issued a fascinating album of Jimmy Murphy's music. It was heralded as a 'comeback' in some quarters, though very few people had heard of him in the first place. In conjunction with that album, folklorist Richard Spottswood conducted what appears to have been the only primary research into Murphy's life. (Two things we ought to clear up early on: this is not the Jim Murphy who cut rock'n'roll for Phoenix labels, nor the Jimmy Murphy who played steel guitar for Carl Smith's Tunesmiths and recorded 'Big Murph' for Columbia.)

An only child, Murphy was born on 11 October 1925 in the small mining town of Republic, Alabama, some miles from Birmingham. Spottswood established that Murphy's father, a miner, liked blues and bought records by Blind Boy Fuller and Leadbelly. The family also listened to WSM's *Grand Ole Opry*. Jimmy told Spottswood that he liked

Uncle Dave Macon, the black harmonica player DeFord Bailey, Asher Sizemore and the McGee Brothers, Sam and Kirk, who'd helped celebrate the *Opry*'s first birthday. Roy Acuff, who first appeared on the *Opry* in 1938 (Jimmy was twelve at the time), became a personal favourite.

As a small child, Murphy played harmonica. At the age of nine, his parents gave him a guitar. The subsequent influence of Bee Coleman, his friend and guitar tutor, is acknowledged in Murphy's 'Open E' tuning in which the guitar was tuned to the 'E' chord. Coleman was the offspring of Dutch Coleman, a singer-guitarist who recorded for Vocalion in 1929 and became a Holiness preacher by 1940 when Murphy first met him and his son. In 1952, Coleman made a couple of records for RCA-Victor as Brother Dutch Coleman and it's just possible that Murphy, who recorded for RCA in 1951, tipped the company to the talents of Brother Dutch. The Pentecostal Holiness churches, which also produced the aforementioned Brother Claude Ely, had an enduring influence on the musical development of many rock'n'roll singers, particularly Elvis and Jerry Lee Lewis. As a Baptist, Murphy's own singing was more restrained. His prosaic vocals don't try to catch up with his busy guitar playing which so often sounds like a two-guitar tussle competing with a speeding train.

Murphy Sr. gave up the mines in 1940 and turned to construction work. Jimmy followed him around, serving an apprenticeship as a brick mason. He also played music in his spare time eventually making his radio debut on the *Happy Hal Burns Show* over WBRC in Birmingham. Eight years later, he travelled to Knoxville, Tennessee where he appeared on Archie Campbell's *Dinner Bell Show* over WROL. The station had played host to Roy Acuff in 1934; the Alabama-born Louvin Brothers cracked WROL in the mid-Forties. Jimmie Skinner appeared on the *Dinner Bell* programme at the dawn of his career. Rural radio stations were the stepping stones for dozens of aspiring C&W singers.

In 1950, Archie Campbell introduced Murphy to guitarist Chet Atkins, already a session player of note and about to become Steve Sholes's part-time assistant at RCA-Victor. Atkins encouraged Murphy to submit an audition tape to music publishers Acuff–Rose, and this, it's said, led to a one-year contract with RCA, for whom Murphy recorded a total of eight songs.

There were hints of Jimmie Rodgers ('Big Mama Blues'), Hank Snow ('That First Guitar Of Mine') and Alabama's most celebrated C&W singer, Hank Williams ('Ramblin' Heart'). Murphy embraced all these popular influences, but his own very distinctive style had little or no commercial impact. As Colin Escott has pointed out, when Tennessee Ernie Ford was topping the C&W charts with the proto-rock 'Shotgun Boogie', Murphy was heading in the opposite direction with songs like 'Electricity', recorded in Nashville with nothing but Anita Carter's stand-up bass for support.

'Electricity' was the first song Murphy ever recorded. His intricate but bluesy guitar playing and religious themes (electricity and God are equal certainties even though you can't see either) remained essential elements of his music for the rest of his life.

Murphy didn't get another shot at recording until 1955 when he signed with Columbia, where producer Don Law paired him with Onie Wheeler, one of the most active harmonica players in country music. They cut four tunes including 'I'm Looking For A Mustard Patch', a jittery answer to the Carlisles' 'Too Old To Cut The Mustard'. Murphy sounded as if he was pushing fifty but he was only three days away from his 30th birthday. The sequel was too late to capitalise on the Carlisles' Top Ten hit of 1952; Murphy was the loose marble of hillbilly, always out of step and behind the times.

As country music took a hammering from rock'n'roll, Murphy tried to get to grips with the new music. His second Columbia session produced four unusual rockabilly songs including the much-loved 'Sixteen Tons Rock & Roll'. Ernie Ford's version of Merle Travis's 'Sixteen Tons' was a huge hit in the USA (and Britain) just months before Murphy adapted the idea ('Go cat, dig that coal!'). But as much as rockabilly fans liked the record, the coalition of Onie Wheeler's harmonica and Murphy's avuncular vocal lagged way behind contemporary tastes. Wheeler, a staunch fan of the Delmore Brothers and Wayne Raney, shifted from a classic honky-tonk style to a country boogie approach after touring with Elvis in 1954. He always thought that this change of direction pointed to the future but his affection for the Alabama-born Delmores — at their peak in the late Forties — imparted an in-built obsolescence some distance from the frantic, skipping rhythms of conventional rockabilly.

Murphy's brush with rock'n'roll made little difference to his fortunes. He continued working in and around Knoxville, leaving WROL for a spot on WNOX's *Mid-Day Merry-Go-Round*, an important showcase in its nineteenth year of operations by 1956.

As with most old-time hillbillies, the 1960s folk revival also bypassed Murphy, who turned up next on Ark Records, a Cincinnati label owned by Roy Shepard and Bill Lanham. Ark paired Murphy's 'I Long To Hear Hank Sing The Blues' with a steel guitar instrumental by Paul Smith. Hank Williams, of course, had been dead for ten years.

The second release on Ark coupled 'Wake Me Up Sweet Jesus' and 'My Feet's On Solid Ground'. Both songs, written by Murphy with assistance from veteran C&W singers Jimmie Skinner and the lesser-known Estel Lee Scarborough, were probably cut in Cincinnati where Skinner owned a world-famous record shop on East 5th Street.

Murphy was soon back in a record studio cutting a one-off and typically anachronistic single for the Michigan-based Midnite label (as Jimmie Murphy).

In 1964, Murphy fetched up on Rem Records, a Lexington, Kentucky-based company whose owner, Bob Mooney, gained a reputation for recording country roots performers with the occasional rockabilly twitch. Mooney made records under his own name for other Kentucky labels and also owned Fayette Music, named after Kentucky's Fayette County. He was a songwriter too, collaborating with Jimmie Skinner on many occasions (Lexington is only thirty miles south of Cincinnati where Skinner was based). No-one on Rem made it big, though Charlie Monroe had been popular and some of the rockabilly acts made records which now command vertiginously expensive prices. Eddie Noack's 'Snowbird' was also recorded a few times, mainly by people who mistook it for Anne Murray's mega-hit.

According to Ray Topping, who owns the releases on Ark and Rem, the first of Murphy's Rem singles was a reissue of the Ark pairing, 'Wake Me Up Sweet Jesus' *c/w* 'My Feet's On Solid Ground'. Publishing credits on Ark were attributed to Sheplan Music (Shepard and Lanham) as well as Mooney-Lee, indicating that Bob Mooney had some involvement with Jimmy Murphy and Ark Records two years before the singer-guitarist appeared on Rem.

Another Rem single, 'Half A Loaf Of Bread', which credits Mooney as producer, was issued in 1965. It ploughed that same distinctive bedrock hillbilly gospel sound, one which normally carried secular whiffs of moonshine or epiphanies to mother. There are similarities with Billy Wallace, another Alabama-raised singer-songwriter whose homespun wit and small, nasal voice turned self-deprecation into an art form. Reviewing Escott and Hawkins's pioneering book, *Catalyst*, in 1975, I advised: 'Don't be dismayed if you've bid for Billy Wallace or Jimmy Murphy singles to find downhome hillbilly blues or religious bluegrass in place of the slapped bass orgy you thought you were getting. Escott and Hawkins have gone to great lengths to point out that it's all grand stuff which deserves a wider hearing.'

Although most of Murphy's Sixties recordings fall into what *Cash Box* called 'the hillbilly sacred field', they're a far cry from what was selling. Tennessee Ernie was probably the biggest white gospel artist with a collection of easy-listening hymns which went platinum by 1963. Murphy's music, which reached back to the gospel idioms of previous generations, demanded more commitment than large audiences were willing to give. Versions of 'Little Black Train' had been circulating in the Thirties (Seven Stars Quartette) and the Fifties (the Dominoes). 'John The Baptist' (attributed to Brother Dutch Coleman) and 'Jesus Is My Only Friend' have longer pedigrees, with many a recording going back to the Twenties. Oft-recorded quartet stalwarts like 'Little David' (check out Brother Claude Ely's version) were also couched in a fresh vitality and shimmering guitar figures.

Murphy's immaculate guitar playing, loose thickets of jangling, trebly sound like some sort of supercharged autoharp, was truly assured. There may be a second guitarist on, say, 'Half A Loaf Of Bread' and others, but, as Colin Escott has explained, Murphy's Open E tuning allowed him to play rhythm and melody at the same time. It's also possible (though I'm guessing) that his wife, Florine, strummed the cool rhythm accompaniment to tracks like 'Jesus Is Coming To Reign'.

'He's Always The Same' — a song Murphy revisited a few times — is the most effective of several stark detours into keening and not-so-close harmony singing with his wife. They were married in 1945. Florine also takes a solo, 'I Feel Jesus', in an untutored, peg-on-nose voice which could scare cats to death and put the wind up the Holy Ghost. Judged harshly, this qualifies as damaged goods; there could scarcely be a greater contrast between Flo's ragged hollering and contemporary gospel singing, so often indistinguishable from bland and glossy soul music.

'Shanty Boat Blues', a highspot of Murphy's secular recordings, offers firm evidence of his familiarity with pre-war blues styles. In this instance, chiefly white blues, since the song was written by Jimmie Skinner with an obvious debt to Jimmie Rodgers. A 'shanty boat' is 'a kind of roughly-constructed house-boat used by lumbermen' (OED). Skinner would subsequently cut the very similar 'Riverboat Blues' for Vetco Records. 'Tears In The Eyes Of A Potato' and 'Hub Cap', co-written by Bob Mooney, blend Murphy's fluid fretwork with a cornpone wit.

One of Murphy's gospel tracks, 'You Better Get Ready', cropped up on the Starday anthology, *Country Bluegrass Favorites*. The album was reissued on Wayne Raney's Rimrock label but retitled *Where Will I Shelter My Sheep Tonight?* Two other tracks, including 'He's Always The Same', were included on Rimrock's *The Family Gospel Album* in 1968. 'He's Always The Same' also appeared on a Jimmy Murphy EP for Walter Bailes's Loyal label in 1969.

The early Seventies saw at least one more obscure release; Murphy revived 'Electricity' c/w 'The Legend Of Joe Haney' for Rusty York's Cincinnati-based Jewel Records. Incidentally, Bill Lanham, the man who recorded Jimmy Murphy's belated tribute to Hank Williams, played bass on Rusty York's 1959 hit, 'Sugaree'.

Nothing more was heard of Murphy until 1978, when Dick Spottswood tracked him down to Corbin, Kentucky, once home to Ernest Phipps whose Holiness Singers cut the first exuberant, hand-clappy recordings of holiness hymns for RCA-Victor in the Twenties. Spottswood persuaded Barry Poss of Sugar Hill to record Murphy again. The 'rediscovered' Murphy, who still worked as a brick mason and shunned the folk and bluegrass circuits, finally got to make a wonderful album which fully communicated his varied musical personality. He was accompanied by a team of young bluegrass players including Jerry Douglas on dobro and Ricky Skaggs, then a member of Emmylou Harris's Hot Band, on mandolin and fiddle. The music, including a version of Johnnie Temple's 'Louise', was unlike any you would have expected to hear in 1979.

Barry Poss remembered taking six and twelve-string guitars from Durham to Lexington's Lemco Sound studio because Jimmy no longer had an instrument of his own. 'There's really no question. He was a very singular fellow,' Poss recalled. 'The idea of playing with other musicians was a little foreign to him. Most of it was just keeping a close eye on

Jimmy. Whenever he would start, you'd have to be ready. There was really no such thing as a count down.'

Murphy's persona may not have endeared him to promoters or deejays. 'I also remember booking him to perform at the *National Folk Festival* in Washington, DC,' Poss continued. 'He agreed to come and he drove fifteen hours to get there. He pulled up where all the performers were staying at this private school which looked like, maybe, Oxford to me. But to Jimmy it looked like an institution. He got a bit nervous. He just decided he felt uncomfortable and got in his car and drove back. I spoke to Hal Durham at the *Opry* later on. They were very, very excited by Jimmy Murphy at one time, but they also had the sense that he was totally unpredictable.'

In 1980 I reviewed the Sugar Hill album for *Melody Maker* and set about getting an interview for that paper's *Echoes* column. Barry Poss was only too keen. *'Let's try it,'* he wrote. 'Send the questions to me and I'll forward a cassette to Jimmy. The reason I say "forward", is that Jimmy is being elusive again. I think he unwittingly lives more of the life of a Fifties rebel than the ones who make such an effort to affect such a lifestyle. Communication is a little difficult but occasionally I seem to get through. Jimmy is not against publicity. In fact, he would love it. I even talked to him about touring Europe and he thought that was a good idea. It's just that Jimmy does not always act in his own best interests. It's really a shame since he is so incredibly talented. On the positive side, he did send me a cassette of some material we were thinking of doing for a second album — some great rockabilly!'

All these plans were pre-empted by Murphy's death from a probable heart attack on 1 June 1981. Some accounts suggest that he'd split up with his wife and moved in with a nineteen year old woman. His wife, Florine, survived him by seventeen years. He also left eight children and a large number of grandchildren. One thing he didñ't leave was a closet full of gold discs but, as all roots music fans are aware, chart success has never determined talent or originality and Jimmy Murphy had both in abundance.

Liner note to CD *Southern Roots* (Ace CDCHD-714) 1999.

2

ROCKABILLY RULES

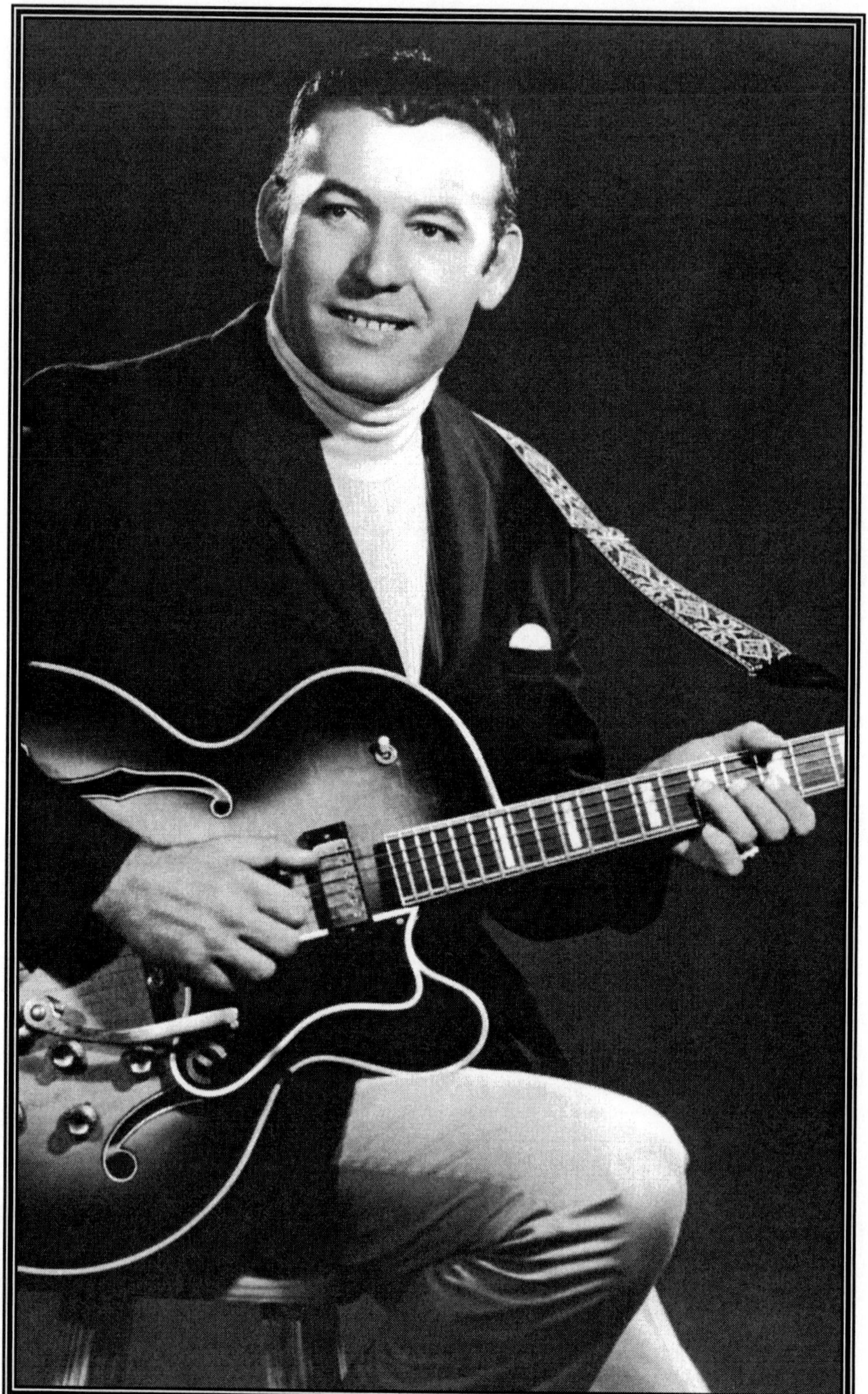

2.1

CARL PERKINS
The Decca Years

Few rock'n'rollers combine Carl Perkins's musicality, his easy wit or the controlled vehemence which made 'Blue Suede Shoes', 'Gone, Gone, Gone' and 'Dixie Fried' among the most memorable of all rockabilly records. Those elemental Sun anthems led to a major label contract with Columbia, where some of his singles had almost as much to commend them. This essay takes the Carl Perkins story through the Decca years, another incident-packed phase.

By the early Sixties, Perkins was as close to the artistic and economic bottom as any terminally unfashionable performer could get. Totally unaware of having achieved any lasting critical respect, he played airport lounge rock in Las Vegas and wondered whether the 40,000 citizens of Jackson, Tennessee could support another grocery store. Now read on...

In August 1965, Perkins signed a two-year contract with Decca and recorded four titles in Nashville where MOR-country had co-opted rockabilly beyond recognition. The session got off to a sluggish start with two of the least exciting songs in the Perkins canon. 'After Sundown' and 'For A Little While' work as dolorous country weepers, but they lack the strong melody which makes country sentiment bearable and show all the signs of compositional fatigue. 'I had very little input at all,' Carl told me. 'It was Owen Bradley's arrangements. He would have players there that he wanted and they worked up the arrangements. Well... to tell you the truth, it wasn't a happy period. I was getting frustrated because I couldn't get a [hit] record and I was drinking way too much. I went through a period where I was contemplating just getting out of the business and I got into alcohol way too heavy. I liked a few of the things I cut on Decca and I loved Mr. Bradley who was producing but... I was letting alcohol write my songs.'

The session picked up when the brass section and steel guitarist left the studio. The folk-rock craze could have inspired the purposeful, jog-a-long feel to 'Help Me Find My Baby', and 'I Wouldn't Have You' is a jaunty rocker despite Mitchell Torok's mawkish lyrics. The Jordanaires added the sort of vocal effects which enveloped a number of early Presley hits. 'That song was played for me by Owen Bradley,' Carl continued. 'I hadn't met Mitchell Torok then. Bradley said: "Here's a song I think you could really get into." I did write 'Help Me Find My Baby' and I played the acoustic guitar on that. My dad, he really liked that song. I remember going to his house with the raw tape of the session and he said: "Yup, that's gonna be the best thing you ever recorded. You gotcha one, son."'

Decca issued 'Help Me Find My Baby' c/w 'For A Little While' in October 1965 ('It never happened; we could never get anything together that would really sell') and 'After Sundown' c/w 'I Wouldn't Have You' in February 1964. 'But y'know, 'After Sundown' almost liked to have been a hit record. It got on regional charts, Top Five in a few places. One in particular, like Albuquerque, New Mexico — there, for some reason, it was a Number One country record on the local chart. It almost broke... it *did* break in a few places.'

Brunswick (the British outlet for American Decca) released 'Help Me Find My Baby' c/w 'I Wouldn't Have You' to coincide with Perkins's first tour of England. *Record Mirror* described the A-side as *'a middle-of-the-road song and not too commercial'*; the *New Musical Express* thought it was *'watered-down Perkins'* and far from being the best he could do. The fifty-two year old arrived during the first week of May; he appeared on ITV's *Ready Steady Go* (8 May) and BBC Radio's *Saturday Club* (9 May). That same night he opened for Chuck Berry at London's Finsbury Park Astoria, where he shared the bottom of the bill with the Nashville Teens and a girl duo, the Other Two.

The media were not prepared for the intensity with which Perkins performed or the strength of his reception. *'Carl Perkins also came in for adulation,'* wrote the *NME*, adding *'... surprisingly'*. Don Arden's office explained Perkins's lowly billing: 'He was such an unknown quantity to us. We just didn't realise how great he is.' Of course, no-one was more surprised than Carl himself. This hero-worshipper saw the package at Hammersmith (on 10 May when the audience stampeded the stage after only four numbers from Chuck); at Woolwich (on 25 May when Berry read out an imaginary letter to his folks back home about prison life and the lack of sex on the inside) and on 31 May when the tour returned to Hammersmith Odeon. It was here that John Lee Hooker made an appearance, completing a line-up that included the Animals, the Swinging Blue Jeans and Kingsize Taylor & The Dominoes, as well as Chuck and Carl. Mates of mine (hi there to Paul Sandford and Roger Osborn) unfurled a mammoth 'CARL PERKINS – KING OF ROCK' banner while other fans jumped on stage and clapped him on the back as if he'd just run a four-minute mile. At each date, he paused in front of the footlights. 'You don't know,' he said — tears trickling down a chubbier face than the *Dance Album*'s lantern-jawed visage had led us to expect — 'just how happy you've made this lil' ol' country boy feel.'

'Well,' Carl explained almost exactly 25 years later, 'I hadn't seen audiences like that in America for years. I'd almost given up. To find out that there were kids out there who knew me and who cared for what I was trying to do with my music... the British fans are the greatest in the whole world, and I say that back in America and I do not beat around the bush about it. I was drinking, I'd lost my brother, I couldn't get a hit... and in London I'm treated like a hero. I owe so much to the loyalty and support of the British fans during that tour.'

Decca A&R man Dick Rowe arranged for Perkins to cut a rock'n'roll single for immediate release, and on 22 May he entered the company's West Hampstead studios with the Nashville Teens, who'd backed him on tour. They laid down six tracks. Apart from 'A Love I'll Never Win' — a croaky ballad in the tradition of 'Turn Around' — it was one good rocking session with a very attractive feel. With its hard-hitting edge and sparse presentation, the date pulled into focus all the finer aspects of Perkins's art. In short, this stuff has credibility. The band was well-rehearsed and under-miked, so that 'Big Bad Blues' and 'Say When' are loaded with Perkins's ingenious licks and masterful solos. 'Say When' was originally intended for Brenda Lee, while Carl told the *Melody Maker* that he'd written 'Big Bad Blues' for the Beatles: 'People tell me I'm one of the Beatles' favourites. I don't know. I've written some numbers that I think they might use. There's one they are going to use — I think — but when and where, I don't know. It's called 'Big Bad Blues' and I'd like for them to record it. I've heard the Migil Five are recording my latest too. It's great to have all this going on.'

Apart from the wrongly punctuated intro that offends purists, 'Blue Suede Shoes' is a fine, slightly hysterical version with two excellent breaks. Ditto 'Lonely Heart', which has the most adroit guitar solos of any Perkins record since 'Movie Magg'. It's true that the new songs don't say very much; they don't give expression to Perkins's rural background (as do all his very best works) and they lack the observation or wry humour of, say, 'Restless' or 'Dixie Fried'. But they sure do sound right, with not so much as a hiccup surplus to intention. I'm glad they were cut in London with the Nashville Teens (as opposed to Nashville recordings with older musicians) and Carl agreed: 'I enjoyed that session very much because I knew I was closer to the feel and the sound *[of rockabilly]* than I'd been since I left Sun Records. Those boys knew the music better than the Nashville people did. There's no question about it. That applies today... like, Dave Edmunds knows my music better than I do, he remembers every little bit of it. And George Harrison remembers the guitar licks that I've forgotten.'

'Big Bad Blues' *c/w* 'Lonely Heart' was rush-released on 1 June. The *NME* review had the flavour of a school report: *'Carl Perkins manages to inject a certain plaintive quality even at speed, and the Nashville Teens provide a most commendable rockabilly backing.'* That date — 1 June 1964 — is historically resonant for another reason; Perkins attended a Beatles session at Abbey Road where his Scouse admirers completed five takes of 'Matchbox' between 2.50 and 5.50 pm.

Carl closed his first trip to Britain with a second appearance on

Ready Steady Go (5 June), but he'd recorded enough tunes — 56 in all, including 'John Henry', 'Hi-Heel Sneakers', 'I Can't Help It', 'The Old Spinning Wheel', 'Mean Woman Blues', 'Marie', 'What'd I Say', 'Jambalaya', 'San Antonio Rose' and 'You Win Again' — to keep him on the airwaves until early August. Breathless Dan Coffey, then President of his UK fan club, would subsequently present him with an acetate of performances from *Saturday Club*, *The Joe Loss Pop Show* and *Top Gear*.

Back in the USA, Perkins worked clubs with George Morgan, Webb Pierce and Faron Young. In mid-July, he caught his left hand in the blades of an electric fan at a club in Dyersberg, Tennessee. He was taken sixty miles to hospital in Jackson while blood dripped through the floorboards of his Buick. The surgeon was persuaded not to amputate two of his fingers: 'It took a long time to recover. My hand was in a cast for eight weeks and when the cast came off it looked like a skeleton's hand. I started squeezin' a rubber ball day and night but I still can't use my little finger on that hand. I only play with three fingers. My playing was definitely hampered by the fact that I can't use my little finger, but then I've been told that I put the other three to work a lot harder so some people think I'm playing better than ever.'

Dates for an autumn tour of Britain were announced in July. Carl was to join a package which included Tommy Tucker and Gene Vincent but, in the event, Vincent was replaced by the Animals, who topped the bill; Don Arden probably figured that two alcoholics on one tour was a recipe for disaster.

On 8 October, Perkins recorded 'The Monkeyshine' and three other tunes in Nashville with a stellar cast of musicians including James Burton and Alan Price, organist with the Animals. 'They were on tour in America and they were in Nashville that night. My session was supposed to start at 6.00 pm but I went and talked to Mr. Bradley. I told him I wanna go see the Animals because I'd worked with them in England and I knew 'em real well. I said I'd like them to come back to the studio, and he said: "That'd be great. Invite 'em." Which I did. Alan graciously came and played some real good hot organ on that thing. The session took place about midnight. We'd all had a few nips and it was a lot of fun.'

This session, Perkins's last for Decca, is something of a curate's egg. His deep, virile voice is suited to the Memphis beat of 'Let My Baby Be', while 'Monkeyshine' blends Sixties dance-craze mania with a long and grand blues tradition (one with which Carl was familiar from such recordings as Smokey Joe Baugh's 1955 version of 'Signifying Monkey'). The other cuts are less appealing. The nicest thing about 'Mama Of My Song' — clumsy mock-gospel inspired by 'I Got A Woman' — is the bass-slapping fade. 'One Of These Days' is a tad routine too; Carl's exhortation, 'Let's go, let's rock' fails to inspire a particularly feeble break. The session files point to Wayne Moss as guitarist, but Carl (who had good reason to recall the first session on which he was incapable of playing himself) credits James Burton, whose presence was probably illicit; ordinarily based in California, he was not, after all, a member of the particularly cliquish local branch of the musicians' union.

In mid-October, Perkins flew to London for a second tour of England. It was tabbed *The R'n'B Show '64*, and Carl topped the first half of a bill which included the Animals, Tommy Tucker, Elkie Brooks, Ray Cameron, the Quotations, the Nashville Teens, the Plebs and, at selected venues, Barry St. John.

I saw the package on 20 October at Edmonton Regal. Carl couldn't play guitar and weighed in well under par; Tommy Tucker, a stocky, little modern bluesman, told the audience they were 'lousy' and he was right. On 2 November at the Kilburn State, Carl stole the show with a vigorous stage presence and a lot of animated bopping: 'I was only attempting to play lead guitar then. I don't think a lot of people knew this, but at the time I was into that vodka bottle very heavy in an attempt to disguise what I couldn't do.' After the show, Perkins sang 'Dixie Fried' outside the theatre. I'm not making this up; there we were, half a dozen of us, jigging about on the pavement while the mighty Carl Perkins — suede jerkin and the pork-pie hat he wore outdoors in those far-off, pre-toupee'd days — gave an impromptu concert before climbing into his taxi-cab.

Perkins remained in Britain until late November. He appeared on BBC TV's *Beat Room*, *Top Gear* and *Saturday Club*. On 19 November, the

NME reviewed 'Monkeyshine': *'Great stuff for shaking and twisting'*. Carl spent that Thursday on the set of *Be My Guest*, the film in which an irrepressible Jerry Lee Lewis sang 'My Baby Don't Love No-One But Me'. He wound up his second visit to Britain with a solo engagement at Kingston Cellar Club on 20 November, where he sang an unaccompanied 'I Love You Because' as a tribute to Jim Reeves who'd perished three months before.

'Mama Of My Song' *c/w* 'One Of These Days' was issued in May 1965. It didn't sell at all and the Decca contract was not renewed. By the end of the following year Perkins had stopped drinking; he bought a farm with royalties from the Beatles' versions of his songs; returned to the C&W charts with 'Country Boy's Dream', and generally got his act together — a feat which this brave, kindly, humble and spirited man always deserved to accomplish. Thankfully, the Decca recordings cannot be described as Carl Perkins's last major work; indeed, there are elements which failed to meet his own high standards. Nevertheless, in my book, they still deserve a hero's welcome.

Note 1   Extracted from the liner notes to *The Classic Carl Perkins* (Bear Family BCD-15494) 1990. The booklet also contains Colin Escott's essay on the Sun and Columbia recordings.

Note 2   Carl Perkins died in January 1998 after several strokes and a long battle with throat cancer. He was, as Colin Escott so rightly said, 'a prince of a man who could no more be rude or dismissive towards his fans than Mary Poppins could beat babies'.

2.2

JERRY JAYE
The Last Of The Rockabillies

*Well I can see what happened to Jerry Lee
And I want the same thing for me.
I know exactly what I wanna do.
Conway did it and I can too.*

These words, a verse from 'I Wanna Go Country' by Otis Williams, portray the feelings of many other rock'n'roll performers. They provide a Seventies parallel to Carl Perkins's time-honoured shout, 'All my friends are boppin' the blues'. Country steel and fiddle, instead of country blues guitar, now dominate the records of Mac Curtis, Jerry Lee, Bobby Lee Trammell, Conway Twitty and any ex-rockabilly lucky enough to be making records today — including Jerry Jaye whose 'My Girl Josephine' is regarded by many as being the last of the genuine rock'n'roll hits. I spoke to Jerry, now carving out a new career in country music, in Mega's offices in Nashville where he was doing promos for the many C&W jocks who converge on Music City during convention week.

Born on 19 October 1937 in Manila, Arkansas, Jerry (real name Gerald J. Hatley) grew up on a cotton plantation. 'Basically, in North-East Arkansas there were almost as many whites as there was blacks picking cotton. Back in the Forties, we were all more or less equal at the bottom. We were sharecroppers, which means that the guy that owns the land gets the biggest part and we got the least, but we were still just a little bit better off than the day-workers. I was too little to pick cotton so I was the water-boy. The first music I heard down there was blues, country music and — on the radio — the big bands too, although I can't really put my finger on anyone in particular.'

Around twenty years of age, and having learned guitar from an older brother, Jerry organised his own three-piece combo with Tommy Baker (bass), Carl Fry (drums) and himself on rhythm guitar and harmonica. They played club dates in the West Memphis area but did not, apparently, record at the time. I say 'apparently' because there are Jerry Jaye records all over the place — on Stepheny, DeLuxe, Carlton, Swan and Quality. There's even another white-sounding 'Jerry Jaye' singing Fats Domino's 'Going To The River' *c/w* 'Cottage For Sale' on a label

2.2 - Jerry Jaye

called... Label. *[Years later, in a postcard to Colin Escott, Gerald Hatley confirmed that none of these records had anything to do with him.]*

A decade elapsed before Joe Thompson at KBIB in Monette, Arkansas, a radio station where Jerry deejayed during the day, persuaded him to cut his first record. He related the amusing story of how 'Josephine' came to be made: 'To me it was a freak record. I went to Roland Janes's Sonic Recording Studio with Tommy and Carl and we cut this thing. I rented the studio for ten bucks an hour and my tape cost me three dollars. I was gonna distribute the record myself and, first of all, I had it on my own label, Connie, named after my baby daughter. I asked a friend in the jukebox end to buy some of 'em and he said he'd take a few, and a little while later he said: "Jerry, I'd like a few more," and soon I was gettin' calls: "Bring me 75, bring me a hundred." I went into Joe Cuoghi's office at Hi Records and he said he didn't have time to talk to me but if I wanted to leave 25 with Bill Biggs at Record Sales, which Joe also owned, it was okay by him. Bill said: "Leave 25 and I'll take 'em round the stations," and, golly, in about a week Joe was knockin' on my door. So I signed with Hi Records who re-cut the thing for stereo.'

The Connie title, 'Hello Josephine', was issued on Hi Records as 'My Girl Josephine' and it climbed to No. 29 on *Billboard*'s Hot 100 in 1967. In Britain, 'My Girl Josephine' appealed to guys who hadn't bought a new record in ten years. Some of us couldn't believe what was happening. Wild Little Willie wrote to *Record Mirror* about it. Rockabilly was back in the Top Thirty right in the middle of the Summer Of Love!

Sadly, as Jerry says, it was nothing but a freak — even freaky: 'We did it with three pieces in mono on a two-track machine. I told the engineer: "What am I gonna do?" — 'cos I couldn't do no overdubbing and that's gonna leave it so empty with me playing the ride and just the bass and drums. Roland *[who played guitar on Jerry Lee's 'Whole Lot Of Shakin' Going On']* was gonna put some reverb on my guitar, not knowing that I had some reverb turned on my amp. He jammed too much on and it caused a feedback. When we were through, I said: "Ain't there somethin' we can do to get that squeal outa there?" but he reckoned: "I don't know, leave it there." And, y'know, I done shows with a lotta groups back then and they'd say: "Jerry, how in the world d'ya get that feedback? That's great, man."'

Jerry did not, however, become a psychedelic pioneer but followed 'Josephine' with nice, equally old-style, rock versions of 'Let The Four Winds Blow', 'Brown Eyed Handsome Man' and a solid album on which he was accompanied by Bobby Emmons (piano, organ), Jerry Arnold (sax), Reggie Young (guitar) and other Bill Black people. There were five Fats Domino hits on it.

'Joe Cuoghi chose the songs. When 'Josephine' got big, Fats sent Joe a whole catalogue of other songs he'd recorded and asked if I could do 'em. So I did, and he got composing royalties on most of 'em and probably made more money than I did! Hi had the idea that I sounded like a young

Fats but I wasn't trying to sing like that. I wish I could. What knocked me out was when people would come out to a show and 80% of 'em would think — before they had seen pictures in the trade papers — that I was a black man. In fact, 'Long Black Veil' was my countrified record with twin flutes and harmonica, yet it was Number One on a Top Fifty soul station in Augusta, Georgia. I visited the station and thought they had shoved it up there just 'cos I was passing but I asked to see all the previous week's playlists and sure 'nuff it was climbing those!'

Until 1969 Jerry continued to obtain work on the strength of 'Josephine'. Then he met Bob Tucker who ran the Bill Black Combo after Black's death and agreed to be managed by him. Through Tucker he was happy to come to Mega with a three-year contract. His country sides, four singles to date, have been sufficiently well-received for Jerry to have been nominated the most promising C&W artist of the year in *Music City News*, but, while beautifully sung and exquisitely arranged (by Tommy Allsup), Nashville is unhappily bent on the kind of merger between C&W and easy-listening which can only make a rock'n'roll fan shudder. Jerry sold a million with a record that cost thirteen dollars to make. Mega now spend thousands of dollars on his sessions without setting the world alight. Nonetheless, if the perfect modern country sound excites you, check out 'Love's A Job', 'Tiny Praying Hands' (both on Mega) and 'Here's To You Darlin'' (on Raintree). Soul fans might prefer Jerry's straighter but heartfelt version of Bobby Bland's 'Share Your Love With Me' (another Mega recording). I do.

Note 1   This feature was originally published in *Let It Rock* (May 1973). The magazine changed the title to *Last Of The Hillbillies*, presumably for reasons to do with typesetting.

Note 2   Jerry Jaye enjoyed further C&W hits on Columbia in 1975 and back on Hi Records in 1976. 'Honky Tonk Women Love Red Neck Men' (No. 32 C&W) was also the title of his sadly underrated second album for Hi. Another cut, 'Standing Room Only', contains the mordant line *'You must think my bed is a bus stop, the way you come and go'*. He appeared at Oxford Street's 100 Club in 1995.

2.3

BENNY JOY
Rockabilly Party Crasher

Benny Joy fulfills all known rockabilly criteria. Like Carl Perkins, he claimed to recognise a kindred spirit as soon as he heard Elvis. Like Charlie Feathers, he made a tiny handful of records prized as much for their rarity as their musical value. In common with most rockabilly singers, he never had a hit and his original 45s now command extremely high prices.

Benny's records bristled with images and values central to Fifties teenagers in the small-town American South. They've also encouraged the fantasies of European collectors who know that Benny had a distinctive grasp on what made rock'n'roll so attractive. Few other performers sang of girls, high school, jukeboxes and parties in quite so ardent and impassioned a manner. Benny Joy wasn't well known beyond the brotherhood of rockabilly enthusiasts but within that discerning circle he'll be remembered as a man with a steadfast commitment to what he saw as the music's essential character. 'Rockabilly is American,' he explained to Derek Glenister, 'and true rockabilly is Southern. From the South — Dixie!'

Benny Joy was born Benjamin Joy Eidson in Atlanta, Georgia on 5 November 1935, the youngest son of Albert and Verna Eidson. Their surname, pronounced 'Idson', derived from the Southern enunciation of 'Eizen'; the family can trace their ancestry to a specific group of German settlers. Benny's unusual middle name came from an Uncle Joy who grew up to be a light-hearted soul. Benny was christened in his honour.

Albert Sidney Eidson worked on a farm in southern Georgia until 1935, when he took a job with an oil company in Atlanta. In 1941, the company relocated to Tampa, Florida and Benny's family moved with it. They lived in nearby Plant City, the Strawberry Capital Of The World.

Benny belonged to the Port Tampa City First Baptist Church and sang in the choir when he was eight years old. His father bought him a cheap guitar when he was about twelve and his brother, Charles Eidson, still remembers the family's astonishment: 'He never had a lesson in his life. Nor could he read a note of music. I was there together with my sister, Jean. Much to our amazement, he just picked the thing up and started playing it.'

At Plant City High School, Benny became President of the Guitar Club and invited other kids to play with him. His brother believes Benny met guitarist John Wilkie Taylor around this time, even though the two friends attended different high schools: 'Big John stayed at my house more than I did. He was like another brother to my brother.' Taylor had moved to Tampa from Tennessee, where he was born on 5 January 1937.

Around 1951, Benny formed his first band. They played in the high school gym and further afield at drive-in theatres during the intermission between movies. Benny was familiar with country music and grew up to the sounds of Red Foley, Ernest Tubb and the Hanks — Williams and Snow. Bobby Lord, soon-to-be star of the *Ozark Jubilee*, also attended Plant City High School. A year older than Benny, he sang country music with the unbuttoned vigour of a blues shouter. In fact, Lord caught on to rockabilly real fast; check out his supremely eccentric take on Monroe Jackson's 'No More, No More, No More' recorded for Columbia as early as October 1954.

Notwithstanding his pride in most things below Mason and Dixon's boundary, Benny Joy had no truck with the semi-apartheid that prevailed in the Old South and his love of black music ran deeper than most white kids' fascination with R&B: 'He was always attracted to Negro singers,' Charles Eidson told me, 'be it farm labour or in the oil company plants where his father worked until he died. The blacks always sang and my brother loved that feeling, that spirit. He would sooner spend a day with a bunch of Negroes —picking up humming, picking guitars, slapping on cigar boxes — than anything else in the world. You hear of the hostility between the black and white races in the South, but my brother automatically got along with black people and they loved him. He would sing and imitate them. He would even get on the phone and talk in their dialect. There are songs that have never been released, songs like 'Night Owl Man', that he got from the black community.'

Benny plainly dabbled in C&W at high school. 'We had this guitar-player who never caught it,' he told *Tampa Times* staff reporter Dale Wilson in 1980. 'He couldn't make the change from country to rockabilly.' But he also maintained that rockabilly came to him in a fully-conceived parcel which combined the look, the swagger and the raw emotion: 'We were like rebels, man. James Dean, Marlon Brando, all those guys. I felt that; I felt what they were feeling. And I leaned to a combination of country, blues and rock. It was just a natural thing I had. I didn't know Elvis Presley and others were doing the same thing.'

If Benny claimed not to have changed the way he sang or played because of Elvis, he evidently recognised the hybrid energy of Presley's first records for Sun and it was Elvis who showed what could be achieved with the new music. After graduating from high school, Benny took a trip to Memphis where he met Sun Records' Sam Phillips, who told him to

2.3 - Benny Joy

return when he'd written some more songs. He went back and played his new material to Jack Clement who told Benny his name could adorn the bright yellow label providing he moved to Memphis. This story, told to Dale Wilson, had altered a little by the time Benny spoke to *Kicks* magazine in 1984. By then, he'd met Jack Clement on both occasions and his second journey took place after he'd had a couple of records on other labels. No matter: Benny didn't get on Sun because he had a job and a girlfriend in Tampa and didn't want to risk leaving either of them.

Back in Florida, Benny worked for the A&P grocery chain and the Trailways Bus Company. His parents wanted him to go to the University Of Tampa like his brother, but Benny was intent on making music and continued rocking in his spare time. He and Big John Taylor played all over Tampa — often in association with Gene Watson & The Rockets, a local band who recorded for Tri-Dec Records co-owned by Dar Dodds, a WGTO deejay who ran the label from a box number in Haines City. 'My Rockin' Baby' and 'Drummer Boy Rock', the produce of radio WGTO's studios, are among Watson's best known recordings.

In July 1957, Joy and Taylor gathered around the microphones at WGTO for a session of their own. The precise details are not well documented but, as far as we can determine, this first foray into a recording studio gave rise to a handful of numbers including 'Spin The Bottle', 'I'm Doubtful Of Your Love', 'Steady With Betty' and 'Hey High School Baby'.

Tri-Dec issued one single, 'Hey High School Baby' *c/w* 'Spin The Bottle' (Tri-Dec 8667), which was probably released around September 1957 when Benny signed a publishing contract with Tri-Dec Music. He and Taylor promoted the disc on personal appearances at high school gyms, recreation centres and drive-ins sharing the circuit with Gene Watson, who claimed to have played rhythm guitar on both sides. 'Gene wasn't that serious about music,' Benny told *Kicks*. 'It was just a fun thing for him.' In truth, Watson's records barely scrape the mustard and his lesser celebrity can't be blamed on a cavalier attitude to fame and fortune. Benny, on the other hand, had motivation in bucketfuls, firmly believing that he was destined for rock'n'roll stardom, subject only to a major label contract and the right promotion.

Tri-Dec arranged a further session at their own studios in Auburnville, Florida. Again, details are uncertain, but the Auburnville recordings probably included 'Kiss Me', 'Ittie Bittie Everything', John Taylor's instrumental 'Money Money', 'In Study Hall' and 'Rollin' To The Jukebox Rock', which Benny wrote at a drive-in restaurant on Bayshore where he and his pals hung out.

For the most part, these were excellent tracks aimed straight at Joy and Taylor's own peer group. But Dodds kept them in the can, probably because 'Spin The Bottle' — the B-side of the Tri-Dec single — had somehow snagged the attention of Shelby Singleton, the half Scottish-half Cajun hustler who handled field promotion for Mercury–Starday

Records on behalf of Pappy Daily. Singleton was charged with finding fresh talent for Dixie, Starday's affiliated label: Benny Joy's 'Spin The Bottle' c/w 'Steady With Betty' (Dixie 2001) and two more Florida recordings, Gene Watson's 'I'll Always Love You' c/w 'Life's Valley' (Dixie 2003), were among the records which helped kick-start Starday's subsidiary. *Billboard* carried the news in a feature dated 20 January 1958. The trade paper noted that Dixie was a new firm specialising in rock'n'roll records; that it's first release introduced Benny Joy from Plant City, Florida, singing two of his own songs; and that Mercury would distribute the Dixie label throughout the South.

The following month, *Billboard* reviewed both sides, describing 'Spin The Bottle' as *'a strong, country blues effort'*. In their opinion, the vocalist had a *'good down-country sound'* that could go well in pop markets. 'Steady With Betty' was tabbed *'an out-of-breath heavily echo'd upbeat blues directed at the teeners'*.

It's been said that 'Spin The Bottle' on Dixie is an alternative take, but that's not the case. The Tri-Dec 45 comes with prominent percussion while the Dixie single has no audible drums. Since the vocal on both discs is identical, Shelby Singleton obviously acquired a Tri-Dec tape without the snare drum overdub. Whatever the wrinkles behind that curiosity, Singleton followed time-honoured tradition by adding his name to the composer credits on 'Spin The Bottle' and 'Steady With Betty'. Both copyrights were assigned to Starrite, Starday's music publishing arm.

' 'Spin The Bottle', 'Hey High School Baby', 'Steady With Betty'... they made some noise. They were our best stuff,' Benny told Dale Wilson. 'But I should have gone to Memphis,' he added. 'I didn't know too much about the music business back then. I saw this chance in Florida and I took it. That may have been an error.'

With records out on two small labels and something of a local following, Benny was beginning to look like Tampa's answer to Elvis. His very own Colonel Tom Parker arrived in the shape of Samuel 'Buck' Ram, a middle-aged lawyer who'd got the Platters on Mercury Records and guided the group to international fame.

It was in 1954 that Buck Ram and Jean L. Bennett launched Personality Promotions & Productions. Bennett, Ram's associate for over 35 years, moved to Los Angeles from Missouri to try her luck as a singer. She met Ram when she was referred to him as a music coach. She made her name in the industry by breaking the Platters' 'Only You' into a national hit. By 1957, she was handling publicity and promotion for over forty acts.

Bennett, who now runs the company from Las Vegas, thought Benny had sent a demo of 'Little Red Book' and other songs to Personality Promotions. Buck, she said, had talked up the tapes in conversations with Mercury's founder and president, Irv Green. He also played the tapes to other Mercury executives. 'Well... go get 'em!' they said.

Ram and Bennett flew to Florida and signed Joy and Taylor to

2.3 - Benny Joy

management and recording contracts and to Ram's music publishing company, Argo Music. 'They were signed together,' said Bennett, 'because that guitar was very important to Benny. Big John's guitar was a speciality. He was great. We took them to New York and introduced them to people. They went down to the Turf restaurant by the Brill Building and they asked the waiter for grits. Benny came back hassling about it: "They don't even know what grits are!" They were two big ol' gawky kids. I didn't even know Florida had hillbillies!'

Billboard announced Ram's new acquisitions in March 1958: *'Buck Ram made a trip to Florida last week and pacted three new pieces of talent. He also picked up ten masters for soon release. Talent includes Benny Joy, rock'n'roll singer set to record for Antler Records; the Canon Girls, aged 15 and 17, who write and sing; and Big John Taylor, a guitarist who will also cut sides for Ram's label, Antler.'*

Buck Ram and Jerry Blaine had set up Antler Records in New York in 1956, but Blaine, the owner of Jubilee, soon sold his half of the company to Ram, who moved the operation to Los Angeles. Ram would eventually discover that his creative attachment to black culture was no basis for running a record company but, in the meantime, he signed a host of R&B artists including the Flairs, Gerald Wilson, the Jewels, Eddie Beal, the Colts, Dimples Harris, Earle Warren and Ray Scott *aka* Walter Spriggs. The roster also contained two white acts, Johnny Olenn, who starred in *The Girl Can't Help It* (he's the potato-faced singer in the glowing red suit), and the Blockbusters, a rock'n'roll combo who recorded for Aladdin/Intro and appeared in the trash teen epic, *Rock All Night*. At first, Antler was distributed by George Goldner's Gone Records, but distribution was soon taken over by Mercury in a double-act similar to the aforementioned Mercury–Starday imprint operative during 1957-58.

The ten masters to which *Billboard* referred included tracks which Benny had cut for Tri-Dec — titles like 'Miss Bobby Sox', 'Little Red Book' and 'Rollin' To The Jukebox Rock'. Jean Bennett couldn't be sure if 'Crash The Party' was on the tape which excited Mercury's top brass, but for many it's the one stupendous lightning-in-a-bottle achievement for which Benny Joy is probably best remembered. According to a note in the Ram archives it was recorded on 2 March 1958 with a band consisting of John McCullough (piano), Big John Taylor (guitar), Mike Savas (bass) and Bill Peck (drums). Released on 1 May, 'Crash The Party' (Antler 4011) was reviewed in *Billboard* on 19 May: *'Benny Joy turns in a rocking reading of a pulsing blues effort on his debut for the label. Lad can sing... a cat to watch'*. *Billboard*'s panel also liked the flip, 'Little Red Book': *'The warbler comes thru with a good quivering type of reading of a rockabilly effort.'*

A close-to-three minute version of 'Crash The Party' surfaced on a *Record Mart*-initiated reissue in 1978. This unholy racket of a rock'n'roll record is bursting with primal energy, lascivious exhortations and a passion to match the achievements of the music's acknowledged leaders.

Buck Ram may have thought the shorter and rather badly-edited Antler single (2:26) stood a better chance of airplay. As it turned out, Mercury were hot on pop and R&B but lacked commitment in other areas. They'd turned down Elvis Presley (Irv Green decided he couldn't afford Sam Phillips's asking price) and they dumped Conway Twitty just before he made it. The Mercury–Starday deal was about to come to an end with acrimony on all sides and Shelby Singleton, who could usually sense a smash hit, was still a regional promo-man in Louisiana. Mercury's executives had difficulty understanding a grassroots movement like rockabilly and, in the summer of '58, there was no-one there with any appreciation of C&W-orientated rock'n'roll. 'Crash The Party', a record which should at least have bopped around the lower reaches of the Hot 100, failed to make any headway. Benny plugged the song on *American Bandstand*, but without Mercury's full support — or their ruthless use of payola — sales were disappointing.

Buck Ram subsequently recorded Benny in Nashville with a cadre of the city's finest session musicians including Boots Randolph (saxophone), Hank Garland (guitar), Bob Moore (bass) and Buddy Harman (drums). A noticeably powerful batch of recordings — 'You're A Bundle Of Love', 'Button Nose', 'I'm Gonna Move' and a fresh, piano-drenched version of 'Hey High School Baby' (Mel Robbins at the keyboard) — were dispatched to Mercury's Sound Studios in New York, but the company evidently rejected them all.

Buck Ram dipped into his cache of Tri-Dec masters and pulled out 'Ittie Bittie Everything' *c/w* Big John Taylor's 'Money Money', releasing the record on a subsidiary of Antler (Ram 1000-1) in 1959. The top deck sounds like a title Bobby Vee might have come up with, but it's a thunderous rocker fuelled by Taylor's churning electric guitar. According to John W. Taylor Jr: 'Daddy wrote that song about my mother.' The record was issued as by 'Benny Joy–Big John Taylor' and they also shared the songwriting credits. Both sides have also been listed on the Mercury-distributed parent logo (Antler 1107) but I've not seen a copy on that imprint. A note in Mercury's ledgers tells us that all the Benny Joy titles were returned to Buck Ram on 14 July 1959.

There can scarcely have been a more surprising development in Benny's life than the decision to tour Europe in the late Fifties. As various factors contributed to rockabilly's demise in the USA, Benny Joy and Big John Taylor were bringing the guitar-driven style, sound and image to European audiences — first with a package of Buck Ram's artists in 1958, and then on a six-week tour of their own in the summer of 1959. First time around, they appeared in France, Italy and Yugoslavia with an entourage of twenty-two people including Linda Hayes, Walter Spriggs, the Fraternity Brothers, Barry DeVorzon, the Blockbusters and the Flairs. The Platters joined them when they played major cities. 'Crash The Party' was issued in Italy (Broadway 1004) and the same company released an album called *Festival Of American Songs* (Broadway 3002) containing both sides of Benny's singles on Antler and Ram. I'm told it also includes his version of Paul Anka's 'Lonely Boy', which has never surfaced anywhere else in the world. Benny told *Kicks* that he'd recorded the song in Italy, where he encountered the most enthusiastic audiences of his career: 'We were possibly the very first rockabilly act that toured Europe. The response was wild... In our stage shows, we did our own songs and stuff like 'Baby Let's Play House'. We encored time and time again. In fact, I think it was as wild, or wilder, than it was over here (in the USA). One time in Trieste, Italy, someone pulled me off the stage and I ended up in the crowd. It took six policeman to break this up and I just went flying through the air back up on stage with my coat torn off.'

Jean Bennett didn't go on the big tour but remembers the event: 'It was arranged by a part-Italian, part-Egyptian promoter and it was supposed to be an annual festival. Buck sent his brother, Michael Ram, with the artists. Benny got kinda sick over there. John Mangano, the piano player with the Blockbusters, he was rooming with Benny and he told us... he said: "I gotta tell you this about Benny Joy. He was constipated and he came into me one day and said: 'I want you to look at these pills the doctor wants me to take.' He held up these long suppositories and he said: 'How am I gonna swallow *these*?"'

Benny Joy and Big John Taylor left Buck Ram after a number of disagreements — mostly over money, though Benny's friends also reckoned Buck didn't much care for Benny's act. 'The Elvis gyrations. That's on the way out,' Buck told him.

Jean Bennett agreed that Buck would have encouraged Benny to do more of his own thing without imitating anyone else. There was, she maintains, no abiding rancour: 'Buck liked Benny and there was nothing really unpleasant about it. Every young person who went through our stable came out of there a lot smarter, and Benny got a good solid foundation from us. Many years later, John Taylor called me and he said: "Y'know Jean, we were kids, we were so impatient, we thought everything had to happen immediately. Now, as we look back, we were fools to split with Buck. He really did an awful lot for us."'

Although Benny long complained that he had not been properly paid 'on any of my early work as a writer and artist on my Tri-Dec and Antler/Argo Music recordings', his brother Charles agreed with Jean Bennett's assessment: 'In a strange way, there was a love relationship between Benny and Buck Ram. My brother also admired Jean Bennett. It felt like a family relationship. My father also liked Buck, and Benny had nothing but praise for him. There were times when Buck would go to my father and get him to approve things that my brother didn't want to do. But, in the final analysis, Benny loved Buck Ram and would most probably have done anything Buck asked him to do.'

Joy and Taylor also parted company in 1959 following an argument over the division of royalties and concert fees. Taylor went to Florida State University and graduated in 1961. For a while he led his own group, Big John's Untouchables, but eventually settled for a post in local government. At the time of his death from cancer on 13 April 1995, he was the city administrator of Auburnville.

Benny stayed in Nashville, where he signed a contract with Decca in 1961. The company issued two singles, 'New York Hey Hey' (Decca 31199) and 'Birds Of A Feather Fly Together' (Decca 31280). 'My brother wrote 'New York Hey Hey' back in '59,' recalled Charles Eidson. 'He was flying back from Italy via London, and he was afraid of flying. There was a black man on the plane who was crying 'cos he was so terrified. When the plane landed in New York, the black man jumped up and hit the floor on his knees and hollered "New York, hey hey!" My brother wrote the song.'

The patronage of a major label failed to lead to a career upswing and Decca left at least five tracks in the can. 'They wanted to make me the male equivalent to Brenda Lee with violins and strings,' Benny grumbled on more than one occasion. 'I wasn't allowed to record rock'n'roll. It changed my image and I had no control over it, although I had lots of good rock'n'roll tunes.'

A handful of Benny's earlier recordings admit reminders of greater or more charismatic talents; the influence of Presley looms large over some, while 'She Cried For Me' leaps out of the Buddy Holly songbook. (Writer credits are actually attributed to Joy and Taylor though Benny has said he'd often cut Taylor in on songs which he wrote himself: 'Many times, he contributed little or nothing because he wasn't a great writer. But he was a great guitar player and he had a lot of potential.')

Other cuts are quite exceptional. There are ballads which he sang with more flexibility than one might have suspected and rockers which sound absolutely fresh. 'Gossip, Gossip, Gossip', recorded at Benny's home with Big John Taylor, is a prime example. It's brilliant rock'n'roll, and Benny knew it. His voice has the coarse-edged, self-possessed attack which gift-wrapped all his best lyrics.

In June 1962, Joy joined Cedarwood Publishing Co. as a contract writer. He was a prolific tunesmith with some two hundred songs to his name. He wrote by himself and with other Nashville-based songwriters including Larry Kirby, Hugh X. Lewis, Marijohn Wilkin, Mel Tillis, Kent Westberry and Rodney Smith. He explained his methods to *Country Song Roundup* in 1965:

'As for how I go about writing a song, I always write from a title or an idea. Then I try to create an original melody, and fit the title and idea to it. The next thing I do is work out a construction and, if necessary, a rhyming pattern to fit the lyrics of the song.

'There are many different kinds of writers. There are story-writers, heart-writers, trend-writers, specialty-writers like the ones who only write children's songs, Christmas songs, etc, and I believe it is good for a writer to be versatile. A writer should try his hand at all the different types and classifications of writing if he is so inclined. This is especially important from a commercial standpoint. Although a person might be successful in several of the types mentioned, I believe that every writer has one particular type of songs which he writes best.

'I think you definitely have to be inspired to write 'heart' songs, and most of my inspirational ideas and thoughts have come from true life experiences. Many great songs have been written by persons who have had a sad experience in love, or who have had a tragedy occur in their home life. The ability to express such experiences in words and music, so that the listener may identify his own troubles with those which you have experienced, is the greatest gift a songwriter could possess.'

Benny's songs, often cloaked in doom and despair, were recorded by a broad range of artists. His most recognisable numbers include 'Hey Bossman' (Ray Smith), 'Big Old Ugly Fool' (Red Sovine), 'I Need A Whole Lotta You' (Johnny Hallyday), 'Holding Back The Tears' (Bobbi Martin), 'One Dozen Roses' (a Top Thirty C&W hit for George Morgan), 'She Loved Everybody But Me' (Charlie Rich), 'Home James' (Burl Ives), 'A Time And A Place For Everything' (Marty Robbins), 'Take The Ring Off Your Finger' (Carl Smith), 'Call The Zoo' (Darrell McCall), 'We'd Destroy Each Other' (Carl & Pearl Butler) and 'Touchdown' (Jimmy Isle).

Other customers included Glen Garrison, Warner Mack, Jim Pierce, Mel Tillis, Carl Perkins, Webb Pierce, Debbie Reynolds, Jackie Wilson and Johnny Rivers, but his biggest client was probably Stonewall Jackson who hit Number One C&W with 'B.J. The D.J.' in 1964. According to *Country Song Roundup*, Benny wrote the song with Hugh Lewis; Benny's name isn't in the credits, but he may have sold his share. (Incidentally, the 'B.J.' stood not for Benny Joy but for Byron Johnson, the Mississippi-based disc-jockey who recorded for D Records). Stonewall Jackson's follow-up, another of Benny's songs called 'Not My Kind Of People', also went Top Thirty.

Benny recorded a single for Dot Records in 1963, but the company took a bath trying to promote 'Somebody Else's Heart' (Dot 16445). His recording career finally petered out with four tracks for Mercury in 1965. The label issued one stillborn single, 'The Only Woman', as by Benjamin Joy (Mercury 72450), but all four songs carry a pronounced emotional impact. In black hands, they'd be called 'soul ballads'; as *Billboard* had indicated back in '58, the lad could sing.

Benny remained in Nashville for ten years. He got married and he got divorced. 'The marriage lasted several years,' said Charles Eidson, 'but the break-up did something to his psyche. He'd had a lot of country hits, but his entire writing changed. It affected him spiritually, physically and mentally.' There were no children.

Jim Newcombe, who met Benny at a Nashville disc-jockey convention, recalled sharing a taxi cab to a party. 'Hey man, where's all the pussy?' Benny asked the driver, who responded with prices and other details. Benny would have sympathised with the Platters, four of whom were arraigned on charges of aiding and abetting prostitution in 1959.

(They were acquitted, but their wholesome image took a bit of a dent.)

In 1972, Benny returned to Florida where he lived with his mother in Tampa. John Burton, rockabilly collector and researcher, visited Benny in 1979. They talked Fifties, football and girls. Benny, he said, was always ready for a laugh. Burton also noticed that Benny's singing and guitar-playing were unaffected by the passage of time. Benny badly wanted to play concert dates in England, but plans were shelved when he was found to be suffering from cancer.

Benny Joy's premature death on 28 October 1988 brought to a close one of the more colourful footnotes in the history of rock'n'roll. He is held by many to be one of the most individual writer-musicians which rockabilly has produced.

Note   Published in *Now Dig This* (February 1999). This feature was an expanded version of the liner notes to *Benny Joy: Crash The Rockabilly Party* (Ace CDCHD-703) 1998. I can also recommend a wonderfully self-indulgent, garage-thrash collection called *The A-Bones Crash The Party With The Wild, Wild Songs Of Benny Joy* (Norton CD CED-254) 1996.

MAC CURTIS

2.4
MAC CURTIS
Bluejean Heart

Rockabilly invites as many descriptions as there are people to describe it; hillbilly with the brakes off, white man's R&B, the snarling face of raw sexuality. Mac Curtis is at the forefront of the resurgence of interest in this twenty-five year old musical hybrid serving up coolly professional but uninhibited helpings to a fourth generation of teenaged fans. He's one of the founding fathers and a Texan rockabilly legend but there's nothing cobwebbed about his most recent performances, still full of fire, honesty and slithering excitement.

Mac's first records — roughly commensurate with instant Nirvana — command a $50 price-tag although, happily, reissues are now available to anyone who wants them. The Sixties, a bringdown for any rockabilly singer, still brought many an acceptable Curtis record, the kind I play once a year and find myself saying: 'Hey, that's nice.'

Offstage, Mac is neither inarticulate hayseed nor egocentrically flash. If that makes him sound bland or uninteresting I'm sorry, 'cos that wouldn't be true either. Tall, eloquent, youthful, he retains the enthusiasm of a superfan with a scholastic appreciation of rockabilly's finer points (*New Kommotion* issues 19 and 23 carry his no-detail-spared reminiscences about Ronnie Dawson, the Chaparrals, Gaylon Christie, Bill Mack and other musical obscurities from Texas). Despite his easygoing professionalism, it transpires that his many recordings are in the nature of a sideline — an inseparable but rarely profitable adjunct to school, the armed forces or regular employment in radio ever since he joined KZEE when he was eighteen years old ('They needed someone to play the kids' music').

From Fort Worth, Texas, where he was born on 16 January 1939, Wesley Erwin Curtis grew up with his grandparents in Olney, a hundred miles from the city. An uncle, William Dunn, played upright bass with swing bands and also sang quartet gospel music with friends. These, and the western swing of Bob Wills were among Mac's earliest musical memories, but he also listened to Dallas's *Big D Jamboree*, where he was drawn to the music of Hank Williams, Lefty Frizzell and seminal country boogie bands like the Carlisles and Maddox Brothers & Rose. In 1952, he visited a Fort Worth junk shop and discovered the records of Piano Red;

'race music' or rhythm & blues had entered his vocabulary, and his infatuation increased when T.M. Mills, an elderly farmer and community church member, taught Mac to play the East Texas blues on a cheap rhythm guitar: 'T.M. had gnarled-up, knuckled-up old fingers, but he taught me chords and rhythm. It was a treat to see that Merle Travis–Chet Atkins sound live and I'd watch him for hours, just as long as I could keep him awake.'

In 1954 Mac moved to Weatherford, where he won second place and $15 in a talent contest held by the Rural Electrification Administration. He formed a hillbilly band with the Galbraith brothers, Kenneth (mandolin) and Jimmy (guitar), and the group played local parties and rotaries for all the food they could eat. The following year, in Cliff Herring's Fort Worth studio, Mac recorded a couple of demos, including 'What'll I Do', issued very much later on Rollin' Rock. Elvis Presley's Sun records had now reached the jukebox in the local dairy mart and they showed the way. Mac's sedate country band dropped the Eddy Arnold numbers in favour of the Sun sound, and in 1956 the group appeared over radio KNOK where black deejay Big Jim Randolph introduced them to Ralph Bass, talent scout for Syd Nathan's premier King label. 'The first session,' Mac recalled, 'took place with Ralph Bass and Bernie Pearlman at the Jim Beck Studios in Dallas where Sonny James and Lefty Frizzell recorded all their big hits. Unbeknownst to me, every record label was looking for an Elvis Presley and, as a matter of fact, I walked up into the control booth as they were doing some playbacks and Bernie Pearlman had a copy of Presley's first album; he would play a little bit of it and compare it with what we were doing to see if we were getting close to the sound.'

The style and content of the King records were determined not so much by Elvis's RCA album as by his Sun singles and, if those have no equal, Mac's sides are also passionately admired. The top decks from the first session — 'If I Had Me A Woman' and 'Grandaddy's Rockin'' — are perfect examples of Texan rockabilly. Light and airy but unarguably powerful, they lift you up and bite your ankles at the same time. Curtis sang with massive authority and the records radiate charm, zest and exhilaration — enjoy the slurs, the mumbles, the trembles, the glottal stops and the spontaneous echo of Bob Wills in the falsetto cry of 'Guitar!'. Jimmy Galbraith, Mac's classmate from Olney High School, emulated Scotty Moore on several volcanic breaks while brother Kenny tangled with Bill Black's trademark, switching from mandolin to string bass, which he slapped with keen precision. The group had worked with a drummer before (Mac had recruited one after seeing Presley and D.J. Fontana on the *Big D Jamboree*), but Ralph Bass preferred Bill Peck, an experienced sessionman. Bill Simmons, another seasoned *habitué* of Dallas–Fort Worth studios, played the subdued but bluesy piano especially noticeable in the bouncy Piano Red feel of 'Half-Hearted Love'.

It was Mac's personal manager, William Thompson, who contacted songwriters Joe Price and Jim Shell. Price had tried to make it as a singer, while Shell worked for the Dallas Cotton Exchange. The partnership provided songs for a host of local rockabillies, though 'If I Had Me A Woman' — all the more exciting for the sharp economy of its blues couplets — is probably their most effective composition.

The Galbraith brothers, disappointed to find that they were not included in the King contract, left Curtis in the summer of 1956. They were replaced by Kenny Cobb, bass-slapper *par excellence*, and Bill Hudson, a Merle Travis soundalike, on lead guitar. Both played on the second King session along with Simmons and Peck.

'That Ain't Nothin' But Right' is a delight: cute words from Shell and Price, and plenty of room for a piano chorus and two sparkling guitar breaks. The similarly-titled 'You Ain't Treatin' Me Right' was written by Don Johnston, an ex-Marine who lived in Fort Worth and slid into music via his mother, Diane, who wrote Hollywood film scores including *Destination Moon*. A rockabilly singer himself, Johnston also penned 'I'll Be Gentle' and 'You're My Special Baby'. Years later he changed his name to Bob Johnson and produced Bob Dylan: 'I'd seen the name on Columbia Records,' Curtis recalled, 'but I didn't know it was the same guy until he came up behind me at a Nashville convention and gave me a great big bear-hug'.

'You Ain't Treatin' Me Right', a dark, sultry bopper, tugged the emotions of North-Eastern bobby-soxers ('I began getting fan-mail from New York and Pennsylvania') and, in December 1956, Curtis joined Alan Freed's *Christmas Shower Of Stars* at the Brooklyn Paramount: 'George Hamilton IV and I became big cronies 'cos we had similar backgrounds, but the show also had the Moonglows, Screamin' Jay Hawkins, Jesse Belvin — whom I loved — the Cadillacs and Barbie Gaye, the little cherub who first did 'My Boy Lollipop'. Teddy Randazzo was like the star of the show 'cos he was big in New York. We did five shows a day separated by a film. The place was mobbed and we couldn't go anywhere. Just incredible, we had police escorts to get us in and out and we couldn't leave until 4.00 am.'

Following a tour of Connecticut with Little Richard, Curtis cut his fifth single, 'I'll Be Gentle' *c/w* 'Say So', at Cliff Herring's busy Fort Worth studio with a new lead guitarist, Jay Brinkley. Major Bill Smith, Cowtown's biggest independent producer, has described Brinkley, known for his instrumentals on Dot and Kliff, as the finest guitar picker to emerge from Fort Worth; the man flicks off a couple of feisty breaks on 'Say So'. Another song from the same session, 'Bluejean Heart', is entirely new to vinyl and, while it's not the rocking discovery it might have been, it's a nice enough ballad from the pen of Don Johnston. The whole date was produced by Louis Innis, who slapped his name on the credits of 'Goosebumps', a hiccupy rocker first unearthed for Polydor's *Rockabilly Kings* album in 1974 (though originally recorded by Mac's King labelmate, Delbert Barker).

In November 1957, Curtis entered the US armed forces, where he remained for three years working in AF Radio and TV as broadcaster and deejay. His final session for King, held in Fort Worth during Christmas home leave, advanced a fluffier, slightly more sumptuous feel attributable to a vocal group who aped the Jordanaires. They were led by Bob Kelly, an Olney High School student who wrote 'What You Want'. Kelly, who became a Dallas disc-jockey, produced the Nightcaps' 'Wine, Wine, Wine' and wrote 'Somebody Help Me' recorded by Gene Vincent (as well as Mac Curtis, whose King version has never been found). The last date for King also spawned Mac's song 'Little Miss Linda', a torrid rocker written before the session in about five minutes, though arch-hipster Ralph Bass was even quicker in putting his name to it.

On leaving the forces, Curtis returned to Texas and began to build a reputation as a country deejay. In 1959, he re-signed with the *Big D Jamboree*, enabling him to work for a radio station during the day and travel in a 200 mile radius for nightly shows. During the Sixties, he cut frequent sessions for Major Bill Smith who issued a stream of Curtis records on Felsted, Dot, Limelight, Shah, Shalimar, Maridene and LeCam. Rockabilly had virtually ceased to exist and rock'n'roll had changed beyond measure; Mac, however, kept close to his roots, waxing David Orrell's magnificent 'You're The One' and glorious, rolling Gulf Coast ballads like 'Dance Her By Me'.

By the late Sixties, Curtis was an influential deejay at WPLO in Atlanta, where he broke many a C&W hit including David Houston's 'Almost Persuaded': 'Epic's promotion man brought me the record and 'We Got Love' was the 'A' side. I told them to turn it over, and I started playing the other side. It was a big hit *[No. 24 pop in 1966]* and the Epic people thought: "Yeah, this guy knows what he's doing." Billy Sherrill, who produced Houston, came down to Atlanta for promotion — like, this is where the record broke an' all — and he took me to Nashville, where I signed with Epic. They were good years, but Billy Sherrill didn't react very well to the rockabilly feel I was trying to recreate. Glenn Sutton took over as producer and, finally I told him: "Look man, I just don't feel comfortable with a lot of the ballads. I'm not a George Jones and you're tryin' to make me too country, which I'm not. I think the time is right to do what I think I do best, and then we'd all be better off." I wanted to cut 'Your True Love', but Glenn thought that was a little obscure so we settled for 'Honey Don't'."

Mac's updated rockabilly resulted in half-a-dozen chart entries including 'Honey Don't', and the pattern continued when he moved to GRT in 1970. A fervid version of Buddy Holly's 'Early In The Morning', taken from an album on which Mac revived the rock'n'roll classics of Fats Domino, Jimmy Reed, Chuck Berry and Ray Charles, also made the C&W charts. But again there were problems. Tommy Allsup, who'd worked with the Crickets, was no longer into downhome rockabilly. Nashville producers were not in tune with rock'n'roll as Mac remembered it and that, he felt, was their loss. In 1971, he moved to Los Angeles where Rollin' Rock's Ronny Weiser soon tracked him down.

Weiser's happily restricted vision led to many intense reincarnations of the rockabilly style, as Mac and fellow legend, Ray Campi, invested a slew of obscure boppers with their own timeless brand of down home Texan 'cat music'. Some of us felt that Rollin' Rock records suffered from a certain homogeneity, but Mac's younger fans, those who read *Cat Talk* and snap up all the many rockabilly compilations, thought these new recordings were as exciting and relevant as anything else around.

In 1975, Curtis formed his own label, Emcee, and leased material to Ranwood. He cut a gospel album for Sunshine in 1977 and three tracks for Hot Rock in 1980; these echoed the past without a hint of self-parody. A year earlier, Curtis relocated to Fort Worth as general manager of radio station KXOL, where he and Tom Wayne developed a popular comedy show. Today, they operate a production company which markets comic features and commercials on a nationally syndicated basis. Apart from local performances and several tours of the UK, Curtis has appeared in Finland (1981), Holland (1982) and France (1984).

The history of Mac Curtis is a mini-history of rockabilly telling us very nearly all we need to know about the music's gestation and maturity.

Note   A good proportion of these unedited notes accompanied *Mac Curtis: Rockin' Mother* (Radarscope LP RAD-22, 1979) and *Bluejean Heart* (Charly CDCHARLY-264, 1991).

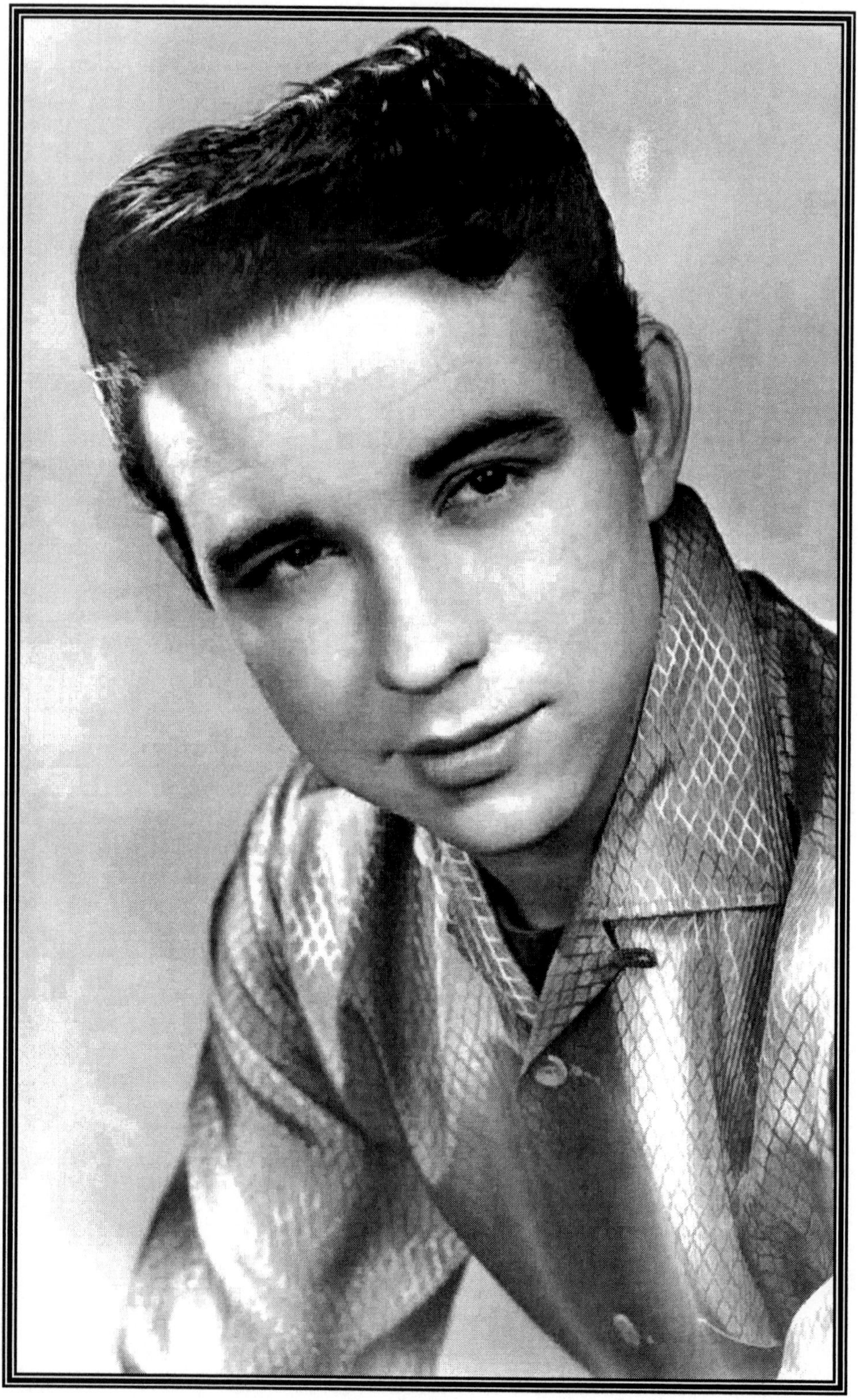

2.5

JOHNNY CARROLL
Rock, Baby, Rock It

Johnny Carroll's full-throttle brand of snarly-faced rockabilly has always been considered a trifle wilder than the rest even by the hardcore standards with which the music is generally best judged. Although they slipped between cup and lip at the time, his generic wild-man records eventually helped shape the taste of the rockabilly community — particularly in Europe where the music became a growth industry in the mid-Seventies.

Carroll was a comprehensive artist. He could deliver trembling blue note cameos of Gene Vincent's balladry, but he was at his best when he personified rockabilly's most potent image: the sexy, half-crazed fool flailing away at a guitar and hollering his guts out. If commitment means anything at all, then Carroll deserved greater celebrity. Paul Menard, who appeared with him in the film *Rock, Baby, Rock It*, paid this tribute in the English magazine, *Now Dig This*: 'I never saw anyone perform with as much passion. Of all the rockabilly guys, there was Elvis and then there was Johnny. No-one else even came close. And Johnny never had a down night. He never let up, whether it was SRO or nobody in the house.'

John Lewis Carrell was his real name, and not Johnny or even Carroll which was a Decca misspelling he failed to correct. He was born on 23 October 1937 in Cleburne, Texas and raised in nearby Godley where he would have been born if the tiny community had had a hospital. His father, William Lewis Carrell (the whole family called him 'W.L.') was a schoolteacher, a cattle rancher and a dairy farmer. He died around 1975, leaving the Carrell dairy farm in the hands of Johnny's younger brothers, Roy and Kirk. It didn't hurt that Johnny's mother, Ina Mae, came from a long line of musicians, mainly breakdown fiddlers and accordionists. She was his greatest supporter and taught him how to play guitar. His siblings took little interest in music, though Roy Carrell and his wife sing duets in church.

Carroll went to school in Godley, only thirty or so miles from Dallas and Fort Worth but light years away from the metropolitan bustle. 'Godley,' he told me in 1980, 'is still the same size now as it was in 1900. It's a very small community. About 427 people. They're happy with the size of it. In fact, they vote against new housing or industry of any kind.'

Radio was an early fascination in Carroll's life; he struggled to catch Roy Acuff, Tex Ritter or Ernest Tubb before the battery faded altogether. He bought his first guitar after working as a water-boy among wheat-threshing German internees: 'I was on a horse and I carried water around to several hundred workers stacking the corn. It must have been during the war because there were a lot of German prisoners there.'

Armed with his new acoustic guitar, Carroll, aged nine or ten, sang and played on Cleburne's KCLE on Saturday mornings. Pals from elementary school strummed along. Electricity came to Godley in 1947: 'From then on we had big, big radios that looked like a jukebox.' The Rural Electrification Program was especially important to a kid growing up on a farm in North-Central Texas. Carroll could tune into WBAP in Fort Worth, the hour-long *Grand Ole Opry* programme on Saturday nights and other strong 50,000-watt stations that played the blues during the early hours of the morning: 'That got to be the 'in' thing,' he recalled. 'Blues had such an impact. We were getting it out of New Orleans and on WLAC in Nashville. I also had a cousin in the jukebox and coin-operating machine business who was always giving me 'race' records. I got a lot of discs, all 78s of course. I don't remember labels, but Big Joe Turner was one of my favourites. B.B. King too. While I was in high school we were all getting into the Clovers and the Charms. We were basically country people, but we were getting into, like, 'Hearts Of Stone' and we started doing those songs. We didn't have the instrumentation they did of course, we still had a hillbilly band. But there was no segregation musically.'

W.L.'s tolerance of the black man may have extended further than most farmers in 1950s Texas. 'Besides all else,' Carroll continued, 'my dad was a greyhound breeder. He imported dogs from England. In fact, he shipped 'em both ways. The coloured people were very heavy into greyhounds and they were out at our place all the time. Dad invited them to greyhound races at the property, so there'd be 50 or 75 coloured people there every week. I didn't know about 'race' as such. I'd heard about 'nigrahs' and all that stuff, but I never associated the ones I knew with the ones they were talking about.'

Carroll's high school band, formed in 1952, were called the Texas Moonlighters because of the many nights which he and his friends spent milking cows or baling hay. 'They sounded like Slim Whitman,' he told John Blair, 'but with a little touch of the Clovers.' They performed at talent contests sponsored by the Future Farmers Of America organization and on KCLE, where the programme directors, Ronnie Hall and Gene Echols, helped them obtain other bookings. At high school, and on graduation in 1955, the band included Bill Hennen on piano and Billy Buntin on bass. Lead guitarist Jay Salem from Burleson, Texas was brought in when he came second in a talent contest at which the Moonlighters won first prize.

The Moonlighters never made a dime more than subsistence living even though, in Carroll's words 'we played anyplace we possibly could and just tried to get on stage anywhere we could. We'd managed to play in a few shows and got some reviews and credentials even though I wasn't recording for anybody. Then, I went to a show starring Ferlin Husky and Hank Snow at the Northside Coliseum in Fort Worth. I got backstage and talked to Ferlin. I told him we were a local band trying to get started and that we'd had write-ups here and there. Ferlin said: "Let me hear a little bit of what you do." So, I got my band, which was Bill Hennen and Billy Buntin and Jay who was probably with us then. No drummer, just a hillbilly band. Ferlin heard us and he said: "I tell you what I'm gonna do. There's a lot of important people out there. You go out and do the first fifteen minutes of my show." And we did, and that's when this J.G. Tiger came up...'

J.G. stood for Jack Goldman, who added a flamboyant but fictional surname to increase his prestige. He was a big man, six foot four, with a booming Texan diphthong and a black, untamed, Santa Claus beard. He chewed on raw garlic and bits of the pungent tuber would lodge in it. He may have been a wrestler at one time. Johnny thought he was pushy but positive. He was impressed by Goldman's patter: 'At the time I thought he was fifty years older than me, but it turned out he was only 28 or 29.'

J.G. Tiger took the band, now renamed the Hot Rocks, into Dallas where he owned or had an interest in the Top Ten Recording Studio. 'It was a beautiful-looking studio,' remembered Johnny, 'but the sound was *horrible*. Next door had a bunch of transformers and every tape that came out of that studio had a buzz on it.' The group added a drummer, one Dude Cohn, and made their recording debut at the Top Ten in 1955.

'Why Cry', 'Hearts Of Stone', 'Sexy Ways', 'Crazy Little Mama' and 'Stingy Thing' are among the tapes or acetates which survive and the R&B titles demonstrate how quickly Carroll and his chums jumped on this stuff. 'Hearts Of Stone' and 'Sexy Ways' had been around for a year or two, but the Eldorados' 'Crazy Little Mama' *aka* 'At My Front Door' didn't enter the *Billboard* R&B chart until September 1955. I'm not sure which tracks were submitted to Paul Cohen, Decca's A&R chief in Nashville, but whatever he heard (probably 'Crazy Crazy Lovin' ' and 'You Two-Timed Me One Time Too Often'), Cohen was impressed.

In the meantime, Carroll continued playing sock hops, school auditoriums and hillbilly pisspots all over North and West Texas. He often appeared with Mac Curtis but also recalled opening a show for Elvis, Scotty & Bill and Hank Snow. He played the *Big D Jamboree* when Elvis was there, but thought this Hank Snow bill-topper took place in Waco or Fort Worth. 'Hank hated Elvis with a passion,' he said. 'I can tell you that Hank Snow did not like Elvis at all. He may have later, but I know from being backstage that he really had some vile things to say about Elvis.'

Johnny Carroll recounted the story of his Decca sessions many times. Here's what he said to me in 1980: 'Tiger called me saying: "I've got you a deal, but the regular boys in the band can't come to this session." Dude Cohn had gone off immediately to Sonny James, but the rest of the band were very disappointed. After we got to Nashville, Tiger tells me we can't record unless I give them the publishing rights to 'Crazy Crazy Lovin'', which was my song, and I can't do that unless I give him writer's credit on it.

'We went down and did three tunes and next day we did three more. They were cut in the basement of a house that belonged to Owen Bradley. There was Grady Martin on lead guitar, Owen Bradley on piano and Bradley's brother, Harold, on rhythm guitar. I've no idea who the bass player or drummer were. Y'know, I was swept in there... "Okay, let's do it" and right back out again. 'Crazy Crazy Lovin'' was the one song I wanted to do. The session guys listened to our demos and copied 'em almost exactly. 'Trying To Get To You' I'm real fuzzy on. I'm sure it was one they said I had to do. They gave me a Johnny Cash demo of 'Rock & Roll Ruby'. It was just Cash singing and, if I remember correctly, there wasn't anything but a guitar on it. I liked it, anyhow. I thought it was a good song to go with. But then it seems like everybody in the world put it out. Warren Smith did a real good job. Rusty Draper's was too laid-back. Mine might have been a little too frantic. I liked Warren's best...

'Tiger had the words to 'Hot Rock'. He came in with fifteen pages of words, and we edited them and put a tune to it. They played me Joe Turner's record of 'Corrine, Corrina' and said: "We're gonna do a country version of this." It was probably Paul Cohen's idea. He was in charge of the whole thing, although he left most of the decisions to Grady Martin and Owen Bradley. On 'Wild Wild Women', Ruth Brown had a song called 'Wild Wild Young Men' and I did some various changes on the thing. That was the basis for what we were doing. The Maddox Brothers & Rose also recorded it. They were one of my favourites. They were really rockabilly pioneers along with Jumpin' Bill Carlisle.'

The Decca singles were played in the South and North-East. Most of the fan mail — enough to fill two suitcases — came from New York and New Jersey. But on a national scale, teenagers paid more attention to ads for pimple cream. 'Wild Wild Women' and 'Hot Rock' were also issued in Britain in 1956. For James Asman, English record columnist, they fell into the category of *'rock-billies'* music, though the description had not caught on in Godley, Texas. 'We called our music "country rhythm'n'blues",' said Carroll. 'Rockabilly? That was a term which, say Faron Young or Hank Snow would use. It was a term for belittling — it was a put-down.'

The UK issues (on Brunswick) didn't sell either. It was scant reward for such genre-defining classics. The entrepreneurial Goldman decided that a movie would best promote his nineteen year old protégé. According to John Blair, he approached his mother who gave him $10,000 in return for shaving off his beard. Johnny Carroll agreed that: 'Tiger's family was rich, they had a lot of money. He seemed to be the one that wasn't making any, but he was taking it off the rest of 'em.' The newly-shaven Goldman financed *Rock, Baby, Rock It*, filmed — not in Memphis as the *Rock & Roll Movie Encyclopedia Of The 1950s* would have it — but mainly in Dallas. Distribution came via Free–Bar of Dallas; Johnny thought they distributed the Japanese horror flick, *Godzilla*. The plot concerned a group of youngsters who thwart gangsters threatening to evict them from the building in which they run their 'Hot Rock Club'. As always in this type of movie, the teens look as if they graduated about ten years earlier. The 'kids' save the day by putting on a show and raising sufficient cash to pay the overdue rent. Anyone requiring full details of the synopsis is referred to John Blair's excellent article in *Goldmine* No. 41.

Filmed in October 1956 and released in the summer of 1957, the movie featured Kay Wheeler, president of the Dallas branch of the Presley Fan Club, as a dancer and a number of Goldman's wrestling pals as heavies. Musical interest centred on exceedingly generous clips of the Five Stars, a black group signed to a Memphis label owned by B.B. King, the Belew Twins (backed by the Hot Rocks), the Cell Block Seven (whose version of 'Hot Rock' degenerates into a corny instrumental after one couplet), blues shouter Rosco Gordon, Don Coates & The Bon-Aires and Preacher Smith & The Deacons, whose guitarist supplied a forty-five second solo of harsh, Ike Turner-ish intensity.

Johnny Carroll and the Hot Rocks, including Billy Buntin and the pug-faced Jay Salem, injected their own kind of blues — a wild, passionate, thoroughly abrasive music which still retains the capacity to excite and disturb. Four numbers — 'Crazy Crazy Lovin'', 'Wild Wild Women', 'Sugar Baby' and 'Rockin' Maybelle' — were recorded especially for the film at Pappy Sellers's Studio in Dallas. The magazine *Box Office* quoted an Alabama exhibitor: *'Just what the teenagers want,'* said Charlie Webb. *'It did top time business on a two-day change.'* In truth, it played in a few venues and was quickly withdrawn. Johnny hated the film when it came out. In later years, he found it amusing, realising that it was no worse than many celluloid banalities of the day.

Carroll and Goldman parted company in acrimonious circumstances: 'I dropped by a Dallas theatre where we'd played before. The manager was discussing the fact that he was paying me $1,000 a night, whereas I'd been getting $100 a night from Goldman. Tiger would shout: "Here, Johnny, here's your pay, sign here!" and I'd sign the back of the cheque without looking at the front. On top of that, he'd take ten per cent out of my $100. I took him to court but he got a 'cease and desist' order until the hearing was set, so I couldn't work for six months. I could mow lawns or dig ditches, but I couldn't work as an entertainer. Decca wanted no part of anything like that going on.'

At some point Carroll played the *Louisiana Hayride,* renewing an acquaintance with Bill Black and Scotty Moore who'd reached a temporary impasse with Elvis. 'They felt they weren't being paid enough. They were madder'n hell. Elvis was calling Scotty and Bill two or three times a day trying to get 'em to go back.'

Carroll began playing lead guitar under Moore's tuition and it was Scotty or Bill who suggested that he ought to approach distributor Bill Emerson about a record deal with Sun. Emerson called Sam Phillips who took four songs which Carroll had recorded at Cliff Herring's Fort Worth studio in June 1957. Two sides were issued on Phillips International: 'I flew to Memphis because Sam wanted to talk to me. He said he was gonna start this new label. Now Sam would be the last person to admit this, but he went into great detail. He said: "I know Philips *[the Dutch electrical giant]* is planning on coming to the US. I want to establish Phillips International as a known label, so they'll have to buy me out." That's the gospel truth. It was a business move. Sam told me: "You can be released on Sun now or you can wait a couple of months and go on Phillips International. I'm gonna release five records in one package and, whichever one the disc-jockeys start playing, I'm gonna put everything behind that one record and go with it as hard as we can. I'm gonna make a star out of whichever one hits." I said: "I'll take my chance," and I did, and then 'Raunchy' came out...'

Sam Phillips failed to renew Carroll's one-session contract and the singer remained in Dallas under the care of Ed McLemore, a new manager who also booked acts onto KRLD's *Big D Jamboree*. Carroll met Gene Vincent in McLemore's office at the Dallas Sportatorium. He was impressed with Vincent's intense, even dysfunctional lifestyle and mightily influenced by his singing, especially those shimmering, high-voiced ballads like 'Peace Of Mind'. The two men became fast friends and for a while their lack of good fortune was intertwined. Carroll stayed at Vincent's house in Dallas, drove him around and went on tour with Vincent when he wasn't working himself. The song, 'Maybe', on Gene Vincent's fifth album, was written by Carroll. On occasion, they shared the same musicians including Grady Owen, Howard Reed and Juvie Gomez.

There were no vocal innovations on the songs which Carroll cut for Warner Brothers in 1958-59. Gene Vincent's masterful technique influenced all four. Carroll's group, known as the Spinners, included Bill Hennen (piano), Howard Reed (guitar), former Blue Cap bass-player Grady Owen and Royce McAffe (drums). 'Bandstand Doll', produced in Dallas by Johnny Hicks, benefited from additional musicians: Artie Glenn, the writer of 'Crying In The Chapel', slapped a string bass while Marvin Montgomery plucked a mandolin. The mix was as intriguing as it was unlikely and the record came close to being a hit in Texas, especially Houston where the Spinners were surprised to find themselves sharing equal billing with Fats Domino. The second Warner Brothers single, 'Sugar' (a revival of 'Sugar Baby' from *Rock, Baby, Rock It*), was cut in New York during a gap in a string of one-nighters. There was a third single which featured the band, including Carroll on rhythm guitar.

Ken Nelson, Capitol's A&R man in Nashville, engaged the Spinners for sessions on which they accompanied a number of vocalists:

'He liked us, 'cos the band was basically the Blue Caps.' Nelson said he'd like to put out an instrumental by the Spinners, but word got back to Warner Brothers who didn't want Carroll recording for them while his band recorded for another company. Warner Brothers finally agreed to issue two Nashville-recorded instrumentals, but the disc made no impression and the company subsequently dropped the whole group. Carroll smiled at the games of businessmen: 'When we went with Warner Brothers they were building artists 'cos it was a brand new label. Six months later, they had a meeting and decided that in future they'd buy contracts from other labels. They had us set up for a tour with Edd Byrnes and Connie Stevens but cancelled everything.'

Carroll next recorded for Duchess, a label inaugurated by a Warner Bros. executive who was fired when the roster was pruned, and for W.A. (which stood for 'William Armstead', owner of a Dallas booking agency). Johnny, however, dealt with Roy Armstead Stamps, cousin to a singer in the Stamps Quartet. Both labels issued different recordings of 'Run Come See', Carroll's adaptation of an old calypso about a hurricane which destroyed much of the Gulf Coast in 1929.

For the rest of the Sixties, Carroll's recording career lay dormant. 'There was a rock'n'roll depression. To get work, I was travelling from Toronto, Canada all the way to South Texas for a gig. I finally said "this is ridiculous" and quit.' He became a booker and fixer at a Fort Worth nightclub, with similar affiliations in Houston and San Antonio. He hired musicians, put them together and generally ensured that the owner had three bands playing each night of the week. He also ran a club in Dallas — a move which proved calamitous when a hot-tempered customer shot him in the stomach. Mac Curtis heard that Carroll had been killed. He wrote and recorded a tribute, 'Johnny Carroll Rock', which came out on Ronny Weiser's Rollin' Rock label. Although Carroll's injury healed, he reportedly contracted hepatitis from an infected hospital aide and the illness would eventually necessitate a liver transplant.

Record-wise, Carroll's situation improved in the early Seventies. Ronny Weiser drew his attention to the rockabilly renaissance and persuaded him to cut 'Black Leather Rebel', an immaculate Vincent tribute which enjoys an afterlife as a strong addition to the visibly increasing Vincent legend. Carroll subsequently teamed up with Judy Lindsey, a former Miss North Texas beauty queen and modelling instructor from Austin. 'When I first met Johnny,' she told *The Dallas Morning News*, 'I was the 'Dodge Girl' for the Texas Regional Dodge dealers. I was travelling the state making television commercials and local appearances. I was also singing part-time in a local Fort Worth club called Buddy Fudputter's. Johnny came into the club one evening wearing a black leather jacket, black sunglasses and scared me to death. He said: "Honey, I can make you a star." I said: "Oh yeah, sure." But I went over to the recording studio he was managing and cut a commercial. Then we cut a single record together. About three weeks later, he called me and we formed a band.'

The Judy & Johnny band became the Sonny & Cher of the Texas hillbilly circuit, making numerous records for QCA and Gypsy. In 1978 there was a solo album, *Texabilly*, on Rollin' Rock.

Carroll and Lindsey made the first of many visits to Europe in 1980 — way too late for the complete orgiastic package. A roly-poly figure with a full set of whiskers, Carroll looked to be a disturbing prospect for hardcore rockabilly freaks and you had to listen real hard to hear what was thought to be so outrageous about his mid-Fifties music. But warmth of personality and a jovial physical presence came through on stage. Now and then, he would fine-tune his Gene Vincent impression, always a crowd-pleaser in Britain and France. He appeared in Europe again and again (no fewer than eleven tours) and helped proselytise the British rockabilly scene among other Texans including Joe Poovey, Sid King and Ray Sharpe.

Johnny Carroll underwent a liver transplant at Baylor Hospital in Dallas on 13 January 1995. He appeared to be making progress, but suffered a relapse and died on 18 February. He is survived by two ex-wives, his brothers, a grandson and several thousand rockabilly rebels.

Carroll was an ebullient entertainer and his musical contributions will continue to be heard as long as rockabilly is performed. He was also an unassuming, courteous and generous man with a powerful gift for lasting friendships.

Liner note to *Rock, Baby, Rock It* (Bear Family BCD-15928) 1996.

2.6

BOB BERTRAM
Hawaiian Hillbilly

'Hawaii? The music's enough to make you stay away from the place.' Those unkindly words were uttered by the leading character in *Soap*, who was probably listening to Radio London when Charlie Gillett was playing Gabby Pahinui's Hawaiian Band. Hawaii might, at first blush, prompt a mental image of short fat men in colourful shirts strumming away on tiples, but there's more to it — the influence of Hawaiian guitar in blues, the eccentric hillbilly hulas of Jenks 'Tex' Carman, Screamin' Jay Hawkins's tribute to the surfers' paradise, Oahu and, not least, the rockabilly records which Bob Bertram produced for Bill Lawrence, Robin Luke and others.

The avuncular Bertram, Hawaii's Man of Music, was born in Sharon, Massachusetts on 30 April 1916. He now lives in Concord, California and has packed most experiences into his 62 years: musician and vocalist (his last single was 'Welcome Home Elvis'), artist (his oil painting of Franklin D. Roosevelt hangs in the White House) and author (several volumes including *The Business Of Music* and *How Loud Can I Scream*). Bertram dabbled in country music on the West Coast during the early Fifties, recording Jack Pitts, Eddie Dean and himself for Ode and acquiring the Lariat label (famed for discs by Joe Maphis, whose guitar playing would later serve as a model to aspiring rockabillies). Bertram's songs — over four hundred ASCAP compositions divided into categories like C&W, Blues, Folk, Polkas and Service (eg 'Gotta Find My Foxhole Dream') — have been recorded by Dave Edwards, Eddie Dean and Roy Hogsed, who's a must for any Capitol hillbilly boogie set. Lately, Bertram's been collaborating with an old colleague, Eden Ahbez, who wrote 'Nature Boy' for Nat 'King' Cole. Two of their songs reached the finals of last year's *American Song Festival*. Back in 1958, another Ahbez–Bertram song, 'Yes Master', was recorded by Don Carson & The Casuals. Although Bertram acquired the master, he never released it. He tells me that just the other day he came across a long-forgotten document which indicated that J.P. Richardson *aka* The Big Bopper had cut the number under the pseudonym of Carson whilst under contract to Mercury and enjoying hits like 'Chantilly Lace'. (I don't think I give much credence to this story, but trivia buffs will be intrigued by it; Don Carson recorded

Bob Bertram with the Lawrence Brothers Combo (Bill Lawrence centre).

for Crest and wrote songs for the parent company, American Music).

Bertram's parents had retired to Hawaii and, in 1956, he went there to comfort his father on the occasion of his mother's death. Intending to stay a year, he began to put down roots, started a record rack-jobbing business and began to record the local talent on his own labels, Bertram International and Polynesian. The latter is devoted to discs by native islanders on songs and chants with eye-boggling titles.

Bertram was also interested in local country and rockabilly hopefuls, and I first came across him when I was trying to locate the publisher on Bill Lawrence's 'Hey Baby', a track included on *Imperial Rockabillies (Volume 2)*.

The Lawrence Brothers Combo consisted of Bill (lead guitar and vocals), Freddy (rhythm guitar) and Manuel *aka* Sonny (bass). They all grew up in Kaimuki, Hawaii, where Bill Lawrence was born in 1925. 'Hey Baby' was cut at Associated Recorders in Honululu. Freddy was absent on this occasion and Bill, who sang and played lead, dubbed in a rhythm guitar. The record also includes Bob Bertram on drums and a female chorus, namely Bertram's daughter, Karen Ann, and the Cousins — Linda and Charlene Lewis. Despite its unusual origins, the disc has a genuine downhome flavour comparable to any number of fine rockabilly records from Tennessee or Mississippi.

Bertram wasn't too surprised to be told that he had helped write and produce a rockabilly classic: 'Well, I haven't thought much about it to tell you the truth. But a lot of people have commented on how the devil we got such a sound over in the Islands. The Lawrence boys were basically oriented towards country music, and at that time I'd done quite a few shows with the military bases. They always loved C&W performers and the shows we'd put on would always feature country musicians. Bill entertained at numerous shows throughout the Islands and was a great favourite with the military personnel. Bill and his brothers, Sonny and Fred, were outstanding individuals in every respect.'

'Hey Baby' was originally issued on Bertram International and sold to Freedom, a subsidiary of Liberty, in 1958. The Lawrence Brothers cut a variety of follow-ups for the Hawaiian market including an instrumental 'Marine's Rock' (local Top Thirty in 1959) and 'Billy Boy', pressed up in 1963 but not released. They also doubled as the Five Finks ('Boss' and 'Crying Guitar' on Bertram International).

The Lawrence Brothers accompanied other Bertram acts including the Tilton Sisters, Ken Craig, Dave Edwards, Danny Dalton and Robin Luke, whose 'Susie Darlin' ' bounded up the Hot 100 after spending weeks at the top of the Hawaiian best-sellers. 'I was told that Robin was appearing in his high school show, and that he had a song I should check out. Which, of course, I did.'

'Susie Darlin' ' was cut on a $300 tape recorder in Bill Lawrence's bedroom. 'It was strange, because we kept rehearsing with amateur musicians including a ukulele player who couldn't get it right — I don't know whether you can hear a ukulele on that record, but it's there. We'd come in every few days and try again, and this went on for weeks. I must have... oh... 75 takes of 'Susie Darlin' '. Incidentally, the beat was the sound of two sticks pounding away at a ballpoint pen in my pants pocket. My leg was black and blue, and if we'd gone for take 76 I'd have been crippled for life!'

When the performance was taped to everyone's satisfaction, Bertram had copies pressed in New York. Art and Dotty Freeman, record distributors from Cleveland, heard the disc while honeymooning in Hawaii and phoned Randy Wood, who bought the master for Dot Records. 'Susie Darlin' ' remained on the Hot 100 for four months becoming a million-seller for Luke, who's generally bracketed in a list of one-hit wonders at the back of various tomes on the Fifties. A sixteen year old blond with the kind of face that once graced untold numbers of teeny mags, Luke still has his fans and you'd be wrong to dismiss him as typical of so much Rydell/Avalon mishmash. Dot issued another nine singles including 'My Girl' (No. 3 Hawaii and No. 97 in *Cash Box*), 'Strollin' Blues', 'Five Minutes More' (both Top Twenty locally) and 'You Can't Stop Me From Dreaming', a spiky cut that rockabilly collectors speak of in reverential tones. The guitar — Bill Lawrence again — is superb and Luke handles this Presleyish vehicle with a total absence of cutesy-poo. His later recordings — 'School Bus Love Affair', 'Everlovin' ', 'Poor Little Rich Boy'

— were produced by Dot Records, who signed him after his contract with Bertram expired. They're insufferably poppy, but I can tap my foot to the rest. As long as Bertram's thoroughly economical production recalls the soft rock of Sanford Clark, Wally Lewis or Ricky Nelson, the predominant elements of high school wimpery are pardonable.

Luke thought he'd do better with Dot Records, but, although he appeared in all the right places — older readers may recall a spot on the *Perry Como Show* — only 'Susie Darlin'' and Bertram's composition, 'My Girl', made the national charts. Randy Wood and Bob Bertram became close friends — they're both health and fitness enthusiasts — and Bertram acted as Dot's local A&R man until 1964 when he returned to California, where he continued to work for himself on a whole variety of projects.

Recently, however, he revived Bertram International Records: 'We have an album called *Rockabilly 1958*. I'd bought thousands of records as a rack-jobber and they'd been in storage for years. Then came the oldies revival and I found I was sitting on hundreds of dollars-worth of collectable records, so I started offering them on set sale and auction lists. I began to realise that there was a tremendous interest in rockabilly especially in England and on the Continent, so I went back over my old masters and compiled a rockabilly album.' The new compilation — put together with the help of English and German rockabilly fans who looked up Bertram on their US travels — is a 16-tracker with cuts by Robin Luke, Bill Lawrence, Ken Craig, Tom Moffat and Hawaiian acts like the Cousins and the Tilton Sisters.

Note 1   Originally published in *Melody Maker* (6 January 1979). Bob Bertram died on 1 May 1994 in Paradise, California.

Note 2   The complete Robin Luke recordings, including his cover of Marty Wilde's 'Bad Boy', have been gathered up on Bear Family Records (BCD-15547, 1991). Luke's slightly different account of the recording of 'Susie Darlin'' ('the percussion was provided by the hitting together of two pens on a Capitol Records box') is related in Colin Escott's thorough CD booklet biography. Bear Family have also reissued Roy Hogsed's work (*Cocaine Blues*, BCD-16191, 1999), though his version of Bob Bertram's song, 'Babies And Bacon', originally recorded by the Gallion Brothers on Ode (with Bertram on vocal), isn't included.

2.7
BIG AL DOWNING
The Story Behind The Story

I spoke to Big Al Downing, courtesy of Warner Bros. here, in April last. We spent an hour on the phone discussing the European interest in his early records and his remarkable position as the most successful black country singer since the advent of Charley Pride. Al was in great form, full of good humour and delighted to be speaking to someone who knew a little of his past. A year before, Ray Topping and I had spoken to Vernon Sandusky and Rodney Lay who came to this country with Roy Clark. Vernon — you could make him out on BBC-TV's *Sing Country* with his stetson pulled low over his eyes — is one of those real good ole boys you hear songs about. He talks with a drawl and it takes him half an hour to turn around. Rodney Lay, Clark's bass guitarist, played behind Al's brother, Don Downing, when the Poe-Kats moved out of the Kansas plains. He's a live-wire full of stories about Tulsa Bop and the people who played it. This feature amalgamates information from all three sources; it reveals the mysteries behind those enigmatic Downing–Poe–Sandusky credits and pays tribute to the many fine records on which they appeared.

Apart from 'Down On The Farm' — perhaps the greatest of all 'non-hit' rock'n'roll records — I don't think it's possible to make any Messianic claims for Al's prolific output. Our readers will be familiar with his uncanny ability to sound exactly like Fats Domino or Little Richard, and soul fans will tell you that he's also perfected Brook Benton ('I'm Just Nobody'), Garnet Mimms ('All I Want Is You') and Levi Stubbs ('Medley Of Soul'). For me, his shot-silk soul sides — those from the early Sixties — are as unforgettable as the rockers. They're all artistically seamless and, as a vocal chameleon, Big Al has no peers. But, while he never made a mediocre record, his most devoted fans would have to admit that originality is conspicuous by its absence. Al too confesses it's been a problem: 'Everyone has always had a different idea about what I ought to be doing. One guy thought I should be the new Fats Domino, while another wanted to make me into the next Little Richard. Sure, my piano influences were Fats Domino, Jerry Lee, Richard and Nat Cole, but it wasn't until I finally began singing country that I started to become successful.'

Born on 9 January 1940 in Centralia, Oklahoma, Downing moved to nearby Lenapah at the age of six or seven. His country roots stem from an upbringing as one of a dozen children on his father's farm. His siblings include Walter Downing, a session musician with Motown on the West Coast, and Don Downing, a minor soul star with a comparatively recent disco hit to his credit. As an infant, Al heard Muddy Waters and B.B. King, but developed an equally strong taste for C&W while loading trucks with hay and hearing Bob Wills and Hank Williams on the truckers' radios. At sixteen, he left school and went straight into a three-piece rockabilly band with Vernon Sandusky (lead guitar) and Bobby Brant (vocals).

Sandusky and Brant (*aka* Bobby Poe) had met at college during the fall of '56. Brant, a twenty-three year old from Coffeeville, Kansas, was looking for a rock'n'roll band to manage. Sandusky, born 30 June 1939 in Earlham, Iowa, had learned to play guitar and piano before reaching his teens. His father, a farmer of Polish descent, had offered much encouragement and, on moving to Kansas in 1948, Sandusky appeared on talent contests and radio stations as a singer-guitarist. The Poe-Kats (a name chosen by Bob Polk who ran a nightclub in South Carolina) played dances and bars around Coffeeville throughout 1957. 'It was a whole new idea,' recalled Al. 'Up to then, they didn't have a rockabilly band that could do Fats Domino or Ray Charles properly. The audiences were getting the best of both worlds, 'cos Bobby Brant could sing Elvis Presley while I did Fats Domino and Little Richard — all to a rockabilly backup. Not that the audiences saw any real distinction — they danced just the same whether it was R&B, rock'n'roll or rockabilly. But that was our trademark throughout the years: me playing the black songs and Bobby playing the white.'

Towards the end of '57, the Poe-Kats added a drummer, Joe Brawley, and cut an audition tape at Moose Hall in Coffeeville. Brant sent copies to a number of companies including Sun, but Sam Phillips was evidently unimpressed with the mixture: Jerry Lee Lewis tunes, 'Rip It Up' and some early Elvis stuff. One such tape was sent to White Rock in Dallas, who'd placed an ad in *Billboard* seeking new talent. The owner, a deejay called Jim Lowe (not the 'Green Door' singer), called Brant and arranged a session at Cliff Herring's Fort Worth studio, where the Poe-Kats cut 'Down On The Farm' and 'Oh Babe'. 'Rock'n'Roll Boogie' and 'Rock'n'Roll Record Gal', sung by Brant (although Downing contributes a devastating verse from 'Good Golly Miss Molly') also appeared on White Rock. According to Sandusky, 'Down On The Farm' went to Number One in Texas before Lowe sold the master to Challenge. The group received no royalties or session fees and Al had no idea the record had been bootlegged and reissued in Europe. He wasn't particularly perturbed: 'Money isn't that important and it always goes to the record company anyhow. I think the more people who hear the music, the better and if I don't get paid from the records I figure I'll benefit somewhere down the line, maybe from touring Europe.'

Before 'Down On The Farm' was released, the Poe-Kats came to the notice of agency boss Jim Halsey, who signed them up to accompany Wanda Jackson, already a C&W star with several hits on Capitol. The group spent a year with Jackson travelling throughout the South.

'Bobby and I would do solo spots,' said Al, 'warming up the audience before she came on. Frankly, there wasn't as much prejudice as you'd expect even though I'd stand beside her and sing with her. She liked my playing and she'd introduce me to the audience which helped. Sure, there'd be times when they'd sneak me into a hotel with a towel over my head, but I didn't hear many racial remarks.'

Sandusky agrees: 'There were problems in Texas, where we'd have to sleep in the car 'cos we couldn't get Al into a motel. And sometimes a cowboy came up on stage and asked what a nigger was doing with a white group. But Al always kept his composure and the guy was usually thrown out of the club. Al was such a great entertainer. Boy, did he sweat — I don't care if you're black or white, you had to go along with someone who was that good.'

During April 1958, the Poe-Kats joined Wanda for a recording session in Hollywood, cutting eighteen or more titles in four days. Most of these appear on Wanda's first Capitol album (T-1041), which contains four rockers including Thelma Blackman's 'I Wanna Waltz', 'Money Honey', 'Let's Have A Party' and 'Long Tall Sally', where Big Al Downing repeats the glorious piano solo he introduced on 'Down On The Farm'. The ballads, including 'Happy Happy Birthday Baby', feature Downing and Sandusky on background vocals, while Sandusky plays lead guitar on every track except 'I Wanna Waltz', where Buck Owens takes over. 'Mean Mean Man', cut at the tail-end of these sessions, is also studded with Al's staccato piano. 'We'd only just done 'Down On The Farm,' recalls Vernon, 'and we didn't know if it was gonna be a hit. So, recording with Wanda was a brand new experience for all of us. I was as thrilled as a kid with a candy bar.'

2.7 - Big Al Downing

Throughout 1958, the Poe-Kats continued looking for fresh deals. Capitol, who had Esquerita and didn't need another singer who sang like Little Richard, were not interested in the group under their own name. During the summer, they returned to Fort Worth and laid down further tracks for White Rock including 'Miss Lucy' and 'Just Around The Corner', which Lowe leased to Carlton. 'Piano Nellie' c/w 'I Found A New Love', on which Brant sang, were sold to Atlantic's subsidiary, East–West. Downing, of course, played piano, while Lowe hired a bass player and a saxophonist to fill out the sound. If *Atlantic Rockabillies* ever sees the light of day, 'Piano Nellie' will take pride of place. But it didn't sell at the time and Brant moved away from singing to concentrate on managing the group.

In 1959, the Poe-Kats moved to Washington where Phil Ladd arranged a one-shot record deal with Carlton's promo man, Lelan Rogers. Al was taken to New Orleans, where he recorded 'It Must Be Love' and 'When My Blue Moon Turns To Gold Again', patterning Gene Sullivan's old C&W hit after the hugely successful style of Fats Domino. Cosimo's sessionmen increased the similarity and Domino's influence remained to the fore on Downing's next three records for V-Tone. Cut at Philly's Reco-Art studio, 'Yes, I'm Loving You', 'If I Had Our Love To Live Over' and 'So Many Memories', feature a new band including Sandusky (guitar), Eddie Kopa (sax), Johnny Dubas (bass) and Chib Holmes (drums). The strings on the magnificent swampy ballads were overdubbed in New York. Sandusky and Dubas cut their own discs for V-Tone and the Len subsidiary (named after V-Tone's owner, Len Caldwell) under the cognomen of Spic & Spann. Downing plays piano on both. The Poe-Kats also appear on Clyde Stacy's Len sides cut in Washington during 1961; originally from Oklahoma, Stacy became popular in Canada where he was managed by Phil Ladd, then a deejay at CHUM in Toronto.

Al Downing and Vernon Sandusky remained in Washington until 1964. They appeared at Rand's Rock'n'Roll Club, a residency which attracted mention in *Billboard*. In 1962, they and Poe formed their own label, Kansoma, and issued records by the Choralettes ('three black chicks out of Washington') and the Magnificents (the Al Downing band with a cover of the Raging Storms' 'Dribble Twist'). Al himself revived Marty Robbins's country-pop hit, 'The Story Of My Life', and, in March of '62, his bluesy rendition — harmonica from Johnny Dubas — was sold to Leonard Chess and heavily promoted. Chess turned down 'The Saints' c/w 'Heartbreak Hill' but probably signed Downing to a standard one-year contract because his next record, a Lelan Rogers production, appeared on Popline under the pseudonym of Big Rivers. 'The Land Of Make Believe' — a dead-ringer for 'Valley Of Tears' — and 'No-One Else' (a facsimile of 'But I Do') were written by the usual team but credited to 'Nelson', 'Raye' and 'Alex' to help preserve anonymity. Alex equals Al, and Raye equals Sandusky (Ray is Sandusky's middle name), but I'm not sure why Poe equals Nelson.

Fats Domino, who played with Al at Rand's ('if you hadn't been watching you couldn't tell the difference,' said Vernon), subsequently recorded 'The Land Of Make Believe' and a clutch of other songs which he and Downing wrote together. 'Mary, Oh Mary' appears on *Fats On Fire*, while 'Reelin' And Rockin' ', 'Heartbreak Hill' and the memorable 'The Girl I'm Gonna Marry' grace *Getaway With Fats*. Songs by Downing, Poe and Sandusky have also been waxed by Mickey Gilley (Lynn), Billy Lewis (Jin) and, I suspect, a good many others. Years after the Poe-Kats left Wanda Jackson, she cut the Downing–Sandusky song, 'I'm Gonna Walk Out Of Your Life' (Capitol 3143).

In 1963, Lelan Rogers teamed Al Downing with Esther Phillips, the one-time child prodigy who'd secured a Top Ten renaissance with 'Release Me'. The duo's 'You Never Miss Your Water' — a charming but none too subtle ripple at emulating Brook Benton and Dinah Washington — reached No. 73 on the Hot 100, providing Al with his first taste of national chartdom. Lenox issued another single by Al which coupled 'Mr. Hurt Walked In' and a reissue of the earlier V-Tone side, 'If I Had Our Love To Live Over'. Bobby Brant wrote 'Mr. Hurt Walked In' on the plane from Washington to the session in Nashville; it's a terrific country soul ballad which rivals the best of Solomon Burke. It also typifies the material Al was performing at Rand's during the early Sixties when Roy Buchanan played with him. 'It was like no country you ever heard,' said Roy. 'He played piano himself and really moved everybody. He's one of the most really soulful cats I've ever known.'

In 1964, Sandusky took the band — himself (guitar), Vince Gideon (sax), Johnny Dubas (bass) and Chib Holmes (drums) — to Sam Hodge's Mutual Records in Philadelphia, where they recorded 'She's The One' as the Chartbusters. This Beatle-like slice of opportunism became a big hit (No. 33 in '64) and the follow-up, 'Why Doncha Be My Girl', also dented the Hot 100. The Chartbusters were flooded with bookings and, although Al shared the financial action, he had to find a new band to fulfil his contract at Rand's. At the same time, Bobby Brant negotiated a solo contract with Columbia where Clyde Otis produced Downing on 'All I Want Is You'. Another marvellous soul record, it was far too similar to Garnet Mimms's 'Cry Baby' to go anywhere. The follow-up, 'Georgia Slop', could well be the finest rock'n'roll record to come out of 1964. Downing listened to Jimmy McCracklin's version before he recorded it and he's glad it's well liked: 'Commercially, it was a dead record but whenever I searched for a sound that I could use, I always ended up using what I could do best and we instinctively reverted to rock'n'roll. I guess we didn't know how to change. It all goes back to rock'n'roll — it's one of the simplest and purest forms of music there is, and it's still the best.'

By 1965, however, Downing couldn't find anyone else who wanted to play it: 'Certainly, none of the bands wanted to play rockabilly. I formed a seven-piece black band and started doing James Brown and stuff.' In 1966 he travelled to Luxembourg and Germany, where he

2.7 - Big Al Downing

played military bases. In 1967 he cut 'Jivin' Jean' *c/w* 'Yeah Yeah Yeah', at a Frankfurt studio using army musicians; the record was issued on German CBS. Returning to the USA, Downing cut further sides for Lelan Rogers's soul labels, Silver Fox and House Of Fox. 'Cornbread Row' and 'Medley Of Soul' are to be found on Charly's *Music City Soul* (CR-30107), but 'Buffalo Soldiers' remains unissued.

Vernon Sandusky, who'd played with the Chartbusters throughout the late Sixties (they also recorded for Crusader in L.A.), rejoined Al for European tours in 1969 and 1970. Totally unnoticed, they appeared at USAF bases like Mildenhall and Lakenheath. Al reckons they played civilian clubs too ('there was one in the North of England called Smith's... Ringo Starr came in').

During the Seventies, Al enjoyed some success with soul and disco records on Janus and Chess ('I'll Be Holding On' reached No. 85 on the Hot 100 in 1975), but through it all he continued to harbour the desire to make the transition to C&W: 'All these years I've been playing country but couldn't record that way myself. It's not really a switch, 'cos that's how I started out with Wanda Jackson. A couple of years ago, I'm in the studio looking for disco records with my producers, Tony Bongiovi and Lance Quinn. I'm sitting at the piano playing my C&W songs like 'Mr. Jones'. Tony says: "What's that? It's better than disco, let's do that." We paid for the session ourselves and out of the seven companies who wanted it, we chose Warner Bros.'

Vernon Sandusky has also reverted to C&W. Throughout the early Seventies, he toured with many established country artists including

Jody Miller, Freddy Fender and Merle Haggard. He joined Roy Clark as rhythm guitarist in 1976 but continues playing on sessions when the opportunity arises. As lead guitarist with Rodney Lay & The Wild West, Sandusky has cut a lot of tracks for Sun: 'Singleton signed us in '78 and we did an album of old rock'n'roll stuff by artists who had died. He was gonna call it *Rock'n'Roll Heaven* but decided not to release it' (a rare attack of good taste). Sun have put out an album of modernised cowboy songs ('Tumblin' Tumbleweed', etc) and, while I've not heard it, I'm sure Singleton would be better employed hunting for the Poe-Kats demo tape. Brant himself made one further record as Bobby Allen Poe in 1966 ('Concrete Jungle' c/w 'Gotta Find A Way' on Monument 957). The following year, he hocked his wristwatch and formed a Top Forty tip sheet business in Washington. Called *Pop Music Survey*, it now exerts a powerful influence over East Coast radio stations.

Big Al Downing is now well into the ascendancy. He's reached the C&W charts with self-written songs on five occasions since January 1979. 'Mr. Jones' and 'Touch Me (I'll Be Your Fool Once More)' made the Top Twenty, while 'Midnight Lace' and 'I Ain't No Fool' notched the 70s. 'The Story Behind The Story' is climbing the Top Forty as I write.

Last year, Al shifted his booking to Tandy Rice's Top Billing Inc. in Nashville and received *Billboard*'s *'Number One New C&W Artist'* award: 'I can see it's odd,' he chuckles, 'but I'm now playing with many of the top C&W artists... Tom T. Hall, Conway Twitty... they grab my hand and say: "Great!" And I can still do all the Jerry Lee and Little Richard things in my show. Oh yes, I still stand up and hammer that piano. I'm just sticking with the heritage I grew up with and it's going down better now than all the other things I have done put together.'

Note   This article first appeared in *New Kommotion* (No. 24, 1980) and then, without my say-so, on the back of a bootleg album, *Big Al Downing* (Jumble 111). Some of the very worthwhile demo tapes have since surfaced on two CDs from a German company, *Rockin' Down The Farm (Volume 1)* (Eagle EA-R-90116, 1994) and *Rockin' Down The Farm (Volume 2)* (Eagle EA-R-90125, 1998).

ROLLIN' ROCK RECORDS
RAY CAMPI
ROCKABILLY REBEL
Ronny Weiser, P.O. BOX 8174, N. HOLLYWOOD, CALIF. 91608, TEL. 781-4805

2.8

RAY CAMPI
Eager Beaver Boy

For the first two decades of his recording career, Ray Campi remained a resolutely mysterious figure known only to a handful of European collectors. A faceless name on a string of obscurities, he was one of many unobserved talents whose publicity rarely escaped the confines of rock'n'roll auction lists. All that's changed: a passion for rockabilly, the music that Elvis and Sun Records pioneered, circled the world in the mid-Seventies and Ray Campi, one-time musical comma from Austin, Texas, became one of rockabilly's international heroes. He's toured Europe several times and his albums are well into double figures.

Though born in New York City (on 20 April 1934), Campi moved to Austin at the age of nine. Honest, danceable 'roots' music excited his imagination; he'd heard black music in New York — chiefly Louis Jordan and Cab Calloway — but his interest increased in Texas, where he was introduced to the chilling declarations of Johnny Ace, Clarence 'Gatemouth' Brown and other black singers on the well-distributed Duke and Peacock labels of Houston.

Hillbilly mingled with the blues to form the common aural heritage of the South and Campi's love of that music borders on the obsessive. Here, for example, is some routine Campi on the C&W stalwarts of yesteryear: 'My cousins, Harold and Harvey Layman, had moved to Austin from Fogo, Newfoundland, my mother's birthplace, and brought with them many country records they'd bought there. They loved Hank Snow and brought many of his Bluebird and early Victor records, and used to listen to him when he had radio shows in Canada. The first record I remember hearing by him was 'I'm Gonna Bid My Blues Goodbye', a great rolling blues number with lots of round-hole Martin guitar as only Hank Snow could play it. Soon, 'My Two-Timing Woman' was a big hit and I began to try to learn the guitar breaks copying Hank Snow's style of picking. Actually, I had heard country records as a small child in New York when another cousin from Newfoundland, Nellie Saunders, came to live with our family. She bought records like Montana Slim's 'Old Barn Dance', Tex Ritter's 'Rye Whiskey', Elton Britt's 'Patent Leather Boots'. I still have those records today and get a kick out of them. Soon, my cousin Harold and myself were spending whole weekends just listening to, and playing along with, the records of Al Dexter, Bob Wills, Hank Williams, Lefty Frizzell, Ernest Tubb, the great, one and only Merle Travis, the Delmore Brothers, and of course, Jimmie Rodgers.'

Austin teemed with struggling musicians and, throughout his high school years, Campi patronised the rawest dives imaginable — joints like the Diamond Bar, where the cedar choppers listened to Gene Snowden singing 'Quit Your Triflin' ', or the adjoining Ritz Theatre immortalised in one of Campi's best known compositions. By 1948, he was leading a hillbilly band of his own appearing as Rambling Ray on Austin's KNOW and further afield, in Taylor, Texas (the home of Jimmy Heap, to whom Campi has dedicated a recent Bear Family collection: BCD-15486). Local label owners told him to come back when his voice had broken, but a few audio discs and demonstration tapes survive including 1954 cuts of 'Scrumptious Baby' and 'I Didn't Mean To Be Mean'.

Two years later, after obtaining a BA (Drama) from the University Of Texas, Campi formed a fresh group with Johnny Maddox (guitar) and Henry Hill (bass) and recorded the oft-reissued 'Caterpillar' c/w 'Play It Cool' for TNT owned by Bob Tanner, who was looking for a local rockabilly with Presley's appeal. The disc was heard by a New York publisher who arranged a deal with Dot, for whom Campi recorded the sought-after 'It Ain't Me' in 1957. He promoted the record on *American Bandstand* but soon returned to Texas, where he recorded for Domino and D.

'My Screamin' Screamin' Mimi' (Domino) was written with Little Richard in mind, while 'The Ballad Of Donna And Peggy Sue' (D) was recorded with the Big Bopper's musicians including Link Davis. None of these discs sold well, and songs he had written for Jim Lowe (Dot), the Slades (Domino) and Jimmy Craig (Imperial) fared no better.

Disenchanted, Campi moved to California, where the glamour of Hollywood had already attracted many Southern rockers including the Burnette Brothers and Gene Vincent. He joined the McCoy Boys (ex-Cheers) for a solitary Verve single and also recorded for Colpix. Apart from occasional trips to Texas, resulting in one-off discs for Windsor and Sonobeat, be remained in California.

Campi was teaching English in the San Fernando Valley when he met Ronny Weiser and decided to help this Hebrew hillbilly to realise his dreams of recording yesterday's rockabillies in a Californian setting. Weiser grew up in Austria, France and Italy, where the arrival of Presley's *Loving You* at a Como cinema instilled a devotion to rock'n'roll and its land of origin. By the time he emigrated to Los Angeles in 1965, rockabilly was long dead and his idols severely neglected. In 1970, after graduating from UCLA with a degree in electrical engineering, Weiser founded the Hollywood Rock'n'Roll Fan Club and produced the first issue of *Rollin' Rock*, his own magazine. The sexy graphics and Ted-English might have been a constraint to those who read their fanzines on the 8:29 commuter special, but the need for a subscription was readily apparent. Weiser declared his intention to put the clock back by rediscovering and

2.8 - Ray Campi

Ray Campi & The Snappers - Austin, Texas 1957.

re-recording all the never-has-beens he'd read about in European rock'n'roll magazines. If anyone laughed at the apparent naivety of this swiftly-Americanised Teddy boy, they're keeping quiet about it now.

Weiser began Rollin' Rock Records by persuading small independents to lease their ageing master tapes. Thereafter he set up a four-track studio in the living room of his Los Angeles home and taped the then forty-four year old Ray Campi, an instrumentalist of nonpareil ability. Campi created the Rollin' Rock sound by playing virtually all the instruments behind a host of rediscovered legends on the Rollin' Rock label. Years after rock'n'roll had been co-opted and smashed, he delighted a fourth generation of teenaged fans by successfully recreating one of rock's most elemental strains.

On stage, he's a whirlwind of motion, whether slapping his upright bass like a masseur with convulsions, switching to guitar for a sparkling 'Steel Guitar Rag' or urging his band through tightly-routined but spectacular antics. Offstage, this rockabilly Action Man® still retains the enthusiasm of a superfan with an awesome knowledge of all things hillbilly; tapes unspool in his head as he quietly recalls an endless fund of memories and anecdotes about Slim Willett or Jimmy Heap, the Maddox Brothers & Rose, the Short Brothers or Lonnie Glosson — neglected musicians whose work suggested the vitality of rockabilly long before Presley, Perkins and other crazed individualists gave it dimension.

2.8 - Ray Campi

This nostalgia has permeated the very core of his music, showing up in beautifully-conceived and often sensitively-executed tributes to Johnny Horton, the Delmore Brothers, Gene Snowden, Cactus Pryor, Bill Carlisle and Hank Snow. Campi enjoys bringing the material of such pioneers to wider notice and he gives a volatile treatment to a host of hillbilly favourites including a clutch of Jimmie Skinner tunes. Skinner's jaunty compositions readily lend themselves to a rockabilly treatment, and although Campi, the son of middle-class parents from Yonkers, New York, lacks a Southern twang, 'How Low Can You Feel' and other Skinner songs are none the worse for that. In any event, collectors who generally pissed on anything that wasn't cut in the Fifties were forced to change their habits when they heard a lot of this stuff.

As a rockabilly jukebox Campi has few equals. His lifelong commitment has evolved into a special kind of erudition and conferred an intense but easy confidence within the idiom. Witness his versions of 'Ballin' Keen', from the pens of Bobby & Terry Caraway; Sleepy LaBeef's Houston bopper, 'All The Time'; Buck Owens's debut 'Hot Dog' and George Jones's impossibly raucous 'Rock It'. The spirits of these men lurk behind every growl, hiccup and falsetto skirl — traits which Campi employs to the brink of exhaustion. Not one of the original recordings was a hit in any significant sense, but together they provide a solid picture of this restricted but dynamic music. When Campi sings 'Let 'Er Roll' or 'Pretty Mama' — twenty years after Sid King and Marty Robbins — his trodden-on voice pays tribute to those who first added a country beat to the blues, and his performances radiate pleasure and conviction.

Rockabilly lyrics are not ordinarily renowned for their wit, but 'Major Label Blues' is perfectly illustrative of new-wave rockabilly at its most allusive and ironic. Still, above all else, it's the sound that counts and, at their best, as in 'When Two Ends Meet', 'The Thought Of Losing You' and 'Dobro Daddio From Del Rio', his own compositions sound like resuscitated classics, conveying the genuine feel and uncanny aura of records by his boyhood idols.

Campi has found success by sticking with the music that serves his needs as an artist and, in the process, he's reaffirmed the enduring appeal of rhythm-centred, blues-influenced C&W without diluting its 'uncommercial' qualities. He helps preserve the very purest of rockabilly sounds and his work stands out as one of the finest contributions to the rockabilly renaissance.

Note   This essay has appeared in two forms; in liner notes to *Rockin' At The Ritz* (Rounder LP-3046) in 1980 and *Eager Beaver Boy* (Bear Family BCD-15501) in 1990.

3

A SHOT OF RHYTHM & BLUES

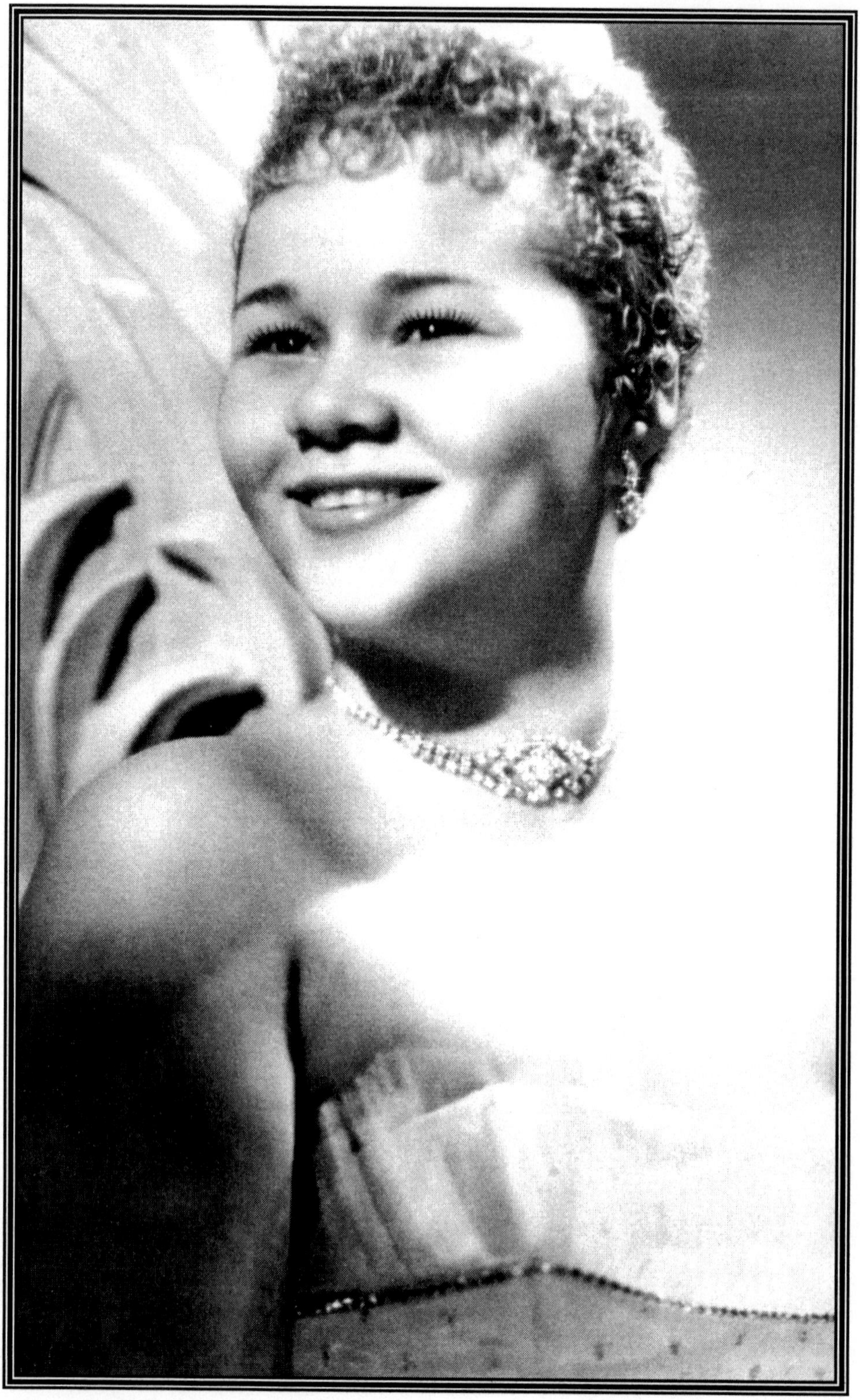

3.1
ETTA JAMES
Payin' The Cost

You can enjoy Etta James as a throwback to the rockin' Fifties. You can admire her as the apotheosis of Sixties soul, performing ghetto clubs while the more decorous Aretha triumphed over white concert halls. If your taste in black music extends no deeper than Little Eva, you'd like Etta doing 'Pushover'. Sophisticates are soothed by the restrained voice and shot-silk strings of 'At Last' and 'Fool That I Am'. Deep soul pervs find solace in 'I'd Rather Go Blind', 'Take What He's Got', 'The Love Of My Man' and two dozen others. There's simply too much of Jamesetta Hawkins to cover all at once and, while she has a fund of anecdotes for current devotees, it's our duty to go back, way back... to the mid-Fifties when she made what Charlie Gillett describes as his favourite rock'n'roll records by a woman. You see what that means? Better than Janis Martin, LaVern Baker, Wanda Jackson or Ruth Brown. It's an assessment with which many would agree.

Etta grew up in Los Angeles, where she was born on 25 January 1938. She divided her infancy between St. Paul's L.A. church choir (age five) and summers with a great-aunt in San Bernardino, where the kids next door introduced her to the 'real old blues', Smokey Hogg and Lightnin' Hopkins. At eleven, she moved to San Francisco with her real mother, a songwriter and jazz fanatic who introduced Etta to Billie Holiday, Dinah Washington and Lester Young. At fifteen, she was a bobby-soxer, tomboy and sometime delinquent who sang with the Peaches — Abbye (short for Abyssinia) and Jean Mitchell — two older girls who followed the Midnighters around town.

The groupies had written 'Roll With Me Henry', a song directed towards Hank Ballard, lead with the group whose 'Work With Me Annie' provided blacks with a national anthem and the girls with the wherewithal for a sequel. Abbye, Jean and Etta cornered the Midnighters in a hotel room but they'd declined the song if not the invitation. Abbye, nine years older than Etta and a go-ahead girl, subsequently fixed a meeting with Johnny Otis, L.A.'s Godfather of Rhythm & Blues: 'He came down and he seemed real jivey. He had three or four band boys with him, and I thought "Oh-oh, one for each of us", y'know. I thought it was a trick, but I was a tough teenager so I went anyway — I was always heavy, stocky built and thought if one of these guys tries to take advantage, I'll just pop him or somethin'. But Johnny was really serious, and I was too shy and ashamed to sing. I agreed on condition that I sang in the bathroom. They stayed in the room and I went to the bathroom — after all everyone sings in the bathroom. We sang jazz 'cos the Hi-Los and the Four Freshmen were big at the time, but we had 'Roll With Me Henry' as our finale.'

Otis took the girls out to Modern Records' Culver City studio on Thanksgiving Eve 1954. His all-star band — Don Johnson (trumpet), Big Jim Wynn (baritone sax), Devonia 'Lady Dee' Williams (piano), Pete Lewis (guitar) and Otis himself (drums) — provided the accompaniment while Maxwell Davis (tenor sax) and the exceptionally-creative Richard Berry helped out: 'The song wasn't written as a duet, but Richard thought we should do more to it: "How about me putting somethin' on the front?" And he came straight out with "Hey baby, what I have to do to make you love me too" and he hollered: "No, Abbye" — turning to the girl with the real squeaky voice — "*You* holler that", and she hollered and — bam! — we were into the song. Richard is a great songwriter, great musician and a great singer, he was such an artistic cat. Golly me, I just can't understand why he's not the biggest thing around.'

The disc was pressed the next day and five hundred copies were in local shops the day after. Four months later, 'Roll With Me Henry' — retitled 'The Wallflower' — was Number One on the R&B chart. Georgia Gibbs took a cover version, 'Dance With Me Henry', into the national charts. A lot of money was at stake: 'You and the girls wrote it, but Johnny's got his wife's name in the credits?'

'Yeah, Phyliss and Shuggie and every other kind of Otis I expect. We had a big falling-out over that tune 'cos Johnny didn't put Jean or Abbye's name on it. I had a fourth of it, but I had to split my share with them and I didn't get the fourth until I was twenty-one. By that time everyone was suing everyone else: the tune had sold four million copies (including the Midnighters) and everyone wanted a bit of the action, Hank Ballard, Syd Nathan, Ralph Bass — Ralph was a partner of Johnny Otis, but he was also hired by Nathan to look after the Federal label, so Ralph was well in there to prevent Johnny from gettin' sued to death. Modern Records — the Biharis — they'd give me $100 every time I went into the studio, but royalties were a different matter. Under California law, record companies can't turn royalties over to a minor, they go direct to court. Whenever I needed money, I went to court with my lawyer, my mother and the record company. I told the judge what I needed it for — a new car, new gowns whatever — and he might give me some.'

Turned sixteen, Etta no longer had to attend school and she went out on a criss-cross tour of the South with Jim Wynn and Johnny 'Guitar' Watson, who cut up the crowds by playing guitar with his teeth. L.A. boiled with cliques of black talent: they rehearsed together, swapped songs and sang on each others' records in a loose and informal manner with scant regard for contractual agreements. Richard Berry, the Cadets, Johnny Watson, the Flames, Jesse Belvin... 'We hung out together all day, in and out of the studios. Saul Bihari was trying to learn how to be an engineer, he'd stay there piddling around while we were cutting records.'

They were exceptionally fine records: Etta cut ten singles for Modern and a number of other cuts appeared on a couple of Crown albums. Most were written by Richard Berry and Frank Gallo, another of Otis's partners whose father owned the famous Gallo Wine Co. Rough, strident, old-time rock'n'roll, they were geared to white audiences with references to artefacts of the era, Sputniks and blue suede shoes. The best include 'Hey Henry', with rattling piano from Devonia Williams, 'Good Rockin' Daddy' (Top Twelve R&B in 1955), 'W-O-M-A-N' inspired by Muddy Waters, vocal group things like 'I'm A Fool' with the Cadets and 'Tears Of Joy' which Jerry Leiber and Mike Stoller had previously written for Linda Hopkins. 'Oh no,' exclaims Etta. 'I didn't know that. I've done so many of Linda's songs she must think I'm running around copying her. People bring me a tune saying "It's a great song Etta", and then I find out that Linda Hopkins did it first. It's happened again with 'Deep In The Night'. 'Tears of Joy'? 'I was really tight with Mike Stoller, who produced that while Jerry was back East.'

In 1957, the Biharis flew Etta to New Orleans for a stab at the Little Richard audience ('Modern thought we were in the same groove'). She cut six titles at Cosimo's with Dave Bartholomew, Earl Palmer and the rest including 'Tough Lover' and a cover of Richard's 'By The Light Of The Silvery Moon'. Intentional Richard copies, they nonetheless rank high in anyone's Top Ten of distaff rockers: formulaic to be sure, but gut-wailing gospel inflections, sired by the church music of her infancy, were never far away. Hey... here's one to delight collectors of rock'n'roll *curiosa*: 'Come What May', the reverse of 'Silvery Moon', was one of the first songs Allen Toussaint ever penned: 'I did background vocals on his last album. I didn't know I'd met him before, but he says "C'mon, you remember me" and then it clicked.' 'Come What May', written under the pseudonym of 'Tableporter', became a Top Twenty R&B hit for Clyde McPhatter the following year.

Touring Chicago in '58, Etta met Harvey Fuqua, lead singer with Chess's premier vocal group, the Moonglows. Harvey was under contract to Leonard Chess while Etta was now on Kent, the Biharis' successor to Modern. No matter, they looked at 'Frankie And Johnny' and decided on Betty & Dupree. This incipient soul duo recorded 'We're In Love' (they really were) and 'I Hope You're Satisfied', an indelibly catchy song which Etta's mother had written for Bobby Bland. His version — 'You Got Me (Where You Want Me)' — graces the *Blues Consolidated* album, but Don Robey, rather than Hawkins, claimed the copyright. Betty & Dupree's revival got a lot of reaction in L.A. — Jesse Belvin and Richard Berry sang background vocals — but Etta was stranded in Chicago and couldn't get home without help from the Biharis, who didn't want to know. Harvey

Fuqua fixed up a deal with Leonard Chess and began grooming Etta for super-stardom: 'We sat up all night side by side. Harvey had one of those little Wurlitzer pianos and a book of a hundred standards. We'd get it out every night and he'd play the changes to all these different old songs.'

Etta's voice and material underwent considerable change. A natural contralto, she'd been afraid to be anything but basic; under Fuqua's tutelage, she began to sing higher, ornamenting her style with a variety of tricks from the smooth phrasing of a Sinatra ('I was trying to be bourgeois') to the wild abandon of the Baptist Church.

Two further hits with Harvey Fuqua, 'If I Can't Have You' and 'Spoonful', crashed the R&B charts in 1960, while a solo hit the same year, 'All I Could Do Was Cry', launched the second and most fruitful phase of Etta's career. It was written by Billy Davis and Berry Gordy, and Etta relates a gripping — if novel — account of Motown's origins: 'Leonard Chess actually lent the Gordys money to start the Anna label, which was distributed by Chess and notionally owned by Berry's baby sister, Gwen. She was engaged to Billy Davis, but Harvey Fuqua was sent to Detroit to handle business and he fell in love with Gwen and stayed there. Billy Davis came over to Chess and did 'All I Could Do Was Cry' with me. I never worked with Harvey again. I was heartbroken and everythin'.

'The song came right on time... that and 'Stop The Wedding' and 'Something's Got a Hold On Me'.' Etta picks up speed. 'See, all that stuff was written about what was going on at the time. Like, here's Etta James and she's in love with Harvey Fuqua, and he's gone to Detroit and he's taken Leonard's money to start this record company, and no more Harvey Fuqua. Over to Leonard, and Leonard's mad at Harvey and he wants to make a big, big star out of Etta to show Harvey he should never have left.'

The rest is... er... history. But, while 'All I Could Do Was Cry' led to an increasingly assured stranglehold over the Hot 100 — 26 hits in eleven years — Etta's success was still confined to ghetto clubs like Nashville's New Era, where she cut the mind-blowing *Rocks The House* in front of an audience from the then all-black Fisk University. The sleeve carried pictures of Etta with a bandage around her arm, barely disguising a problem that helped contribute to the lack of Ed Sullivan spots and primetime TV: 'I was an addict. Everybody asks me, especially little kids: "Oh Etta, you broke your arm?" and I'd say: "Yeah, I broke my arm", but really I had bad marks and sores on there. I didn't think those dumbheads would take a picture of my arm like that, but you could be laying down in the toilet and they'd take a picture and make an album cover out of it.'

Chess had little respect for his artists then? 'Leonard didn't really know anything about music. He came to every session, counting money, counting time and beating on a box. He would stand in the booth with me and tell me to sing higher. He thought that if he poked me in the side, it'd make me holler and scream.' He'd actually poke you in the side? 'Yeah, sing it mother, sing it you mother and — bam! — an elbow in my side, almost crack my ribs.'

Those who've found *Deep In The Night* to be less than wholly satisfying will be recommending rib-poking lessons to producer Jerry Wexler. I've a better idea. Wexler has startled R&B fans by declaring an infatuation with Southern country belles and, surprise, surprise, Etta shares his enthusiasm: 'Country & western is my favourite music — Kenny Rogers and Hank Williams... Yeah, I know there's some difference between the two, but I'm trying to update and go back. Charley Pride, Waylon Jennings... Leonard was planning to release a strictly country album before he passed away. I went down to Nashville with Marshall Chess and Paul Simon and we cut a country album without any R&B or black flavouring, just plain country songs with fiddles and steel. To this day I don't know whatever happened to that album.'

There's a direction, huh? Female Otis Reddings are thin on the ground, but a female Charley Pride — now *that* would really be news.

Originally published in *Melody Maker* (23 September 1978).

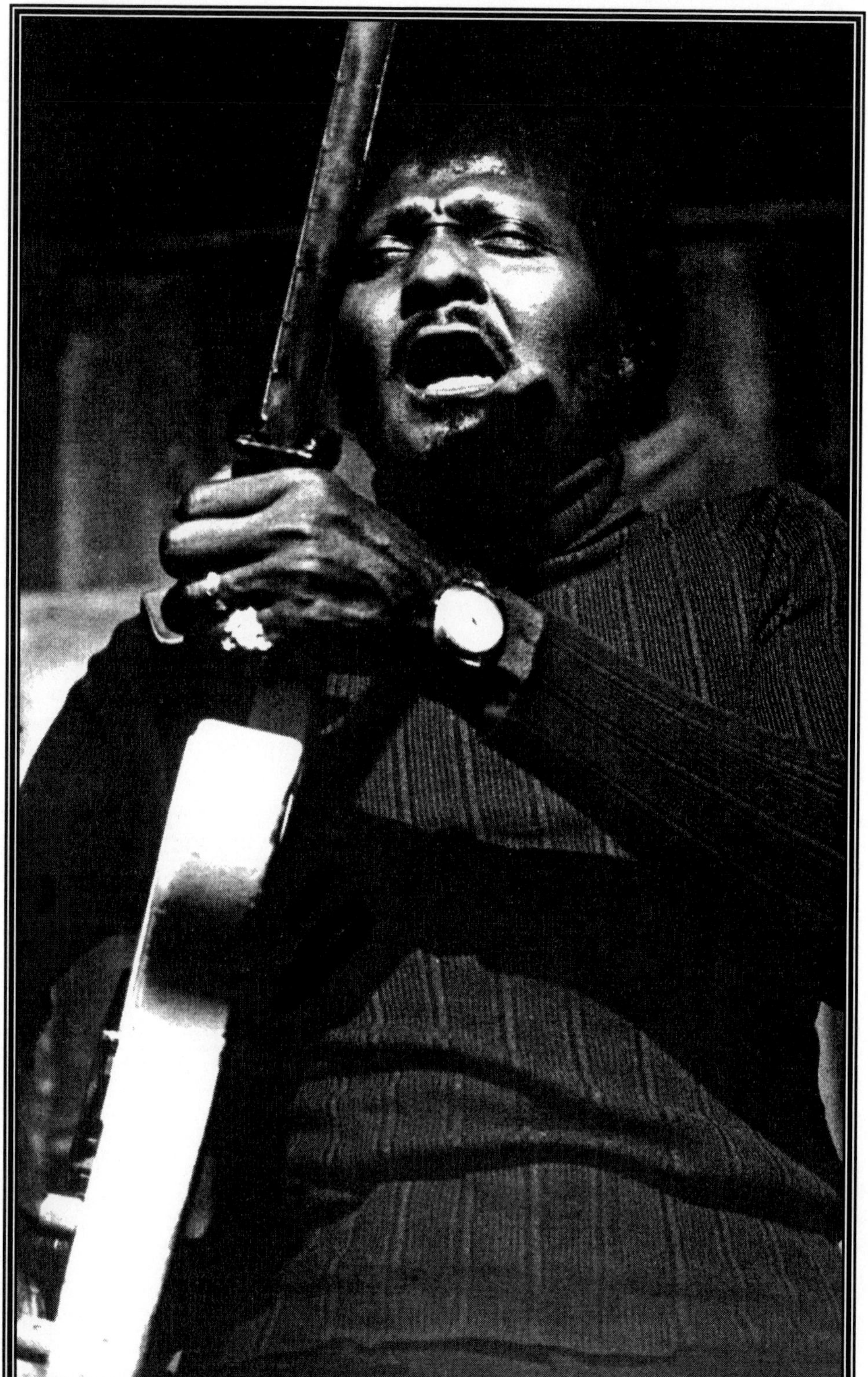

3.2
ALBERT COLLINS
Albert Collins Keeps His Cool

Albert Collins, who some have described as the most underrated blues guitarist in Texas, in the USA or maybe even the whole world, sailed into England on a Wednesday, destroyed Dingwalls on Thursday (4 January) and flew out to Chicago on Friday. This lightning stopover undertaken with considerable discomfort — Collins took a boat from Holland to Harwich and drove down to London in a freezing blizzard — left most of his admirers unawares and this one aching with frustration. I didn't make the gig (Dingwalls tend to put people on long after any sane blues fan has gone to bed) but, from what I've heard, some of the largely appreciative patrons were bemused by this peerless, seldom successfully imitated master of modern blues. 'Why does he copy B.B. King?' was one remark. 'You can see where B.B. King got that,' was another. Collins can afford to be amused by this; his reputation was earned among more discriminating critics — musicians like Albert King who's stated that Collins is his favourite guitarist, John Lee Hooker who declares 'I'm an Albert Collins *freak*' or Canned Heat's Henry Vestine, who was chiefly responsible for bringing him out of Houston and onto the West Coast where he recorded three albums for Imperial during the late Sixties and early Seventies.

Collins's instrumental blues, crisp shuffles incorporating organ and super-tight horns which he helps to arrange, are entirely his. He's recorded other kinds of blues and, occasionally, he sings — though without, as he's the first to admit, any real distinction. His cool, Texan shuffles are something else again; it might be a narrow prowess but it requires considerable technique and he sticks with it. After all, the first few bars of 'Frosty' (sorry — that sounds like a sweet) or 'Sno Cone' are unmistakably Albert Collins and no living guitarist comes close to what he does best. On stage and very often off it — wandering about amongst the audience, even out into the street and back again, playing all the while — Collins is also a devastating showman.

Modest, ingenuous, soft-spoken, he seemed slightly amazed that anyone should take a keen interest in his work and, to begin with, my questions were generally twice the length of his replies. When discographer Ray Topping spread out his maps of Houston, some colossally rare records and lists of others that Albert didn't even know he'd made, his interest increased, but I still got the impression that he's more than willing to let his music speak for itself.

Born in Leona, Texas on 3 October 1930, Collins moved to Houston in 1939. Although his father was something of a downhome guitarist, he initially preferred the bands of Jimmie Lunceford, Artie Shaw and Louis Jordan ('I liked the horn sections, I wanted to play a guitar like Louis Jordan played his saxophone'). During his teens, an acquaintance with Houston's popular Lightnin' Hopkins ('he's related to me by marriage, but it would take my mother to explain how') led to an increasing interest in blues guitar.

His first real instrument, made by a white man who'd played with Ernest Tubb and owned a carpentry shop which Collins helped to clean up, was carved out of oak and contained the rattles of a rattlesnake to improve its tone. A cousin showed Collins some of the rudiments, and his expertise grew by watching and listening to T-Bone Walker and Gatemouth Brown, who often played in Houston. By 1946, he was leading his own trio — Judge Davis (piano) and Charles Washington (drums) — to which he added horns during a lengthy engagement at the Manhattan Club in Galveston. The suggestion came from club-owner Rudolph Wiley, who bought Albert his first Fender Esquire. After a Southern tour with Piney Brown, Collins returned to Houston, where he spent the next fifteen years, largely unknown outside Texas and the South-West.

While Goldstar session files might denote an earlier excursion into a studio ('Harmonica Rock' and 'Marita'), his recording career can be said to have commenced with 'The Freeze' on Kangaroo in 1958. The band, a unit he'd assembled in Galveston — Frank Mitchell (trumpet), Big Tiny *aka* Cleotis Arch (tenor sax), Henry Hayes (alto sax), Herman Hopkins (piano), Bill Johnson (bass) and Herbert Henderson (drums) — backed by a female group, the Dolls, cut a couple of instrumentals when there was some studio time to spare. 'The Freeze' was a distinctive debut, but Collins had turned down offers from Duke's Don Robey, whom he didn't trust, and Robey retaliated by covering the record with Fenton Robinson.

Robey also used his enormous influence to prevent the R&B jocks from playing Collins's original, which still sold enough to attract steady engagements. Collins's next record, 'Defrost', on Great Scott, was picked up and reissued by Bill Hall, a kind of poor man's Huey Meaux who'd helped produce Johnny Preston, Rod Bernard and Moon Mullican. Hall's Beaumont studio attracted a bunch of teenage girls who listened to his tapes and proffered their opinion as to what might sell: 'I cut 'Frosty' while Janis Joplin was there,' Albert recalls. 'She used to hang around Bill Hall and Jack Clement, who knew her family in Port Arthur, just across the bridge. She came to the studio to shoot hookey, just one of seven little girls who listened to Bill's playbacks. She picked out 'Frosty', the one she really liked.' It became his biggest single to date, breaking all over the South without denting the national charts.

3.2 - Albert Collins

Between 1962-68, Collins recorded a slew of singles for Hall-Way, TCF-Hall, Tracie and 20th Century Fox. Coinciding with the vogue for modern electric blues, they were bought by increasing numbers of white blues fans and prompted Pete Welding's observation that Collins was one of no more than two or three artists to have demonstrated any great originality in the handling of contemporary blues idioms. His assessment, written prior to the death of Collins's competitors, Magic Sam and Earl Hooker, graced the sleeve to *Truckin' With Albert Collins* (Blue Thumb 8), a beautifully repackaged set of TCF-Hall recordings originally titled *The Cool Sound Of Albert Collins* (TCF-8002). A tight, well-rehearsed collection of instrumentals as diverting as any recorded by Earl Hooker or Freddy King, this is the yardstick by which all of Collins's studio performances are judged. His sharp, clipped, intense guitar-work was supported by most of his working band together with pianist David Dean and two organists, Bobby Alexis (on 'Frosty') and Walter McNeil (on 'Sno Cone'). Horn lines, like those on 'Don't Lose Your Cool', were inspired by Bill Doggett, while the single-chord thrashes 'Thaw-Out' or 'Kool Aide' will appeal to those who dug the monotony of the Mar-Keys. Although Collins insists he's no singer, the solitary vocal, 'Dyin' Flu', proves otherwise. Keith Richards paid $50 for the original album (a high price at the time), while Eric Clapton borrowed a copy from Ray Topping.

Despite interest of this kind, Collins was still playing black clubs in the Houston ghetto: 'Occasionally, six or seven white guys would come in but they wouldn't stay around too long, not in Houston. The places I played — joints like Blood Alley in the Fifth Ward — were kinda rough. I was scared to go in 'em myself. I grabbed my guitar and ran from a million fights.' Albert remained unscathed, but one of his vocalists was shot by mistake when a bullet passed through its intended victim and into the singer's stomach.

Throughout the Sixties, Collins continued to lead one of the best bands in the city and was called on to provide the accompaniment for local acts — Jimmy Nelson, Joe Fritz, Big Walter Price — as well as national R&B stars like O.V. Wright and Jimmy Hughes. But, by 1968, he'd had enough of Houston: 'Canned Heat found me in a little club called the Ponderosa. They came in with beards and long hair, which people in Houston weren't used to seeing... what's this... Jesus... but we talked and they got me interested in going to California, where Bill Hall made arrangements for me to record for Imperial.'

Collins's three Imperial albums lack the clean drive of the earlier sessions for Bill Hall, but often reveal far more about his own surprising tastes in blues. Current favourite Albert King is echoed on 'Chatterbox', while a debt to Guitar Slim, who also used a 100-foot guitar lead so that he could walk offstage, around the tables and back again, is evidenced by 'Talking Slim Blues' *aka* 'The Things I Used To Do'. His near-obsessive and relatively unusual love of organ blues has encompassed Bill Doggett, Jimmy McGriff and Booker T. The popularity of 'Green Onions' persuaded

3.2 - Albert Collins

Albert to continue playing instrumentals, and his 'Cookin' Catfish' was not unlike Booker T's million-seller. Collins also recorded Jimmy McGriff's 'All About My Girl' under the title of 'Left Overs'. This, and 'Talking Slim Blues', were credited to Collins — an obvious nonsense which arouses slight distress: 'I loved 'All About My Girl'. I met Jimmy McGriff in Kansas City and listened to him a great deal. Bill Hall changed it slightly and called it something else, same with 'Talking Slim Blues'. I'm not sure why he wanted to do that. When I play it, I announce it correctly. I could never take anything away from Guitar Slim or Jimmy McGriff.'

After recording for Tumbleweed in 1972, the label was bought out by ABC who'd already acquired B.B. King and Bobby Bland, leaving little room for Albert. Now, however, he has a brand-new contract with Alligator and an album, *Ice Pickin'* — his first for six years — is released here on Sonet this month. He records another in June and hopes to return here this year. Many more blues fans are about to savour the in-person discovery of Albert Collins and he appreciates their support: 'Back in the Sixties, whites weren't really into my kind of music, but today white audiences are just like a dream to me. I still ain't got used to it, but it feels so good 'cos a lot of blacks don't care anything 'bout blues. It's like a brainwashed thing, if you're not Marvin Gaye or the Commodores they don't want to hear you. It's too slow for them.'

Note   Originally published in *Melody Maker* (27 January 1979). Albert Collins died of cancer on 24 November 1993.

3.3

HERB HARDESTY
The Sax That Rocked The World

If you look over the credits on the Fats Domino reissue series — a chronological set of six albums which United Artists released in 1977 — you'll find the names of three musicians on every one: Dave Bartholomew (trumpet), Buddy Hagans (tenor sax) and Herb Hardesty (trumpet and tenor sax) remained with Domino for over twenty years and they saw it all.

The first Domino records, based on upfront, boogie-blues piano-work, gave New Orleans its reputation as the stylistic seed-bed of rock'n'roll. During the mid-Fifties, this chubby, middle-aged singer attracted large numbers of white teenagers. He played the music he had always played and, to his surprise, became a star in a new industry, recording fifteen songs that became million-sellers and a dozen more that came close.

Bartholomew, who led the band and helped write many of the songs, has been interviewed by John Broven (*Walking To New Orleans*, Blues Unlimited, 1974), while Hagans was well-covered in 'Domino Men' (*Jazz Monthly,* July 1967). No-one, as far as I can gather, has spoken to Herb Hardesty, very much the pillar of the band with whom he remained throughout the Fifties and Sixties.

Hardesty appeared at the London Palladium with Tom Waits last month, but the Musicians' Union prevented him from joining Waits on *The Old Grey Whistle Test* and he was glad to fill a hole in the evening by talking to Ray Topping and myself. Waits had not penetrated our innermost thoughts but, on the face of it, the combination seemed bizarre.

Herb lay back on his bed, flexed his long, trim fingers and spoke politely and precisely: 'I'm a session musician, and my career has really taken off since I left Fats in 1972. I divide my time between Los Angeles and Las Vegas, where the opportunities meant I could better myself. I do TV soundtracks like *Starsky And Hutch* and I've worked the lounge-shows with some of the real superstars including Duke Ellington, B.B. King, Count Basie, Ella Fitzgerald and Frank Sinatra.

'I didn't know Tom until Earl Palmer called me to L.A. to do an album with him, but he's got a very personal style. He specialises in musical freedom — if you feel like jazz you put it in, if you wanna get a little bluesy you put that in too. There's complete freedom of playing — it's one of the most interesting groups I've ever worked with.'

Born in New Orleans in 1925, Hardesty grew up surrounded by jazz. His immediate family circle contained no musicians, but his father encouraged his propensities by buying a trumpet on which Herb hoped to emulate Louis Armstrong. He played the instrument in his grammar school band, learned to read music and joined professional musicians during the summer season. His repertoire included standard tunes and Armstrong originals: 'Every trumpet player copied Louis's style 'cos he was the only one making records.'

At sixteen, Herb enlisted and travelled to Europe: 'When I wasn't fighting a war in Italy, I'd play with much more experienced musicians. Frankly, I loved every minute.' He returned to New Orleans in 1945 and worked with several bands before forming his own combo with guitarist Roy Montrell. Dave Bartholomew heard them play and, in 1948, invited Hardesty, who now played tenor saxophone, to join his own band — a unit which had recorded for DeLuxe the previous year.

Bartholomew's band accompanied most of the local singers on recording dates and, before Domino tours fully curtailed his studio work, Hardesty recorded with Roy Brown ('I went on tour with him for eight months. He was the first black singer out of New Orleans'), Jewel King, Shirley & Lee, Smiley Lewis ('Fats cut a lot of his tunes and, although Smiley did 'em just as good, he didn't go out on the road so much'), Jesse Allen, Professor Longhair, Sugar Boy Crawford, the Spiders, Eddie Bo, Lloyd Price ('Fats played piano on 'Lawdy Miss Clawdy'. He wasn't booked to come in the studio, Lloyd asked him to sit in with us') and a host of lesser-known names.

It was Hardesty's busiest period: 'Club engagements didn't pay and you couldn't make it on club work alone, you had to have a second job. But the studio musicians survived, and I was in Cosimo's studio fourteen or fifteen hours a day. I knew the labels we were recording for, but the union transacted all the arrangements — the companies sent the money directly to the union and you had two weeks to pick up your cheque.'

Hardesty blew a tenor saxophone on Fats Domino's very first record — 'The Fat Man' — in 1949 and soloed on most of the big ones: 'Going To The River', 'All By Myself', 'Ain't That A Shame', 'Poor Me', 'My Blue Heaven', 'I'm Walkin' ', 'Sick And Tired', 'Margie' and the rest. No slouch for detail, he'll gaily contradict the published evidence identifying soloists as readily as I might recognise voices of friends: 'To begin with, Fats used Bartholomew's session band including myself and Alvin Tyler (tenors), Ernest McLean, who helped with the arrangements (guitar), Frank Fields (bass) and Earl Palmer (drums). I played baritone only once, on 'Blue Monday', and Wendell Duconge played alto on 'So Long'. We were studio musicians and we didn't tour. Fats rarely brought his own band to the studio. I only agreed to go on the road with him when I was having a little domestic problem in 1952. People told me: "Aw, you won't wanna stay out of New Orleans", but I stayed out there for twenty years and it was the biggest mistake of my life.

'It was a good, secure job but working with one person for so long puts a musician in a rut where you're playing the same thing every night and you're not able to expand yourself. The only outlet you'd get from your music would be to go and jam with someone like Big Al Sears or Sam Taylor — jazzmen who weren't making any money playing jazz so they joined Alan Freed's rock'n'roll shows in New York.'

Readers who saw Domino's week-long engagement at the Saville Theatre in 1967 will recall Hardesty's vigorous contributions with delight; he'd take a familiar riff and push it over the edge, creating exhilaration out of exhaustion. Was it all a sham? 'It was a fine feeling, like jumping ten feet in the air. Rock'n'roll audiences were happy and that gave me the energy to apply myself into making them even happier. I'd turn somersaults... there were no limitations to what I'd do and it cost me a fortune to get my clothes cleaned, 'cos every night I'd come off with my shoes all scuffed and my suit completely wet and filthy.'

While Hardesty toured with Fats, saxophonist Lee Allen was used in the studio with increasing frequency, taking solos on 'I'm In Love Again', 'The Big Beat' and others. 'I blow with more style,' smiled Herb. 'Lee Allen was completely different: he was a hard blower. I'm jazzier, softer and a little more melodic.'

Towards the end of the Fifties, Imperial began to use band-tracks, leaving even less room for Hardesty who was normally on the road. The practice took an absurd twist when James Booker and, later still, Allen Toussaint, played piano aping Fats's style so well that, to this day, the problem of who plays piano on what becomes intractable if not academic: 'None of the musicians got any credit or recognition back then. I was just another sax player. On jazz records they'd always list the soloists, but on rock'n'roll it was only the artist. You could play behind a rock'n'roll singer all your life and you'd never be known as a musician.'

Hardesty's bids for solo recognition were short-lived but

fascinating. During a Domino tour, he and drummer Cornelius Coleman stopped off in Chicago, where they accompanied the Diamonds on an album which the Canadian doo-woppers made for Mercury in 1958. Nat Goodman, the Diamonds' manager, cut Herb on a collection of tenor instrumentals for the same label, and the pair flew to New Orleans where they spent three days recording Little Sonny Jones. Nothing came of either venture and Hardesty was back on tour before his A&R career had a chance to blossom.

In 1959, he sloped off from the Domino band and recorded four titles for Paoli and Mutual in New York. The masters were bought by Federal whose owner, Sydney Nathan, invited Hardesty to Cincinnati after watching his performance at a Domino concert. The band, with Walter Nelson on guitar and vocals, cut another four titles including 'Just A Little Bit Of Everything' and 'Chicken Twist". It was the last occasion records appeared under Hardesty's own name, although 'Everything' glossed a scurrilous King album, *James Brown Presents His Band And 5 More Great Artists*.

Addicts for the ineffable New Orleans feel would now derive greater satisfaction from Nelson's triplet blues ballad, 'It Must Be Wonderful' (12444) and the fierce instrumental, 'Beatin' And Blowin'' (12410), although both releases were ignored in 1961.

There came a time when the media also overlooked Domino's records, although he appeared to roll along without making any debilitating accommodations. Herb believes Fats controlled his own destiny: 'All he lost was fresh royalties. He'd become a legend and eventually he made more money in engagements than when he had the hottest records out. I think he stopped recording through choice. He thought that Lew Chudd cared, and that Imperial really pushed his records.

'Chudd was responsible for that success and his instincts were impeccable. We'd often cut thirty or forty takes, but he'd choose the first or second and he'd speed up a record when he mastered it. It always worked. Other companies didn't get so involved and Fats got a little disgusted at that. But it didn't bother him. I've never seen him sit down and say: "I've just got to get another hit." Let's face it, he needn't have another hit for the rest of his life and he'll still be a draw.'

We left Hardesty backstage at the Theatre Royal, where he talked with old friends like Mickey 'Guitar' Baker and Hal Singer prior to the *Roots Of Rock'n'Roll* show. The concert was more on the lines of an ill-conceived seminar — stiff, antiseptic and very dull. Herb Hardesty, shoulders rotating like pistons or flat on his back, blowing the reed out of his instrument, could have taught the participants something they lacked: the rorty essence of rock'n'roll.

Originally published in *Melody Maker* (19 May 1979).

3.4
GATEMOUTH BROWN
The Country-Style Blues

Although R&B and country are pretty well polarised today, there was not — as recently as twenty-five years ago — that much difference between the music of Southern blacks and whites. Wynonie Harris offered a kind of orchestrated country boogie, while the Delmore Brothers played some scintillating blues. These cross-currents were meaningful and enjoyable, amply squelching any assumption of a gap between blues and hillbilly as little more than a racist myth. Occasional cross-pollenisation is now limited to the empty gesture — Porter Wagoner's excursion into disco or James Brown's appearance on the *Opry* — but if one man is genuinely attempting to re-marry blues and C&W it's premier Texan guitarist Clarence 'Gatemouth' Brown, who brought a dazzling combination of each to the stage of the Dominion Theatre last month.

In the space of a year or two, Brown can record a fiercely black tribute to Louis Jordan (Black & Blue 33.053) and a clutch of contemporary Cajun songs (Barclay 90.002) with some of the hottest fiddle-playing you'll ever hear. This last, *Down South In The Bayou Country*, evokes all the images of South Louisiana — pots of gumbo, the muddy pirogue and oxbow swamps — but his voice remains bluesy, soulful and unmistakably black.

Pushing further into this extraordinary story of cross-cultural influences we find that Brown, long renowned as the jump blues guitarist who influenced Albert Collins, Johnny 'Guitar' Watson, Frank Zappa, Roy Buchanan, Cal Green and Guitar Slim was, first and foremost, a C&W fan with a more than peripheral understanding of that music's offshoots.

Born in Vinton, Louisiana in 1924, Brown moved to Orange, Texas, within a week of his birth. Two of his three brothers became musicians: Bobby, a vocalist and drummer, left music after marriage and James 'Widemouth' Brown, the singer/guitarist who recorded 'Boogie Woogie Nighthawk' (Jax), died of cirrhosis in 1971.

They were all taught by their father, Clarence Brown Sr, who played Cajun and bluegrass in a string band. I asked Clarence Brown Jr, country music's blues legend, to explain more of this unusual background. As thin as a rake and very tall, Brown placed his white stetson on the table next to him and raised a bony arm to slick back his processed hair:

3.4 - Gatemouth Brown

'My father was a better musician than me, 'cos we both played guitar, mandolin and fiddle — but he could also play an accordion, which I've never been able to do. I started to strum a guitar with him at five and he put me on a fiddle when I was ten. At the weekend, we'd kick the furniture back in the living room and have a shindig all night — fiddles, guitars, accordions, banjos — it was a wonderful experience for me. We didn't play zydeco — that's the Negro version of Cajun — but real Cajun and bluegrass because Daddy was raised by a Caucasian and my mother, who was born in Opelousas, spoke French.

'I got Negro, French and Choctaw Indian blood in me; in fact my two-month old baby girl looks like an Indian papoose (the child was sleeping upstairs with her mother, classical pianist Yvonne Ramsey, who plays in Gatemouth's band). I had no knowledge of musicians outside the family until I went to school and sang spirituals in the choir. One morning, the PA system went out and I kept on singing — the teacher remarked that I didn't need a microphone 'cos I had a voice like a gate, meaning it was real powerful. Some kid shouted 'Gatemouth' and the rest got to sniggering. I tried to shake it for a long time, but in the end I decided to take advantage of it.'

During the early Forties, Brown was firmly hooked on Bob Wills, Gene Autry and Roy Rogers, but Orange, a small town with a thriving shipbuilding industry, began to attract a number of jazz giants and, after seeing Count Basie and Louis Jordan, Brown began to play blues on guitar and drums. After leaving the USAF, he was given a job by Hoyt Huge who led an orchestra at the Keyhole Club in San Antonio, where Gatemouth made his professional debut in 1945.

Don Robey, a successful gambler from Houston, heard the

youngster sing and invited Brown to look him up. After hitchhiking to Houston, Brown went to see T-Bone Walker who was playing at Robey's club, the Bronze Peacock. The house was full but T-Bone, who suffered from a stomach disorder, was taken ill during a performance. As he ran off to the dressing room, Gatemouth got up out of the audience, grabbed his guitar and began to sing.

The words came out of nowhere and they rhymed: 'Gatemouth Boogie'. The crowd were ecstatic. Brown made $600 in tips, T-Bone told him never to lay a finger on his guitar again, and Don Robey moved in with indecent haste. He paid for a room in Houston, bought the kid a $750 Gibson L5 and had half a dozen uniforms made by a flash Negro tailor on Dowling Street. Gate is wearing one on the front of the Red Lightnin' album, *San Antonio Ballbuster*.

Robey flew Brown to Los Angeles in 1947 hoping a record release would help the singer to fill his nightclub. Aladdin, the West Coast label, issued two discs, including 'Gatemouth Boogie', but Robey chose not to renew a one-year contract, believing the time was right to enter the record business himself. Peacock, christened after his nightclub, was formed in 1949 and Brown kicked it off with 'Atomic Energy', a fast, jazzy side with Jack McVea's band. Brown remained with Robey for almost twenty years, witnessing the growth of a one-man operation into the mightiest black-owned record company in the South. Robey acquired Duke in 1952; Willie Mae Thornton, Johnny Ace, Bobby Bland and Junior Parker were just a few of his biggest stars. But, while he continued to release records by Gatemouth Brown, the singer never repeated the success of 1949's 'Mary Is Fine' *c/w* 'My Time Is Expensive', his only chart entry.

With the passage of time, he's better known for later records, including 'Pale Dry Boogie', a commercial for a beer company, 'Ain't That Dandy', recorded with the band which became Little Richard's Upsetters, and 'Okie Dokie Stomp', named after a New Orleans disc-jockey. But they were not chart hits and the potential of this multi-talented performer was never maximised.

It's a sordid tale: Robey, who died at the age of 71, behaved like a tzar of the black underworld and he ran his company with an unscrupulous fist. Clarence wrote and recorded a song about him ('You Got Money' — Peacock 1607):

> *You got money and I don't have a dime,*
> *While you in a hurry I got lots of time,*
> *You may have more money but you won't be havin' it long,*
> *I'll still be around when you dead and gone.*

'I really hated Robey. The moment I signed with him, I went to climbing a hill. A twenty-year contract, iron flush.' Brown leans forward, removes his shades (which he needs to wear following a recent cataract operation) and begins to finger my tie as if to underline the confidential trustworthiness of his words: 'It wasn't that I didn't have any education, 'cos I did — it's just that he was a smart businessman and when he drew up papers, they were in his favour and not yours.

'He beat everyone, Bobby Bland, Junior Parker, Jimmy McCracklin... he burned us all, but he got me first and he got me the most. He didn't want me to be too successful, 'cos as long as I was broke I couldn't buy a lawyer to fight him with. Dick Boone, the agency manager, offered him $20,000 for my contract but he refused; he could make more money by keeping me moderately successful and out of reach of anyone else.

'Now I was hot in the R&B field, I'd hear my records on the radio and on every jukebox, but he was stealing my tunes by putting 'D. Malone' on my records, when he couldn't write a song if you pushed a gun to his head. He reaped what he sowed, 'cos he died a very lonely man who couldn't look anyone in the face — he'd talk to me and Bobby Bland while looking at the wall.'

To add to his frustrations, Brown was unable to record country music. He'd always mixed it up, even during the Fifties when he led a 23-piece black orchestra for the blues clubs and a group of white guys from Houston for the honky-tonks. Few black artists could get away with this two-way street, although Jimmy Newsome, another black guitarist from Houston, followed Gate's example. You can hear Newsome on the *MGM Rockabilly Collection (Volume Two)* rocking up Hank Williams, but of Brown's pioneering endeavours in this area nothing survives. He had no control over his choice of material and, although he slipped some country feel into 'Gate's Tune' and 'Just Before Dawn', his records were always confined to blues or jazz.

Between 1949 and 1960, he cut 54 titles, most of which can be found on Japanese compilations or bootlegs (Python and Red Lightnin'); wherever you get them, you'll hear a superb guitarist, a fine singer, a proficient harp-player and the most important violinist in blues. While it's true that British enthusiasts have yet to regard Brown as highly as they should, he's become a star on the Continent and the man himself has a firm appreciation of his talent, reserving the merest scintilla of praise for T-Bone Walker and despatching other important guitarists in a sentence or two: Guitar Slim ('a clowner, but not much of a musician'), Goree Carter ('started off with me but never did go noplace'), Albert Collins ('he'll tell you I taught him to play'), even Muddy Waters and Lightnin' Hopkins fail to attract his allegiance: 'I won't play Mississippi Delta blues 'cos it's all based on hardship, whereas my blues are more sophisticated. I can't give the others much credit. In some ways, I'm an egotistical man, but before I recorded I decided I was gonna create a style that nobody else had.'

Brown finally broke his contract with Robey in 1964 when he recorded for Cue (a bossa-nova version of 'Summertime') and Cinderella (six tracks, including a remake of 'Okie Dokie Stomp'). These small Houston labels were owned by Jimmy Duncan, who lacked the distribution to get much airplay beyond the Tri-State area, where Brown played regularly.

In 1965 he recorded in Nashville at the behest of WLAC's Bill 'Hoss' Allen, who borrowed $3,000 from Chess to finance the session. One single, a cover of Little Jimmy Dickens's 'May The Bird Of Paradise Fly Up Your Nose', appeared on Hermitage and, although it sold well enough,

Hoss Allen killed his girlfriend and went to prison for seven years. Chess retrieved the rest of the tapes — thirteen titles — and where they are now is anybody's guess.

Quickly-out-of-print curiosities emerged from time to time (Gatemouth Brown & The Beats accompany Gary Ferguson on Pam) and, although these did little for his reputation, he remained a legend. In 1971, French promoter, Jean-Marie Monestier, lured Brown to France ('he searched for me for six years') where albums have now been issued on Black & Blue, Barclay and Blue Star. These, and many European tours, reserved a place for Gate in Jean-Claude Arnaudon's *Dictionnaire du Blues*.

Although this column has focused on Gatemouth's past, this is not one of those stories that peters out in the Seventies. He has a stupendous new album with C&W star Roy Clark, and his management contract with Jim Halsey ensures the kind of exposure he has lacked up to now. There should be more to write about Gatemouth Brown in future and, whether it's blues, jazz, Cajun or country, he's bound to provide a lot more music that's well worth hearing.

Originally published in *Melody Maker* (18 August 1979).

3.5
IVORY JOE HUNTER
Blues, Ballads And Rock'n'Roll

Any one album by Ivory Joe Hunter can only hint at the depth and breadth of a career which spanned five decades of entertainment experience. His R&B and pop hits — over twenty between 1945 and 1960 — are catalogued in almost every history of popular music. Hunter, who played the *Monterey Jazz Festival* and the *Grand Ole Opry*, transcended barriers between blues, pop, jazz, C&W and rock'n'roll. Hearing the 'blues-singing, piano-playing' Ivory Joe Hunter prompted Alan Freed to follow his 1951 classical radio show with a rhythm & blues programme. Johnnie Ray, Charles Brown, Nina Simone, B.B. King and Elvis Presley are among those to have cited Hunter's work as a prime influence. Elvis recorded five of his songs (six if you count a snippet from the *Million Dollar Quartet* session).

Hunter's impact on soul was no less substantial. Long before Ray Charles sang Don Gibson, Ivory Joe Hunter combined gospel piano, country songs and blues feeling. This triple alliance inspired much Sixties soul — particularly Solomon Burke, who first hit big with a C&W song and went on to record 'I Almost Lost My Mind', 'A Tear Fell' and 'Since I Met You Baby', all of which echoed Hunter's earlier and definitive versions. According to Atlantic's Jerry Wexler: 'Ivory Joe set the stage for the merger of black blues ballads and white country music in the Sixties.'

Hunter's country roots ran very deep indeed; at least as far back as March 1944, when Jimmie Davis, hillbilly singer and Governor-elect of Louisiana, recorded Joe's song, 'Love, Please Don't Let Me Down'. Hunter eventually returned the favour by including 'Worried Mind', a song Davis wrote with Ted Daffan, on his second Atlantic album.

Ivory Joe — a colourful name, but the one with which he was christened — was born in Kirbyville, a sawmill town in the backwoods of East Texas. He told interviewers he was born in 1914, but Bettye Berger, who managed Joe during the last years of his life, confirms an earlier date of 10 October 1911. This was also the date Joe supplied on a King Records biographical form in 1947. His father, Dave, was a preacher who played country breakdowns on guitar. His mother, Anna, who played guitar and piano, also sang spirituals. They raised four daughters who harmonised on the front porch and nine other sons, four of whom became pianists or drummers in local bands.

Hunter began playing piano by ear at thirteen and sang with a number of spiritual quartets. His parents prohibited other forms of music, but he picked up the blues from a less religious family who lived nearby. He left Port Arthur's Lincoln High School in the eighth grade and toured with vaudeville shows and carnivals. In *American Ballads And Folk Songs*, published in 1934, John A. Lomax described Hunter as a 'barrelhouse pianist extraordinary'. Lomax had recorded the youngster on a wax cylinder for the Library Of Congress. The location was Wiergate, Texas and the song was 'Stackolee'.

Hunter continued playing in clubs along the Gulf Coast. Singer-pianist Charles Brown saw him perform at an aunt's rent party in Texas City in 1936: 'He was a young, tall, nice-looking man. A guy that played piano and sang beautifully for $20 a night. He could turn around backwards and play the piano with his hands on the keys.'

Hunter led bands throughout the late Thirties. His dedication and leadership attracted many musicians who became significant figures in jazz and blues. Arnett Cobb and Illinois Jacquet, who stood shoulder to shoulder in Hunter's Houston unit, would accomplish mighty CVs of their own.

Following the outbreak of World War II, Hunter moved to California. The land of opportunity attracted thousands of blacks looking for work in the defence and shipbuilding industries, but Hunter said he left Texas because he didn't like being treated as a second-class citizen.

As the big band era waned, West Coast musicians fused the sound of bebop, jazz and Louis Jordan's jump'n'jive with the boogie-woogie and blues ballads of performers newly arrived from Texas and Oklahoma. There were two main strands: jump blues, a fierce and exhilarating dance music popularised by Roy Milton and Joe Liggins, and cocktail blues, a lighter, sophisticated, often introspective style typified by Johnny Moore's Three Blazers including pianist Charles Brown, who accompanied Hunter on 'Blues At Sunrise' in 1945.

'I financed the record myself,' Hunter told Tony Standish. 'I pressed five hundred copies on the Ivory label. But it was during the war and the pressing plants couldn't get material to press with, so they cut me off. I took it to Exclusive Records and asked them to continue pressing. They shelved it for a while as Joe Liggins — the Honeydripper — had a hit going. When it came back out, it did very well.'

'Blues At Sunrise' made the R&B best-sellers in December 1945. By August 1946 it had sold almost 90,000 copies. The words — entirely different to Leroy Carr's 'Blues Before Sunrise' — made an impression on B.B. King, who could still quote the risqué final verse some thirty years later.

Hunter never looked back. In 1946, he made a series of records for Pacific, a label he owned with a local disc-jockey. 'Pretty Mama Blues' reached No. 1 R&B. In 1947, he joined Syd Nathan's King Records, a company which pioneered the black/white musical interchange. Hunter recorded in Cincinnati with members of Duke Ellington's orchestra and in Nashville with white sessionmen like Harold Bradley, whose guitar-playing amazed him. He enjoyed a slew of R&B hits on King including 'Guess Who' and 'Jealous Heart'.

Occasionally, composer credits were attributed to the first of his three wives — a move Joe may have come to regret: 'Joe told me to be careful with women,' Floyd Dixon recalled. 'His wife stole everything he had after the divorce.'

Hunter's career reached a crescendo on MGM Records in 1950. The anthemic 'I Almost Lost My Mind' peaked at No. 1 R&B. 'I Need You So', another pop-tinted blues ballad, followed suit. These songs had a sentimental impact on young singers who preferred doo-wop to bop. James McGowan of the Four Fellows described their Friday night get-togethers: 'We'd put on soft blue lights, lean heavily on the shoulders of the girls and dance the slow drag to Ivory Joe Hunter's ballads.'

In the light of Hunter's huge popularity, King, MGM and 4-Star (who bought the Pacific masters) began issuing new singles almost every month. The overkill soon contributed to chart dropout, and by 1955 he hadn't had a hit in four years. Jerry Wexler and Ahmet Ertegun, who resuscitated the careers of Big Joe Turner, Ray Charles and Chuck Willis, were set on turning bewildered veterans of R&B into major rock'n'roll stars. In December 1954, they announced that Joe had been signed to Atlantic.

The neat line in tweeds, the horn-rimmed spectacles... Joe did not look like one of rock'n'roll's crucial images. The urbane, balding, pipe-smoking figure had the physiognomy of a diplomat or civic dignitary, but Wexler and Ertegun soon applied their clean, streamlined production, thoroughly-conceived arrangements and unfailing sense of good taste. 'It May Sound Silly', Joe's first Atlantic single, broke out in New York where he was sharing top billing with LaVern Baker at the Savoy Ballroom. By April 1955 it reached the R&B chart, though pop success was thwarted by the McGuire Sisters' Top Twenty cover version.

'I'll Never Leave You, Baby', Hunter's second song for Atlantic, borrowed a melody from Blind Lemon Jefferson's 'Prison Cell Blues'. Hunter knew Jefferson and was familiar with his songs. 'In fact,' he told Tony Standish, 'Lemon was uncle to my sister-in-law.' Hunter was eighteen years old when Jefferson died.

Most of Hunter's records suffered from the cover syndrome. 'Heaven Came Down To Earth' lost out to Jerry Vale (Columbia) and Helene Dixon (Epic). 'A Tear Fell', written by Dorian Burton and Eugene Randolph, had stronger legs (No. 15 R&B in March 1956), but Teresa Brewer's pop version made it all the way to No. 5 on the Top 100.

In the summer of 1956, Pat Boone took a revival of Ivory Joe's 'I Almost Lost My Mind' to the top of the charts. This million-selling record inspired the arrangement to Hunter's fifth Atlantic single, 'Since I Met You Baby'. Jerry Wexler described the situation to Rob Finnis: 'Ahmet and I are not musicians, but we listen. We're 'ear' people, and we steal from any place we can — licks, rhythm patterns, voicings, combinations. And we were very hipped on what Pat Boone was doing. He lifted a technique and a style from Ivory Joe, and we went back and lifted from Boone. We took the idea of using the vocal chorus and alto sax in harmony, that whole gentle approach. And another thing: Joe used to come in and 'woodshed'. We'd say: "Play us some old train blues" or "What do you remember from Texas, Joe?" And he played this blues called 'The Santa Fe'. It had a right-hand fill in it, a little off-time lick running through the treble. We made him put that in, and that's what made the record: that great piano sound.'

Joe claimed to have written the song in 1942 (as 'Since I Met You Jesus'), but the similarity to 'I Almost Lost My Mind' was obvious and compelling. The sentiments were reversed of course, and Taft Jordan's trumpet phrases were replaced by Leon Cohen's soothing alto. Joe, as ever, sang softly and sweetly. He attributed his sleek, velvety touch to the difficulties of playing in bars before the War. Improved microphone techniques produced a volume that irritated drinkers and encouraged performers to sing quietly. The bell-like piano fills were, as Wexler indicated, the most important components in Ray Ellis's sublime arrangement. Hunter was influenced by Clarence Williams and Earl Hines, but Fats Waller also made a deep impression. Santa Fe and the Santa Fe railroad were eulogised by a number of Texas-born blues musicians; Lee Hunter, one of Joe's brothers, cut 'Going Back To Santa Fe' for Goldstar in 1948.

And so, Ivory Joe Hunter had a rock'n'roll smash (No. 1 R&B and No. 12 Pop) with ancestral ingredients of a kind he'd been singing and playing for over two decades. The flipside hinted at this paradox: 'You can't stop this rocking and rolling, it's been here for years and years.'

'Since I Met You Baby' beat out cover versions by Mindy Carson and Molly Bee (as well as Edna McGriff), but white covers generally dominated the R&B records they imitated. Hunter's follow-up, 'Empty Arms', was trounced by Teresa Brewer, who reached No. 13 Pop. Joe's original barely disturbed *Billboard*'s Top Fifty, though it reached No. 2 R&B and No. 18 in *Cash Box*. The flip, 'Love's A Hurting Game', also dented the R&B chart. 'Shooty Booty', a departure from Joe's ballads, wasn't a hit but Solomon Burke filched the tune for 'Be-Bop Grandma' in 1961.

Hunter left Atlantic on the crest of 'Yes, I Want You', a R&B hit in December 1958. On this occasion, the woodshedding picked up on the melody of Joe Pullum's 1934 Bluebird recording, 'Black Gal, What Makes Your Head So Hard'. Pullum used it again for 'My Woman' on Swing Time in 1951, incorporating lyrics about the Santa Fe railroad and some crystalline piano licks. Joe was the first to admit that he couldn't sing like Smokey Hogg ('it wouldn't be accepted') but 'Yes, I Want You' confirms that he was fully *au fait* with the details of the Texas blues tradition.

Joining Pat Boone at Dot Records, Hunter donned spurs and stetson for a final pop C&W hit with 'City Lights' in 1959. That same year, Elvis reached No. 12 with 'My Wish Came True', a song Hunter had delivered to Graceland. Joe told the *NME* that he and Elvis 'spent hours and hours sitting at the piano singing spirituals and blues numbers'. Presley's mother told Joe that her son had made a special point of collecting his records. Elvis's arrangement of 'It's A Sin' — to which he added the piano chimes from 'Since I Met You Baby' — could not have existed without prior knowledge of Joe's version.

In 1961, Hunter took a European vacation and appeared on BBC-TV's *Juke Box Jury*. Despite poor-selling records for numerous labels — record contracts were never hard to come by — he remained a prosperous man on the strength of songwriting royalties. He lived in New York but maintained a summer home near Monroe, Louisiana.

By the Seventies he had relocated to Nashville, where he worked as a country songwriter, subsequently performing at the *Grand Ole Opry*. His career received a notable lift in 1970 when he appeared at the *Monterey Jazz Festival*, where five thousand fans sang along to 'Since I Met You Baby'. This led to a minor resurgence with a soul album on Epic and a C&W album on ABC-Paramount.

In December 1973, Hunter was told he had terminal lung cancer. Shortly before his death, the *Opry* held a benefit concert featuring George Jones, Tammy Wynette, Isaac Hayes, William Bell and Sonny James (who'd had No. 1 C&W hits with 'Since I Met You Baby' and 'Empty Arms'). Elvis sent a telegram (*'Your music will always be a part of us'*) and a donation of $1,000. Ivory Joe was airlifted from a Memphis hospital and sang a couple of songs from a wheelchair. He died on 8 November 1974.

Liner note for *Blues, Ballads & Rock'n'Roll* (Ace CDCHD-747) 2000.

3.6

STICK McGHEE
Drinkin' Wine Spo-Dee-O-Dee

Stick McGhee is unlikely to share the position in which his much-loved brother is so rightfully placed. Alert and articulate, Brownie has been called the smartest blues singer who ever recorded, and his long partnership with Sonny Terry has had incalculable effects on all phases of blues revivalism. Stick made hustling his life's work. He was a cab-driver, a street-singer, a pool-player, a dancer, a gambler and a small-time racketeer. When he had time, he made records which fuelled and invigorated both rockabilly and blues. One of these, 'Drinkin' Wine Spo-Dee-O-Dee', has been recorded a hundred times or more. It was hastily translated into hillbilly (Loy Gordon), rocked unmercifully (the Treniers, Jerry Lee Lewis) and revamped again and again in the blues field (Big John Greer, Wynonie Harris, Champion Jack Dupree, Lightnin' Hopkins, Lionel Hampton, Larry Dale). There are easily recognizable variations (Johnny Jano's 'She's Mine', the Nightcaps' 'Wine, Wine, Wine', Vince Maloy's 'Soda Pop') and a slew of classic and not-so-classic rockabilly versions: Johnny Burnette, Matt Lucas, Sid Starr & The Escorts (whose version of 'For You My Love' segued into 'Drinkin' Wine Spo-Dee-O-Dee'), Glenn Reeves, Wally Dean, Malcolm Yelvington, Marcus Van Story and Whitey Pullen spring to mind. This truly seminal example of grape-rock has inspired artists as diverse as Charlie Daniels and Pere Ubu. The song is everywhere but, while few versions are superior to the original, Stick himself is barely remembered. Emaciated and down on his luck, he died in 1961 before the folk-blues revival could diminish his music or change his hapless fortunes.

The youngest of four children, Granville Henely McGhee was born on 23 March 1917 in the country slums of Kingsport, Tennessee. His father, George Duffield McGhee, worked as a 'wheeler', digging gulleys and canals and loading the earth on to a horse-powered wagon. 'Duff', as he was called, also played guitar and sang in an integrated group performing reels, rags and hillbilly songs as well as blues. An uncle, John Evans, played fiddle in a manner characteristic of black and white country dances, and the children were also exposed to blues and hillbilly on shellac.

3.6 - Stick McGhee

Stick's mother, Zelda, was fond of Jimmie Rodgers, Bessie Smith, Lonnie Johnson and the Carter Family, whose records were played on a hand-cranked Victrola. The McGhees were poor nonetheless. Kingsport was a rat-infested town without electricity or running water, and both boys helped supplement the family income by grazing cows for 25¢ a week. In 1919, Brownie was stricken with polio leaving him with a permanent and pronounced limp. Unable to walk fast enough to keep up with his younger brother, he constructed a four-wheeled cart which Granville propelled by means of a stick inserted into a tin can on the back. It was an efficient form of transport, particularly after throwing rocks in the white section of town. Granville, who was rarely seen without this locomotive device, became known as 'Stick' McGhee — an appellation which remained for the rest of his life.

The brothers went to school at Oklahoma Grove in Kingsport. While Brownie graduated, Stick left in the ninth grade. A carefree, happy-go-lucky individual, he shined shoes outside Kingsport's billiard parlours and studied the town's finest pool-sharks. In the black neighbourhood, where his pool-playing ability went unrecognised, Brownie would place bets on him and the duo cleaned up. Stick learnt to play C&W-style guitar before Brownie; he also played piano and he could tap-dance with distinction. He was tall, very good-looking and he had a disarming way with women, marrying twice before the end of World War II. During the Thirties, Stick worked as a labourer for service stations, restaurants, the WPA, the Red Cross and the Eastman Kodak Co. As a dancer, he joined shows which Brownie devised with singer/guitarist Leslie Riddles and they played riverboat parties for wealthy white clientele. The brothers parted company in 1938. Brownie travelled North — initially to Chicago, where he made his first records in 1940, and then New York, where he eventually settled; Stick moved to Knoxville and then Portsmouth, Virginia where one of his two sisters lived. In 1942 he joined the army, where he drove a truck for the laundry unit.

The inspiration for 'Drinkin' Wine Spo-Dee-O-Dee' occurred during boot training at Petersburg, Virginia. It began life as an obscene barrack room chant: *'Drink wine, motherfucker, drink wine / Pass the goddamn bottle to me'*. Stick posted the lyrics to his brother and asked him if he could clean them up a bit. In the meantime, he travelled around the world on active service and fought in the Pacific, where he was wounded by shrapnel which seriously damaged his left hand. After an operation, and further service in Japan and Korea, he left the army and moved to New York where Brownie was firmly established. In June 1946, Stick made his first records as second guitarist with Dan Burley & His Skiffle Boys. They were issued on Circle, owned by Rudi Blesh who gave Stick the name 'Globetrotter' because the back of his guitar — an Epiphone — was covered with the names of the countries in which he'd travelled. Willie Moore referred to Stick's residence around Kester, North Carolina during the same period (*Living Blues* No. 5) but, by 1947, Stick had a day job in a cosmetics factory and worked New York's streets with Bob Harris, his bass-player who subsequently recorded for Derby, Jackson and Par. The pair popularised the newly-revised 'Drinkin' Wine' to which Brownie had added the now-famous nonsensical syllables. Brownie, who had realised you couldn't say 'bed' on a record, let alone 'motherfucker', claimed to have plucked 'Spo-Dee-O-Dee' out of the New York air, but Sam Theard, a vaudeville comedian, cut something called 'Spo-Dee-O-Dee' for Vocalion in 1937. Theard, who wrote 'I'll Be Glad When You're Dead, You Rascal You', also used 'Spo-Dee-O-Dee' as a stage-name; he died in 1982.

Stick McGhee and Bob Harris first recorded the song — which opened with 'Down in Petersburg...' — for J. Mayo Williams. (Contrary to other sources, Brownie did not play on the original version; most of the biographical details here came from Brownie, and I have chosen his information whenever it contradicts entries in various works of reference.)

Formerly recording director at Paramount, Vocalion and Decca, Williams was a sharp black man who bought half the songwriting copyright for ten dollars. According to Brownie, it was a legal contract and, until his death in 1980, Mayo Williams continued to receive half royalties from numerous revivals. 'Drinkin' Wine', released in 1947 on Williams's short-lived Harlem label, originally made next to no impression and Stick returned to the streets. However, Brownie kept him busy whenever he could and in 1949 the pair recorded Irving Berlin's 'Yesterday' (Sittin' In With 538), with Stick on guitar. The disc was released as by Blind Boy Williams, but Berlin discovered who was responsible and sent them a letter telling them to stop messing up his songs.

Stick began to worry about his ability to play with an impaired hand. He frequented the local park and drank to excess. The story might have ended there, but Mayo Williams had off-loaded his Harlem pressings to a distributor from New Orleans, where the record began to receive airplay. Local shops soon ran out of stock and news of the demand reached Herb Abramson, co-owner of the then-emergent Atlantic Records. Abramson asked Brownie if he'd heard of Stick — was he, perhaps, a relative? The record was making a noise in Louisiana and maybe they should re-record it with New Orleans in mind. (Brownie's account of these events is matched by Herb Abramson, whose recollection, and another by Ahmet Ertegun, appears in Charlie Gillett's Atlantic history, *Making Tracks*.) Brownie pulled his brother out of the park and set up a date which was supervised by Abramson and Ertegun. Stick played the introduction and Wilbert Ellis, a bar manager from Birmingham via Harlem, played piano. Brownie contributed the single-string solo and shouted the 'mop mops'. 'We forgot about the original version,' Ertegun told Gillett. 'Next thing we know, Decca is competing with us. They had bought the rights to Mayo Willams's version and put it back on the market. But we outsold them, which gave us confidence in both our production techniques and our marketing.' 'Drinkin' Wine Spo-Dee-O-Dee' hit the R&B chart in April 1949, reached No. 3 and sold over 300,000 copies. Atlantic were on their way and Stick, who signed a contract for $700, was their first R&B star. Some have said his contract was for three years; Brownie thought five.

During the next three years, Stick cut no fewer than twenty-five titles including 'Southern Menu' (the title was supplied by Brownie who didn't play on it), 'Drank Up All The Wine' (whose author, the late Rudolph Toombs, frequented Brownie's school-cum-studio on Harlem's 125th Street), the magnificent 'House Warmin' Boogie' and the equally lovely 'She's Gone' (originally waxed by Wilbert Ellis on Sittin' In With in 1949). These were popular records and, under the agency of Jimmy Evans, Stick toured the country appearing in *Battle Of The Blues* concerts with Wynonie Harris, Roy Brown, H-Bomb Ferguson and others.

Stick was not a prodigiously gifted musician. It's been said that he became infuriated when he couldn't duplicate his brother's dexterity and went so far as to hire saxophones in order to disguise his weaknesses. Brownie thought he was a fine singer and a good guitarist, and these are probably the highest superlatives one can use. His guitar-playing is deceptively simple, relying on strategy rather than technical brilliance. All the same, few would criticise that solid boogie figure on 'Drank Up All The Wine' or his solos in 'Blue Barrelhouse' and 'House Warmin' Boogie'. And his voice — while not intense — is wonderfully warm, without menace or introspection. At fast or slow tempos, it reflects an easy, good nature. Sonny Terry, Brownie himself and, in particular, Van Walls helped create unfaltering performances which verge on the inspired; these records are among the best novelty R&B, evoking a spirit of 'togetherness' and the mellow, friendly conditions in which they were made. Drums were usually played by Gene Brooks or Philly Joe Jones, while bassists include Gene Ramey and Bob Harris, who screams in the middle of 'House Warmin' Boogie'. Brownie, of course, adds vocal frills to 'She's Gone' and 'Let's Do It', which was written by Atla Williams. A huge woman from Mississippi, she sang around New York in company with Stick, Jack Dupree and Sonny Terry.

Stick's last national hit, 'Tennessee Waltz Blues', was planned as a rush cover job. Atlantic needed a R&B version to compete with Patti Page and, although Stick wanted to sing it, he'd had too much booze the night before and was simply too hoarse to reach the notes. Withdrawing 'Blue And Brokenhearted' (on sale for a month or less), the company substituted 'Tennessee Waltz Blues' as an instrumental with Stick (guitar), Van Walls (piano) and a saxophonist whose name escapes my R&B dragnet. It reached No. 2 on the R&B chart in 1951. The same year, while under contract to Atlantic, Stick, Brownie and Van Walls recorded 'Oh, What A Face' for London. While the London record didn't sell, Atlantic protested and their relationship with Stick was evidently strained beyond repair (the trade papers reported that London Records were obliged to pay Atlantic a royalty equal to McGhee's royalty on 'Oh, What A Face'). After a final session in December 1951, which produced a duet with Brownie on 'Wee Wee Hours', Stick and Atlantic parted company.

During 1952 he worked as a cab-driver, making only one record for Dave Miller, who was unable to recall the circumstances in which Stick came to record 'My Little Rose' (Essex 709). Late the same year, Stick signed with King and cut at least a dozen sides, the best of which concern booze in one form or another. Stick plainly enjoyed a drink. 'Whiskey, Women And Loaded Dice' also bears witness to his rural background. Performed to the tune of Jimmie Rodgers's 'In The Jailhouse Now', it was revived a year later by C&W singer, Jack Cardwell. There are two formidable 'Spo-Dee-O-Dee' clones: 'Head Happy With Wine', a solid, stop-time grape-rocker, and 'Six To Eight', a relentless litany of bootlegged bottle labels. 'Double Crossing Liquor' speaks for itself, while 'Get Your Mind Out Of The Gutter' addresses a drunken partner. Down-in-the-bottom partying also characterises 'Sad, Bad, Glad' and 'Jungle Juice'. They're all set to a backdrop of riffing saxes, a handful of flawlessly structured sax solos and Stick's elastic, high-toned guitar playing.

Stick also cut a solo session for the Savoy label in 1954. Three years earlier, he had joined Brownie for the Savoy session which produced 'Diamond Ring' and 'So Much Trouble'. According to Brownie, they were recorded in Herman Lubinsky's office on Market Street and feature two guitars; the one you hear most is Stick — which might interest George Thorogood, who revived 'So Much Trouble' for Rounder in 1978. Stick can also be heard on New York blues records by Champion Jack Dupree (including Vik and Red Robin) and Sonny Terry (Red Robin, Groove and Folkways, where they revamped 'Drinkin' Wine' in 1958). The year before, he returned to Atlantic/Atco, but the titles ('Wailin' And Sailin' ', 'Be A Playboy' and 'Pigalle Lover') have never been issued.

In 1960, Stick went for a check-up and was found to be suffering from lung cancer. There was nothing anyone could do. He recorded his final single for Herald with — in all probability — Sonny Terry's nephew, J.C. Burris, on harmonica. 'Money Fever' *c/w* 'Sleep In Job' do not sound like the work of a dying man, but his weight had dropped to less than one hundred pounds and he passed away in the Bronx Veterans' Hospital on 15 August 1961.

Note 1   This essay on Stick McGhee is a confluence of the notes to *Drinkin' Wine Spo-Dee-O-Dee* (Crown Prince LP IG-401, 1980) and *Stick McGhee & His Spo-Dee-O-Dee Buddies* (Ace CD CHD-502, 1994) with a number of corrections from Chris Smith's superlative discography, *That's The Stuff: The Recordings of Brownie McGhee, Sonny Terry, Stick McGhee and J.C. Burris* (Housay Press, 1999).

Note 2   Tony Collins told me that Jack Kerouac referred to 'spotioti' in *On The Road* (1957) and other books. It is, in fact, a mixture of wine and whiskey or, seven pages later, *'a shot of port wine, a shot of whiskey, and a shot of port wine'*. Kerouac's other works also referred to *'wine spodiodi, whiskey, beer and wine'*, while novelist James Lee Burke has defined wine spotioti as *'a mixture of muscat and whiskey that can fry your head for a week'*. Thanks also to Keith Briggs and Dave Moore who listed these references in *Blues & Rhythm* (October 2003).

3.7
BIG JAY McNEELY
Roadhouse Boogie

In August 1983, Big Jay McNeely flew to London for the *R&B Jamboree* at Camden's Electric Ballroom where he topped a bill which included Willie Egan, Chuck Higgins and the grievously underrated Young Jessie. The companionably crowded audience gave the fifty-six year old Grand Master a tumultuous reception, and he played to the gallery in a vulgar, rough-hewn style unseen in Europe since Big Jim Wynn toured with Johnny Otis over ten years before.

A hugely charismatic figure, McNeely performed a variety of anatomical tricks from rolling his belly like a stripper to projecting his eyeballs on stalks — this last coinciding with the fruitiest of lowdown notes from his long-suffering Selmer saxophone. Dressed in black from head-to-toe, he squealed, roared and stuttered, reducing his cotton suit to a fistful of wet rag and raising the temperature to the verge of hysteria. It was a fearsome display: he laid on his back and kicked his legs in the air, proffered a hand to the prettiest girls on the premises and roamed, hunch-backed, through the throng blowing all the while. Finally, the house lights dimmed and his luminous golden saxophone bobbed about in the dark.

Thirty years earlier, McNeely established a reputation as the very wildest of the tenor saxophonists to walk up and down the bar-tops of ghetto America's long, narrow saloons. The most substantial of rock'n'roll contortionists, he was born Cecil James McNeely on 29 April 1927, the third and last child of Dillard and Armonia McNeely who lived in Watts, Los Angeles. Compared to many black families, the McNeelys were several rungs up the social ladder. Dillard McNeely worked as a porter on the *SS Tango*, a floating casino moored some miles out from the coast. The ship attracted a wealthy clientele and the tips were high. Armonia turned the spare cash to profit by making blankets and multi-coloured quilts; she was proud of her Red Indian ancestry. Both parents played piano; Dillard McNeely Jr, the oldest brother, eventually played bass and Bob McNeely, born circa 1922, took up baritone saxophone during the late Thirties. There was talk of his joining Cab Calloway's Orchestra, but Armonia thought he was too young and refused to let him go.

Cecil McNeely became enamoured with swing and jazz at Jordan

High School where he formed his first band: 'It was called the Earls Of '44 because Earl Hines was big then. We played little kids' dances and stuff, in fact I formed the band 'cos the older guys wouldn't let me join their band. We had about ten pieces. It was an integrated high school and the band was mixed: black, white and Spanish kids.' McNeely's tastes gradually expanded to include Dizzy Gillespie, Howard McGhee and Jack McVea of 'Open The Door Richard' fame. He patronised the Basket Room where McVea played frequently. Three other musicians, Arnett Cobb, Charlie Parker and Illinois Jacquet, excited McNeely's interest: 'All the tenor sax players. That's the first music I ever heard that seriously intrigued me. I used to catch Jacquet doing 'Flying Home' with Lionel Hampton. It was such a big tune, it was like a standard, the melody sold it more than the opening chorus. Everybody waited for the solo that Jacquet played. Later, I jammed with Charlie Parker when he was out in L.A., and I'd have to say that he was the musician who inspired me most. I was very close to him — my mother even washed Charlie Parker's clothes one time.'

At seventeen or thereabouts, McNeely took a short-lived job with the Firestone Rubber Company. The monotonous work disagreed with his temperament and he returned to full time study at Los Angeles Polytechnic High School. At the same time, he began to give firm consideration to a musical career: 'At Jordan I used to pick up the saxophone, try to play a couple of numbers and then throw it under the bed. Now, I decided I'm gonna have to learn how to play this thing properly. I 'd tried a regular job eight hours a day and the last four hours was killing me. I really felt music was a better way to make a living.'

Clutching a borrowed alto, McNeely cycled up town for a course of 50¢ lessons from Miss Hightower, aunt to the singer-saxophonist, Vi Redd, and tutor to a number of jazz musicians including Lorenzo Holden and William 'Sonny' Criss, both of whom would later work with Johnny Otis. During these tutorials, McNeely switched to a tenor saxophone (left behind by Bob McNeely when he joined the army) and formed a trio with Sonny Criss, on alto, and another Polytechnic student, pianist Hampton Hawes. Of roughly comparable ages (Hawes was a year older than Criss and McNeely), the three young men played a polite form of gospelly jazz at a club on Central Avenue called The Last Word.

McNeely and Criss remained at Polytechnic High School for one semester and then attended Jefferson High School, where they graduated together: 'In fact, we played a Chopin waltz as a duet at the ceremony.' McNeely also attended Johnny Otis's newly-opened Barrelhouse Club and absorbed first-hand the emerging synthesis which became known as 'rhythm & blues': 'I was nineteen or so when I went down there by the Santa Ana tracks. Johnny Otis's partner, Bardu Ali, put on a lot of good shows often emceed by the deejay, Hunter Hancock. They had the Robins with Bobby Nunn, and Cathy Cooper. It was very exciting.'

In 1947, McNeely was advised to see another music tutor, Joseph

Cadaly, who played saxophone and clarinet in the orchestra at RKO studios: 'I studied everything... counterpoint, vocal harmony, classical conservatory, clarinet too. But I got real legit, my saxophone began to sound like a cello and it seemed like my soul had just left momentarily because of studying so hard. I was losing my soul, getting too legit. I stopped and recorded 'Deacon's' Hop'! Until then I'd been obsessed with notes — with 'Deacon's Hop' I abandoned all that and just let myself go.'

Like many an important record, 'Deacon's Hop' resulted from a confluence of coincidence and happenstance. Prinze 'Candy' Stanzel, guitarist and Barrelhouse habitué (he also recorded for Johnny Rand's Jay-Ree label) introduced McNeely to Ralph Bass, then working as a West Coast talent-scout-cum-promoter for Savoy Records. Bass caught McNeely playing at the Barrelhouse and discussed the terms of a record contract: 'At that stage I had no idea what I was gonna record. I wanted a record under my own name, but I didn't have a band of my own or any original material. I was a regular visitor to Pete Canard's Record Shop, just going by listening to records to get some ideas. Eventually, Pete played me Glenn Miller's 'Nothing But Soul' and that was it... that drum sound: *tch tut tut tch*... From that I wrote the tune, just from that little introduction. When I got it all together, I played it to Ralph Bass and he called Herman Lubinsky, the owner of Savoy, who flew out from New Jersey. I only met him that once. He came to my house in Watts and paid me for the session. He didn't think Cecil was a good enough stage-name and asked me my nickname. I told him 'Jay' because everybody called me Jay for short. "Big Jay," he said. It was all Lubinsky's idea. Funny thing, I wasn't really big at all.'

'Deacon's Hop', the tune McNeely originally played to Ralph Bass, was not recorded until his second Savoy session. The first, which took place at Radio Recorders in Hollywood on 29 November 1948, spawned 'Benson's Groove', dedicated to Al Benson, the popular Chicago disc-jockey (it was later retitled 'Deacon's Groove' and 'Cool Blood'). Other tunes from the first session, 'Wild Wig' and 'Man Eater', were given titles which expressed the angry, frenetic nature of the music. Some three weeks later, McNeely returned to Radio Recorders where, in addition to his famous signature tune, he laid down 'California Hop', 'Cherry Smash' and 'Artie's Jump': 'That was named after a little girl who lived on the West side of L.A.. We were not very close or anything, but her name was Artie and I wrote the tune for her.'

Apart from Bob McNeely who played baritone sax, the Savoy cuts (all eight can be found on *Honkers And Screamers – The Roots Of Rock'n'Roll, Volume 6*, Savoy 2234) employed session musicians including the late John Anderson on trumpet ('he and Buddy Collette ran a progressive, non-profit making organization to help musicians'), Jesse 'Streamline' Ewing (trombone), Jimmie O'Brien or Jimmy O'Bryant (a pianist who attended Jefferson High with McNeely), an unidentified bass-player (possibly Ted Shirley) and William Streetser (drums).

3.7 - Big Jay McNeely

'Deacon's Hop' became a bestseller (No. 1 R&B in February 1949), releasing McNeely from his self-imposed musical straitjacket, creating interest on a national scale (Raymond Hill's 'Bourbon Street Jump' was a crafty re-creation) and persuading the twenty-one year old tenor-man to form a band of his own: 'I would have gone East on the strength of 'Deacon's Hop', but Bardu Ali told me not to go. The New York agency wanted me to play the Apollo but I felt I was too young. I asked if my brother could come too but they wouldn't let him, so I didn't go either. Bardu Ali, he kinda schooled me as to how those guys take your money and misuse you. What they'd do is rob musicians, tell you big stories, and when you come off the road after a year you owe everybody. Bardu Ali hipped me to that — they'd buy you cars and suits and you'd end up owing them the money. I may have lost out 'cos the record was big, but it was probably best that I didn't go. Right after that I got a band together in order to work locally. We also toured the South.'

The longest-serving members of the McNeely aggregation included Leonard Hardiman and both of McNeely's brothers. Dillard was recruited in a fit of nepotism: 'We just bought a Fender bass — he started out on Fender bass because we didn't have room in the trailer to carry one of those big string basses, that would have got broken up, and anyway the Fender had the coming sound. We wrote out his parts and told him: "You just play this and don't ask no questions." And that's what he did. He had a good mind: you played him a tune once and he could remember it for five years. We had a fantastic guitar player, Melvin Glass — he played bass too — and he would teach Dillard the parts. Dillard also acted as road manager. Leonard Hardiman, the drummer, he was called 'Tight' because he was so small I guess, no bigger than a pair of scissors.'

That trio accompanied McNeely throughout 1948-56, the years of 'pre-rock rock', when his wild-man stage persona became the stuff of myth and legend. Trailed by his baritone-playing brother, Big Jay marched back and forth across the stage, or off it, down into the aisles or through the crowd. He would take off his coat, lie down on his back and kick his feet in the air: a band-member would hold a microphone over him to catch every decibel. At least one older saxophonist claimed to have pioneered such antics: Big Jim Wynn, a veteran of countless West Coast sessions, was probably the first to combine sax-playing and acrobatics.

McNeely, however, refers to a slew of gimmicks and devices which sprang forth in a flash of spontaneous, attention-getting combustion: 'I'll never forget that moment. I was twenty-two years old and we were playing Clarkville, a little town in Tennessee. I had a fantastic group with me including Bob and 'Tight' as well as Carl Peterson, the jazz pianist, and a girl singer out of Michigan. The club had an upstairs and a downstairs and we played upstairs. We played for two hours before taking a break and the people just didn't respond — they just sat there like a bad spell, couldn't reach them at all. During the intermission, I was too worried to change clothes. I just sat there thinking: "What can I do?" I thought: "I'll get on my knees," and during the second show that's just what I did. Still no reaction. I laid down... and that did it. That broke the spell and people began screamin' and hollerin'. People from downstairs came upstairs and we packed the place. After that night I thought: "I'm gonna try that again," and it worked everywhere, all through Tennessee and Texas. I bought lots of beautiful suits, bright canary yellow and so on. I'd be walking outside in the mud, lying down in all the dirt and people would say: "Oh please, don't lie down in that pretty suit!" This was for the blacks first, of course, but when I got back to the West Coast and began doing it with the white kids... Wow!'

In 1949, McNeely's booking agency introduced him to Leon Rene, owner of Exclusive, for whom he made a clutch of remarkably fine singles at Radio Recorders. Although McNeely's powers of recollection do not fully extend to the Exclusive sessions ('I don't recall half the tracks even though I produced them myself') many listeners will prefer these recordings to the one-paced Savoy material. Indeed, their variety undermines the sterility associated with a good deal of archetypal honking. Witness 'Blow Big Jay', an April 1949 heart-stopper on which McNeely's relentless, roller-coasting tenor is uplifted by a Latin lilt. Hear too 'Tondalayo', which begins like an Oriental-flavoured tone-poem and features Bob McNeely on alto, or 'K&H Boogie', a showcase for sublime piano-playing authored by Jimmie O'Brien. 'Willie The Cool Cat' (which stroked the ego of New York WHOM deejay, Willie Bryant) does little to disguise McNeely's reverence for Charlie Parker while 'Gingercake', 'Boogie In Front' and 'Hoppin' With Hunter' (dedicated to KFVD's deejay Hunter Hancock) illustrate his command of all the techniques associated with the honker's art. The blues ballad, 'Midnight Dreams', was written and performed by Clifford Blivens, a young singer from Dawson, Texas whom McNeely first engaged as a chauffeur. Blivens cut solo discs for Exclusive including 'Hobo Boogie' and 'Unhappy Woman Blues'. His plummy voice also adorned 'Junie Flip' while bass-player Theodore 'Ted' Shirley sang on the humorous and wildly exciting 'Roadhouse Boogie'. (Thirteen years later, Shirley's son, Everett, played trumpet on McNeely's *Live At Cisco's* album).

1950 brought a swift four-track session for Aladdin whose titles — 'Jay's Frantic', 'Let's Split', 'Real Crazy Cool' and 'Deac's Blowout' — presaged the brainbending excitement of rock'n'roll by half a decade. Ironically, 'Let's Split' (not issued until May 1954) was based on an elderly music hall tune, 'One Of The Ruins That Oliver Cromwell Knocked About A Bit'. All four tracks conform to the wildest traditions of McNeely's chosen genre; as a blueprint for honking at its most mantra-like there is little to compare with 'Jay's Frantic' or 'Real Crazy Cool' — actually one long performance split up. Midway between a desperate, chaotic mess and a marvellously invigorating noise, they did not sell well; as Jay himself concedes: 'The saxophone was a little too black for most white kids comin' on.'

The following year McNeely joined Imperial, where the band featured a slew of vocalists including seventeen year old Jesse Belvin, whom McNeely had met at a gig in L.A.. 'Jesse was a fantastic artist,' Jay eulogised, 'a very, very handsome fellow and a wonderful person. He came out to my house in Watts and we broke bread together. He was always writing songs, he could sit down and write a tune in five minutes. And he gave them away. Of course, we really didn't know anything about publishing — nobody would tell the blacks anything, and you were blackballed if you tried to learn. Jesse's mother didn't really want him to go on the road but I was the first one to carry him around. Jesse and Jimmy Huff — another singer who used to play drums in his own band until he joined mine — they were over at my house all the time.'

Belvin sang as a single ('Sad Story') and as part of a group, Three Dots & A Dash — namely Jimmy Huff, Marvin Phillips and a girl remembered only as Betty. Their half-dozen cuts have been reissued on *Big Jay Rides Again* (Pathé-Marconi 1546691) together with instrumentals from the band and one song, 'Insect Ball', by the comedians, Dope & Skillet *alias* Little Arthur Matthews and Ernest Mayhand. Matthews recorded for Johnny Otis while Mayhand had appeared during the Forties as part of Pan, Pot & Skillet with Jimmie Lunceford's Orchestra. He spent the Sixties creating a wealth of smutty comedy routines as half of Leroy *[Daniels]* & Skillet on Laff Records.

Before leaving the Imperial sides, I should incorporate a note of caution for those who want every McNeely disc. 'Blow, Blow, Blow' (Imperial 5170) plus dubbed audience noise equals 'Deacon's Express' (5219), which was re-titled 'Hometown Jamboree' on Bayou 014. 'Teenage Hop' (the reverse of Bayou 014) is a re-titled 'Night Ride'. McNeely's second Bayou coupling (018) is more complicated: 'Calamity' equals 'Night Ride', but with an ending spliced on from 'Deacon Rides Again', while 'Catastrophe' is a mixture of several records spliced together, the longest segment being 'Deacon's Express'.

By the early Fifties, McNeely was a huge draw, primarily because of his onstage antics and spectacular walks. He talks proudly of a concert with Lionel Hampton circa 1950: 'Wrigley Field in Los Angeles, a baseball stadium, a black promoter and 25,000–30,000 people. Jesse Belvin sang his stuff and I went on. I did one number and Hamp's wife pulled me offstage — she didn't want anyone else to steal the show and wouldn't let me go on. When Hamp marched his band down to the front, I ran out past third base and right on up into the audience and started blowing. Hamp's wife was mad but there wasn't nothin' she could do. I was up in the audience and all the kids were hollerin' and screamin' for me, the hometown boy. I marched all the way around the stadium... Hamp wasn't gonna be outdone though — he took his whole band offstage and marched right round the stadium to where home plate is. When I saw that, I started crawling on my back from second base all through the dugouts. And he still had to follow me. We all ended up in the dugouts and I got big write-ups in the papers after that.'

McNeely's walks were nothing if not photogenic. *Ebony* carried a spread of him blowing in the street outside Los Angeles' Club Oasis; he would honk at passers-by and compete with car drivers who honked at him. He'd cakewalk to the dressing room in a green suit and emerge in a purple one. At the Band Box on New York's 51st Street, he would blast his way next door to Birdland, go walkabout amongst the customers and then leave with a dozen or more people jigging along in his wake. On one occasion, in San Diego, he was detained for disturbing the peace: 'I was working with Hunter Hancock at the Eagle Ballroom and I start to march around and entertain the people. Bob, on baritone, and the trombone player are following behind me. I manage to get past the policeman on the door — he's clapping his hands and enjoying himself — but the crowd is packed tight and Bob couldn't follow me. I'm playing in the street when an off-duty policeman comes up and arrests me. He called in and a police car came and picked me up. I was in the cells for half an hour before my brother came down and bailed me out. The rest of the band was still inside the club playing when I got back.

'We used to have *Battles Of The Saxes*,' McNeely continued. 'Myself, Vinny *[Vido]* Musso, Chuck Higgins, Joe Houston — I introduced Joe to the West Coast and put him on a lot of sessions — all those guys. That was like a constant happening when the sax was the thing before the guitar took over. They'd be advertised like a boxing show. I'd created a lot of excitement by lying on the floor and stuff, and other saxophonists began to copy my act. There were dozens of 'em doing it.' *[In 1954, Down Beat listed a string of McNeely imitators including Wild Bill Boone, Frank Lewis and Eugene Jackson; 'Lewis,' wrote Down Beat's reporter, 'arranger and saxman with Bruce Dybvig's Royalaires, turns into a Big Jay at 11.45 pm nightly upon instructions from the boss.']*

'I thought: "I'm gonna have to come up with something a little different." I was in an after-hours club, the Nitecap. They had a striptease show and one girl came out... they turned off all the lights... she just had panties on and they were fluorescent. I thought: "*That's* what I'll do!" I stripped the horn, painted it with gold leaf, and then put on the real vivid transparent paint. When the lights go out, it just glows, all you see is the horn moving.'

In 1952, Ralph Bass signed McNeely to Federal and, over the following two years, his normal working band cut seventeen titles. The first session produced a schizophrenic pairing in 'Just Crazy', a ferocious honker, and 'Penthouse Serenade', a warm, grainy jazz ballad. 'The Goof, another track from the same session, featured 'Porkie' Harris, a white guitarist from a hillbilly band. 'He was a fat little kid,' said Jay. 'When I first saw him he was working with Roy Rogers. Y'see, the Mexicans were now into R&B and the white kids too. I used to play at all the high schools in L.A., and often had a mixture of a band with different lead singers. Johnny Torres, he was a kid from Philadelphia — a mix of Italian and black. I used Smokey Lands, a black stand-up singer from L.A., and Duke Thomas, a white kid from Eagle Rock. He sang just like Frankie Laine.'

William 'Buddy' Woodson, who stood in for Dillard McNeely, had attended Jordan High School: 'He was a quiet, reserved sort of fellow who played upright bass. He went off and played with good single acts at cabaret and supper clubs. I replaced him with one Texan after another — including Ike Brown — and Cecil Harris, who worked with me quite a while in the band as well as on sessions. He was out of Denver.' Other stalwarts of the McNeely band circa 1952-54 included pianist Boyd Dunlop, drummer Darnell Cole (Hardiman's cousin who came from Fort Worth) and organist Dwight David (he wrote the Federal track, 'Rock Candy'). Uncharacteristically, King–Federal owner Syd Nathan paid McNeely for each session ('$1,000 a date — that was my share'), but one disappointment still rankles: 'I was supposed to record 'Fever' with my singer, Johnny Torres, but he was fooling around with some chick in Providence and wouldn't come down to New York for the session. They gave the tune to Little Willie John.'

By then McNeely had recorded 'Jay's Rock' and 'Big Jay's Hop' for Vee-Jay, backed by two new sidemen, Earl DeWitt (piano) and Johnny Walker (drums). (Ignore, incidentally, the Vee-Jay session files which reverse those roles.) 'Johnny was a fabulous drummer from Chicago,' recalled McNeely. 'We played with Gene Krupa in Philadelphia and, after Johnny took a solo, Krupa wouldn't let him take any more. He was tremendous... but he died of heart trouble — his heart never developed. I picked up Earl DeWitt in San Bernardino. I used to have an organa, a small organ which Earl tried out with us on the road. I think he's now in Las Vegas playing a Hammond organ and making a living at it.'

The mid-Fifties brought numerous tours including the *Top Ten Revue*, a series of Southern one-nighters with the Moonglows, Joe Turner ('I accompanied the performers, but Joe tried to act like we couldn't read his music; really, he just wanted Choker Campbell to back him 'cos that's who he was used to'), the Five Keys, Bill Doggett and headliner Little Richard, who once told McNeely: 'You're the only cat who can warm 'em up for something like me.' Other performers were less magnanimous; according to McNeely, he was cut out of tours with Ray Anthony, Kay Starr and Johnnie Ray. One *Down Beat* feature (*'Big Noise in R&B: McNeely, McSqueally — Either Way You Pronounce It, Means Box Office'*) explained why a number of established acts refused to appear with him at his peak: *'McNeely has been busy hereabouts since 1949, both in clubs and on records, but he came into his own with the big boom in rhythm & blues business. He started doing concerts in outlying communities, where he caught the high school and junior college set (both white and coloured). Then things started to happen. Last fall, Big Jay and his boys were engaged to bolster the bill on the Eckstine–Basie–Shearing concert here, and Big Jay stole the show. He was engaged as one of the subsidiary acts to appear on the Johnnie Ray show here at the Shrine Auditorium last month. Not only did he steal the show again, but it was obvious that of the crowd that turned out, a larger number had paid to hear Big Jay rather than Johnnie Ray or his other supporting attraction, Harry James.'*

McNeely encountered similar hostility from Nat 'King' Cole: 'Kinda sad, that. My drummer's wife knew Nat's first wife, Nadine, and he came by the little garage where we used to rehearse. "Keep up the good work," he told us. "You gonna make it." I always respected him for that, but later we played a gig together in Oakland. I really got the people built up. I'm really walkin'. I got the crowd in such a frenzy, they didn't want to hear no singing. Nat came over and told me: "You'll never work with me again." I thought he was kidding, but I was all set up for a GAC tour with Nat Cole and Sarah Vaughan and they ended up putting Louis Jordan in there. It hurt me, but I've always had the highest respect for the guy.'

In 1956, while appearing at Birdland with Bill Doggett, McNeely recorded for Atlantic. He doesn't think he signed a contract, and British efforts to liberate all fourteen titles have met with a 'can't-find-the-tapes' response. Two years elapsed before McNeely recorded again and then, with Little Sonny Warner, he enjoyed the biggest hit of his long career.

Little Sonny's version of 'There Is Something On Your Mind' entered the Hot 100 on 31 May 1959, peaked at No. 44 in July and remained on the chart for sixteen weeks. The tune reached No. 5 on the R&B chart and remained in the Top Thirty for six months. One year later, Bobby Marchan's version topped the R&B list and climbed to No. 31 on the Hot 100. Baby Ray (No. 69 Pop in 1966), the Jolly-Jax, Tommy Ridgley, Little Johnny Taylor, the Cupcakes and Professor Longhair have all helped to increase the popularity of one of R&B's most valuable copyrights. Ironically, McNeely didn't write the song: 'I bought 'There Is Something On Your Mind' from Rocky Wilson, the guy who sang with the Rivingtons. He wrote the tune in San Francisco and we had jammed around doing sessions, so I had heard it for some time. Rocky liked Fats Domino and had the tune going like Fats. I told him: "What you need to do is cut everything in half," and I slowed everything down and rearranged the tune. I *knew* it was gonna be a hit. We were playing in Seattle. I wanted to record it with Rocky, but he was in a hurry to get back South and needed the money to get there. He said: "I'll sell you the tune for $25," and so I bought it. Then I recorded it with Little Sonny, who I'd met around 1955. He came up to us when we were playing a little town out of Washington, DC. He sang with us that night and I thought he sounded exactly like Ray Charles. I was so impressed. He reminded me of a Baptist preacher, he could just tear a house up, he had that enthusiasm. A tremendous entertainer too — he was about twenty-one when we cut 'There Is Something On Your Mind'. We recorded it in a guy's basement in Seattle after we got off work one night. It was the regular band, Bob and Dillard, Leonard Hardiman and my new guitarist, Wendell Johnson.

3.7 - Big Jay McNeely

He was a tall, nice-looking kid who played so loud I had to go turn the switch down on the back of his guitar. He quit because of that, but he's on 'Something On Your Mind'! I told Sonny: "Sing the song exactly like it is here on Rocky's tape, no Ray Charles or nothing, just like this." That's what he did. I took the tape to Hal Zeiger, a promoter in L.A., but he didn't like it. Then Hunter Hancock was getting ready to open a label, Swingin' Records, and I took it out there and he said: "Okay, we'll try it."

Now, at that time I wasn't making but maybe $150 a night. I was playing behind Bobby Darin and Chuck Berry, and trying to support a six-piece band. After I had paid my musicians, gas and 10% travelling tax, I was down to four or five dollars. We went up to Frisco where I knew a guy named Rocky Lucky, who played the dub on his show, *The Midnight Shift*. He put the dub on the air and, with no records in the stores, everybody started clamouring for it. Eventually, the record broke all over the country and when I came back to the Oakland Auditorium with B.B. King I was getting $1,000 a night!' (The story has a further twist. In 1957, Rocky Wilson was singing with Jacqueline Baldain *aka* Jackie Day, and he wrote 'There Is Something On Your Mind' at her home in San Francisco. When Jackie heard the record over the air, she called McNeely and politely enquired as to how he'd got hold of the song. They corresponded back and forth, met up and, eventually, in 1960, they were married.)

Between Swingin' singles, Warner and McNeely recorded for Liberty who issued 'Riff Runner' *c/w* 'San Antonio Rose' on their Freedom subsidiary. Both sides were produced by Billy Ward, vocal coach behind the Dominoes. In 1960, Warner left the band to pursue a solo career. He recorded 'My Love For You' (Concertone 200) with Jesse Herring's orchestra in 1961 and a couple of duets with Marie Allen for the Bee Bee label in 1962. 'Bell Bottom Blue Jeans' and a revival of the Pastels' 'Been So Long' (Checker 1151) constitutes his last generally known coupling in 1966. Although little has been heard of Warner since then, the Imperial vaults contain an unissued four-track session (including 'My Love For You') which dates from 1955, adding credence to McNeely's final recollection on the subject: 'I carried Sonny around for four or five years before I could get him on wax. He sounded so much like Ray Charles that nobody would record him.'

Little Sonny Warner was replaced by Leon Haywood, a top soul star during the Seventies: 'Leon came out to my house from Houston. Somebody had told him about me and he asked for a job as a singer and organist. I was the first one to carry him on the road.' In 1961, Haywood sang and played on McNeely's last Swingin' single, 'Without A Love' *c/w* 'The Squat'. He also wrote the top side. McNeely himself played on Little Johnny Taylor's 'One More Chance' (Swingin' 639). Thereafter the company collapsed in a welter of legal proceedings. Hunter Hancock was accused on three counts of tax evasion (ie neglecting to report payola received during 1956-58) and eventually placed on probation and made subject to a suspended term of four years' imprisonment.

In 1962, McNeely joined Warner Brothers for a celebrated live album recorded at Cisco's on Hermosa Beach. He and his brothers were joined by trumpeter Everett Shirley and guitarist Arthur Wright: 'We're all of the same faith — Jehovah's Witnesses. Everett has played on a lot of L.A. sessions, he's a teacher in electronics. Arthur Wright worked for John Dolphin as an A&R man but now has his own recording studio and produces many albums.' Fred Thompson (organ), Ramon Martinez (drums) and 'Little Walter' (harmonica) completed the personnel. While McNeely had no reason to suppose that the harmonica player was not *the* Little Walter, his description of the man ('a very big, tall guy') confirms the identity of the late George Smith who used to bill himself as 'Little Walter Jr'. Smith played on three tracks only: 'You Don't Have To Go', 'Cisco's' and 'Farther On Up The Road'.

All three McNeely brothers left the music business during the early Sixties. Bob, who suffered from poor health, retired altogether, while Dillard now operates a one-man custodial business. Jay McNeely took jobs with Alfa Car Wash and the National Cash Register. Now and again, Maxwell Davis would use him as a sessionman, dubbing his horn parts onto tracks for records by Lowell Fulson and B.B. King. McNeely also recorded the backing track for his wife's revival of the Leon Haywood song, 'Without A Love', in 1965. 'She's a tremendous singer,' he says, 'good on soul stuff like 'Knock On Wood' and 'Land Of A Thousand Dances'. 'Without a Love' was a big tune on Modern.' Mrs. Jay McNeely, whose records were issued under the name of Jackie Day, recorded 'What Kind Of Man Are You' (Modern 1037) in 1967 and several sides for Specialty including 'Free At Last' in 1969. By then, McNeely himself was an infrequent visitor to the studios. Modern issued a re-recording of 'Deacon's Hop' with Maxwell Davis on piano, and Davis supervised a blues record by Roscoe Holland with Big Jay McNeely playing tenor ('Endlessly' *c/w* 'Troubles, Troubles, Troubles' on Rand 3143). McNeely has no recollection of the session, but could have helped to provide a backing track for a singer he has never met. In 1962 McNeely formed his own label, Armonia, after his mother's name and issued one record, a Coasters-type novelty by the Sonics entitled 'I Get That Feeling'.

When R&B historian Norbert Hess interviewed McNeely in 1973, he was playing weekends at Tiki's in Monterey Park and making his living as a postman. 'I joined the Post Office in 1971,' he recalled. 'I also became very active as a Jehovah's Witness. I didn't have the incentive to record and didn't want to go into the studio with just anything, but I never stopped playing. For a long time I played five nights a week; now it's just two club dates a week and the occasional concert.'

McNeely remained with the Post Office for twelve years and was filmed there by Geoff Hayden in 1983: 'The film opens up in my apartment with me playing flute, and then they came down to the Post Office and shot a scene on me putting mail in the hamper and delivering my first stop. And then they come out to a club in Santa Fe Springs and shot 'The Big Jay Shuffle'. We ended up at the Variety Arts Center on Figueroa with Charles Brown, Margie Evans, Lowell Fulson and Big Mama Thornton. Joe Liggins opened the show and I closed it. I had a black suit and they dropped a black curtain... so all you could see was a gold horn. That's the movie!'

1983-84 were Big Jay's busiest years in quite a while. He formed an organ trio with 'Moments' hitmaker Jennell Hawkins ('she can play like Jimmy Smith, she can outplay Shirley Scott, she's *bad*'), he signed a four-man soul group, the New Creations, to his own production company, and his performance at the Penguins' 30th anniversary concert was recorded and issued in both Britain (*Big Jay Meets The Penguins*, Ace CH-101) and America (*Jay's Loose On Sunset*, Big Jay 101). During a second European tour, he played a string of dates in London including the 100 Club ('*the best live gig of any kind in two years or more*' — *Black Echoes*, 28 April 1984) and the *Caister Rock'n'Roll Festival*: 'We had all the little pink-haired kids. The man said: "You gonna be a total success or a total flop." He was really afraid. We came out screamin' on 'Night Train' and we stood 'em up, no problem. I had to go back three times.' McNeely's Swingin' records were released as an album (Big Jay 103) and Ace Records issued *From Harlem to Camden* (Ace CH-111), his first studio session in over fifteen years.

Big Jay McNeely still believes the best is yet to come. He plans to manage a nightclub on Catalina Island (a summer resort twenty miles off Long Beach), persevere with the Big Jay Production Co, and alternate those honks and screeches for as long as his lungs can take the strain. He told Jim Dawson: 'Heck, there's a lot of kids that don't know who I am, but as far as I'm concerned they ain't nothing but Big Jay fans I ain't blowed my horn for yet.'

Liner notes to *Roadhouse Boogie* (Saxophonograph LP-505) 1985.

3.8
YOUNG JESSIE
Shuffle In The Gravel

Young Jessie epitomised the primal blend of R&B and rock'n'roll. Ironically, he can trace his lineage back to the portly crown prince of rural blues, Blind Lemon Jefferson. The triple strains of country blues, gospel and the slick jump'n'jive of Central Avenue came together in his early work and have long remained the touchstones. In recent years, his bebop scat singing has taken him back beyond his roots in rock'n'roll, but the hipster's shades, so useful for leaving a jazz club at dawn, cannot disguise his feel for the primitive shaking music we all know and love best. Young Jessie's catholic taste has served him well. It's helped him survive the changing times without having to sing 'Mary Lou' twice a night for drunken yahoos or middle-aged couples trying to relive their first fumble. He's able to move with consummate ease from the early days of R&B to supper-club jazz to reggae and, without a genuine hit to call his own, he is nothing if not a true survivor.

Obie Donmell Jessie was born in Dallas, Texas. His father, a cook, had no musical accomplishments, but his mother (maiden name Malinda Harris) enjoyed a brief professional career under the name Plunky Harris. By the time she gave birth to Obie, on 28 December 1936, she was a housewife who confined her piano-playing to home and church. She could, Jessie has said, play anything. Although he did not see her perform, she introduced him to a wide variety of popular tunes as well as blues and hillbilly. The maternal side of his family was rich with musical cousins including the aforesaid Blind Lemon, once the most popular country bluesman among black audiences.

Jessie spent the first nine years of his life in a house on a dirt road in Lincoln Manor, a small community to the south of Dallas. David Newman, who became a saxophonist with Ray Charles, lived nearby as did Shorty Clements, a locally famous bandleader with whom Jessie first sang in public. When the USA entered World War II, Jessie's father moved to Los Angeles for employment and Jessie attended Manual Arts High School until the family returned to Dallas in 1950. Malinda gave birth to Dwayne Jessie the following year; now a Hollywood actor, Dwayne is best known for roles in *Car Wash*, *Bingo Long* and *The Scott Joplin Story*.

3.8 - Young Jessie

Back in Lincoln Manor, Jessie listened to blues and gospel on the radio, and to a number of local musicians. One distant relative, Lenis, played piano in a Corsicana-based band led by Pete Gabriel Cooley. On finishing junior high, Jessie returned to L.A. and enrolled at Jefferson High School, a hothouse of aspiring black talent whose students numbered Johnny Watson, Don Cherry, Etta James, Frank Morgan and a host of amateur harmonisers, Jessie included: 'We modelled ourselves on New York groups like the Clovers and the Dominoes. We were crazy about them. I also admired Joe Williams, the singer with Count Basie, and Roy Brown — he was my first inspiration.'

Jessie transferred to the integrated Fremont High for one term but completed his education at Jefferson, where he also met Richard Berry, founder member of the Flairs and one of the most important figures in West Coast groupdom. The Flairs — Cornelius Gunter (lead tenor and utility voice) Beverley Thompson (first tenor) Thomas 'Pete' Fox (second tenor), Obie Jessie (baritone and lead) and Richard Berry (bass and lead) — have as many beginnings as there are participants.

Jessie remembers it this way: 'We all met doing doo-wops on streetcorners. Richard and I went to Jefferson, Cornelius attended Jefferson and later switched to Manual Arts, Beverley was at Fremont. That's what made the Flairs so popular — we had members in each of the three high schools. We had two guiding lights in Richard and Cornel, maybe three with myself. We did the lead vocals and most of the writing. Beverley had a car and wanted to sing, whereas we had a group but no transport. Beverley took us around to house parties and eventually began to sing with us. Pete, Beverley and I did most of the dancing things. We made them up and, if a cat couldn't follow it, he'd stand back and clap his hands. In those days, I was much thinner and much faster. I'd do anything: jump offstage, do the flips. The Flairs were wild; Screamin' Jay used to say there was only one cat that could out-scream him, and that was me. We first recorded for John Dolphin when we were called the Debonaires. We made a demo with Pee Wee Crayton's band, but Dolphin issued the record ('I Had A Love' on Recorded In Hollywood) as by the Hollywood Blue Jays, and we never called ourselves that. Dolphin had an earlier group of that name, older gospel-oriented people. We were pretty dissatisfied and thought: "We gotta find ourselves a real record company." We ditched school for the day, Beverley picked us up and we went riding around Hollywood until we passed a sign, "RPM Records". We went in there and sang. Joe and Jules Bihari got real excited and told us they were gonna set up a recording session.'

Cash Box pinpointed the Bihari brothers' interest in August 1955: *'The Flairs, five 16 year old schoolboys, have been signed by Joe Bihari for his Flair label. The boys debuted at the Gene Norman Jazz Concert held at the Shrine Auditorium in Hollywood.'*

'She Wants To Rock', the group's first outing on Flair, was produced by Jerry Leiber and Mike Stoller. It was a playlet featuring

Richard Berry in the lead and the rest of the group responding with lines which continued the story in the kind of sparkling arrangement which Leiber & Stoller would soon perfect with the Robins and the Coasters. The original Flairs cut four more singles under their own name and an unknowable number of tracks under other names, of which 'Down At Hayden's' by the Hunters was the first example. Jessie again: 'Hayden's was a place on Stark Street in Dallas, around the corner from where I lived as a child. It was a very rough bar. Mr. Hayden was a real dark cat with straight, yellow hair. Boy, he was mean, that was the reputation he had; didn't nobody mess with Mr. Hayden. I sang lead on that and Pete Fox took the narration on it.'

During 1954-55, the Biharis encouraged Jessie to aim at a solo career. He recorded 'I Smell A Rat' and called himself Young Jessie: 'It came about because I sounded like I was forty — like, ancient for a boy. I had this deep baritone voice and the Biharis wanted me to get close to the rock'n'roll market. I could have called myself Obie Jessie but I didn't want people to think I was old.'

'Mary Lou', Jessie's biggest seller, was inspired by an aunt, Emma Green, whom he remembers as a cunning, worldly person. His father told him stories about her including a court appearance during which she approached the bench, sobbed on the judge's shoulder and picked his pockets. It's in the song of course: *'She picked the judge to go her bail'*. 'Mary Lou' was the highlight of Jessie's solo career. He was signed to Buck Ram's Personality Promotions and toured widely with Ram's other acts including the Platters, Dolly Cooper and the Blockbusters. He played the Apollo on three occasions and joined a Southern package tour with Little Willie John, B.B. King, Guitar Slim and Bobby Bland. Although 'Mary Lou' is best remembered by Arkansas rockabilly Ronnie Hawkins (No. 26 Pop and No. 7 R&B) there have been some thirty versions of this Culver City classic including those by Bob Seger, Buddy Knox, Frank Zappa, Sonny Burgess and Steve Miller. 'I never got paid for the 1959 hit,' said Jessie, 'but I talked to Ronnie Hawkins and he never got paid for it either. Since '74 I've been paid by the publisher, and nowadays the more people who do it the better.'

On leaving Modern ('I was fed up seeing names like 'Ling' and 'Josea' on the record. They'd say: "That's Joe's other name, we do that with all the artists".'), Jessie hooked up with the Coasters, appearing on that most famous of Coasters' records, 'Searchin'' *c/w* 'Young Blood'. Four months later, in June 1957, he recorded 'Shuffle In The Gravel', the first of his post-Modern solo singles. Like the Coasters' discs, 'Shuffle In The Gravel' was produced by Leiber & Stoller, of whom Jessie has nothing but warm memories: 'We go back a long way... originally, like on 'She Wants To Rock', they were sort-of understudies to the Biharis, just learning the trade. We were in our teens then and we partied together. They wrote 'I Smell A Rat' and 'Here Comes Henry', and I used to do Elvis demos for them including 'Don't' and 'Hot Dog'. Elvis wrote and thanked them for the way I did the demos.'

Buck Ram has claimed production credits for 'Shuffle In The Gravel', but the way Jessie tells it, Ram was cold-shouldered by the Atlantic bosses after he had negotiated an Atco contract. In the event,

'Mike and Jerry came to my house and I showed them the tune. I wrote it as a dance craze. The shuffle was a genuine Texan dancehall thing, my mother used to do the dance and we kept a sandbox for it. They'd spread the sand on the wooden floor and the whole crowd, hundreds of people, would create a shuffle-noise as they moved back and forth. Lester Sill (Leiber & Stoller's partner, head of Screen Gems, etc), he could do it — in fact, he's making the noise on the record. There were a lot of takes and Lester was sweating, he was real tired.' Jessie first cut the tune with trumpeter John Anderson, but Jerry Leiber preferred a second arrangement by pianist Ernie Freeman. Freeman's piano licks were clearly inspired by a famous Joe Turner hit, 'Shake, Rattle And Roll'. The vocal group on both 'Shuffle In The Gravel' and 'That's Enough For Me' are the Sharps, who did so much background work for Thurston Harris and Duane Eddy before changing their name to the Rivingtons.

'Margie' also bears the hallmarks of a Leiber & Stoller production. Here the whizz kids convert a flapper-era novelty into a tawdry, bar-roomish vehicle for Jessie's vociferous shouting which, on this occasion, is a dead ringer for Screamin' Jay Hawkins.

In 1959, Jessie recorded 'Lula Belle' and 'The Wrong Door' for Capitol: 'Buck Stapleton, the house producer, had no idea I was coming. I went into Capitol and asked "Who's producing here?" The receptionist called Stapleton, and when I walked up he had a *Cash Box* on his desk; the page was open at a picture of me in a white suit with a cane in my hand. He said: "Man, I was just looking at this page when you called."' This weird happenstance did not produce a hit: both sides of the record resembled Bobby Darin's pop-jazz finger-snappers and 'Lula Belle' — rock'n'roll lyrics to a jazz arrangement — seemed least likely to appeal to either camp. Thereafter, Jessie took an eighteen-month sabbatical. His disillusionment was fuelled by business malpractice — at one stage he was being booked as Jesse Belvin and got tired of telling audiences who he really was — but the fragmented sounds of the early Sixties didn't help ('the whole thing kept changing and nothing ever came back to that hard rock period').

An association with Bumps Blackwell rekindled Jessie's enthusiasm and led to a Mercury contract in 1961. If truth be known, Blackwell was signing his friends (Joe Liggins, Sonny Knight, Grady Chapman) and greatly overspending the label's budget. The Mercury sides reflected Jessie's uncertainty but remain, for the most part, effervescent examples of black pop music. A Coasters sound is well represented both in the juvenile rhymes of 'Teacher Gimme Back' and the sneaky-voiced mewlings of 'My Country Cousin', performed — somewhat cheekily — to the tune of the Coasters' 'Run Red Run'. 'I'm A Lovin' Man' has a Cameo–Parkway flavour (it was A&R'd by Steve Douglas, who probably contributes the saxophone solo), while 'Be-Bop Country Boy' leans towards the strident orchestrations of Lloyd Price. 'Big Chief' — this in the wake of 'Running Bear' and 'Rocking Redwing' — is the kind of desperate hokum to which many a fine rock'n'roll singer succumbed during the era of pop-slop and pimples.

In 1962, Jessie produced himself on the bluesy soul ballad, 'Make Me Feel A Little Good'; he was rewarded with a reasonable seller in San Diego, L.A. and San Francisco. The label, Vanessa, was owned by Walter Douglas, the proprietor of a cleaning chain. Junior Rogers, ex-Roy Milton guitarist, helped put the band together. 'Young Jessie Bossa Nova' was cut live at a party-cum-recording session in a Hollywood club. Orchestra leader Jerry Long put up the finance and the disc appeared on his Bit label in 1964.

Jessie has since recorded for Jake Porter (soul which remains unissued) and for Jerry Williams in a group called the Seeds Of Freedom on Stone Dogg in 1972. There's also an album's worth of as yet unheard material owned by Harvey Fuqua. In 1982, Jessie toured Germany, Belgium and Holland with the Superlites, a Dutch jazz group who knew nothing of his career as a R&B singer. In 1983, he travelled to London for the *R&B Jamboree* at Camden's Electric Ballroom, where he astonished the audience with a truly charismatic performance. He sang with the raw authority of the best soul singers, stomping the stage and falling to his knees, creating as distinctive an emotional climate as, say, Solomon Burke or Nappy Brown.

When Ray Topping and I spoke to Jessie a few days later, he was writing a reggae tune and seemed wholly familiar with the idiom ('Rosco Gordon had that feel and Richard Berry has a natural bent for it too').

Today, Jessie lives near Venice, L.A. with his wife, singer Barbara

Prince, and their four children. Two children by a previous marriage live nearby and sing in the group, Wizdom. Jessie plays with a jazz trio and hopes to record a slew of fresh blues-cum-reggae songs with local musicians. 'I'm adaptable,' he told me. 'I've always been serious about my career and I never want to make it doing something other than singing and playing music. Nothing else is important to me. If I got rich from doing something else, I'd feel like I'd been cut short.'

Liner note to *Shuffle In The Gravel* (Mr. R&B LP-1004) 1986.

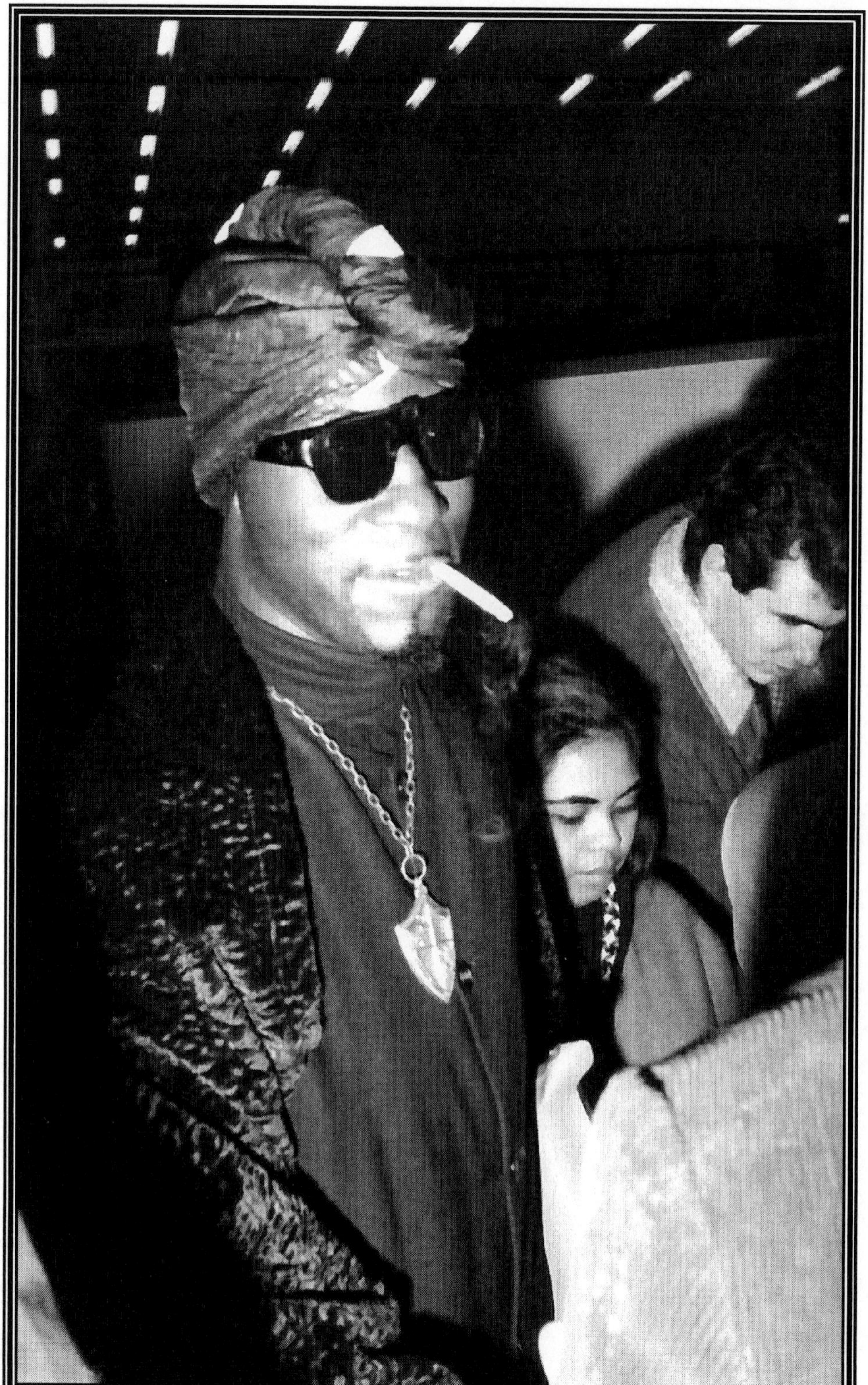

3.9
SCREAMIN' JAY HAWKINS
A Most Singular Man

'Why not be at London Airport to welcome Jay?' That was the invitation in the late Roger Eagle's *R&B Scene*. And so, on Monday 25 January 1965, Cliff White and I travelled to Heathrow to be told that Jay had forgotten his passport and missed his TWA flight. Gloria Cann, his manager's wife, bought drinks and handed out Roulette promo copies of 'The Whammy'.

The following morning, Jay appeared on the steps to the Customs Hall. You couldn't miss him: floor-length astrakhan cape (black, and dyed blacker), two-tone turban, black shades and — on a three-foot pole — a white skull ('Henry') which gleamed in the winter sunshine. He walked into the public lounge, where he decided to test the efficacy of his flash-powder. He magicked his beard into flames and couldn't put them out. There he was, the hero of 'I Put A Spell On You', slapping his chin and hopping from one foot to another. This was clearly a most singular man, one to whom we immediately took a liking.

Cliff and I left the airport in Don Arden's Jaguar along with Jay, Mr. and Mrs. Cann, and Ginny, Jay's pretty Filipino wife of eleven months. Jay played to the gallery: he broke into bloodcurdling screams for no apparent reason and shook Henry at bewildered passers-by. We behaved like star-struck fans and asked the sort of questions which star-struck fans ask. He told us that his favourite singers were Roy Hamilton, Frank Sinatra, Nappy Brown ('Man, that cat's got so much soul'), Big Maybelle and Brenda Lee. He signed pictures with the phrase 'I Love You Madly' — a near hit for Charlie & Ray with whom he'd shared an Apollo billing (*The All Gold Oldies Show*) only three weeks before.

Wonderful stories emerged, some taken with two pinches of salt: of Little Willie John who was standing trial for murder; of Huey 'Piano' Smith who allegedly stole 'Don't You Just Know It' after seeing Jay at a Baltimore concert; of Larry Williams who interred Jay in his coffin together with a diarrhoeic monkey. (Bowel problems would, er, resurface from time to time. His French lavatory paper — he spent the last seven years of his life in Paris — was reportedly printed with staves of music: ordinary tissue wouldn't do. There was nothing bog standard about Jay.)

Back at the hotel, he unpacked two mammoth scrapbooks and brain-bending goodies tumbled out: adverts for Apollo label-mate Solomon Burke (billed as *'The 14 year old Wonder Boy Preacher'*) and a magnificent pictorial essay from *Ebony* which took me another twenty years to find.

A group of us flocked to almost every London show including the opening night (2 February) at Wallington Town Hall. Hawkins was never in better form: he ran on and off stage, did the splits, played piano, waved his cloak like a rabid bullfighter and screamed a slew of rock'n'roll classics for well over an hour. Sadly, the louder his half-dozen fans cheered, the more the locals booed. They came to the Town Hall every Tuesday to get pickled and practice their chat-up lines regardless of whoever was on that week. They certainly didn't want anyone to complicate things by putting on a show. Eventually, fighting broke out and we escaped via the dressing room and car park, skulking along in the dark behind the former Golden Gloves Middleweight Champion Of Alaska. I don't think Jay was quite so wild again, but elsewhere audiences were ecstatic.

At Soho's Flamingo on 3 February, he was more subdued but he fed Henry with cigarettes and the first three rows went apeshit. The *Melody Maker* couldn't understand why people clapped him on the back as if he'd just broken the lap record, but *Record Mirror* called it a *'fantastic display'*.

At Bromley Court Hotel on 7 February he assaulted Henry with a tambourine, blew a saxophone during 'Ko Ko Mo' and ran around the ballroom trashing an amplifier in the process.

On 13 February he was back at the Flamingo in top hat and tails, looking like the Duke of Earl with facial hair.

It was two-and-sixpence to get into the Black Cat Club at Woolwich (17 February) and the venue resembled a refrigerated container, but the sound was terrific and Jay danced like a dervish (keeping warm I guess).

A third visit to the Flamingo on 13 March attracted admirers from Yorkshire and Wales including Breathless Dan Coffey, the architect of rock'n'roll's first real UK fanbase.

The spring of 1965 was memorable. Jay, who was here for over four months, appeared on ITV's *Thank Your Lucky Stars*, where he disturbed the sepulchral quiet of the English teatime by miming 'The Whammy'.

On 6 April, we saw Larry Williams cutting his live album for Sue — hence the inclusion of impromptu verses like *'Saw Screamin' Jay Hawkins with Long Tall Sally in the coffin / She don't love him but she do it very often'*. We went to the zoo, and to the movies (*The Curse Of The Coffin*, actually). We spent long evenings at Dave Hastings's house in Streatham (we were amazed to find that Jay had already pasted photos of us in *his* scrapbooks), at the flat I shared in Shepherd's Bush (Jay entertained callers with impressions of John Lee Hooker and Jimmy

Reed), and at Jay and Ginny's apartment in the White House overlooking Regent's Park.

On 4 June there was a dramatic bust-up with Don Arden and Jay decided to fly home immediately. We'd gone up to his rooms with a view to catching Donnie Elbert at the Flamingo, but ended up deflecting threatening phone calls from the promoter and nervously watching Jay while he oiled a revolver.

Jay couldn't pack his luggage in a hurry and started to trash his belongings, tearing up his suits like a man in the grip of dementia. Ginny told us not to worry; this happened periodically. When we finally said our goodbyes, we were loaded down with Henry, two capes, several gonks, a pair of zebra-striped moccasins, a small but highly-prized record collection (including his first LP, *At Home With Screamin' Jay Hawkins*), a foot-high jar crammed with threepenny bits, and a suitcase full of flash-powder and fuseboxes. Cliff took custody of the apparatus; my flatmate baulked at storing these unpredictable magnesium devices which had already caused second-degree burns to Ginny's predecessor.

On leaving Britain, Jay relocated to New York, hanging out with Little Joe Cook and Titus Turner (on a wave because RCA had just released Elvis's version of his song, 'Tell Me Why').

Jay brought social conscience to R&B with 'Poor Folks' and sent cartons of the Providence 45 to fans in England. The song was originally intended for Nina Simone, whose sombre version of 'I Put A Spell On You' had reached No. 23 R&B in 1965.

Jay's letters were always rich in affection and anecdote: he and Ginny had guested at Lady Iris Mountbatten's wedding; Esquerita had gotten into a tussle outside the Colony Record Shop with someone who questioned 'her femininity'; did I know that 'Hi-Heel Sneakers' was really written by Dean of Dean & Jean? I was also told to take good care of Henry and that Charlie the Gonk liked to sit next to Henry and talk to him now and again (yeah... I know what you're thinking — not mad at all). Then, after a brief sojourn in Hawaii and another Apollo appearance, some exceptionally welcome news: *'I must let you know that, on 30 March 1966, I shall be putting in a very weird appearance at London Airport for a thirty-day tour. I hope that Henry, the fuseboxes and the capes are ready to be used again.'*

In the event, Jay arrived on April Fool's Day and played the Ram Jam in Brixton that same night. Luminous-socked rockers turned out in force, displacing Afro-Caribbeans for the evening, and Hawkins came on as if it were still rock'n'roll's finest hour. He eclipsed everything around at the time, agitating his way through 'The Whammy' and concluding with 'Shout', a feast of improvisation.

The rest of the tour, for Roy Tempest's Global Promotions, proceeded without difficulty. Only ten people, including Lee Dorsey, turned up at the Scene on 14 April, but Hawkins was no less vigorous or affecting. Before a crowd of black servicemen at Douglas House US Air

Force base on 17 April, he completely transformed his act with an earthy recital of jokes and far fewer songs, though a version of Bobby Lewis's 'Mumbles Blues' electrified this hippest of audiences. Another frenzied night at the Flamingo on 22 April completed the London dates.

Our correspondence continued and, as ever, Jay's letters were packed with gossip and good humour. Sample: *'Larry Williams was also in "American Hot Wax" but he made such a fool of himself that they cut out his part completely.'* The letters eventually ceased, probably when Jay and Ginny separated in the early Eighties. By most accounts, Jay became an irascible man of moods. Friends pogo'd up and down his Shit List, and he chased enemies real and imagined.

When he wasn't busy falling out with those who loved him most, he went on to further triumphs on record, in concert and in cult-favourite films — a medium that had once shut him out. Harvey Keitel listens to Jay's 'Hong Kong' in Wayne Wang's charming drama, *Smoke*. Jim Jarmusch's *Stranger Than Paradise* featured another mega-fan, a young Hungarian woman who listens to nothing except 'I Put A Spell On You'. The same director's *Mystery Train* cast Jay as an impassive night-clerk in a retina-detaching red suit. In January last year, *The Independent* reported that Jarmusch had made a soon-to-be-released film about Jay's life but I don't know what happened to that.

Another mystery is how on earth I managed to get from nineteen to fifty-four in about five years. Jay had a related difficulty: 'I'm middle-aged,' he once confessed, 'but I still feel like I'm twelve years old.' Screamin' Jay Hawkins enriched my life beyond vinyl and celluloid and the part of me that first saw him off his plane, on stage and off his trolley will always be nineteen.

Note   Screamin' Jay Hawkins died on 12 February 2000, at the Ambroise Pave Clinic, Neuilly-sur-Seine, near Paris after emergency surgery to treat an aneurysm. This obituary was published in *Now Dig This* (April 2000).

3.10
BIG JIM WYNN
Saxman

R&B saxophonists are generally anonymous. After King Curtis and Junior Walker the list of household names gets a bit slim. With the current accent on blues guitarists, the world has largely forgotten musicians like Red Prysock, Sil Austin, John Greer, Lee Allen and Jimmy Wright.

Big Jim Wynn is another whose name is unfamiliar and whose instrument is now unfashionable: but out front with the Johnny Otis Revue he is a solid, unforgettable gas. Heaving those fruity notes from his baritone saxophone and quaking his legs in a reincarnation of the Fifties rock spirit, Wynn's performance is a severe contrast to his workaday life offstage, and his story demolishes a lot of romantic misconceptions about the way in which R&B records are made.

Born in El Paso, Texas on 21 June 1908 (though he told me it was 1912), Wynn moved to L.A. as a child, got a paper-round and put a down payment on a tenor saxophone before he was ten. In the late Thirties, he experienced the breakdown of big swing bands into smaller R&B units first-hand and recalls a fund of anecdotes from this important era: 'I began to play blues in the Harlem Club in Watts in 1936. A fellow came to town, name of T-Bone Walker. He was dancing and picking up tables with his mouth. He'd dance on a table and then grip it in his teeth and whirl it around. That's what Miss Brown booked him for, as a dancer. He started singing with the first small band I had and the people went mad about him. He had a funny little box he'd play, a contraption he had made himself but his fame soon began to spread, and when he went off to Chicago or Cleveland to do a sit-down date, my agent would keep my band busy by sending me out with other stars like Joe Turner or Marion Abernathy.'

Jim, who has made over twenty singles under his own name, didn't record until 1945. It was then that Jim Wynn's Bobalibans cut his best known composition, 'Ee-bobaliba', for 4-Star Records with Claude Trenier on blues-shouting vocal. He was outsold by Helen Humes, who recorded her version, 'Be-Baba-Leba', for Philco a month or two before Wynn. There was more competition from Estelle Edson (on Black & White) and Bull Moose Jackson's Band (on Queen). The best of the lot came in 1958 with

Photo © Norbert Hess, Berlin

Thurston Harris, whose storming rock'n'roll treatment paid proper homage.

Claude Trenier also became a rock'n'roll star. 'The Trenier Twins were a regular part of my line-up. Claude came from Alabama and joined me at the Cafe Society in 1944. He brought in his brother, Cliff, and a very light-skinned fellow, name of Don Hill. They formed the Treniers when they left me.'

Other vocalists on the early 4-Star and Gilt-Edge records by Jimmy Wynn's Bobalibans included Pee Wee Wiley and Luther Luper, but he also attracted a steady flow of fine blues sidemen like Freddie Simon (tenor), Teddy Shirley (bass) and Robert 'Snake' Sims (drums) who stayed with him for fifteen years. Steady sales generated work further afield and Jim began touring up and down the West Coast, often accompanying Percy Mayfield, Lowell Fulson, the Robins and many more. 'I took out Etta James, Richard Berry and Johnny 'Guitar' Watson from L.A. to Boston, all as a result of 'Roll With Me Henry'. I was the manager of the troupe and all the contracts were in my name. Johnny was a good salesman. The people would come to see Etta James, but Johnny was the one who was breaking it up on the show. He'd play guitar with his teeth, lay on it, kick it. He's a wonderful fellow, he came down from Texas and when we'd pass through Houston his mother would have us all out to dinner.'

Jim is an engrossing live performer. 'I was the first sax man in L.A. to lay on his back and play the horn. Jay McNeely was a little kid when he used to come in and watch me play at weekends. Two or three years later, he was laying on his back and playing. He's a great musician but he got the clowning from me. Sometime after that, my band ended up playing his tunes when that Little Sonny Warner got popular with 'There Is Something On Your Mind'. You have to play what's popular if you wanna stay in business.'

Throughout the late Forties and Fifties, Wynn recorded for Modern, Specialty (as Jim Wynn & His Groove-Masters), Supreme, Mercury, Million and Recorded In Hollywood, sticking as ever to the raucous jump blues format popularised by Roy Milton and Jimmy Liggins, and continuing to attract the cream of the city's musicians including Zell Kindred (piano), Shifty Henry (bass) and Charlie Norris, who played guitar on the Robins' sides for Spark. His last single, 'Rubberlegs', a fast guitar-prominent shuffle, was made in Hollywood for Great Records in 1959 and reissued on the tiny Pico label in 1960.

As jump blues became unfashionable, Jim could no longer afford to keep a band together and, with a casual stoicism, he turned to session-work. He explains how the system works: 'In the Fifties, you'd just set up and play, and everything's done at once. I recorded with T-Bone Walker, Jimmy Witherspoon, Lowell Fulson, a little crippled fellow name of Ray Agee, George Smith, even Peggy Lee. In the Sixties, I done hundreds of sessions but I don't even know who they were for. We'd go in the studio and lay down a track and then the singer comes in later. That way, if the singer makes a mistake you don't have to hold the band up too long. If you wanna hang around, you can ask who the star is. Y'know when you gonna record him? Next week? Too bad! Most of the time I'm not interested enough to go back and see who it is. Sometimes the singer might come down and watch the band putting down the track. Like Jimmy Robins — he's a hard guy to get along with — and Little Johnny Taylor. I'm the man playing baritone sax on Johnny Taylor's 'Part Time Love'. He was there when I was putting that down but he never sang. He started to sing when we was through making the track, just when the band was packing up to go home. He could've done it over and over twenty times to get the best.'

While, until recently, Little Johnny Taylor has had to eke out some sort of living on the strength of that particular hit, Big Jim Wynn has drawn a steady wage as a session musician for the past ten years. 'Your pay goes through the union and they take out union tax and withholding tax. I keep a list of what sessions I do and what should be coming to me. They make out a slip and you go down to union headquarters to get your money. They have two working weeks to pay you, and if the company don't send it on time the union will fine the company so much. The scale is around $65-$70 for four numbers — that's the basic union rate, you all get the same, even the cat shaking maracas. After tax, that's about $52 out of $70. There's a lot of ways you can get beat, a lot of records I played on and didn't get paid. Some of Ray Agee's things I ain't been paid for. That's why guys do bootleg sessions. Some companies will offer you a session and give you $50 in hand and get through with it. Sometimes, that way it's even better for you. The union don't strictly allow it. But they do it — period.'

Note 1   Big Jim Wynn died in Los Angeles on 19 July 1977.

Note 2   This feature appeared in *Record Mirror* (4 November 1972) and *Blues Unlimited* (September/October 1975). I've added a couple of significant corrections from Dave Penny's liner note to *The Chronological Jim Wynn: 1945-46* (Classics 5043) 2002.

3.11
BULL MOOSE JACKSON
Handsome Is As Handsome Does

With the best will in the world, you could not describe Bull Moose Jackson, one of the first R&B vocalists to enjoy a million-selling single, as a handsome or glamorous man. Contemporaries like Roy Brown were worried by the competition until they saw what he looked like, and Charles Brown tells a joke about Bull Moose and his one-time lady friend, Annisteen Allen: 'Their children just had to be beautiful because they were two of the ugliest people around.' In an era of velvet-voiced crooners who exploited their looks to stimulate female passions, Jackson was a rarity whose popularity rested entirely on his music and showmanship. His band, the seven-piece Buffalo Bearcats, with their bright uniforms and fur-hunter's caps, decried bop as too irregular for dancing and too advanced for public consumption. Their own music invites descriptions which could apply to any number of post-war R&B records, but the sheer variety of styles was uncommon. Jackson's R&B embraced blues, boogies, jazz, novelty songs, hillbilly tunes, pop and even out'n'out rock'n'roll; the high-energy 'Watch My Signals', recorded for Encino in 1956 is comparable to T. Tyler's 'Sadie Green' or Al Downing's 'Down On The Farm'. This small, owlish man with the silvery baritone voice was not only capable of crooning that would rival Billy Eckstine, his tenor-playing on fast jump numbers could compete with the best rock'n'roll honkers.

Born in Cleveland, Ohio in 1919, Benjamin Clarence Jackson began his musical career as a soloist with the Junior Choir of the Avery M.E. Church. His parents provided him with violin tuition, saxophone instruction and vocal coaching. By the age of six, he was playing violin in his grade school orchestra, later doubling on saxophone with a school band at Central High, where he and Freddie Webster formed the Harlem Hotshots, who played around Northern Ohio. Moving to New York State, he became a local favourite, appearing with small dance bands at the Moon Glo, Little Harlem and other popular venues in the Buffalo area. In the early Forties, Jackson returned to Cleveland and joined the Cedar Gardens Club dance band, where he was discovered by Lucky Millinder in 1943. He replaced saxophonist Lucky Thompson in Millinder's orchestra, a seminal organisation which became the house aggregation for Cincinnati's King label, and also recorded for RCA-Victor with great

3.11 - Bull Moose Jackson

success during the late Forties.

Rechristened 'Bull Moose' by members of the Millinder troupe, Jackson first sang with the band during a gig in Lubbock, Texas when their vocalist, Wynonie Harris, was unavailable. When Harris returned, Jackson was given his own repertoire.

Jackson first appeared on shellac when, as alto saxophonist, he joined the band of drummer Big Sid Catlett during a session for Capitol

Records in 1945. In truth, he remained part of the Millinder troupe and recorded as such for Decca between 1945 and 1947.

According to *Who's Who In Rock'n'Roll* (Fredericks, 1958), Millinder specifically trained Jackson for solo stardom, securing a contract with Syd Nathan's Queen label (King was then confined to C&W), choosing top instrumentalists to accompany him and providing a team of songwriters to come up with original material. That was the publicity blurb; songwriting credits suggest no such team, although saxophonist Ernest Purse, Millinder himself, Syd Nathan (under the pseudonym of 'Sally Nix') and — more importantly — Henry Glover, appear in various combinations. Millinder was certainly an infallible judge of sympathetic and dextrous sidemen (his own band contained Eddie 'Lockjaw' Davis, Bill Doggett and Panama Francis), and when Jackson left Millinder to form the Buffalo Bearcats, Bill Mann (piano), Harold Johnson (trumpet), Sam Taylor (tenor), Ted 'Snooky' Hulbert (alto and baritone) and Jimmy Meard (bass) went with him. More often than not, Les Erskine played drums.

Henry Glover, Syd Nathan's A&R man and ex-Millinder trumpet-player, wanted his old boss on Queen; since the bandleader was tied up with Decca, Glover agreed to record Jackson with Millinder's sidemen and to issue the records under Jackson's name. The wide-ranging results — contemporaneous hits like 'The Honeydripper', sedate swing and a session with Annisteen Allen — proved only moderately successful, but his final record for Queen, 'I Know Who Threw The Whiskey In The Well' (an answer to Wynonie Harris's 'Who Threw The Whiskey In The Well') became Jackson's first Top Ten R&B hit in 1946.

In a one-shot deal arranged by Millinder, Jackson switched to Irvin Feld's Superdisc, where he cut 'Memphis Gal' and 'Moose On The Loose'. Superdisc specialised in blues and hillbilly and, on returning to King, Jackson's records often mined a C&W vein. Between 1947 and 1949, he and the Buffalo Bearcats monopolised *Billboard*'s R&B chart with no fewer than ten hugely successful discs including the million-selling, double-sided 'I Love You, Yes I Do' *c/w* 'Sneaky Pete', 'All My Love Belongs To You', 'Cleveland, Ohio Blues', 'Don't Ask Me Why', 'Little Girl Don't Cry' — which was on the list for six months reaching No. 2 — and a cover of Wayne Raney's 'Why Don't You Haul Off And Love Me', which reached the same slot in 1949. It was a lean year for dance bands, but Jackson's gross income from one-nighters and royalties exceeded $200,000. The core of his following resided in the Deep South, where the fast-travelling Jackson held surprising box office appeal for white audiences; in Knoxville, Tennessee during 1949, he played a black dancehall where over 700 whites jammed the upper balcony (reserved for them under segregation laws) and demanded the right to mingle on the dance-floor with the regular clientele.

His success puzzled New York critics who reserved their kudos for 'tasteful' black crooners or bop jazzmen; *Ebony* was particularly snooty, describing Jackson as a voracious reader of comic books and his band as a bunch of mediocre musicians. Clearly, there were many individuals better informed as to the nature and appeal of R&B via jazz, and the demand for Jackson's services outstripped Billy Eckstine, Sarah Vaughan and Ella Fitzgerald. In terms of best-selling records however, Jackson's sensational career was over before the Fifties began, although he remained with King until 1954 and some seventy intriguing and listenable records appeared on the label.

It's impossible to enthuse over every one. R&B was a new music of uncertain antecedents and Bull Moose tried them all. He clearly exploited the emotional taproots of popular sentiment ('It's important,' he says. 'The people wanted melody and I gave it to 'em. They want to hear something they can hum.') and some of his many ballads are simply too sugary to carry much weight today. Arnold Shaw refers to Jackson as a Crosby-style crooner, close to Vaughn Monroe and imitative of Tommy Dorsey's sentimental balladry' — 'more lover-boy Benjamin than horny Bull Moose'.

The rocking covers of hillbilly tunes are far better. Syd Nathan pioneered the black/white musical interchange, producing many cross-cultural King discs which undermine the assumption of a gap between blues and hillbilly. I'm sorry for those who created a black-white animus which would consign Jackson to the trash can because he covered C&W discs, or ignore the talents of Wayne Raney, Moon Mullican or Jimmy Ballard (who covered Jackson's 'I Want A Bow Legged Woman') because their hillbilly records embraced the spirit of the blues. The cross-fertilization of musical ideas enriched the work of almost everyone Nathan recorded and Jackson was no exception. Take a listen to 'Why Don't You Haul Off And Love Me', 'Cherokee Boogie' — where Jackson shouts Moon Mullican's verses over a walking bass figure — and 'Going Back To Cleveland', a distant forerunner of Johnny Burnette's 'Cincinnati Fireball'.

Much of Jackson's best work is unutterably earthy, full of crazy vocals, addictive riffs and sly, often risqué lyrics. 'Big Fat Mamas Are Back In Style Again' has a certain bounce (music to read *Peaches* by), while 'Fare Thee Well Deacon Jones' concerns the tawdry activities of a clergyman who *'sure could shift his gears'*. I'm also partial to the tragic story of 'Nosey Joe', whose olfactory organ was amputated by a jealous husband. This severely moralistic tale was written in 1952 by Jerry Leiber and Mike Stoller — then nineteen years old but already steeped in the world of bluesmen.

No discussion of obscenity and R&B is complete without mention of 'Big Ten-Inch Record', in which Jackson boasts of his extraordinary genital development: *'I cover her with kisses when we're in a lover's clinch / And when she gets all excited, she begs for my big ten inch... record of the band that plays the blues.'* It also explains why he required a bow-legged woman, another of his most suggestive records: *'She's gotta be built like an old bass fiddle / Big bow legs with plenty room in the middle').*

While all these records anticipated the joyous and irreverent hedonism of rock'n'roll, the adult themes — especially sex and booze — were totally unsuitable for white radio stations. Jackson found himself trapped in a no-exit world without access to the white, teenage market. Fats Domino and Little Richard defied all the usual limits, but like most ageing R&B singers — Amos Milburn, Rosco Gordon, Roy Brown — Bull Moose Jackson did not outlive his era. His music was too gutty, and he was altogether incapable of singing about classroom repression or rock'n'roll's harmless fun. He was signed to Marterry, a subsidiary of Chess, in 1956, but the label was short-lived and none of his four recordings saw the light of day. Subsequent records for Encino and Warwick (1960) did not sell well and, from 1958 until the early Sixties, Jackson worked for a number of catering firms. 'After you pass a certain plateau, you get tired of travelling. The road is rough. And jobs in one city don't last too long. People get tired. So, I had to do something else. I got to eat man.' His music no longer supported his family (he met his first wife in 1945 and married again in 1964), although a re-recording of 'I Love You, Yes I Do' for Seven Arts reached both the R&B chart (No. 10) and *Billboard*'s Hot 100 (No. 98) during 1961. The song is now entrenched in the public consciousness with versions by James Brown, Ted Taylor, Willis 'Gator Tail' Jackson, the Merseybeats, Chris Connor, Clarence 'Frogman' Henry and many more. Country boogie singer Chuck Murphy rehashed 'Nosey Joe', while Eddie Fontaine covered another of Jackson's ballads, 'All My Love Belongs To You',

In 1963, Jackson moved to Washington, DC where he worked for B&B Caterers as a waiter, serving guests at Smithsonian Institution receptions. The firm were aware of his importance, and at weekends he was able to lead a trio including cordovoxist Mike Warring and drummer Mort Freed; they played local weddings, parties and bar mitzvahs. He also appeared in the dramatic film, *Sincerely The Blues* (Morback Productions) in 1974.

The following year, he broke a leg and was forced to recuperate in Louisiana where his daughters and grandchildren had settled. They reproached him for turning away from music and, while he returned to catering (he's now with Gourmet Services Inc.), he also joined the Washington Local of the musicians' union and solicited more engagements. Since 1976, he's appeared with a jazz band at the Smithsonian, toured France and North Africa with Buck Clayton's Quartet, and played the *Metro Magazine All-Star Jazz Concert* at Virginia Beach in September 1978. 'I still like to play,' he says. 'When the music comes up, the catering goes out the door.'

Jackson continues to live in Washington and, although he's paid little attention to collectors' overtures, he's spoken of re-recording some of his better songs. Route 66 plan to whet his enthusiasm by reissuing some of his best records on an album in the series which has already rejuvenated the careers of Roy Brown, Floyd Dixon and Nappy Brown. It'll feature plenty of hot, jumping sides hitherto available only on 78s.

The material is now thirty years old but you'll find that the substance more than equals the legend; twelve inches of Bull Moose Jackson is even better than ten.

Note 1   Originally published in edited form in *Melody Maker* (10 November 1979).

Note 2   Bull Moose Jackson died of cancer on 31 July 1989.

3.12
SONNY KNIGHT
Confidential

Sonny Knight looked destined to become an intriguing footnote in the history of R&B, a two-hit wonder whose many less successful records embodied that distinctive Californian strain of light rock'n'roll, a music of fast cars, broken teenaged hearts and what Johnny Otis once impolitely described as 'those jive, bullshit, ice-cream chord changes'. However, in 1981, Knight achieved a genuine first in R&B's tortuous history. It was something none of the acknowledged giants had dreamed of: Knight published a full-length novel under his real name, Joseph C. Smith.

The Day The Music Died (Grove Press) can be regarded as a *roman à clef* or a parable or a positively brilliant thriller fuelled by unstoppable wit and energy. The huge tome bristles with authentic characters and coarse, bitter themes, particularly the corrupt manipulation of black musicians by big business, the insidious influence of the Mafia and the racism that deprives black talent in a rabid quest for easy profit. However much you think you might know about R&B and rock'n'roll, Knight's eye for spectacularly well-researched detail will inform and entertain you. In brief, *The Day The Music Died* is an essential, truly awe-inspiring book, 'as good,' declared the *New Musical Express*, 'as anything ever written on the subject'.

This essay sheds light on the performer behind the writer, and on some of the seventy or so titles which Knight recorded between 1953 and 1964. The general territory — L.A. grease music — will be familiar to fans of Jesse Belvin, Ron Holden, Johnny Flamingo or Little Julian Herrera. It's the sound of the R&B singer whose audience was primarily white teenagers and the young Mexican-American community. More than anything, the tracks reveal a catholic taste which was apparent from Knight's earliest days. Unlike most R&B musicians, Knight might have been found chalking *'Bird lives'* on an apartment house wall, or checking out the latest release by Frankie Laine. One fact stands out: his clear-eyed grasp of the industry's seamy underbelly should not be a matter of surprise. Knight has experienced most of the vagaries of the business and lived out much of his own block-busting plot.

He was born on 17 May 1934 in Maywood — a small town near Chicago, to which he moved as an infant. His father, Joseph Smith Sr, owned a cleaners where his mother, Alice Elizabeth, worked until she became a real estate broker. She also played piano, while his older sister played double bass in her school orchestra. Knight, however, obtained his first piano lessons from an aunt, a lifelong teacher of music in the Chicago school system. Growing up on the West Side he heard a wide variety of music. The ghetto neighbourhood rang to the sound of urban pop ('Erskine Hawkins's 'After Hours', that was like the national anthem') and black musicians like Muddy Waters ('he played in a terrible little tavern at the end of my street') were just beginning to glimpse a new dimension in blues. The jukebox in the local ice cream parlour offered flexible fare: self-pitying ballads by Frankie Laine (' 'That's My Desire' was the first record I ever bought'), the bouncy piano of Sir Charles Thompson and the flashy calisthenics of Dizzy Gillespie attracted coins which Knight earned by delivering clothes to his father's customers: 'I was no more than ten or eleven then. I went over to the jukebox and played Dizzy's 'Salt Peanuts' and a cat at the next table said: "Hey little brother, let me buy you that cone 'cos you're pretty hip, man".'

Knight's early experience of live music was confined to the rehearsals of James Hill, a band led by the father of a school buddy. During one incident-packed evening, he and Hill Jr. sneaked up into the balcony at the Union Park Temple to watch the band. They were set upon by a brace of big kids intent on a public demonstration of their manhood. The twelve year old Knight was about to be hurled from the balcony when Dinah Washington intervened, cuffed his assailant and — he's quite convinced of this — literally saved his life.

In 1947, the Smiths moved to Los Angeles. After a year in junior high, Knight attended Belmont, a forward-looking high school whose integration allowed for music as eclectic as any he had heard in Chicago: 'It was probably unique. In six semesters we had six student body presidents of different nationalities. There were a lot of Mexican kids, so we played 'Cornbread' by Hal Singer and those really popular shuffle things. I met Mike Stoller in the music room — he played good jazz piano at sixteen. Schools in other parts of the city were doing different things, dancing different dances, but Belmont developed its own little culture: it was a combination of blacks, Chicanos and... the Ames Brothers. You could come to our little Friday night sock-hops and hear just about everything there was.'

By the 11th grade, Knight's piano-playing had improved beyond measure and he joined forces with a fellow student who played drums. The duo appeared in talent shows at the Lincoln Theatre and the Barrelhouse. Knight also made a dub for his mother, a version of Larry Darnell's 'I'll Get Along Somehow', and his interest in the music business was further excited when a fellow student at L.A. City College obtained a job at Radio Recorders and invited him to a Rosco Gordon session.

Knight promptly called up Aladdin ('the first company in the phone book') and spoke to label owner Eddie Mesner, who arranged an appointment at which Sonny duly performed 'Dear Wonderful God', a lugubrious tribute inspired by Edna McGriff's 'Heavenly Father'. After a brief conversation with his wife, Mesner returned with the offer of a contract and, in June 1953, with a band organised by Bumps Blackwell, Knight cut three tunes including 'But Officer', an instant classic which still conveys the authentic odour of police harassment. Written by Knight, Tim Inocencio (a Filipino student at City College) and Bob Wainwright (a friend of Inocencio's who threw in a couple of lines), the key to the record's success probably lay in the fiery, puckish quality of J.D. King's tenor playing. All the same, Knight, a nineteen year old college student with a taste for Thelonius Monk, enjoyed one of the first West Coast rock'n'roll hits: 'On the strength of that, I worked with Huggy Boy, a very popular deejay who was in the Mesners' pockets — he put out a Top Ten and seven of 'em would be Aladdin Records. He had a big show, *Autumn's On Adams*. Autumn was a very pretty black woman who resembled Dorothy

Dandridge. Her shop was a hangout for white teenagers who bought R&B, and the first time I went down to sign my record, there were people lined up totally stopping the traffic.' Before returning to College (he studied literature and had already written a rejected novel concerning teenage gangs), Knight toured Texas and New Mexico with Chuck Higgins and Johnny 'Guitar' Watson. The audiences who flocked to their performances in El Paso or Amarillo were almost entirely white: 'Chuck had drawn an audience with 'Pachuko Hop' and, for all practical purposes, we played rock'n'roll. Black record-buyers were into Junior Parker and Muddy Waters, and we weren't in that category. Mexicans and white Texans liked that shuffle thing, and the blacks who came to see us were very few. It was segregated socially and psychologically, and we were unique in one way. Our music kind-of transcended that.'

After a second Aladdin date with Maxwell Davis ('I recorded 'Baby Come Back' on the tail-end of an Amos Milburn session — I was awestruck watching Amos making hits'), Knight saw no sign of the promise held out by his 1¼% royalty rate and well remembers his disagreement with Eddie Mesner: 'Shortly before then, *[another musician]* had gone in with a gun and that was headlines in the black papers. I told Eddie: "Remember what that other guy did. I'm not gonna miss, man!" '

Still working on the borders of blues, ballads and jazz, Knight resumed his long relationship with Bumps Blackwell, who obtained a contract with Specialty under the auspices of Art Rupe ('a cold, self-servicing and unresponsive man who automatically assumes he's superior,' recalled Knight). 'I was hanging around for ages waiting for Bumps to come back from New Orleans with Little Richard, and I asked Rupe when I was going to cut a record so I could get some gigs. He told me: "Well, if you don't have a record out soon, you can come by my house and do some work." I said: "If I wanted to work at your house, I wouldn't have signed a contract. I signed a contract to cut records — not cut your fucking lawn." ' Not surprisingly, Knight's Speciality contract lapsed after a solitary release.

In 1955, Bumps Blackwell introduced Knight to Hite and Dorinda Morgan, white middle-aged music publishers who cared for him, particularly following the death of his mother. They provided the use of their home studio, financed a number of demonstration records (for their benefit as well as his) and generally encouraged his ambitions in an obstinate but kindly way. 'Short Walk', a sinuous, choppy tune resonant of 'Fever', and the ballad 'Dedicated To You', were recorded at Hite Morgan's studio and leased to Cal-West, a Fresno-based label, in 1956. The disc, issued as by Joe Smith on both Cal-West and King Records, went nowhere.

'Confidential', the Morgans' next collaboration, entered the Top Twenty in December 1956, though not before it had been pressed on two different labels and sparked a whole series of puzzles for a generation of discographers. The song was performed in a gentle, conversational tone and the animation with which Knight tells the sometimes sad, sometimes amusing story is regulated by his equally soft speaking voice: 'Dorinda came up with the song. She had written for Kay Starr and had a couple of small hits. She'd probably presented the song to Bumps while I was on Specialty, but Bumps was out hustling and I never got it. Now, she wanted me to do it 'cos she thought I had a confidential sounding voice. I learnt the song and Ernie Freeman came by and made a tape of the piano part. For a long while I wouldn't cut the record because I was very disillusioned. I was working at a club, a really bad club on Central Avenue. They had the front door open and I could see the funeral home where my mother was lying in state, and that was traumatic — the worst three or four days of my life. My mother had never wanted me to be a musician and I thought I was letting her down. At the same time, I was close to getting married and didn't know if I could take care of a wife without getting a Government job. It was a hot, smoggy day and I sat in the cafeteria for hours. Eventually, I thought: "I don't have to spend the rest of my life doing this," and went into the studio.

Hite Morgan produced the song, and he and Larry Mead of Vita Records put up half each — it was a split session at Master Recorders with a girl singer, a model that Larry was goofin' around with. The record came out on Vita and began to sell very well in certain markets, and then Larry sold it to Dot Records — he and Hite got twelve grand in front. Dot put it out, but Vita continued to press it. Don & Dewey worked at Vita's pressing plant and we've cracked up many times over that. Vita pressed and sold thousands of copies, and not just for L.A.. 'Confidential' was No. 1 in Minneapolis for sixteen weeks, and for the whole of that time it was on Vita. Don & Dewey told me that Larry Mead was sneaking it out all over the country. I never knew how much it sold because Hite had sold me to both Dot and Vita, and we immediately went into litigation. The case was settled out of court eventually and I guess I was the one who really lost, 'cos out of the whole thing I got $2,100. With Dot and Vita it was close to a million-seller because there were a lot of copies sold that didn't show up on the charts.'

In the wake of 'Confidential', Knight's earlier work reappeared. Art Rupe dubbed a girl chorus onto 'Keep A-Walkin' ' while Art Laboe acquired the master of 'Dedicated To You', added the voices of the DeVille Sisters and issued the disc on his Starla label. 'Short Walk' underwent similar refinements, while Aladdin issued 'Dear Wonderful God' for the first time (on the flip side of the reissued 'But Officer'). In the meantime, Knight was properly signed to Dot Records (though not without some hassle including a face-to-face confrontation with owner Randy Wood). The Morgans produced a fresh single, 'Worthless And Lowdown', but Dot spelt his name wrong on the label ('Sunny Knight') and, as the follow-up to a big hit, he wasn't too pleased with it. Lee Hazlewood, a staff producer fresh from a huge success with rockabilly Sanford Clark, produced Knight's next session ('Lovesick Blues') but the singer firmly believes his best material, including a self-produced rock-beat version of 'Ghost Of A Chance', remains in some mildewed tape-box. (In a misleading and curious twist, Dot Records acquired 'Dedicated To You' and 'Short Walk' from Art Laboe and issued both titles after Knight had left the label. 'Dedicated To You' became Alan Freed's theme song when he moved to California. 'Whatever they say about Alan, he was a nice cat and we really got along well when he worked at KDAY'.)

After Dot, Sonny Knight switched labels with bewildering rapidity — Starla, Eastman, Kent, Original Sound, Swingin'. He has entertaining stories about them all, but beneath the broad wisecrack lies a sourly-observed corruption which isn't always funny. The songs echoed the formative black pop of the late Fifties, but a Californian oldies flavour spilled over into most of his work — sometimes successfully, as on 'Madness': 'That had a Swallows–Charles Brown type of sound with Ernie Freeman playing on it. I actually got an advance out of the Biharis, but it wasn't a smart move for me 'cos most of my audience was not in the black market but more in the Art Laboe field. I was going to be a — quote — 'white artist in the Jimmy Clanton bag' or some such bullshit. But then 'Madness' wasn't really such a clunker. I never heard anything about it for perhaps a year or more. Then, on a few occasions when I happened to be making a personal appearance on the strength of another record, someone would request it — like, three Mexican girls came up to me in Denver — that never failed to surprise me.' 'Madness' was also issued on Go Go coupled with 'Teenage Party', another of Hite Morgan's studio masters on which Knight plays piano and sings in a manner which recalls the snarling Fender guitars and boppy vocals of Gene Vincent.

The Sixties began in similarly revivalist fashion. Knight cut Johnny Ace's 'Saving My Love' for Fi-Fo ('owned by Bob Markley, a rich kid, one of the heirs to the Texaco fortune — you'd call and he'd be in Aspen for the week') and Nat Cole's 'I Wanna Thank Your Folks' for Mercury ('Bumps had opened a Mercury office in L.A., but he signed everyone who passed through and they fired him a week after that session — he overspent and ran out of budget before he could mix it down'). Knight's unorthodox work for A&M, including a bluesy 'Georgia Town' (revived by George McCurn) and the New Orleans-flavoured funk of 'State Street', displayed a refined intellect, but the company had only just begun and still lacked promotional clout. Then, bang in the middle of the Beatles era, Knight brushed the Hot 100 with a couple of self-assured blues ballads. 'If You Want This Love' (No. 71 in 1964), arranged by Erskine Hawkins vet Bobby Smith, introduced Knight to a world of girl groups, Mersey Beat and the glutinous Dick Clark. Aura, the pop subsidiary of World Pacific, also issued an album containing winsomely arranged versions of 'Confessin' The Blues' and 'I Need Your Love So Bad'. The company was bought out by Liberty, who had already used Knight's services as a producer ('we did some Timi Yuro tracks, stayed up all night coaching her to sing melismatically').

The sleevenote to Yuro's 1963 country-soul collection, *Make The World Go Away* (Liberty LRP-3319) explains: *'Timi had the assistance of Sonny Knight, who guides her vocal career, and the one who was responsible for getting Timi into the music world. He discovered her singing in her family's Italian restaurant. He is the one who has brought out Timi's great capacity of soul in her singing in her previous records and in each and every one of the songs in this album.'*

Towards the end of the decade, Knight recorded Billy Larkin-styled jazz for Celebrity and, before pulling away from the record business altogether, half an album's worth of 'social conscience' tunes for Frankie Laine's SGC productions: 'I left for Hawaii right in the middle of a song.'

In Hawaii (Knight first visited the islands in 1957 on a tour with Chuck Berry and the Five Satins), he returned to his first love — serious writing. At the same time, he continued to work hotel lounges, playing a mix of Hawaiian music, swing, current hits and a smattering of oldies. Today, Knight lives on Maui where he's playing with a new band, Hua Paka (Hawaiian for scrambled eggs) and writing a sequel to his glorious novel. From the vantage point of a sunny beach, he holds no bitterness towards any of the people he encountered as a recording artist: 'No animosity towards any of them. Maybe I'd have enjoyed more success had I chosen to accept their moral values, but it's unlikely. Very few people of my era, good or bad, moral or immoral, survived. I probably wouldn't have either.'

Liner notes to *Confidential* (Mr. R&B LP-107) 1985.

Note 1   There is another Sonny Knight, a white disc-jockey (KTLN in Denver, KRIZ in Phoenix and KENO in Las Vegas) who produced Don & Alleyne Cole for Tollie and Curtis Lee for Mira. He became West Coast A&R man for Columbia in 1968.

Note 2   In 1984, Sonny's younger son, trumpet-player David Smith, visited Britain with the All-American Wind Instrument Orchestra; I took him to lunch at the Home Office. His father and I exchanged frequent letters. In 1995, Sonny wrote: *'I'm now working in a very elegant (boring) dinner room here on Maui; tuxedo, waterfall, playing piano. I haven't sung a note in a year and a half. Let's face it, my days as a teenage semi-idol may be drawing to a close.'* Sonny died on 5 September 1998, two years after suffering a devastating stroke. Everyone should own a copy of *The Day The Music Died*. There never was a sequel; as Val Wilmer wrote in an obituary in *The Guardian*, hassles with publishers, agents and television companies wore him down.

3.12 - Sonny Knight

4

COTTON PICKIN' ROCK

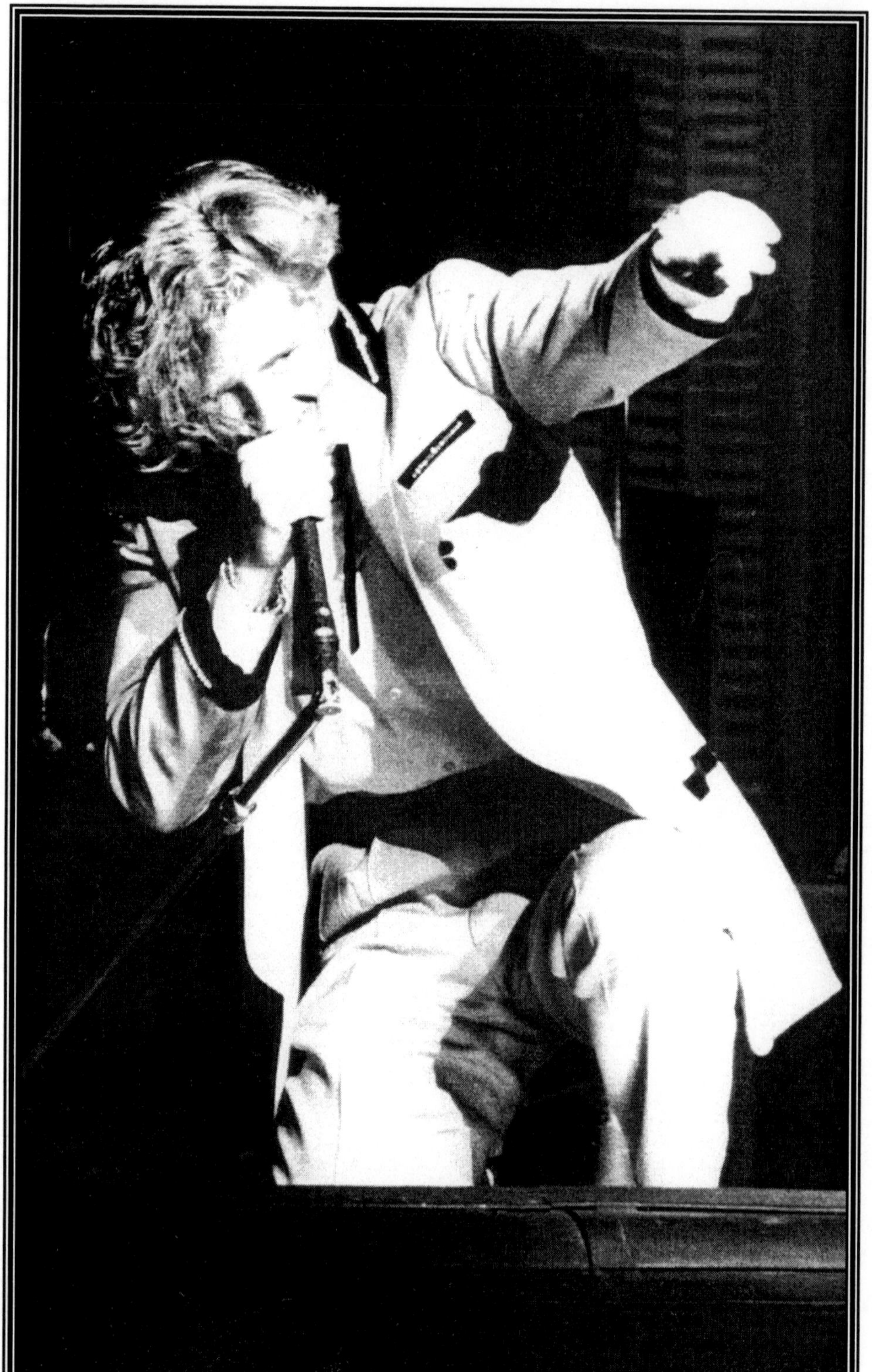

4.1
JERRY LEE LEWIS
Rock's Greatest Entertainer

On 22 May 1958, an Immigration Officer manning the desk for TWA flights from New York to London Airport North scratched his head, sighed, picked up the passport of Myra Gale Brown Lewis and promptly fell off his seat.

Fresh-faced but tall, Myra would have passed for sixteen. But the passport revealed all. Born July 1944, Vicksburg, Mississippi. Thirteen years old and, for the previous five months, housewife to the big, flash, yellow-haired, cigar-eating Southern hustler who waited in the lounge with his father-in-law, Fender bass-playing J.W. 'I ain't got no Christian names' Brown.

The immigration official thought Myra was unusually young for a married woman but noted *'since both parties come from the South-Eastern part of the United States, where the legal age for marriage is lower than other parts of the world, no action on my part seemed to be called for'*.

Folks bringing child brides into the country is more common than you'd think. If, every now and then, the press huffs and puffs about Africans doing so, it's a mild reaction compared to that touched off by the arrival of Jerry Lee Lewis almost fourteen years ago. But he was white, thrice-married at 22 and — perhaps the cardinal sin — he played rock'n'roll.

Lewis blew the lid off Fleet Street. *'Here is a chance,'* crowed one leading Sunday, *'for Britain's teenagers to show that even rock'n'roll hasn't entirely robbed them of their sanity.'* It worked, of course. Sir Frank Medlicott, the Independent MP for Norfolk Central, referred to the 'great offence' caused to many people by the singer's arrival. He also asked the then Minister of Labour, Mr. Iain Macleod, if he would remember 'that we have more than enough "rock'n'roll" entertainers of our own without importing them from overseas'. The Minister agreed that this was a 'thoroughly unpleasant case, ended by the cancellation of the contract and the disappearance of the man'.

Jack Good, who reviewed the opening night at Edmonton Regal, described a hostile audience driven to jeers by Lewis's indifference, contempt and lack of humility: *'Lewis knew he could, by his shattering performance, thrill his audience whether they liked him or not. So did the audience, and for that, they hated him even more.'* Shows at Kilburn and Tooting were stopped in less than thirty minutes and Jerry flew back to New York International within five days.

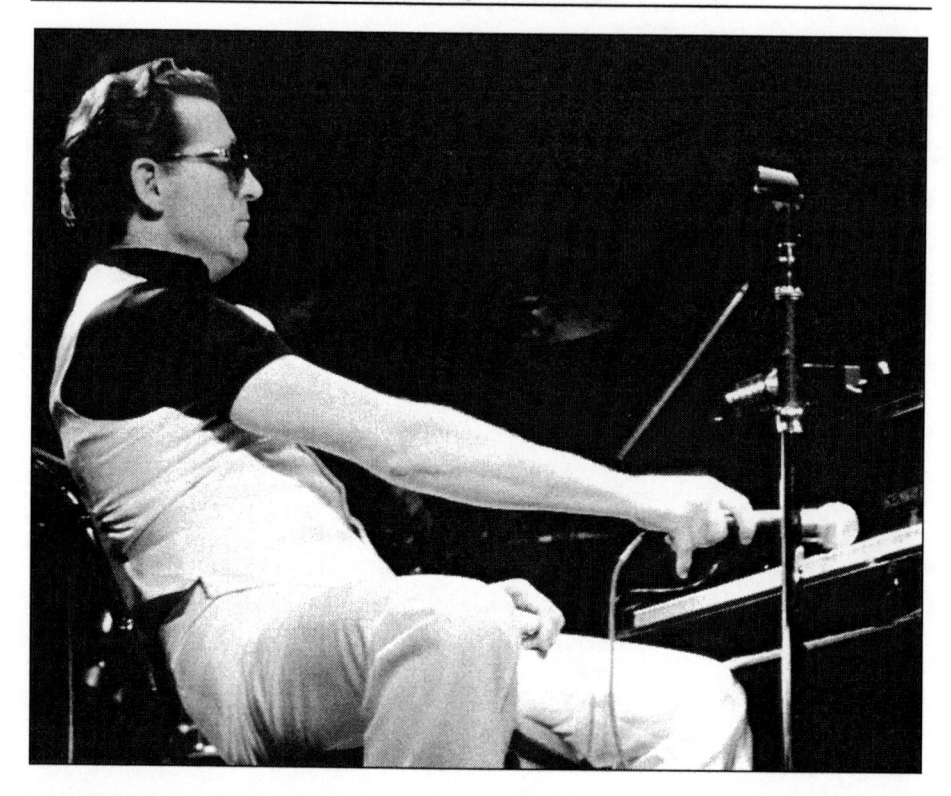

'We had a very good reception in England,' he told reporters. 'I just got homesick. People treated us very nice.'

A bible college dropout from Ferriday, Louisiana, Lewis had taken the world by storm with 'Whole Lot Of Shakin' Going On'. Previously recorded by Big Maybelle, Roy Hall and others, Lewis's immediately identifiable version reached No. 3 in 1957. His irresistibly compulsive style, which appeared to spring fully fledged from no obvious source, is best tabbed 'Jerry Lee Lewis music'. It was an apocalyptic sound as bright and swaggering as the diamanté trimmings on his custard-yellow stage suit. Boiling over with an arrogant Pentecostal fervour, Lewis went one better with 'Great Balls Of Fire' (No. 2), while 'Breathless' (No. 7) completed a run of million-sellers. Despite smaller hits, including 'High School Confidential' and 'What'd I Say', the formidable and truly dedicated performer spent a decade in the wilderness before his recent renaissance as the finest honky-tonk country singer around today.

I've never written about Lewis before. It's too difficult. How do you describe the sort of charisma that has grown men of thirty recalling his concerts with tears in their eyes? Tunbridge Wells 1962. What's so *great* about a guy lifting his right trouser to his knee and combing the blond hairs on his leg? Mitcham the day before. Why pay to see one of those contests where somebody sees how quickly they can dismantle a piano? (It was too small to stand on — he got so annoyed he damn near ate the pieces!) Stratford 1964. What makes a whole theatre roar with one voice at the sight of a maniac who plays piano with his butt? 'Whew! It's gonna git gooooood inah minute.'

There's no answer to these questions. You just had to be there. Dripping with anticipation. Heaving and shaking alongside two thousand others for whom Lewis is 'The Governor' and the rest are just... well, the rest. South Harrow one time. Before he got big again, there were always half a dozen dates within fifty miles of London whenever he toured. Anyway, I'm crushed up the back of someone's drape. Jerry smashes the piano lid down, throws it up again, juts his chin in and out, weaves an imperial hand around the mike and — wham! — three outrageous flourishes in the uppermost register. This piece of pure theatre lasts a couple of blinks. In between *'your cheatin' heart'* and *'will make you weep'*. Drape-jacket's old lady looks up: 'Thinks he's God, don't he?' The response is peculiarly gentle: 'Well, he is, dear.'

Jerry Lee... Jerry Lee... he joins in the cheers, mocking our British accents. He looks at the audience, at the roof, into the wings. Anywhere except at what his fingers are doing. They operate by remote control, falling contemptuously on to notes which are so right. And on the next torrid solo he leans back. Long greasy tresses cascade over ears which stick out at right angles. Dig the killer hair, y'all. The man is in love with himself. Frightening. Drunk on rock'n'roll but equally intoxicated by his own insane talent.

And then he sneers. Forget about Presley's comical upper lip. This is a sneer a mile long. All the arrogance, sex and soul of the White South is in that sneer. How can he sing 'Old Black Joe' and make me believe him? Yeah, he sings as well. Yodels, falsetto howls and blistering, pile-driving hysterics bring life to songs that anyone else would have been forced to bury fifteen years ago. A gravel-corded 'Hound Dog' goes on for twenty minutes. And when he stops rockin' it's no less astonishing. If there's a superficially impudent unconcern about the rest of his talents, he can't disguise the respect he holds for his own voice. Loose, downhome and laced with experience, it turns a country weepie into a desolate expression of real despair.

You didn't see him climb on the piano at Tunbridge Wells. With a wave that said: 'Watch this, cretins,' he minced from one side of the stage to the other and sorta glided up there. Taunting a whole theatre by swinging his paunch round in a lascivious arc. On top of the piano Lewis just overflowed. Looking back becomes sheer fantasy.

There are these crescendos where insolence gives way to aggression; the sneer evaporates, his face disappears into a bloated mess, and his shirt billows and ripples like the obscene figure from a Michelin X advert. First aid would seem to be inevitable but that's Jerry — jest satisfyin' his soul's anguish.

At Birmingham, on his last tour, he was fractionally quieter. I guess he's mellowed a little, if only a little. The killer hair is shorter, darker and he doesn't wear custard-yellow suits any more. His voice is a deeper — dare I say soulful — baritone; the high notes in 'You Win Again' don't come quite so effortlessly and, instead of kicking the piano stool into the orchestra pit, he uses it to climb on the piano. But make no mistake, he can't be beat. As John Grissim, Charlie Gillett, Nik Cohn, Peter Guralnick and the man himself keep telling you, Jerry Lee Lewis is still the greatest performer in the history of universal entertainment.

I had intended to talk about the handful of albums that have been released in secret during the past few months. But waiting for Philips to send them is like waiting for Godot. Meanwhile I'll be at the London Palladium on 23 April. And if you decide to go, you'd better book up for Birmingham and Ipswich as well. Lewis can be a cathartic experience but he's also highly addictive.

First published in *Record Mirror*, 11 March 1972.

4.2
MAJOR BILL SMITH
Fort Worth Boogie

'Listen, I don't know one note from another. A key to me is something you unlock a door with, a chord is something you tie somebody up with. Quarter-inch mono tape, that's all we had, no mixes and no tracks — that's why we got such a great sound. We didn't have to worry about anybody being a hero. Notes and chords and keys don't make a hell of beans to a hit record.'

Major Bill Smith is sprawled on the floor of the lounge in his first floor suite at the Kensington Hilton. He's wearing cowboy boots, check pants and a gold record medallion on a necklace. A black stetson with gold studs rests on the plush sofa behind his back. Every now and then the phone rings: 'Now listen here, I gotta roomful of record people here and they know I'm a big wheel. You want some of the ol' Major's bagful of goodies you'd better get over here fast.' His craggy face splits into a self-mocking smile as he returns to his position on the floor amidst what looks like twenty years of recording memorabilia: stacks of early Delbert McClinton tapes ('they're calling him the new superstar, but he's just playing that old Fort Worth boogie'), new albums by Southern soul duo Pic & Bill ('Bill has the most beautiful falsetto voice, he does 'Funny How Time Slips Away' and goes up to high P') and half a dozen acetates with *'99% Pure Rockabilly'* stamped on the labels ('I'm the king of rockabilly, I started that stuff'). Taken with just the tiniest grain of salt, it's all very engaging because the Major just loves to talk about his music and he has the knack of making his listeners feel as if they're the only persons on earth.

Cowtown's biggest independent record producer, Major Bill ('that's legitimate, it's not like Colonel Tom Parker, Kentucky Fried Chicken or something') is indeed respected for his many chart entries, first gaining recognition with his production of 'Peanuts' by Rick & The Keens (No. 60 in 1961) and consolidating his reputation with enormous hits like Bruce Channel's 'Hey! Baby' (No. 1 in 1962), 'Hey Paula' by Paul & Paula (No. 1 in 1963) and 'Last Kiss' by J. Frank Wilson (No. 2 in 1964). He's sold fifteen million records and produced some two thousand recordings on a great many different labels, mostly his own. Before I can gasp he hands me a catalogue of Le Bill Music and Le Cam Records — 'The "Le" came

4.2 - Major Bill Smith

from Letitia, my wife's name, and the "Cam" from my partner, George Campbell' — a document which contains 1,200 sides by soul singers (Johnny Adams, Pic & Bill, Johnny Copeland), bluesmen (Willie Hobbs, Amos Milburn Jr), rockabillies galore (Steve Wright, Johnny Carroll, Dean Beard, David Ray, Gene Summers) and a few eccentricities like the Legendary Stardust Cowboy ('Boy that was the craziest ever. He was really Norman Odom, a loony — worst cotton-pickin' singer there ever was. Three thousand hippies in Cleveland went nuts over that record').

Born dirt-poor in Checotah, Oklahoma, Smith was raised on hillbilly and western swing, soaking up first-hand the music of Jimmie Rodgers and Bob Wills and attending what he calls 'singing all day and dinner on the ground — where the ol' country people get together on a Saturday night and Sunday and sing gospel hymns'. Following the Japanese attack on Pearl Harbor, he joined a bomber plant assembly, passed a cadet programme into the US Air Corps and flew B-17s out of Molesworth, England on thirty-two missions over Germany. Badly shot up on the thirty-third, he spent several years in military hospital where he began writing songs in the early Fifties: 'A navy photographer came to the base to do a story on the B36. He said: "One time, I had to go down into twenty feet of muddy water and take pictures." That hit me: 'Twenty Feet Of Muddy Water'.' The song, an echoey country blues, became a big hit for Sonny James in 1956 and was recently recorded by Linda Ronstadt:

'I still get royalties on it and they always come to Sgt. Bill Smith 'cos I was a Sgt. then.'

During convalescent leave in Houston, Smith gained the confidence of Don Robey, the owner of Duke/Peacock for whom he worked in a promotional capacity, occasionally producing black artists (Joe Hinton) and local rockabillies (Doodle Owens) for the Backbeat subsidiary.

Robey, one of the few black millionaires in Texas, had built his fortune from old spiritual discs and hair straighteners. He comforted the R&B jocks with white hookers and $100 bills, and used Smith to establish which ones were earning their rewards. Smith was also responsible for one of Robey's first rock'n'roll hits: 'We kicked off the Casuals 'So Tough' on a small station and Robey gave me expense money to go to Philadelphia. I took a box of steaks up there, and when I got to *American Bandstand* I asked for Dick Clark but his producer, Tony Mammarella came out. "Look, our record is 'So Tough' but our steaks are so tender," and I whipped that box of steaks on his desk. Clark came running in: "Man, we've had offers of everything and the moon but you're the first cotton-picker who ever brought us something to *eat*!"' Clark got behind the record, which sold very well in the South. (A cover version by the Kuf-Linx entered the Hot 100.)

Later that year, Smith resigned from the air force and settled in Fort Worth, where he began to haunt Clifford Herring's studio — the origin of virtually every one of those two thousand recordings. He worked with George Campbell, a songwriter ('Four Walls') and pianist, and the pair produced a wide range of material: 'I used to hitchhike to New York in my Major's uniform with the ribbons and silver wings, and take my little ol' bag of masters and get one of those $5-a-night rooms across the street from the Turf Grille at the front of the Brill Building. That's where the action was: you go in the Turf Grille and get coffee and Danish and try and pitch your records.'

It was the tail-end of the rockabilly era and his involvement with Texan greasers like Huelyn Duvall and Tooter Boatman is obscure. But Smith was in the studio when they cut their deservedly sought-after sides for Twinkle and speaks of Boatman, who died in a car crash, with enormous affection: 'He was a terrific rockabilly singer and he could make his guitar walk down the street; Eric Clapton ain't even in it as far as I'm concerned.' By 1959, the Major was pitching his tapes to Felsted (Mac Curtis and David Orrell) and Roulette (the Chaparrals' 'Leaping Guitar'). Nothing really clicked, so he formed his own label, Le Cam, and tried leasing the occasional biggie to a much larger company in the tradition of all Southern record-men. Local hits by the Team-Mates, Ace Dinning ('Mulholland Drive', which was leased to Top Rank) and the Straight-Jackets led to a cataract of Smith-produced discs on literally dozens of other labels: 'I was comin' up with so much stuff and I didn't want to be accused of payola. If I came up with three or four Le Cam records on a chart it was gonna look stupid, but if I put stuff out on Soft, or Troy, or

Pastel, or Shalimar... I could get by with it.'

The Straight-Jackets, the house band behind many of the Major's discoveries, were led by a young Delbert McClinton whose 'Wake Up Baby' on Le Cam became the first record by a white artist to be broadcast on Fort Worth's R&B station, KNOK. The group played at Jack's Place on Mansfield Highway backing up Buster Brown, Howlin' Wolf and Jimmy Reed, who puked up over the Straight-Jackets' brand new microphone. The Beatles' first hit, 'Love Me Do', was inspired by McClinton's harmonica playing on 'Hey! Baby', Bruce Channel's hit of 1962.

Before the Major had ever heard of him, Channel had sent a tape of 'Hey! Baby' to King, but Sydney Nathan ('the hot shovel of the day') had sent it back with *No good* scrawled on the box. Bruce was hanging around Cliff Herring's studio when Smith was cutting Ornette Coleman's sister, Trudy, on 'Come Back Jack'. She couldn't get it right and Channel cut a demo for her to copy, subsequently asking if he could lay down a song or two of his own: 'I had Delbert and the Straight-Jackets kick off Channel's song with the harmonica. I pressed two hundred copies of 'Hey! Baby' and it exploded — a record shop would have one copy and little girls would be fighting over it. Steinberg, the head of Mercury, called me: "You gotta lil' ol' record down there, we'll take it." I said: "Steinberg, have you heard this cotton-pickin' record?" He hadn't. Mercury bought it on the strength of a 'Pick Hit' in *Cash Box* magazine. When you got a 'Pick Hit' in those days it was real and not because you'd taken out a full-page ad. I'd already sent Shelby Singleton at Mercury a tape of 'Come Back Jack' and 'Hey! Baby', and I never heard a word from him. Mercury in Chicago bought it and it went to Number One in the nation in March 1962. In May of '62, I get the tape back from Singleton with a letter saying: *"Sorry we can't use this 'Hey! Baby' stuff."* Ain't that great? I still got the Mercury record on the wall and I've framed the letter from 'em turning it down after they'd gone and released it!'

The Major reaches for a suitcase and records spill out by the armful. 'Here's Amos Milburn Jr. on 'Dearest Darling' — that's a Birmingham, Alabama record if ever I heard one. Here's Doug Sahm, ol' Sir Doug, doin' 'Cry'. This is the best cotton-pickin' soul record in the world: Carolyn Sullivan singing 'Dead'.' Crisp comments like these punctuate each fresh tale; what Fats Domino told his chauffeur when he first heard Joe Barry's 'I'm a Fool To Care', how Smith was beat out of $100,000 when Acuff–Rose used a Roy Orbison tune for the flip of an Everly Brothers' record instead of David Orrell's song 'You're The One', why little ol' pimply face Tony Orlando followed Bruce Channel all around Houston. The stories go on and on but you never get tired of hearing them; it's the next best thing to being in the studio when these million-sellers were made: 'I got $111,000 from 'Hey! Baby' and I spent it all recording everything that could walk. One day I'm supposed to record Amos Milburn Jr. — a heck of great blues singer — and the cotton picker don't show. There's this tall, athletic boy with a crew cut hanging round the studio and this real beautiful black-haired girl with him. I'm mad at Amos 'cos I got four musicians cooling their heels at $5 apiece when my co-producer, Marvin Montgomery, persuades me to listen to these two 'cos they've driven 130 miles from Brownwood. So we go in the studio and the tall athlete puts his foot up on the piano bench and hits the strings of his guitar: *'Hey, hey, Paula...'* It had 'hey' in it, right? Let's go, let's record! The girl was scared to death: "Now?".'

Ray Hildebrand and Jill Jackson took a dub back to Brownwood, where it was played to wild reaction. Smith released it on Le Cam — two hundred records of 'Hey Paula' by Jill & Ray — and sold the master to Philips, who wanted him to beef it up by adding organ and vibes. Philips renamed the duo 'Paul & Paula' and went on to sell ten million copies in eighteen languages. The first two hundred Le Cam pressings have no organ or vibes, and additional pressings on Le Cam (Smith retained the rights to sell the disc as by Jill & Ray in Texas) are the same as the worldwide Philips version: 'I tell everybody who has a copy of 'Hey Paula' by Jill & Ray to listen to it, and if it doesn't have organ or vibes on it you got a $1,000 rarity.'

In April 1963, Paul & Paula were touring England where a radio appearance on *Pop Inn* was scheduled: 'I'm standing there like the proud peacock, the big shot, and this dude in a bowler hat comes up to me: "Major, I used to be in the clothing business, but now I'm getting into the record business and I'd like to talk to you about it. My name is Brian Epstein and my group was supposed to be on the show today, but we got bumped when Paul & Paula came in."

"That's showbiz," I told him. "What's the name of your group?"

"The Beatles."

"Whaaat? Man, we *stomp* on beetles down in Texas!" '

Smith relates this foolish anecdote with some relish; he likes to think it's his Number One weird story, but the man who insulted the Beatles has plenty more and I much prefer the one about J. Frank Wilson who topped the best-sellers with 'Last Kiss'. Smith had been introduced to Sonley Roush, a go-getting promoter from West Texas who became his partner on various deals and drew his attention to a record by Wayne Cochran on King: 'It was called 'Last Kiss' and it was selling like crazy around Lubbock. "Man," I told him, "get somebody into a studio and cover that thing, get some musicians and copy that arrangement!" He took J. Frank Wilson out of a slaughter pen and had three schoolgirls off the street to back him up — they all go as flat as a flitter on the end of the record.' The Major took the master to Mercury where Shelby Singleton turned his nose up again; Josie, who'd released several of Smith's productions, agreed to take it: 'I went back to Texas and nothing happened. Then the Fox, ol' Harry Finfer, he made a deal with Sonley Roush and went and released 'Last Kiss' on his own Tamara label. Harry got in his white Cadillac and he broke that record all over — if he hadn't done that, Josie would have sat on the thing and done nothing, but Harry created the demand. We ended up in a Philadelphia courthouse and we won the case 'cos I had the rights in the first place. When the record began to sell, I went to see J. Frank in San Angelo about a follow-up. He says "Oh Mr. Smith..." — he's sitting with his head in his hands — "if you can do anything to help me. I'm tired of working out there in the slaughter pen, all that blood and all that sweat, oh please Mr. Smith." Six weeks later, he's in a suite at the Park Sheraton Hotel with his feet up on a mahogany desk: "Give me some pretzels, order me some beer..." What made the difference? A Number One record!' It was also a prophetic record; J. Frank and Sonley Roush were driving into Canton, Ohio when they took a curve too fast. Sonley was killed and Wilson was badly injured: 'Now he's living on food stamps and carrying old people around in a rest home in Lufkin, Texas. NBC-TV did a documentary on the guy who went from the top of the pop world to the bottom inside six months.'

Major Bill's last chart appearance came with the Straight-Jackets, who had broken up and reformed as the Rondells, with 'If You Really Want Me To, I'll Go', a lovely, folksy tune written by Delbert McClinton and later recorded by Doug Sahm and Waylon Jennings. It notched the Hot 100 in 1965 — the unlucky thirteenth in a row of previous smash hits.

Smith blames his downfall on the professional jealousy which surrounded a man who, by his own admission, knew nothing about notes, chords or keys: 'Before 'Hey! Baby', I'm a freak. I come up with 'Hey! Baby' and I'm a fluke. Then I'm up there with 'Hey Paula' and I become a crook. I went from a freak to a fluke to a crook in eleven months. I had more Number Ones... Bruce Channel's 'Going Back To Louisiana' was the best record I ever made, and that should've been Number One but politics and things entered into it. It got to where people would try and take my records away from me, the radio stations got jealous, they put 'Going Back To Louisiana' up on the wall at KLIF–Dallas and said: "Don't play this record, it's a Major Bill Smith record." '

Right now, however, the Major is hungry for another hit and before I leave he puts on Amos Milburn Jr. singing 'Long Tall Sally': 'Listen to this, I didn't know I was making a rockabilly record 'cos he's black, see. Now I realise Chuck Berry was one of the first rockabilly artists. Boy, there's your rockabilly guitar, that's a cotton-pickin' smash today.'

Originally published in Melody Maker (29 September 1979).

Note   Major Bill *aka* William Arthur Smith died in Fort Worth, Texas on 12 September 1994. He was 72. Smith aroused some contempt in his later years by claiming that Elvis was alive and in touch with him. He wrote two books on the theory. But the Major was also an altruistic soul who had donated a percentage of his income to a Fort Worth shelter for the homeless since the 1960s.

4.3
CHARLIE GRACIE
Back From The Cold

By the time I got into rock'n'roll, Charlie Gracie was already a folk memory dimly recalled from a performance on *Stars From Blackpool* and a 78 of 'Wanderin' Eyes'. I'd bought the record in 1957, but it failed to spark any lifelong enthusiasm and lay in a cupboard alongside the Five Smith Brothers ('Frosty The Snowman') — virtually forgotten until I *really* saw the light.

Rock'n'roll has become a subject for boundless study and middle-aged rockers are exhumed with alacrity. Men who rarely ventured outside their honky-tonk, truckstop world now appear in English pubs before a thousand rockabilly rebels. Most retain their early talent, using their new audiences to shape revitalised careers. Such is the case with Charlie Gracie, whose career appeared to crunch to a sudden halt in 1958, not long after his second tour of England, where the tiny (5'4") 21-year-old mauled a huge, custom-made Guild guitar and rocked our Granadas and Hippodromes with hits like 'Butterfly', 'Fabulous' and 'Wanderin' Eyes.' Gracie was a big star. He made all the nationals from *The Times* (*'Mr. Charlie Gracie reveals a fabulous stamina. The test of a rock'n'roll expert is presumably whether he can convert his staider audience to the delights of this intoxicating rhythm, and your critic must confess to conversion'*) to the *Daily Mirror*, where Clifford Davis was really on the ball (*'Charlie offered mostly rock'n'roll and its express-paced successor, rock-a-billy'*). The gulf between the aforementioned hits and the rest of Gracie's repertoire — 'Lucille', 'Rock The Joint', 'Hound Dog' — was already wide, and one wondered which direction he'd take when he played England again in 1979.

The audience was noticeably apprehensive: Gracie has, after all, been described as the first purveyor of wimp-rock (with the accent on wimp). I, for one, need not have worried. He strode out and whammed straight into some primitive Treniers stuff. Somewhat pinched features and an absence of grease are the only signs of two decades without a hit — and, yes, he really can play guitar. The flop-haired Ted to my right is waving a bottle of brown ale: 'Bloody brilliant this *[he takes a swig]* Charlie Gracie.' I can't argue. The time machine has burped or Charlie Gracie Jr. has been dispatched in his father's place. It's an immaculate set, tight and generous with an endearing emphasis on songs which aren't actually about anything except rock'n'roll itself.

I asked Gracie at his London hotel shortly after his opening night, why he'd waited twenty years before returning to Britain, where his popularity was always greatest. Sinking deep into his chair and virtually disappearing ('People tell me: "Charlie, no matter how much money you make, you'll never be a big man".'), he speaks with the kind of genuine sincerity that comes naturally to happy and contented people: 'My last tour coincided with my honeymoon. My son was born in '58 and I had a daughter in '61. I thought I should stay about the house and help raise my children. Now they've grown up and they told me they wanted me to come on this trip. We've done okay. I play forty weeks a year around the Tri-State area, so I've never felt it was necessary to leave them.'

A second-generation American of Sicilian ancestry, Charles Anthony Bernard Graci (the 'e' came later) was born in Philadelphia in May 1936. At fourteen, he appeared on the *Paul Whiteman Teen Show*, where his guitar technique earned him many prizes including his family's first refrigerator. During the early Fifties he recorded for Cadillac, owned by Graham Prince, and 20th Century, owned by Ivin Ballen, who'd distributed the Cadillac records. The music he made embraced a wide variety of styles including jump blues, swing, country boogie and something you'd call rockabilly, were it not for the fact that rockabilly didn't emerge until three years later and many miles away. As a whole, this small but lively portion of pop music history is redolent of a cross between Joe Turner and Billy Cotton — an amazing body of music for any young kid to have made several years before most of our rock'n'roll heroes had seen the inside of a studio.

Its fashionable, nowadays, to knock Northern rock'n'rollers. If you don't come from Tennessee or further South you just don't make it. Gracie provides a fascinating antidote to this thinking: 'Apart from reading about it, I don't know what 'Southern culture' is, but I'd say there's a little bit of rockabilly in all of us. I was a sixteen-year-old, Eastern-born white kid playing early R&B, country and pop-gospel with the individual singing-star influence of the Frankie Laines and Johnnie Rays. I began playing guitar in 1946 and the Cadillac records retain the dying influence of the big bands.

'We had a black piano player, Luther Henderson, and a fantastic soprano sax-man plus black girl gospel singers on 'Say What You Mean' and 'No Sin In Rhythm'.' Gracie continues: 'I'd developed a certain style by playing guitar with a backbeat — it would sound like a guitar and a drum together, so although it was a small group, it really sounded like a big swing band. I listened to WHAT and WDAS in Philly — they had Joe Turner and B.B. King. This is 1951 and only us kids knew who they were. My mother was a big country fan, with records by Hank Williams, Roy Acuff, Eddy Arnold and Tennessee Ernie. She took me to see Bill Haley in 1952, when he and the Saddlemen were dressed up in cowboy suits. But they had added drums to a country band, which was kind of unorthodox. He influenced me as much as anybody and I was buying his records before

I made my own. I also bought Arthur Smith, B.B. King and Louis Prima — I love that shuffle thing. My head's so full of all this stuff it feels like it wants to burst.'

In 1957, Bernie Rothbard, Gracie's agent this past quarter-century, fixed a deal with Cameo, owned by Bernie Lowe and Kal Mann. A figure with a homespun integrity rarely found in Philly businessmen, Rothbard also has stories to tell. During the Fifties he owned the largest theatrical agency in Philadelphia. He also owned the Earl Theatre and booked big bands and R&B acts as well as country artists. He's managed a long list of local performers including many of those to appear on Jack Howard's Arcade label. Howard, he remembers, owned a printing shop in Philly and produced photos of the stars (Lulubelle & Scotty, Red River Dave and the Sons Of The Pioneers), which he'd sell during the interval of shows at outdoor hillbilly parks including the Sleepy Hollow Ranch in Quakertown, PA where Charlie Gracie first saw Bill Haley in 1952. At one time or another, Rothbard has managed and/or booked most of Philly's biggest names including Freddie Bell, Dee Dee Sharp, Dave Appell, Screamin' Jay Hawkins, Doc Bagby, Bunny Sigler and Bobby Rydell. Other Rothbard acts were: Billy Duke & The Dukes (known for 'Flip, Flop And Fly' on Casino, they were big favorites at the Cadillac Showbar, where they often topped the bill over Gracie's thirty-minute slot), Jackie Lee (known as 'Mr. Hot Piano', Lee was killed in an automobile accident in 1977 at the age of 52. His biggest sellers, like 'Isle Of Capri' and 'Happy Vacation' revealed his MOR-big band origins, but his rock'n'roll cuts are likely to appear in John Beecher's *Rockaphilly* album series) and Ray Hatcher (a rockabilly from Knoxville whose band, the Tennessee Drifters, played clubs and parks in the Philly and New Jersey areas. Hatcher, another *Rockaphilly* candidate, last appeared on Knoxville's WKGN as featured singer with Clyde King & The Kentucky Ramblers in 1949, but moved to Philadelphia in the mid-Fifties). Jesse Rogers, the Arcade artist from Mississippi, and Frankie Day, the teen artist and originally one of the Dukes, were also on Rothbard's books.

Bernie Rothbard is familiar with many of Philly's mysterious label owners and prefers not to talk about them in any detail. 'They're mostly lawyers — you never get a straight answer from them,' he says, but Kal Mann and Bernie Lowe of Cameo are 'real nice people' and Rothbard produces a sheaf of friendly letters from Mann to prove it. They're along the lines of 'Let me know if there's anything I can ever do for Charlie', which is perhaps as it should be, since Gracie gave Mann and Lowe their first hit. It was 'Butterfly' and it was credited to Anthony September, a pseudonym for Tony Mammarella, then producer of *American Bandstand*.

Gracie, who lived only twenty minutes from the studio, appeared on *American Bandstand* ever since 1952, when it was a local event hosted by Bob Horn. He plugged 'Butterfly' until it took off, and Mammarella subsequently admitted taking $7,000 for a song he had no hand in writing. These machinations propelled Gracie to the top, although 'Butterfly' and his other hits, crafted with the old Tin Pan Alley guile, were right for the times. Expertly assembled at Philly's Reco-Art studios with Dave Appell on rhythm guitar, Gracie playing lead, Jerry Kilgore on drums and Lowe himself on piano, there was no denying Cameo's ability to make commercial records.

Whether you like them or not, those records were (and indeed, still are) a mild reflection of the material which Gracie performs on stage. 'Performing live is a visual thing and I've always liked to make a gutsy impact,' he says. ' 'Rockin' Is Our Bizness' — that's the kind of stuff I like to do, and we call it 'house-rock' back home. It rocks the house all right. I bought that record by the Treniers on the OKeh label in '53 and I'll never forget it as long as I live. But I've never been able to record basic rock'n'roll. The Cameo discs were successful, and I'm not knocking that, but the record companies have always believed that I fell into a different groove and, like most artists — unless they became immediate superstars — I had no control over what I recorded.'

After two big hits, Gracie believed he was owed more money than was actually forthcoming and he filed suit against Cameo. The matter was settled out of court but the company failed to promote his other singles and they never issued an album. 'In order to fulfill the contractual agreement between us they had to release four more singles, but there was no law that said they had to promote them,' Gracie recalls. Evidently, he never appeared on *Bandstand* again. Without that crucial exposure, 'Wanderin' Eyes' failed to duplicate its British success in America and his last three Cameo singles fell by the wayside.

During the Sixties, Gracie recorded, without success, for a slew of labels including Coral, Roulette, Felsted, President and Diamond. In the early Seventies, he was cutting blue-eyed soul for Vince Montana at Sock & Soul. The results (vibes, clomp, clomp, clomp) are rated very highly in the North of England where the last soul fanatics pay inflated sums of money for generally mediocre records much-prized for their obscurity. If any Northern Soul fans got past the Teds at Sunderland's Boilermakers' Club, they were in for a shock, although Gracie can sing like an uptown soul-shooter when he needs to. 'If it's a country song, I'll sound more like a country artist. I sing a song like it's written. If the soul songs call for syncopated vocal qualities, I'll use em. That sounds entirely feasible to me,' he says.

Forties swing to Fifties rock'n'roll to Sixties soul is one peculiar trip, and Gracie hasn't finished his journey yet. I asked him what he thought he'd be singing in ten years time: 'Good question; I hope I'll still be doing what I'm doing now. Y'know, this is the first time in my life that I've seen an audience with people from 16 to 45 all dancing and singing to rock'n'roll. Over here you've really closed the generation gap in this particular field of music and, whether trends change or not, rock'n'roll will always be a part of Charlie Gracie. It's eternal and it's part of my soul.'

Originally published in *Melody Maker* (20 October 1979).

Note   The Cameo recordings, and the earlier singles on Cadillac and 20th Century, have now been collated and reissued on the Cotton Town Jubilee label's *It's Fabulous — It's Charlie Gracie* (CTJCD-2) 1995.

Left to right: Lionel 'Butch' Mattice (bass guitar), Johnny Paris (tenor sax), Dave Yorko (guitar), Bill 'Little Bo' Savich (drums) and Paul Tesluk (organ).

4.4
JOHNNY & THE HURRICANES
Blowing Up A Storm

I'm not the greatest Johnny & The Hurricanes fan in the world, and when rock'n'roll LPs began to fetch fistfuls of notes theirs were the first to go. I kept the singles, however — practically all of them from 'Crossfire' to 'Salvation' to 'Kaw-Liga', right up to 'Money Honey' in 1964. Nothing generated that nostalgic youth-club buzz so much as an instant helping of 'Sandstorm', 'Red River Rock' or 'Sheba'. Those mechanical but once highly marketable rock'n'roll instrumentals tend not to appeal to rock's historians (there's no mention in *Sound Of The City* for example) and, if Johnny Paris has been interviewed before, I've missed the results. I didn't see his February tour either — a group of English musicians masquerading as the Hurricanes isn't my idea of a good night out — but it would have been churlish to pass up the opportunity of talking to the man who once sold almost as many records as Duane Eddy or the Shadows. Paris receives no income from the around-the-globe compilations of those original golden oldies and plans to re-record them, keeping as closely as he can to the monaural simplicity of the era in which they were made. That way, he can sell some more records and get to keep some of the money which would otherwise swell the estates of Irving Micahnik and Harry Balk, the Detroit entrepreneurs who managed and produced Johnny & The Hurricanes during the early Sixties.

From Walbridge near Toledo, Ohio, where he was born in 1940, Paris put a band together at Rossford Catholic High in 1957. Toledo had no legendary blues or hillbilly musicians to speak of, and Paris, of Polish and Czechoslovakian descent (real name Pocisk), followed jazz masters Charlie Parker and Sonny Rollins until the mid-Fifties, when Rudy Pompilli (saxophonist with Haley's Comets) and Sil Austin helped create the Top Forty rock'n'roll hits he was better able to identify with. The nucleus of his high school band became the Orbits who first recorded with Mack Vickery, a local rockabilly singer whose work appeared on the *Roulette Rock'n'Roll Collection*: 'I played sax together with Dave Yorko on guitar and Paul Tesluk on accordion. I don't remember the titles or label *[possibly Princeton]*, but we shot up to a little studio in Detroit and got a few bucks for it. Vickery was a crazy man with a left-handed, cross-eyed lead guitarist called Wild Bill Emerson who wrote 'Sheba' for Johnny & The Hurricanes.'

In 1959, the Orbits returned to Detroit to back up Fred Kelley and the Parliaments, another local group who'd secured an audition with Talent Artists Inc, owned by Micahnik and Balk. The Parliaments flunked the audition, while the Orbits were contracted to an agency whose roster included the Royaltones ('Poor Boy' went Top Twenty in 1958), Jamie Coe & The Gigolos, the Italian singer Mickey Denton, Johnny Gibson (who scored with 'Beachcomber' and 'Midnight') and, later on, Don & Juan and Del Shannon, whose career took off as the Hurricanes began to fade. 'It was a family,' says Johnny. 'We all helped each other out, and I played on a lot of their records — not always sax but tambourine or rhythm instruments too.' Micahnik and Balk — the 'Ira Mack' and 'Tom King' of so many composer credits — signed the band to their own Twirl label at a 1½% royalty rate and then leased the records to Warwick, Big Top and Mala in New York at a royalty rate of 8%. Since they took credit for most of the tunes, their own Vicki Music collected publishing royalties as well. Worse, the band paid for studio time: 'That was one of the misfortunes about being young in the music business. I was simply too naive. Harry Balk had managed R&B star Little Willie John during the Fifties and he had an ear for music. He couldn't read, but he was in the studio all the time and he'd sometimes dictate the tempo or tell the engineer when to turn the knobs up. We contributed everything else to the records and never got the credit — that's all I want to say. Harry's working with Motown in Los Angeles now, but Micahnik died last October, so he's out of the picture. Sure, I could have done with the money but I haven't invoked any long litigation procedures... there's always the artistic endeavour: they're down on vinyl and they're my records.'

In February 1959, the Orbits — Paris (sax), Tesluk (organ), Yorko (guitar), Butch Mattice (bass) and Tony Kaye (drums) — cut 'Crossfire', their first record for Twirl, at Carmen Towers in Detroit: 'It was an old movie theatre. We'd record way upstairs, and they'd pipe the sound downstairs where they'd taken out the seats. The sound would slap around inside this monstrous auditorium, where they had microphones to pick it up and feed it back to the tape machine upstairs. That was the only way we could get a reverb. David Sanderson of the Royaltones helped A&R the session, and he was laughing and sneering 'cos he already had a hit and didn't think 'Crossfire' was any good — we took thirty-two takes to get it right but we still got a live, exciting feel — not like the dry, cold sound you have today.'

'Crossfire', by the newly rechristened Johnny & The Hurricanes, was leased to Warwick and reached No. 24 early in 1959. Other big ones, recorded at Bell Sound in New York with Don Staczek or Bo Savich on drums, included 'Red River Rock', 'Reveille Rock', 'Beatnik Fly' and 'Down Yonder' — all antiquated melodies fired by a supercharged rock'n'roll beat: 'Harry Balk purposely chose material that was in the public domain, any copyright laws were over with and anyone could redo them and claim composers' royalties. It wasn't until the third album that we began to get wise to the legalities of the music business and it was only then that we started to get credit for the tunes we'd written ourselves. Harry still stuck to familiar melodies for the singles... 'High Voltage' ('Stackolee'), 'Salvation' ('Bringing In The Sheaves') or 'Revival' ('When The Saints Go Marching In').'

The exception, 'Rocking Goose' — a much bigger hit here than in the USA — was an accident. The Hurricanes were messing around with a riff when Johnny decided to change the reed on his mouthpiece: 'I'd go in the washroom, wet the reed and blow through it. Harry passed by and heard the squawk. Right off he said: "There's your next record: 'Rocking Goose'." So, after the strain on the organ, I just blew into the mouthpiece without the rest of my horn. It wasn't planned that way.'

Johnny & The Hurricanes toured Britain in February 1963, topping a bill which included Jimmy Savile and a host of *Jukebox Doubles* — English acts who impersonated American stars: Elvis, Brenda Lee and so on. I'd won seats in a *Record Mirror* competition by naming my three favourite Johnny & The Hurricanes records (ticket sales must have been poor) and I now fished around for the programme, a priceless artefact with a 9x6 glossy photo of Paris on the front. 'Heh, look at that, I'm still wearing the same ring,' smiled Johnny proffering a pinkie engulfed by an expensive-looking diamond band, the only visible reminder of stardom. It's often suggested that the Mk. II Hurricanes who came here sixteen years ago — Eddie Waganfeald (organ), Billy Marsh (guitar), Bobby Cantrall (bass) and Jay Drake (drums) — were downright imposters used strictly for tours. Back in New York, a group of black sessionmen led by T.J. Fowler were allegedly laying down the real thing — a precedent which established itself as far back as 'Beatnik Fly' in 1960.

Paris is bewildered by these accusations: 'Now that's funny, that really tickles me. Nobody could be hired to play that sax with that drive on those kind of records and come up with that kind of feel. T.J. Fowler was a big, black, forty year old pianist who wrote 'Crossfire', 'Rocking Goose' and a lot of songs for Harry and Irv, but he never played a saxophone in his life. Sure, there were tympani drums by guys from the New York Philharmonic on 'Down Yonder', Kai Winding's trombone section and Billy Butler from Bill Doggett's band on the *Big Sound* album, but the meaty stuff... bass guitar, lead guitar, organ, drums and sax, that was me and my band everytime. Nobody else could have played that, and nobody else did.'

As the hits faded, personnel changed even more rapidly. There's a clutch of fanzines devoted to rock'n'roll instrumentals and Johnny's suitcase was stuffed full of *New Gandy Dancer*; I'd keep an eye out for that one if you've a thirst for further detail. He'd no idea why his records were switched from Warwick to Big Top to Mala; his contract was always with Twirl and he never answered to any other company. When Twirl dropped the Hurricanes in 1965, Paris formed his own label, Atila, and for the next five years he let his hair grow long and performed a variety of stillborn material including 'The Saga Of The Beatles'. Strangely enough, his name was not among those dragged out of retirement for the *Rock & Roll Revival* shows: 'I was very surprised by it. I sent Richard Nader a bunch of promotional material but he never got back to me. Why, I don't know. Well... if I said what I really thought I'd only surround myself with problems and it might hurt the areas in which I'm doing business now.'

Paris still plays weekends around Toledo with a pool of musicians he can count on but during the week he's plain John Pocisk with Glass City Talent, his own booking agency in South Maumee, Ohio. Of the other Hurricanes, Paul Tesluk operates a carpeting firm in Boston, Dave Yorko works in Rossford, Bo Savich is a taxidermist in Detroit and Mattice clocks in at Toledo's Chrysler plant. Paris kept on playing and he's pleased about it: 'This is my anniversary, twenty years in the music business, twenty years to the month since I cut 'Crossfire'.'

Originally published in *Melody Maker* (24 March 1979).

4.5
LINK WRAY
A Link With The Past

The recordings which stretch from the million-selling 'Rumble' in 1958 to 'Good Rockin' Tonight' in 1965 are what Link Wray is all about; a succession of jagged guitar screams and occasional wild vocals with plenty of enthusiasm and no pretence. His reputation tends to rest on his work as a premier rock'n'roll guitarist, the greasy anarchist with vicious timing and a raw, 'jump-right-into-it' approach. I liked the Robert Gordon albums with their welter of adept guitar styles, but Link in the Seventies has often smacked of a recorded search for a new musical identity when the old one suited him best all along. What with earthy, almost pastoral sounds of white gospel and downtown country via Polydor, derivative blues from Virgin and shades of heavy metal on Charisma, Link's music has fallen into more bags than a wrongly-addressed envelope, generally well away from the harsh, echo-corona'd instrumentals with which he made his name. I'll stick with those; they were the discs that foreshadowed countless garage bands and influenced today's giants: 'This is the King,' Pete Townshend has said. 'If it hadn't been for Link Wray and 'Rumble', I would never have picked up a guitar.'

Fifty years old last month, Wray is still a magnetic figure well-suited to a label with the Charisma tag; the jet-black hair, dark shades and gaunt Shawnee Indian cheekbones evoke an image of prowling malevolence which was crystallised by 'Rumble', but still some way off when he made his first records with the Palomino Ranch Gang in the mid-Fifties.

The bones of the story have been told many times, most engagingly by Michael Watts, who visited the Wray commune at their trailer home in Tucson, Arizona during the early Seventies and returned with a riveting feature, most of which found its way into at least two sleevenotes. It described how an impoverished kid from Dunn, North Carolina, learnt to play the blues, got expelled from school after a violent altercation with the assistant principal, joined the forces, where he contracted tuberculosis and lost a lung, recorded 'Rumble', which opened up the musical possibilities of the electric guitar, retreated in the face of rugged experiences with other companies and, in 1971, emerged from the family farm in Maryland with the first of three Polydor albums.

It's an atmospheric tale, but there are some missing links — notably Wray's first recordings, cut in Washington, DC in 1955 and sold to Starday, the Texas version of the Sun label, when Link was a twenty-six year old Korean War veteran.

Link's older brother, Vernon Wray, who went by the name of Ray Vernon and died of cancer in March of this year, had formed a western swing band in Portsmouth, Virginia, during the Forties. The youngest brother, Doug Wray, played drums, while a cousin, Shorty Horton, plucked a string bass. The Ranch Gang appeared at fairs and rodeos, featuring the material of Hank Thompson and Bob Wills but using twin guitars instead of fiddles. Link played one, while Dixie Neal (brother of Jack Neal who joined Gene Vincent's Blue Caps) picked the other. When the group appeared on live broadcasts hosted by Sheriff Tex Davis in 1949, Vincent himself accompanied the Ranch Gang on rhythm guitar.

Moving to Washington in 1955, the group were encouraged by Ben Adelman who'd discovered a host of C&W stars including Marvin Rainwater, Jimmy Dean, Roy Clark and Patsy Cline. They cut a large number of titles, including 'It's Music She Says', to be issued here on Chiswick, 'I Sez Baby', which appeared on Adelman's Kay label, and 'Got Another Baby', 'Teenage Cutie' and 'Sick And Tired' — which are unlikely to emerge until a British licensee acquires rights to the entire Starday catalogue.

With an opportunist's eye on the sleevenote to some future *Starday Rockabillies*, I asked Link to elaborate on these primitive recordings which, given life's twists, would now sell more copies than a reissue of 'Rumble': 'Ben was a good engineer who genuinely loved country music, and he'd built a one-track studio in the Portland Building, an old Government block which they've torn down. The songs were Ray's idea and he made the deals with Ben, who put them out on his own label or sold them to Starday, who issued them as Lucky Wray & The Ranchhands.

' 'I Sez Baby' was the first time I ever sang on a record 'cos mostly I played guitar behind my brother, who sang rockabilly, although it wasn't much different to what we'd always done. When I said "western swing", I really meant rocked-up versions of songs like 'Tennessee Waltz' or 'Bonaparte's Retreat'. We'd listened to race music just like Elvis in Memphis or Gene Vincent in Portsmouth. It was all a coincidence which didn't even start there. If you listen to Hank Williams you'll find he wasn't a traditional country singer, he was blues. Of course, his music was more controlled than ours. I guess Fred Rose took him in and cleaned him up, 'cos otherwise I'm sure he'd have been a rock'n'roller.'

Wray didn't sing again until 1960, when Epic issued his versions of Ray Charles's 'Mary Ann' and Jimmy Reed's 'Ain't That Lovin' You Baby'. The company let him cut R&B providing he agreed to record a pile of schlock with a big orchestra — 'Claire de Lune', 'Danny Boy', 'Tijuana' and so forth. Fed up with compromise, he joined Swan, a label with a

4.5 - Link Wray

dubious reputation, although Wray much preferred to deal with them: 'Epic was a big company looking for dollars and cents, they'd no feelings and constantly turned down material we sent them. We cut 'Dixie Doodle' and a lot of tracks at the YMCA in Washington, but they made me go to New York and re-cut stuff at the Pythian Temple. Whole albums for Epic never saw the light of day, but I really liked Swan and I have to disagree with anyone who thinks Bernie Binnick and Tony Mammarella were crooks. They were like priests in the music business, almost too good for it, and when they went under I felt so bad about it I didn't want to sign with a record company again: "To hell with it, I'll just put out stuff on my own label." Ray distributed the albums around Washington and we sold them at colleges I played, Dartmouth, Cornell, Colgate — that sustained me for a while.'

Apart from his brother's many records (Ray Vernon cut the original 'Remember You're Mine' for Cameo before Pat Boone wiped him out with a cover version), Link also played on those by Dick Williams for RCA in 1955 ('Steve Sholes sent me a letter saying how much he liked the guitar solo on 'Robber' '), Marvin Rainwater ('He's part Indian, like me, and my brother produced 'Hey, Good Lookin' for Star Dale'), Jimmy Velvet (the hit recorder of 'We Belong Together', who went on to manage a group of Platters and got bad write-ups for selling things that belonged to Elvis) and David Walker, *aka* Bunker Hill, who sang with the Mighty Clouds Of Joy before reaching the Top Forty with the devastating 'Hide And Go Seek' in 1962. One-hit wonder perhaps, but Walker's scream mid-way through Part Two is one of the greatest moments in pop history and he's a worthy footnote to the Wray legend. 'David came in with the song, which he'd written, and asked if I'd sing it. Once I heard him do it, I knew he had to record it, but he was afraid 'cos he was singing nothing but gospel. We thought of giving him another name, so's the Mighty Clouds wouldn't have to know about it. We were gonna call him 'Four H' Stamp *[sociological note: 'Four H Clubs' are for straight-laced country kids who do good deeds — it stands for Health, Happiness, probably Honour and something else, Homosexuality, perhaps]* but we settled for 'Bunker Hill'.

'The record was cut at the Portland Building and me, Ray, Doug and a young kid, Bobby Howard, are on it, playing, screaming and carrying on. David really felt the song and it was down in three takes to keep it fresh. Ray took the master to Amy–Mala and, although it was a hit, we had trouble getting it played on account of the words, lines like: *'Will you put down that thing you got in your hand'* and other doubtful stuff. We tried to make an album, but the Mighty Clouds Of Joy found out and things gotta little haywire; David was mixed-up too, he didn't know whether he wanted to be a religious singer or a rock'n'roll shouter.'

Collectively, the Wray family has made some seventy singles and more than twenty albums – including those on little-known labels like Record Factory, Music City and Vermillion, who put out the curious *Tribute To Shorty Horton* which rounded up Swan out-takes by Link and Roy Buchanan. 'Shorty got him a job in a country band with guys who drank a lot, and he died of cirrhosis of the liver around 1974. I was in San Francisco then and had no say in the album — the same people called when Ray passed away, but I said: "No tributes, it's a small family matter."

'Roy Buchanan, though, is a great friend and a fine guitarist. He didn't become big news until John Lennon tried to hire him, but he was always streets ahead, even on Swan. He made a whole album called *The Jam [issued as by Bobby Gregg]* and didn't even get his name on it.'

Link tells these stories in the sort of friendly, outgoing way which leaves you wanting more, but our time was coming to an end and we hadn't discussed the *Bullshot* album (Charisma CAS-1143), most of which was recorded a couple of years ago when Link and Robert Gordon were produced by Richard Gottehrer in New York. Apart from 'Don't', which Wray recorded as a working track for Gordon (who couldn't sing it as well as Link), 'Rawhide' and 'Snag' (which first saw life as 'The Swag' on the flip of 'Rumble'), it's just another contemporary band record with rock songs on it. To say that the solos are better than the vocals is not to deride Wray's voice, which is as mean, slurred and greasy as ever — just that the best moments ('Snag', 'Rawhide' and 'Switchblade') are those on which the unequalled picker of rock'n'roll instrumentals steps back from the microphone and cuts loose on tracks that would sound great among a pile of ten on the old auto-changer. A whole new album of stuttering guitar crackers would go down a treat but, like Roy Buchanan, Wray believes it's hard to get people to buy a record that has no singing on it. Besides, he's an intuitive musician with a relentless desire to transfer all his emotions to vinyl. 'It's always been hard to express feelings with notes, and if I did another instrumental LP the record companies would claim that I couldn't do anything else, and I don't want to be shut up in a box as an artist. I try to play my music to suit my taste, hoping you'll like what I've done, but I don't try to suit you or anybody else. I've just turned fifty and I don't try to live like I'm thirty again. My mood is today; tomorrow it might change — and if it does, all I can hope is that the public will understand. But in case you don't, then I'll include a tune like 'The Swag' and I'll reach you, even if it's only one song.'

For those who like a lot more songs without words, Charly have just reissued *There's Good Rockin' Tonite* (CR-30171), a collection of seventeen titles which originally appeared on Union Pacific in 1972. It's where we came in: from 'Rumble' to 'Jack The Ripper' to the 'must have' title track, it's as representative of good, early Wray as any album I've heard. Buy the Charisma, but get the classics first.

Originally published in *Melody Maker* (23 June 1979).

Baker Knight

4.6
BAKER KNIGHT
Good Knight

Baker Knight's songwriting — teen ballads for Ricky Nelson and C&W hits for Nashville's finest — has overshadowed an enduring, if less spectacular career as a singer of country, pop and rock'n'roll. Like many a Nashville tunesmith, he sees rock'n'roll as a long-gone fad and can't quite comprehend why anyone should want to dredge up quarter-century old recordings which didn't sell at the time (two of his best, 'Bring My Cadillac Back' and 'Just Relax', have popped up on various anthologies since the mid-Seventies). On the other hand, he's seen his share of dumps, dives and bankrupt record deals and he probably welcomes the royalties.

Thomas Baker Knight Jr. grew up in Birmingham, Alabama, where he was born of Scots ancestry on 4 July 1933. His mother sang with a college band, but he inherited most of his talent from his maternal grandfather who played piano in a variety of styles. On the death of his father, Knight was sent away to stay with grandparents in Florida and Georgia but returned to Birmingham in 1951 and attended the University Of Alabama, where he played guitar in the orchestra. By now, he'd decided on a musical career and was engaged semi-professionally by local radio stations, where he and a friend played chromatic harmonica duets after the style of Wayne Raney and Lonnie Glosson. Influenced by country music, pop and R&B, Knight listened to Dean Martin and Hank Williams. (Very much later, Martin recorded a dozen of his songs, while Hank Williams Jr. took a Knight composition — 'One Night Stands' — into the C&W charts.)

His premier idol was B.B. King; his guitar-playing was 'the greatest thing I ever heard', Knight recalled. 'This was 1952. I was over at the black radio station in Birmingham before white people even knew they had such things. They played B.B. incessantly and I'd copy his licks. But I've always had very small hands which weren't large enough to go around the neck of the guitar — I played it resting on my lap with my fingers pushing straight down the strings.'

In '55 or '56 Knight recorded 'Poor Little Heart' for a Nashville label, Kit, owned by Alvin Bubis, cousin to the better-known Music City entrepreneur, Alan Bubis. Collectors' price guides list another early disc on Kit, 'Bop Boogie To The Blues', but I've not heard either. According to

Knight, 'Poor Little Heart' wasn't rock'n'roll and it didn't sell, but his talents continued to impress Alvin Bubis, who travelled down to Birmingham to produce 'Bring My Cadillac Back' in 1956. Knight's group, the Knightmares — A.D. Derby (piano), Nat Toderice, Glenn Lane (saxes), Shuler Brown (bass) and Bill Weinstein (drums) — cut the disc in a tiny studio with one microphone that picked up everything. Originally issued on Kit, 'Bring My Cadillac Back' casts off energy rays in all directions and shows that Knight could have been a real contender in the rock'n'roll posterity stakes. Bubis negotiated a contract with Decca who shifted 40,000 copies in two weeks, but the big Northern stations refused to play a record which resembled nothing so much as a free commercial. The group's subsequent disintegration had as much to do with Knight's introspection as bad breaks. Their rumbustious act brought Alabama audiences to their feet but Knight invariably flunked big package tours. He enjoyed playing small clubs, but larger crowds scared him to death and he rejected opportunities to tour wider afield. He began drinking heavily too, and his next session, cut in New York in 1957, produced the chaotic 'Reelin' And Rockin''. Semi-plastered, Knight and his saxman carouseltheir way through take after take and turned white when they heard the playbacks. Decca, of course, went ahead and released it. Six months later, in conditions of abstinence, Knight cut 'Love-A, Love-A, Love-A', a better record which was covered by would-be Texan teen idol, Milton Allen.

With few exceptions, Knight's Decca and Coral output (fourteen titles between 1956-59) suffered from hamfisted choral accompaniment and hack, over-orchestrated arrangements. His corpulent ballads snag few threads of attention, but other rockers have their moments including 'Pretty Little Girl' (tough guitar solo) and the Elvis-ish 'Oh Yeah'. But only two tracks have really stood the test of time: 'Just Relax' (with a guitar solo from Eddie Cochran, who also played on 'Takin' A Chance') and, obviously, 'Bring My Cadillac Back', Knight's Decca debut recently revived by Cincinnati's new wave rockabilly band, the Customs.

In 1958, Knight flew to L.A. on the promise of a Hollywood film part. When that fell through, he sat around his hotel pool picking his guitar and condemning Hollywood's phoniness to anyone who'd listen. Jerry Capehart, who managed Eddie Cochran, shared the same hotel and thought the two guitarists had much in common, although Knight admits that Eddie could outplay him three ways from Sunday: 'I'm telling you, the licks Eddie played were truly ahead of his time. I was totally overawed and, in a way, it hurt my confidence. It was party-time, we'd sit around drinking together while he fooled around with ideas. I was taking a nap when he came up with 'Summertime Blues', but I'm happy to say I was there when he wrote it.'

Sharon Sheeley, Cochran's girlfriend, had just written 'Poor Little Fool' for Ricky Nelson, who was looking for further material. She brought Nelson along to Knight's apartment and Knight ran through 'I Got A

Feeling' and 'Lonesome Town', a song which described his emotions when he first arrived in Hollywood. Nelson liked both. 'Two days later, I got a call from his manager who asked if I'd be willing to accept $2,000. I don't think I could talk for ten minutes, 'cos I was down to 37¢ in a glass jar and I'd never had more than $300 in my pocket at any time. Two months later, Ricky's manager took me to Imperial to get another cheque for $8,000 — I couldn't believe my eyes!'

'Lonesome Town' and 'I Got A Feeling' both made the Top Ten late in 1958. Thereafter, Ricky Nelson snatched up Knight's songs before the ink had dried. Apart from the hits — 'Never Be Anyone Else But You', 'Sweeter Than You', 'I Wanna Be Loved', 'Mighty Good', 'Right By My Side', 'You Are The Only One', 'I Need You' (all of them chart entries between 1959 and 1962), Nelson lapped up another fourteen titles including snappy rockers, gospel songs like 'Glory Train' and lots of soppy ballads ripe with teenage angst. 'Every time I finished a song, he'd go right off and cut it.' There were good reasons for this; not only did Rick like the songs, Knight also gave him the publishing. The practice was then so widespread that *Music Reporter*'s *1961 Artist Yearbook* could state, quite simply, that Knight was selling his songs to Ricky Nelson.

Nelson also appreciated the feel of Knight's demos, especially the guitar breaks which enlivened many a dull but fashionable teen ballad. Knight claims that most were played by Eddie Cochran, although incontrovertible evidence is now as elusive as the Holy Grail. 'Eddie played so well on a number of demos. It was one of the things that inspired Ricky Nelson to record the songs.'

Flushed with Nelson's success, Knight hauled his demos around other companies in L.A. including RCA, where he tried to place 'The Wonder Of You' with Perry Como. The A&R man turned it down: 'Ray Peterson was in the office and his manager told me they'd take the song if I gave up the publishing. I refused and walked to the door. They dragged me back and recorded it within a week. The arranger, Shorty Rogers, used a lot of my ideas.' A Top Thirty hit for Ray Peterson, 'The Wonder Of You' was revived by Elvis Presley, who topped worldwide charts in 1970. It's Knight's best-seller (out of eight hundred compositions) and he's glad it's now associated with his all-time favourite rock singer.

The song also gained him a short-lived recording deal with RCA in 1960, but his two singles didn't mean a light. Other discs for Jubilee, Kick (sizzling guitar instrumentals), Chess, Challenge, Everest, Daja, Domain (the novelty rocker 'I'm The Wolfman', erroneously credited to Round Robin), Another Record Co, Checker, Happy Tiger, Reprise and Warner Brothers disappeared down the same chute to oblivion. While the interval between his recording sessions increased, he has never stopped writing and his songs have been sung by artists as diverse as Frank Sinatra, Sonny Knight, Joe Stampley, Eddy Arnold, Jerry Wallace, Pat Boone, the Platters, Sammy Davis Jr. and Dave Dudley, who took 'Cowboy Boots' to the top of the C&W charts in 1963. A witty little number (*'Oh give me a home where the swimming pools roam'*), it reflected Knight's still-thriving cynicism towards Hollywood.

In the Seventies he was based in Nashville, where he achieved further success with 'Don't The Girls All Get Prettier At Closing Time'. Mickey Gilley's Top Five C&W hit won the Academy Of Country Music's *Song Of The Year Award* in 1976. Hank Snow, Dave & Sugar, Sue Richards, Jerry Lee Lewis ('I Don't Want To Be Lonely Tonight') and Hank Williams Jr. have also recorded Baker Knight compositions.

A Top Five country hit can mean $10,000 for its writer, but lately that's more than Knight has been able to achieve. He's still looking for that niche somewhere in between the Twittys and the Kristoffersons. Twice-divorced, he doesn't hide his scars and, although I'm not disposed to lay them bare, the road to Country Music USA has been as painful as that travelled by many a more celebrated singer-songwriter: 'It gets tougher as I get older, and booze, pills and grass don't help me. Funny how it works out — I came up with most of my best songs when I was a kid and I scarcely knew what I'd written. Now, rock music has gone off somewhere I don't even know what it is. But the first song I ever wrote was country and I think I've a future in the country field, where songs still tell a story.'

Note 1   Sleevenote written in 1984 for an unissued Charly album of Knight's Decca and Coral sides. I'm still owed £50 on this one.

Note 2   In 1996, Rockstar Records released Eddie Cochran's previously unissued acetate, 'One Minute To One' (Rockstar RSRCD-010), a Baker Knight song subsequently recorded by Ricky Nelson.

4.7
ROY BUCHANAN
Before And After

Roy Buchanan may be remembered as little more than a guitar player who achieved minor British chart success with 'Sweet Dreams' (No. 40 in 1973) and, if that's the case, it's no surprise that *Mojo* magazine should have left him out of their 1996 survey of *The 100 Greatest Guitarists Of All Time*. But the omission left his many fans as gobsmacked as the wholly disproportionate number of musicians who saw him play at London's Marquee Club and Imperial College back in '73. One reader suggested that the compilers had been looking for the definitive version of 'Hey Joe' in the wrong place. And that's the real point — who else possessed the virtuosity to quote Hendrix solos *and* build on them? A lot of Buchanan's material was undeniably mediocre — and most of his plain, sterile singers made one yearn for the whip-cracking vocal of a Dale Hawkins — but no amount of dreary major label albums could disguise the fact that Buchanan was the stuff of legend, an inspiration to many, and the finest white American guitarist of the Seventies. (That should read 'the Fifties' of course; the tragedy is that Buchanan was discovered some fifteen years too late).

Leroy Buchanan looked like an earnest college professor, but he called himself a typical hillbilly. Born in Ozark, rural Arkansas on 23 September 1939, he moved to the small farming community of Pixley, California during infancy. He told journalists that his father preached at the Pentecostal Church Of God but there's no evidence for that ('Roy,' said his biographer, 'displayed a prodigious talent for forging myth from the most mundane facts'). But his mother belonged to Pixley's Assembly Church Of God where the faithful fell into fits of ecstasy and spoke in tongues. 'There was real soulful music,' said Roy. 'Once a month they'd get together with the black church for a revival meeting and that's how I got into black music. I've always been partial to black guitar players and I used to collect their records. Blind Boy Fuller, Jimmy Nolen, Pete Lewis... the old black cats won't ever be beat.' Buchanan's father bought him his first guitar, a Stella, when he was five and he'd mastered the steel guitar by the time he was ten. He acquired his first Fender Telecaster two years later.

At fourteen, Buchanan was already something of a hobo, travelling as far afield as San Francisco ('I wanted to live with the beatniks') and Tulsa, Oklahoma. At fifteen, he met funk guitar pioneer Jimmy Nolen ('the first guy I saw bend guitar strings') and sat in on Johnny Otis's TV show when Nolen was ill. He continued to copy black musicians until he heard Scotty Moore playing on Elvis's Sun records. He cited 'Mystery Train' and 'I'm Left, You're Right, She's Gone'. Roy Nichols, who lived ten miles from Pixley and went on to play with Merle Haggard, was another white influence. Buchanan also admired Barney Kessel, Hank Garland, Chet Atkins and B.B. King.

At sixteen, he was playing with the Heartbeats, a band whose members included Spencer Dryden (subsequently drummer with Jefferson Airplane), Jim Gordon on sax and Tommy Oliver on piano. They played a number of L.A. gigs and accompanied local acts like Little Julian Herrera, the Pharaohs and Alis Lesley. 'Even then,' Dryden told Todd Everett, 'Roy could play all kinds of things. And he had his own style that was all but unique. There wasn't another white guitarist around who played like Roy.'

In 1958, the Heartbeats appeared on Tulsa's *Oklahoma Bandstand*, where Buchanan first met Dale Hawkins (though one source has them meeting in a Shreveport bar the day before both men were scheduled to appear on Tulsa TV's answer to Dick Clark). Buchanan remained with the 'Susie-Q' hitmaker for three years, taking his first recorded solo on 'My Babe', a zestful, bass-slapping version of the Little Walter tune that outshines all other reworkings. Apart from 'My Babe', early evidence of Roy's hyperkinetic prowess isn't always easy to find; he played on some of Hawkins's pop ballads, where lead picking was subjugated by strings and chorus. But listen out for his bristling, burnished tone on 'Lovin' Bug', the Holly-ish touches to 'Someday, One Day' and his capacity for great tenderness on 'Grandma's House', a folksy story written with Hawkins, who believed that Buchanan was the most proficient guitarist he ever employed (a roll-call which included James Burton, Carl Adams, Fred Carter, Kenny Paulsen and Scotty Moore).

Between tours and recording sessions with Dale Hawkins, Buchanan rapidly assumed veteran sessionman status in Shreveport and Los Angeles. In 1959, he played lead guitar on Merle Kilgore's D recordings, 'I Take A Trip To The Moon' and 'It'll Be My First Time'. Dale's younger brother, Jerry Hawkins, also benefited from Buchanan's expertise; his fretboard skills enlivened Jerry's rockabilly sides on Los Angeles' Ebb label. In June 1959, Buchanan recorded with Bob Luman who, like Dale Hawkins and James Burton, had emerged from Shreveport's *Louisiana Hayride*, the first stepping stone for many aspiring rockabillies. Buchanan played lead on Luman's version of 'Loretta' and rhythm on 'Class of '59'; he also played lead on Luman's second Warner Brothers' single, 'Buttercup', a fine rocker where he spins around the beat with all the little tricks for which, very much later, he was described as *'The Greatest Axe In The World'*. (Parenthetical note: contrary to earlier research, I don't think Buchanan played on Bobby Jay's 'So Lonely', and it

4.7 - Roy Buchanan

was John 'Sonny' Jones, Al Jones's brother, whose guitar backdrop characterises Al Jones's original 'Loretta').

In October 1960, Dale Hawkins played a two-week gig at the Rocket Room in Washington, DC. It was here that Roy Buchanan met his future wife, Judy Owens, who related the circumstances to Washington's foremost rock historian, Mark Opsasnick: 'I'd heard that Dale Hawkins was at the Rocket Room, and I loved 'Susie-Q' and all his songs, so we *[Judy and friends]* decided to go down there. When we went in, we were the only females there. It was all males and I thought: "Oh my God, what did we get ourselves into?" The first thing I heard was a guitar and I looked up and the guitar player had his back to us, which was kind-of strange. When he finally turned around, he was really unusual looking for those days. Picture now, this is 1960 and his hair was long with bangs and he was a weird-looking character. I noticed him right off. And he noticed me.'

Roy wrote 'I Found You' for Judy shortly after they met. They were married in July 1961 but the song didn't appear until 1964, when it was recorded by the British Walkers for Try Records (Try 502). Ex-Rayman Bobby Howard's name appears on the credits, but there's some doubt as to whether he added to the lyrics — it's more likely he may have changed the style of the song, helping to turn Buchanan's guitar instrumental into a Beatles-ish rocker.

Buchanan remained with Dale Hawkins, on and off, until early 1961. He wasn't always the easiest of companions and they fought on occasion. During one incident Buchanan attacked Hawkins with a can-opener and he still bears the scar on his nose. Violence was never far from the surface, particularly when Roy was drunk. He told Michael Watts that he had pointed a gun at members of the Ku Klux Klan in Georgia. 'I get into fights,' he said. 'It always happens to me for some reason. I can't let it pass.' Long but thinning hair, and neatly dressed like a strange, spiritual version of Val Doonican, Roy probably got beaten up a lot.

Buchanan subsequently played with Joe Stanley & The Saxtons and a group of former Saxtons called the Bad Boys. There's a record entitled 'Black Olives' by the Bad Boys (Paula 254) and, while it certainly sounds like Buchanan spitting out double-time notes on this Charlie Daniels-produced guitar instrumental, Roy told Alan Scheflin that the guitarist was Dimitri Callas, who co-wrote 'Black Olives'. The early Sixties also saw Buchanan playing a short gig with the Hawks, the Toronto-based band led by Dale Hawkins's cousin, Ronnie. Experience with Dale and Ronnie, both rockabilly greats, was almost mandatory for an up-and-coming guitarist. Roy Buchanan all too readily insisted he was nothing special but recognised that rockabilly very much depended on what the guitarist was doing: 'I never thought much about my playing. I was adequate, but Dale would really make you work. He wouldn't leave you alone for a second and I was all for that. He would sit and talk after every set, encouraging everyone to play better. Dale and Ronnie's style of singing just fits in with guitars. If they didn't have a strong guitar-player, they weren't half so good. I think Ronnie was looking for a guitar-player when he came to see me and Dale, 'cos his own man, Robbie Robertson, well he couldn't play a note then.'

For part of the early Sixties, Buchanan lived in New Jersey where he recorded with a slew of local performers and cut at least two records under his own name. As far as we can determine, the first solo record stemmed from a session for Harvey Moore, a Philly deejay who placed 'After Hours' and 'Whiskers' with the Swan-distributed Bomarc label in 1961. 'After Hours', originally written and recorded by Avery Parrish with the Erskine Hawkins Orchestra in 1940, was a huge hit in the black community, becoming known as the black national anthem. Unlike the version on Buchanan's second Polydor album, the Bomarc release (Bomarc 315) is a slow, wailing showcase with a ponderous, great beat and lots of little tricks which make your hair stand on end. Another disc for Swan itself is equally dynamic. Originally titled 'Teasin'', 'Pretty Please' (Swan 4088) echoes the then very popular Freddy King, while 'Mule Train Stomp' thunders along like Duane Eddy on a bad trip. I asked Roy about these recordings when he first came to England in 1973. Painfully shy and insufferably modest, he replied in the unassuming manner which only served to add to his mystique: 'To be honest, I didn't bother to hear the playbacks. Play 'em now, I feel like a good puke. 'Mule Train Stomp'? Heh, I was on speed then. It might be freaky for 1960 *[actually 1961]* but believe it or not, I was trying to make it commercial.'

Cut at Philadelphia's Reco-Art studio on 6 October 1961, 'Mule Train Stomp' is a little-known classic which may not have progressed beyond 'demonstration copy' stage. That same session provided two cuts, 'Ruby Baby' and 'Am I The One', by the white vocal/instrumental combo who accompanied Buchanan on 'Mule Train Stomp'. Variously known as Cody Brennan & The Temptations, Bobby & The Temps or Bob Moore & The Temps, they were forced to shorten their *nom de disque* to avoid confusion with the Motown soul group. 'Am I The One' is redolent of Jack Scott's tremulous ballads, while 'Ruby Baby', a cheesy version of the Drifters' hit, is redeemed by a guitar solo which still retains the capacity to surprise some thirty-seven years later: 'I was feeding back and using fuzz and distortion in the Fifties. Stuff white guys couldn't do at the time. I thought fuzz was a good idea then, 'cos no-one else was using it. They've about exhausted that busted-speaker sound now with all the fuzztones and big muffs.'

Billboard reviewed 'Ruby Baby' c/w 'Am I The One' (Swan 4089) in November 1961. The A-side was described as an *'exuberant performance by Brennan and group on lively rhythm-rocker with solid teen appeal'*. The trade magazine was just as enthusiastic about the flip: *'Emotion-packed rockabilly delivery by Brennan on moving rockaballad'*. Both sides were awarded four stars.

'How Important Can It Be', another October 1961 recording, remained unissued until the Nineties, but Buchanan collectors were glad to add this muzak dabble to the artist's legacy. Written by Bennie Benjamin and George Weiss, the song was a Number Two pop hit for Joni James in 1955. Versions by Sarah Vaughan and Teresa Brewer also made the Top Twenty.

The Temps cut other records with Buchanan on guitar including 'Mary Lou' c/w 'The Shuffle' (ABC-Paramount 10428) and 'Trophy Run' c/w 'Braggin'' (Daisy 502). Swan Records also used him as a session player on records by Danny & The Juniors and Freddy Cannon. He played the supercharged intro to Cannon's 'Wild Guy' and crops up on

'Teen Queen Of The Week'; check out the fade for a little flourish that re-occurred on 'Cajun', one of Buchanan's most engaging Polydor tracks.

Swan also issued 'Twin Exhaust' under the name of the Secrets. Buchanan's work with the Temps and Cody Brennan, for example 1962's 'Shake The Hand Of A Fool' (Swan 4103) typifies its era as surely as the chrome on a Cadillac, but the acidic, distorted 'Twin Exhaust' (Swan 4097) is a razor-edged precursor to heavy metal. This, contends Jas Obrecht, could pass for early Jeff Beck.

It was Freddy Cannon who introduced Roy Buchanan to Bobby Gregg, a white drummer who fixed a session at Philly's Soundplus studios in 1962. Roy went along, jotted down some chord changes and he and the renegade jazzers were soon into a funky R&B instrumental. Issued as 'The Jam' by Bobby Gregg & His Friends (Cotton 1003) it was a smash, Top Thirty R&B and Pop. However, it's unlikely that Buchanan shared any of the spoils, as Ellwood Brown, guitarist and bass-player with Link Wray, remembers: 'When Roy recorded 'The Jam', he evidently was promised that it would come out with his name on it and he would get credit for writers. Obviously this didn't happen. Somehow, the record came out and charted but the band was sort-of a composite, not a working band. So, for their first gig they had a large venue lined up somewhere and, of course, Roy was pissed because he didn't get credit, but he didn't let on how he felt. He just didn't show up for the gig! So here they are at the last minute, no Roy, and of course who are they going to find at the twenty-third hour that is going to be able to play 'The Jam'? You guessed it. They had to go on with the show and suffer the embarrassment of not being able to do their hit song. I don't think they ever did find a guitar player to do the song on stage.' The follow-up, 'Potato Peeler' (Cotton 1006) featured the first example of Buchanan's guitar harmonics, creating high overtones by striking a string with pick and thumb almost simultaneously. Roy would tell people that his hand had slipped.

By 1963, Buchanan had settled in Mount Rainier, Maryland. As Mark Opsasnick has indicated, tracking the groups that Roy played with during the Sixties is an insurmountable task. There were further gigs with Joe Stanley & The Saxtons; he was part of Bobby Howard's Hi-Boys; he cut 'I Found You' with the aforementioned British Walkers, and he accompanied wild black rock'n'rollers like Phil Flowers at the Hayloft and Big Al Downing, who was playing to SRO crowds at Rand's, a go-go joint on Washington's Eye Street. During 1965-66, he joined up with the Kalin Twins, best remembered for their 1958 hit, 'When'. Hal Kalin, who spoke to Opsasnick, was awe-struck by Buchanan's abilities: 'He was practically a genius as far as figuring out chord structures. He had the ability to play the guitar in such a manner that it sounded like he was not only playing melody, but chords as well. He could be the rhythm and lead at the same time, and if you'd turn your back you'd swear there were two guitar players on stage.'

During the mid-Sixties, Buchanan immersed himself in the drug culture and gained a psychedelic reputation with bands like the Outsiders, the Outcasts (where he was billed, in 1965, as *'Mr. Guitar Himself'*), the Washington Monuments, the Four Skins, the Jumping Jax, the Devil's Sons, the Fourmost and the Uncalled Four — 'the group everybody's talking about' according to the *Washington Post* in 1966. Jimi Hendrix caught up with Roy Buchanan and the Uncalled Four at Georgetown's Silver Dollar in August 1967. Bass player Stan Doucette watched Hendrix and Buchanan trading licks and thought Buchanan was the winner by several points.

In 1968, Buchanan settled down in Hyattsville, Maryland and joined Danny Denver's Soundmasters as lead guitar-picker, renewing an acquaintance which had begun several years earlier when Buchanan played on a couple of Denver's recordings. Denver, *aka* Cole Ghoens *aka* Sammy Gowans, was born in Hartsville, South Carolina on 23 June 1937. Inspired chiefly by Ray Price ('though I liked Elvis pretty good too') Gowans set out for Washington, DC in 1955. A flourishing club scene promised plenty of work for white Southerners from rural areas. He played piano for Patsy Cline and sat in with other musicians at hillbilly dives all over the city. In 1958, he was spotted by a producer for United Artists and taken to New York, where he recorded the brain-bending 'Rockin' By Myself' (United Artists 114). In the Sixties, Gowans recorded for Go-Go, Chancellor and Deville. 'Baby One More Chance', on Deville, featured Roy Buchanan on lead guitar.

Danny Denver's Soundmasters worked all over Maryland. Ellwood Brown often saw them at the Stardust Inn in Waldorf, 'when Roy would do these renditions of 'Malagueña' and 'After Hours' and just these spectacular leads that are still impressed on my mind today. That's when I thought he was God. That's when I saw the light, man. That's when I figured out there was nobody on the planet as good as this guy.'

Roy cut a handful of these numbers including 'Malagueña', 'Peter Gunn', 'After Hours' and Danny Denver's take on 'Let's Twist Again' live at the Stardust Inn with Danny Denver's Soundmasters, including former Link Wray bassman Shorty Horton and drummer Dickie Maughn. Other recordings, like 'Chowbay' and 'Park Boulevard Blues', were improvised pieces developed at Ellwood Brown's home in Park Boulevard, Marlow Heights, Maryland at around 4.00 am after a gig at the Stardust Inn. *'Those closest to Roy,'* wrote Brown, *'knew that he often played two gigs a night. The first on a bandstand, and a second, possibly in an after-hours club, the front seat of somebody's car or the living room of a close friend. Where, if the mood, the beer, the music and the magic happened to collide, it was not unusual for him to jam and compose through the night until sunrise.'*

During 1969-71, Denver and Buchanan set up shop at the Crossroads in Peace Cross on the Bladensburg Strip in Maryland. This ancient hillbilly nightclub — which played host to stripper Blaze Starr in the Fifties and Jerry Lee Lewis in the Sixties — soon attracted an audience of bikers and college students. Sadly, Denver suffered a major stroke in the Eighties, leaving him paralysed on his left side and unable to sing or play. When I spoke to him in 1996, I asked him if he'd like me to include any particularly fond memory in some other notes I was writing. 'I played with the best guitarist in the world,' he replied. 'The finest guitar player who ever lived. We were so successful in the latter part of the Sixties. Me and Roy, we'd draw thousands and thousands of people.'

It's been said that one guitarist after another — Jimmy Page, Eric Clapton, Jeff Beck — traded bootleg albums of Buchanan's work, and there are rumours of obscure albums on semi-private labels. I know of three: *The Best Of Denver with Roy Buchanan* (Wrayco); some tracks on Link Wray's *Tribute To Shorty Horton* (Vermillion) and *Buch & The Snake Stretchers* (Bioya Sound), which was recorded at the Crossroads and issued in a burlap sleeve in 1972. (It was reissued on Genes in 1992).

Tom Zito praised Roy Buchanan and the Danny Denver band in his articles for the *Washington Post* and *Rolling Stone*, and this led to a documentary film, *The Best Unknown Guitarist In The World*, shown on US public service stations in November 1971.

Thus it was that Roy Buchanan was finally discovered in spite of himself. He signed with Polydor and made a slew of albums, two of which sold over half a million copies each. There were further albums on Atlantic, Waterhouse and Alligator. In the long run, the advance notices were impossible to live up to. Success fuelled problems which revolved around drugs (heroin, mescaline, LSD... he spoke of doing enough dope to kill ten men), hard liquor, suicidal tendencies (he tried to kill himself in 1980) and a sensitive, introverted nature which seemed wholly ill-equipped to handle the limelight.

On Sunday, 14 August 1988, Buchanan was arrested on a charge of public drunkenness and placed in a cell at Fairfax County Adult Detention Center, Virginia. At 11.16 pm, he was found hanging from a grated window by his shirt. He was pronounced dead at 11.59 pm. The Sheriff's Department announced a verdict of suicide but, like many deaths in police custody, unresolved doubts have been cast on the official account. Others pointed out that suicide was consistent with a long history of self-destructive behaviour.

For my money, Buchanan was always more convincing than James Burton. He could do it all: trebly rockabilly breaks; squealing harmonics and the long, sustained notes which aped the steel guitar and the imitative screams of the Pentecostal Church. 'I didn't think people would dig my playing,' Roy once said. 'For a long time the white people didn't want me, only the blacks. I'm from the old school. I played in the Fifties. I consider myself the first white blues cat. I take pride in it.'

Note 1   This essay first appeared as an 'Echoes' column in *Let It Rock* in July 1973. It was expanded to form the liner note to *Roy Buchanan: Before And After* (Rollercoaster RCCD-3034) in 1999.

4.7 - Roy Buchanan

Note 2 In 2001, Backbeat Books published Phil Carson's biography, *Roy Buchanan: American Axe*. It's just the sort of book I most like; there's a huge range of first-hand sources, a discriminating eye for quotation and a lot of skill employed in shedding light on the man's short-lived relationships with a legion of largely unknown musicians. Carson is terrific on the major label shenanigans and all the crash and burn-out stuff. *Mojo* sneered because Carson 'writes as a fan'. All too often the word 'fan' is '*Mojo*-speak' for ocean-going thicko who can't write at all. Richard Younger's wonderful book on Arthur Alexander, *Get A Shot of Rhythm & Blues* (University Of Alabama Press, 2000), attracted the same sort of haughty put-down and it can't conceal the reviewer's professional jealousy. Fan or not, *American Axe* is beautifully written and hugely readable.

Note 3 Danny Denver died of congestive heart failure in Laurel, Maryland on 15 November 2003.

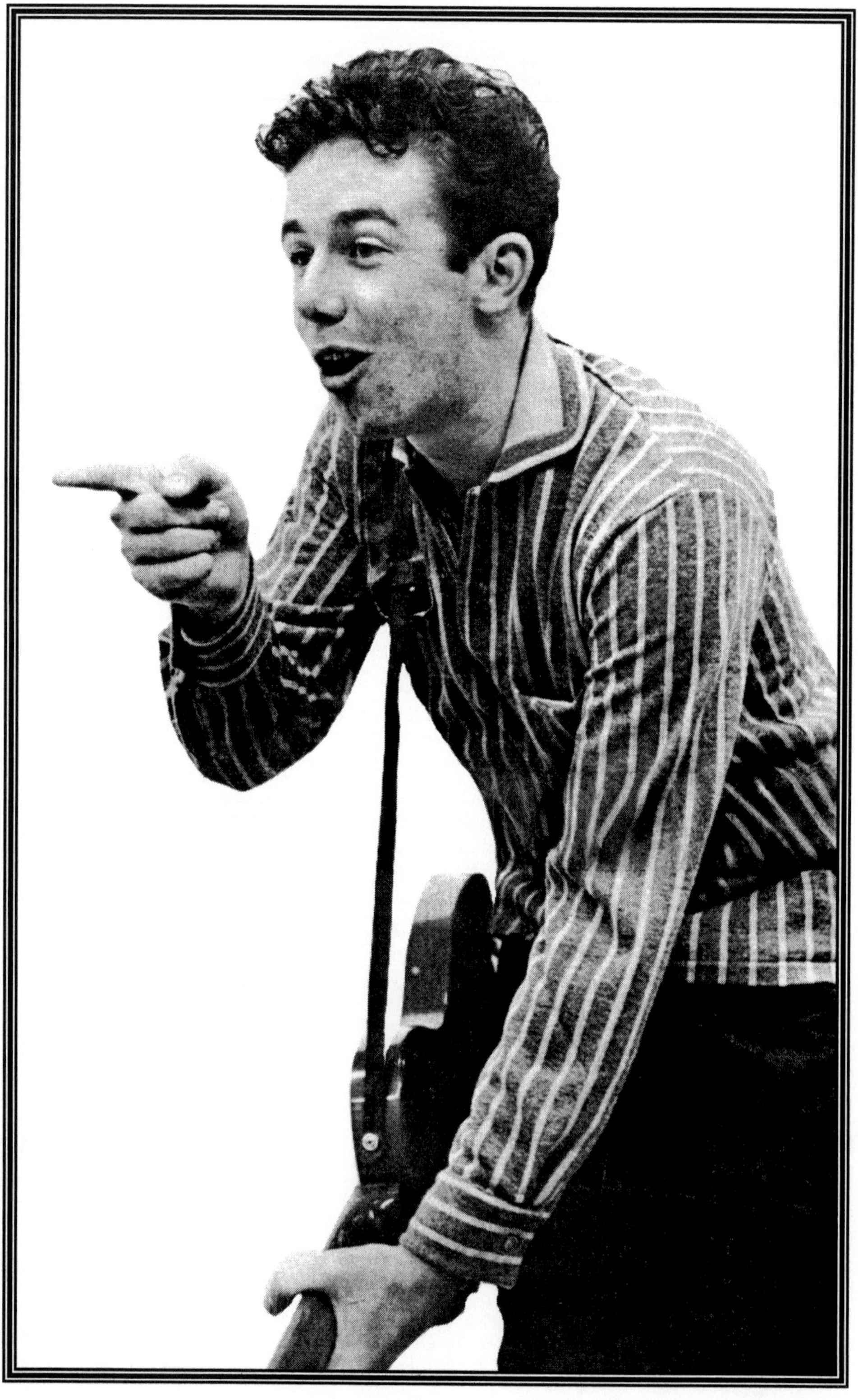

4.8

DALE HAWKINS
The Shreveport Tornado

Dale Hawkins may be short on the recognition that blesses other Fifties rock'n'rollers but that's a blessing of a kind. He's still a legend with records that are sought after and, for the most part, well worth seeking out. Although 'Susie-Q' is the song by which he is best remembered today, there was more to Dale Hawkins — a whole lot more.

Delmar Allen Hawkins was born on 22 August 1936 in Goldmine, Louisiana, a tiny pin-prick on the atlas some thirty miles from Ferriday. His mother, Estelle, taught in the tiny farming community's only school while his father, Delmar Sr, played a variety of instruments in local hillbilly bands. There was one sibling, Jerry (sixteen months younger), whose three singles on Ebb have long intrigued rockabilly collectors, though they made little impression at the time. Hawkins's parents separated when he was three, following which his father died in an accidental fire. Dale was shunted around a succession of share-cropping relatives in Mangham, just South of Shreveport, and Bossier City, where he attended high school.

Black music embraced Hawkins from all sides. He stood outside the local black church where the congregation screamed and rolled in the aisles. He was exposed to country blues in the cottonfields where he toiled alongside black field hands after school. Battered instruments emerged during breaks and Hawkins joined in on a guitar he'd obtained by selling newspapers. The experience left an indelible imprint on all that was to come. At sixteen, he enlisted in the navy, where he remained for a year and a half. After the navy he returned to Shreveport, where he abandoned a college course for a career in music.

Records by Lonnie Johnson, Howlin' Wolf and Guitar Slim filled the jukeboxes and Hawkins, who took a job as a counter clerk in Stan Lewis's Shreveport record store, helped to sell them, becoming an expert on the R&B hits of the day. At night, he sang the blues in clubs along the Bossier City strip across the Red River from Shreveport. This three-mile stretch was crammed with bars and honky-tonks like the Hi-Lo, the Sho-Bar, the Boom Boom Room, the Nite Owl, the Skyway and the It'll Do Club. Servicemen from nearby Barksdale USAF base regarded the Strip as the focal point of entertainment. It was the hot spot for local bands and the stuff of greasy high school dreams.

Hawkins's early bands included young musicians whose experience already embraced work on the *Louisiana Hayride*. This live country music show, networked from Shreveport's radio KWKH since 1948, was now emerging as an unofficial nursery for rock'n'roll wannabes. James Burton played lead guitar in a fluid, apparently effortless style which evolved from hearing the C&W stars he accompanied on the *Hayride* and blues guitarists, Gatemouth Brown and others, which Hawkins made him listen to. Burton was so young, he needed a police permit each time he played in a club. Fred Carter, another *Hayride* guitarist, also figured in some of Hawkins's earliest Shreveport line-ups. He went on to play with Ronnie Hawkins (Dale's first cousin) and Conway Twitty, eventually settling in Nashville, where he joined the A-team — the city's finest session cadre. The inner circle contained bass players like Frank Homer Kirkland who accomplished greater things with Bob Luman and Ricky Nelson, Tommy Mandina, an Italian-American pal of Stan Lewis's, and James 'Sonny' Trammell, an older man who ordinarily played steel on the *Hayride* and greatly influenced James Burton. Drummers included Anthony J. Tuminello and Nick Roppolo who, like Burton, was too young to hold a social security number. There were times, Hawkins told Cub Koda, when the band would ride to gigs on bicycles.

In 1956 Hawkins paid Bob Sullivan, KWKH's engineer, $25 for some post-midnight studio time when the station went off the air for a couple of hours. Hawkins's friend, Bobby Charles, had got on Chess with 'See You Later Alligator' and Hawkins hoped to follow suit with a demo tape of 'See You Soon Baboon'. Things happened in a flurry which becomes more uncertain with the re-telling, but it all boiled down to a management deal with Stan Lewis, who pitched the tape to Chess, the mighty Chicago blues label whose owner, Leonard, was a frequent visitor to Stan The Man's Record Shop, the main Louisiana distributor of Chess Records.

Hawkins's first single, released in June 1956 on the label's Checker subsidiary, coupled 'See You Soon Baboon' and 'Four Letter Word' — both products of the KWKH studio on which John 'Sonny' Jones's guitar licks are overwhelmed by an unknown saxophonist. The Jones brothers, Alton and John, played the same clubs and bars as Hawkins and Al co-wrote 'Swing, Daddy, Swing' for Dale's brother, Jerry. Dale helped Al Jones get a deal with Poplar Records, where Jones recorded the near-hit 'Mad Mad World'; the song appeared as 'Wild, Wild World' on Dale's *Oh! Suzy Q* album, but Dale believes he was the first to cut it.

Dancers were 'Doin' The Susie-Q' — steps which evolved from the Lindy Hop and virtually synonymous Jitterbug — at least as far back as the mid-Thirties, when the song, written by J. Fred Coots and Benny Davis, featured in the *Cotton Club Revue* of 1936. Harlem's Savoy Ballroom was at the forefront of these trends in black choreography, but the dance probably came up from Southern juke-joints along with blacks who sought economic security in the North. Either way, its popularity crossed barriers which divided white middle-class suburbs from rural black communities. Lil Armstrong cut 'Doin' The Susie-Q', but so did white bandleader Joe Haymes and blonde bombshell Ina Ray Hutton, who shimmied in front of her all-femme orchestra in a transparent chiffon trouser-suit. Billy Briggs's western swing band cut a song called 'Susie-Q' for the Time label out of Dalhart, Texas in 1950. Black blues variants had already formed a long queue: Lil Johnson's 'Grandpa Said Let's Susie-Q', 'Harlem Susie Kue' by Victoria Spivey, 'Stop Truckin' And Susi-Q' from Tampa Red and, on Bluebird in 1938, 'Susie-Q' by Sonny Boy Williamson.

None of this pre-rock history necessarily rubbed off on Dale Hawkins or James Burton who played Hawkins's magical creation on his '53 Fender Telecaster, thus supplying one of the most recognisable licks in rock'n'roll. Hawkins also wrote the words, although Stanley J. Lewis promptly copped a third of the credits. (Lewis tells people that he thought of the title because he and Leonard Chess both had daughters named Susan. He also claims to have helped assemble the lyric. Dale Hawkins emphatically rejects both notions: 'Those are the biggest damn lies ever told'). The remaining portion of the songwriting credits was attributed to Eleanor Broadwater, wife of all-powerful deejay Gene Nobles, whose show began with the Tarzan yells which embellished 'See You Soon Baboon'. I don't suppose that dubbed-on hollering was worth one-third of 'Susie-Q', but Nobles had played many a Chess record on the hugely-influential WLAC and Leonard Chess was happy to return a favour. (This sort of 'gratitude' was considered routine; check out your Chess singles for the names of deejays, local printers, programme producers and Alan Freed's bag-carrier).

Roy Buchanan, another of Hawkins's near-legendary guitarists, has said that Dale described seeing Howlin' Wolf in Shreveport circa 1955 crawling on his stomach and shouting Susie-something-or-other. Hawkins denies this, but readily admits that the riff bears a similarity to the Clovers' 'I've Got My Eyes On You' (Atlantic Records, 1953). The whole point, really, is that 'Susie-Q', this gnashing, blues-based maelstrom of sound, bore little resemblance to the fast, skipping rhythms of conventional rockabilly. Hawkins listened to Lightnin' Hopkins, Bo Diddley and Sister Rosetta Tharpe. Black music wasn't a brief flirtation; the pervasive spirit entered his bloodstream as a field holler and coloured his musical palate forever. 'I couldn't be a C&W singer,' he told Hoss Allen back in '58. 'I got to have that beat.'

Like 'Blue Suede Shoes' or 'Be-Bop-A-Lula', 'Susie-Q' helped show the way. Recorded in front of three microphones at KWKH, the combination of Hawkins's whiplash vocal, Burton's hypnotic picking and some extraordinary percussion forged a new and largely inimitable departure from orthodox rockabilly. The cowbell-and-drum patterns were the brainchild of A.J. Tuminello. He'd played with Hawkins in local clubs but couldn't make the date. In the event, Francis Ronald Lewis, one of Stan's relatives, deputised on drums. Hawkins has attributed the bass-playing to Sonny Trammell, whose loud but rudimentary fingering adds a muddy ambiance to the record: 'Sonny had the only electric bass in town. I know it was him.' A contract filed with the musicians' union and dated 14 February 1957, lists Hawkins, Burton and Lewis together with the names of Tommy Mandina, James E. Martin and Edward Lee Copland, but Hawkins is '1000%' sure Trammell played bass (as opposed to Mandina), and he doesn't remember Martin or Copland at all. In any case, if they were there, they're inaudible.

Maylon Humphries — James Burton's brother-in-law — maintains that he and his pal, Gene Scudder, were responsible for the handclaps and

general shouting. Hawkins clearly remembers Scudder's presence ('he was a boy who used to come into the record store') but thinks a couple of black guys were with him. If the exact genealogy is less than precise it's because 'Susie-Q' was worked up over several months, and quite different versions exist. Ragged doo-woppers can be heard on the flip, 'Don't Treat Me This Way', and they croon most effectively on 'First Love', another early Shreveport recording. The very first demo of 'Susie-Q', cut at Shreveport's radio KENT in 1956, also features a black vocal group.

The hit version wasn't released until the last week of April 1957, over ten months after Hawkins's debut. Leonard Chess wasn't too bothered until Hawkins sent a dub to Atlantic and excited Jerry Wexler's interest. 'Tell Leonard to shit or get off the pot,' was Wexler's uncharacteristically crude response.

'Susie-Q' eventually peaked at No. 27 Pop and No. 7 R&B. Hawkins became the archetypal overnight sensation appearing at the Apollo Theatre on an otherwise all-black bill and on the second of *American Bandstand*'s nationally networked editions in August 1957. 'I'd taken the record to a hop,' recalled *Bandstand*'s host Dick Clark. 'I had to play it for twenty-one minutes straight before the kids had enough of it. It went on the playlist the next day.'

While he never enjoyed another hit quite as big, the Fifties were good to Hawkins, who cracked the Hot 100 on four occasions — a tally which, to put this in some perspective, equalled or exceeded the fortunes of Gene Vincent, Larry Williams, Charlie Gracie or Dale's cousin, Ronnie Hawkins. Then again, some of Dale's misses are so well respected that their commercial failure seems all but unbelievable.

As 'Susie-Q' climbed the charts (where it stayed for four months), Hawkins was whisked up to Chess's newly-opened offices on Chicago's South Side. The second floor was rented to the Sheldon Recording Studios, where cowbell-driven rockabilly determined the shape of Hawkins's October '57 single, Dick Glasser's 'Baby, Baby' c/w 'Mrs. Merguitory's Daughter', (named, as it happens, after 'Mrs. Merguitory', a character in a Lon Chaney film). An AFM contract for 29 August 1957 lists Hawkins's musicians as Carl Adams and Fred Carter (guitars) and Leon Post, a *Hayride* pianist who also played with Maylon Humphries. (Chicago blues expert Dick Shurman has suggested that black guitarist Jody Williams is also present, adding a recognisable lick to the solo-less 'Baby, Baby'.)

Carter and Adams were among the Shreveport musicians who accompanied Hawkins on his first trip North. Carter recently told Steve Kelemen that he played on the *Oh! Suzy Q* album sessions while he was up in Chicago, and Hawkins confirms that. (Oddly enough, James Burton, who joined Bob Luman's band within three weeks of cutting 'Susie-Q', also claims to have played on the Chicago sessions, but Hawkins refutes this: 'Absolutely not. I swear to God. Burton was never in Chicago'.) Carl Adams, a former school friend whose contributions galvanised many a Checker session, had shot the first two fingers off his left hand during a boyhood squirrel hunt; the disability aggravated a natural shyness which wasn't helped by having to play a right-handed guitar left-handed with picks taped to his remaining digits.

Solid working bands were always a highlight of Hawkins's records. Adams was present when the unit returned to Chicago for the sessions which produced 'Tornado' and 'Little Pig'. By now, however, the hand-picked entourage also included the Mathis Brothers, the Lewis Sisters and, very possibly, Kenny Paulsen, another plectrum maestro whom Hawkins had met at a show in Boston (Hawkins aficionados sit around discussing the lead guitar parts on 'Tornado' and how much the second solo sounds like Paulsen's guitar work on 'Liza Jane').

Imbued with the tradition of western swing, Louis Aldine 'Dean' Mathis (piano and guitar) and Marcus Felton Mathis (bass and rhythm guitar) arrived in Shreveport from Georgia, where they'd played in Paul Howard's venerable Cotton Pickers. They recorded on Ebb (as the Marcus Brothers) and Argo (as the Brothers), eventually scoring with a cover of 'Tell Him No' as Dean & Marc on Bullseye in 1959. After further twists and turns they wound up as two-thirds of the Newbeats, whose 'Bread And Butter' all but topped the best-sellers in 1964.

Margaret and Rose Lewis, background vocalists divine, also recorded for Chess; one track, 'Come On, Let's Stroll', appeared on the album *Hits That Jumped*, though it was never a single, let alone a hit. Margaret, who came to Shreveport from West Texas in late '57, is best known for her records on Ram, and for writing such country-soul classics as 'Reconsider Me'. She shared Hawkins's obsession with R&B, and her singing is an essential ingredient of tracks like 'Superman' and 'Little Pig', written by Dean Mathis and *Hayride* regular, Merle Kilgore. Margaret recalls the two known versions of 'Little Pig'. The first, she says, was cut in Shreveport in December 1957 and was intended as a demo. An AFM contract for 16 December lists the musicians as Carl Adams, James Trammell and Nick Roppolo. Adams joined Hawkins, Dean and Marc and Margaret and Rose on the subsequent car journey to Chicago, where they re-cut 'Little Pig' at Leonard Chess's suggestion. Issued in April 1958, it was Hawkins's fourth single and another flop. Time for a re-think.

'La-Do-Dada' (No. 32 in 1958) gave Hawkins his second-best shot at the Hot 100. The choppy rhythm motif on this minor classic, moving from a major chord to the next major chord below and back again, was a novel, even progressive invention for the period. Hawkins has ascribed the cracking guitar break to Joe Osborn, who started out on guitar but ordinarily played bass. He's also placed the session in Shreveport in summer 1958 and said he used a second mono machine to overdub the background vocals. Margaret Lewis thinks the song was cut at Sheldon's, that they wrote it during the journey from Shreveport, and that Kenny Paulsen travelled from New York to be there for the session. Everyone agrees that the flip side, 'Cross Ties', was recorded in Shreveport; the alto saxophonist, Shelton Bissell (sometimes shown as Vizell or Bazelle) never ventured to the Windy City.

Hawkins told Stuart Colman that Al 'Puddler' Harris, a pianist from Jigger, Louisiana, played on 'Little Pig', but Harris, who has also been listed on 'La-Do-Dada', isn't too sure. He says he first met Hawkins when the singer drove by his Shreveport house with a guitar sticking out of the trunk of his car. Harris jumped in en route to Chicago, where he played piano on a session with black musicians. Harris's discography has embraced work with Werly Fairburn, Johnny Horton ('Honky Tonk Hardwood Floor'), Ricky Nelson and Paul Revere ('Like Long Hair') but, at this juncture, his recordings with Dale Hawkins remain uncertain. His nickname, 'Puddler', may have stemmed from difficulty in holding his drink. 'He was a trip,' Hawkins remembered. 'He got to drinking, got sick, heaved up all over the piano and never missed a note.'

As 'La-Do-Dada' continued its twelve week chart run, Chess issued Hawkins's only album for the label. This contained a glorious mix of Chicago tracks (distinguished by the sound of Sheldon Studios' state-of-the-art matched echo chambers) and more primitive rockers like 'Take My Heart' and 'Wild, Wild World', most probably recorded at KWKH. 'Heaven', which closed Side One, may also fall into that category though its origins are mysterious. Hawkins has said it was cut in Chicago with the Moonglows on back-up vocals, but the steamy combination of blues and romance (much improved on Werly Fairburn's original Columbia version) paints a luminous picture of humid Louisiana nights — you can practically hear the cotton growing. Carl Adams takes the solo, once described by the *NME* as *'the Bum Excursion Of All Time'*; curious how a record adored by some can be so easily dismissed by others. Adams, who also played with Tommy Blake's Rhythm Rebels and recorded for Dore as T. Carl Adams, was an overweight, myopic and self-conscious soul who finally committed suicide. This churchgoing son of the soil was also hooked on 'bennies', and the addiction increased his mental instability.

The chronology may be too muddy to pinpoint exactly when Telecaster genius Roy Buchanan first recorded with Hawkins, but they met in 1958 on Tulsa's *Oklahoma Bandstand*, where Buchanan was playing with the Heartbeats. 'I really liked his ideas and he liked mine. We both liked to drink,' Buchanan recalled. 'I found a guitarist to replace me, and I went on the road with Dale.' According to Hawkins, Buchanan takes his first and finest solo on 'My Babe'; the song has often been recorded, but this version illustrates Buchanan's uncommon command of touch and tone.

If Dale Hawkins is to be remembered for any one lifetime achievement beyond 'Susie-Q', it'll be for having hired a handful of the most accomplished guitar-slingers in rock'n'roll. How he was able to attract this regular flow of often-doomed but amazing guitar technicians is hard to fathom.

The Hawkinses, Dale and Ronnie, had the best bands in the business, yet neither play any instrument spectacularly well. The insufferably modest Buchanan, who made the electric guitar sound as nimble as an acoustic instrument, put it down to leadership and hard work.

'My Babe' was relegated to the flip of 'A House, A Car And A Wedding Ring', a syrupy cover of an English pop song. 'Class Cutter' *aka* 'Yeah Yeah' has an equally decadent air. Written by Richard Toops and Karl Silbersdorf, the song was first recorded by Dicky Stop on Chicago's tiny BEAT label. Hawkins's effort, also cut in the Toddlin' Town, features a full complement of black session men. The flip, 'Lonely Nights', is graced with a deep-voiced narration by Harvey Fuqua, leader of Chicago's premier doo-wop team, the Moonglows (and not Willie Dixon, who played bass on both sides). While 'Lonely Nights', a revival of Earl King's prototypical swamp pop blues ballad, is pensive and lovely, Hawkins's version of 'Class Cutter' is no tougher than Stop's and the Chipmunk-ish chorus might just be sillier. Nonetheless, it was his third biggest hit, reaching No. 52 in 1959.

Roy Buchanan could see what was happening: 'Dale's best things were never recorded. He always had dreams of Top Ten stuff — he strived for it — and I played what he wanted. I didn't enjoy it, but I liked the shows — not the big shows where we'd do 'Susie-Q' and two others — but the stuff we did in clubs. Then we'd do blues, spur of the moment things. Dale would make them up as we went along.'

For the most part, Hawkins's Checker output continued untarnished by chart-fixated opportunism. 'Liza Jane', recorded at WCAU studios in Philadelphia, features the strongest guitar-work of all. Hawkins's vocals are clean, clear and incisive but Kenny Paulsen's electric lead, kicking off a sonic landscape like a pound of Semtex, is one of the minor marvels in rock'n'roll. Okay, there were a lot of magic moments but this is still something special on a par with the dynamic undertow in cousin Ronnie's 'Who Do You Love' or the astounding solo in Billy Barrix's 'Cool Off Baby'. Simple, but unsurpassed by the pyrotechnics of modern guitar heroes. You could ask yourself why Paulsen, a Steve Allen lookalike who added glitter to Freddy Cannon's 'Tallahassee Lassie', isn't one of them. 'He's just got out of prison,' confided Buchanan in 1973. 'He did five years in there, almost died, got stabbed thirty-two times. He'd get to drinking and he'd be pretty violent — but he's a great guitar player.' Paulsen was a pulverising stage presence too; he attached his guitar to a saxophone strap so that he could twirl the instrument round in a spectacular circle. Asked about Paulsen in 1985, Roy Buchanan affirmed he was dead and mimed the act of injecting a needle into his forearm.

Kenny Paulsen's striking guitar playing also enlivens 'Back To School Blues', a novelty which Hawkins obtained from Eddie Mascari and Dutch Wenzlaff, writers and producers famous for such late Fifties hits as 'Make With The Shake' and 'I Got A Wife' by the Mark IV. They had endurance too, charting with another novelty, 'My Wife The Dancer' as Eddie & Dutch in 1970. 'Back To School Blues', though, was originally titled 'High School Blues' and first recorded by Mack Vickery on Princeton in 1958. On this occasion, Hawkins's version, studded with handclaps, guitar licks and high voice cut-ins, might just have the edge.

Roy Buchanan, another self-destructive guitar wizard, worked with Hawkins until the early Sixties. He also plays on 'I Want To Love You', Hawkins's final Checker single issued in February 1961. Based on the Coasters' 'Searchin' ', it compares very favourably with past glories. Jerry Leiber and Mike Stoller met Buchanan on Dale's New York sessions and went on to produce sides by him including 'Trophy Run' as by Bob Moore & The Temps. Apart from Burton, most of Hawkins's guitarists are now playing harps. Buchanan joined the litany of late greats in 1988.

Hawkins's reputation has received a boost with the emergence of newly-discovered recordings from his most fertile phase on Checker Records. There are fabulous early cuts like 'Teenage Dolly', a staple of Hawkins's 1957 stage show, and 'Boogie Woogie Teenage Girl' and 'Sweetie Pie' from Hawkins's second trip to Chicago with the Lewis Sisters in tow. Margaret reckons they spent a week there recording every day; Rose remembers that it was long enough for Muddy Waters to sit her on his knee. Shreveport veteran Tommy Blake cut a cowbelled version of 'Sweetie Pie' for Sun Records in 1958; a mediocre singer at best, he couldn't hope to better Hawkins's version. Other rockers, 'Boy Meets Girl', 'One Dozen Roses' and 'Caldonia' are hard, fast, loud and always listenable, as are covers of songs better known by Jackie Wilson and Oscar McLollie. Hawkins's love of black music extended to a warm friendship with Wilson and, although he couldn't summon the man's vocal gymnastics, his version of 'Cute Little Girls' has all the playful machismo of early pop-soul. Songs like 'Convicted' may sound dated today, but they shaped the smooth soul direction of black popular music and Hawkins sings this one with a sensuality foreign to most white rock'n'rollers.

On leaving Chess, Hawkins recorded for Tilt, Zonk, Roulette, Atlantic, ABC-Paramount, Go Gillis (a one-off campaign song in aid of Louisiana politician Gillis W. Long), Abnak, Bell, Lincoln and Paula. As his recording career petered out, he threw himself into other aspects of the business. None of his later records meant as much as the mid-Sixties hits he produced: 'Not Too Long Ago' by the Uniques, 'Western Union' and others for the Five Americans, Jon & Robin's 'Do It Again A Little Bit Slower' and Bruce Channel's 'Mr. Bus Driver'. He also produced the Five Jets, Peppermint Harris, Mouse & The Traps, the Blues Kings, John Fred, the Gentrys and the Bad Boys. Bruce Channel's 'Keep On', another Hawkins production, peaked at No. 12 in the British charts in 1968.

In 1975, Hawkins moved to North Little Rock, Arkansas. He licked a reliance on speed and hard liquor and set up a crisis centre for adolescents mired in drug abuse and other problems. Singer, songwriter, producer, rhythm guitarist, textbook rock'n'roll idol — Dale Hawkins has done it all.

Adapted from the liner note to *Rock'n'Roll Tornado* (Ace CDCHD-693) 1998.

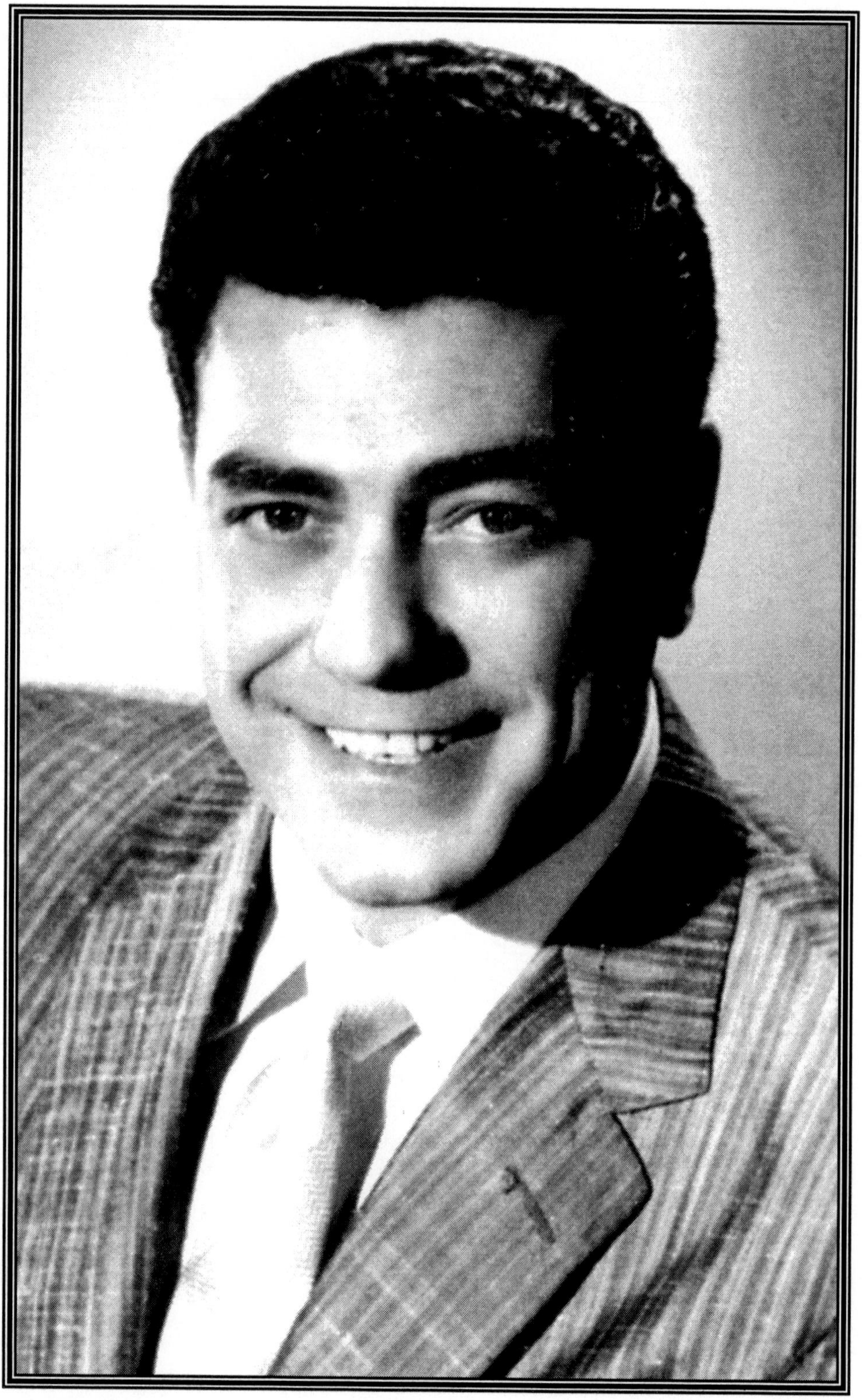

4.9
MIKE PEDICIN
Jive Medicin

To those who live by chart statistics alone, Mike Pedicin had only two hits: 'Large Large House', which hit No. 79 for one week in March 1956, and 'Shake A Hand' which stuttered to No. 71 during its two-week chart run in February 1958.

But there was more to Mike Pedicin than a mere three weeks on *Billboard*'s Hot 100. Coming of age in the era of Benny Goodman and Glenn Miller, he helped to develop a hybrid musical style which incorporated elements of swing and R&B and led directly to the commercial genesis of rock'n'roll. Some called it 'house-rock' — a reference to the casino lounges of Las Vegas and Atlantic City where many of the earliest rock'n'roll combos prospered.

Bill Haley & His Comets formed the vanguard of the movement by revamping Louis Jordan's sound and using Jordan's producer. Any direct comparison with other house-rockers would strain the facts, but there were several prime movers who gained reputations for staying power despite a lack of hit records.

The Treniers, a black band who gained their mass popularity on the New Jersey shore, especially Wildwood, were among the most important. Their handclapping, stomping, shouting blend of blues, swing and slapstick stepped out of Louis Jordan's slipstream and engendered a state of euphoria among clientele who'd lost their shirts at the blackjack and roulette tables.

But most house-rocking bands were white, and they stamped their Italian-American accents on a form of rock'n'roll radically different to the crazed rockabilly pulse of the rural South. The clubs and casino hotels of Philadelphia and New Jersey played host to Freddie Bell & The Bellboys, the Tyrones, Don Haven & The Hi-Fis, Jimmy Cavello & His House Rockers (out of Syracuse, New York), the Playboys, Charlie Gracie & His Wildcats, the Esquire Boys (with Danny Cedrone, who played the guitar solo in 'Rock Around The Clock'), Billy Duke & His Dukes and Dave Appell & The Applejacks (whose pre-Cameo records were Haley-influenced).

Many of these musicians would have been perfectly at home in the rhythm section of a big band, but the wartime economy had waned and big bands became economically unsupportable. Freed of the stiff restrictions imposed by large regimented sections, these bearers of the good news looked mainly towards looser forms of jazz and blues. Charlie Gracie listened to Joe Turner and B.B. King. He also bought records by the Treniers and Louis Prima, and went to see Bill Haley in 1952 when the band still wore cowboy outfits.

For Mike Pedicin, nearly twenty years Gracie's senior, the influence of swing music was deep and inseparable. His greatest inspiration was Charlie Barnet, perhaps the jazziest of the white swing musicians, and he claims not to have heard any hillbilly music before making records of his own. 'I played rock before Bill though,' he insists. 'He played hillbilly with drums added.'

Mike Pedicin was born Michael Pedicine in West Philadelphia on 24 October 1917. His father, a barber from Foggia in Italy, had married a girl from Hammonton, New Jersey and the couple had four children including Mike, who learnt to play alto saxophone at the age of ten. His father acquired the instrument from a local tailor for $50. At eleven, Mike joined the all-kiddie band on Stan Lee Broza's *Horn & Hardart Children's Hour* radio show. He polished his skills at Overbrook High School among kids from all cultures; Dee Dee Sharp and other Cameo acts would attend Overbrook High. As a teenager, Mike led a ten-piece band which played church halls, fire halls and school auditoriums.

Pedicin launched his career as the leader of small musical groups in the summer of 1940. His first combo, the Four Sharps, consisted of musicians from West Philly. Pedicin (alto), Maurice Belmont (vibes), Louis de Francesco *aka* Lou DeFrancis (bass) and the aforementioned Dave Appell (rhythm guitar) rehearsed in the spring and took up their first engagement at the Red Top Bar in Seaside Heights, New Jersey, in June 1940. By then, Pedicin, had married the former Marie Troncelliti and the Red Top booking interrupted the couple's New York honeymoon.

Like most nightclub musicians in the early Forties, the Four Sharps played cocktail music which was smooth enough for dancing, but not loud enough to drown barstool conversation. There was no drummer in the Four Sharps.

The quartet became a celebrated fixture in local clubs, most of which were owned by Frank Palumbo, who hired Pedicin in 1942: 'There was the Click at 15th and Market. And Ciro's at 15th and Walnut. And the 20th Century at 15th and Chestnut. And the Cove at 13th and Locust. And, of course, there was Palumbo's at 8th and Catherine. He also owned the Renault in Atlantic City and the Avalon in Wildwood.' After-hours clubs, like the Treasure in Center City and the East End on Rising Sun Avenue, catered for anyone in search of good times after midnight. Pedicin got to be on speaking terms with Frank Rizzo, the Philly police chief who frequently raided these joints.

House-rock can scarcely be separated from the mob-backed hotels of Las Vegas and Atlantic City (which is still the north-eastern capitol of legalised gambling) but if organised crime ever sank its claws into Pedicin, he isn't saying. The boys did, however, get to play with Frank Sinatra: 'It was 1944. He had just signed with Columbia Records and we were hired to accompany him at a party at the Ritz-Carlton Hotel in Philly. We had none of his music but knew most of the songs he sang. All Frank had to do was call out the song and give us the key. He must have sung at least fifteen numbers and we had a ball.'

By the time drums entered the group's line-up in 1950-51, their name had changed from the Four Sharps to the Four Men Of Rhythm to the Mike Pedicin Quartet (sometimes Quintet). And the personnel had gradually solidified. Belmont had left, as had Dave Appell, who would earn his place in history by writing 'Let's Twist Again' and a host of Cameo-Parkway hits. They were replaced by Sam Cocchia *aka* Sam Cook on guitar and Alexander 'Al' Mauro, who played drums and took most of the vocals. Nicholas 'Buddy' LaPata occupied the piano stool.

The band made their first records for Algonquin, a New York label owned by Robert Mellin, but no-one I know has heard them. In 1952, Pedicin was signed to 20th Century, Ivin Ballen's first label and the first in Philadelphia to record hillbilly music, which he did in 1946. But diversification was the key to Ballen's success. In 1948, he acquired Gotham and, under his direction, Gotham and 20th Century issued all types of music including blues, R&B, gospel, C&W, jazz and rock'n'roll. A handful of Charlie Gracie's best early singles including 'Wildwood Boogie' appeared on 20th Century.

Pedicin cut some twenty-five tracks for 20th Century and the label issued a clutch of singles during 1952-54. 'One Potato, Two Potato' (the Mike Pedicin Quartet with Joe Kuhn's Orchestra) is a jivey, swinging version of the Three Peppers' nursery rhyme on Gotham, while the saxophone-led 'Disc Jockey's Boogie' (billed as the Mike Pedicin Quintet) rivals Tiny Grimes's wilder boogie rockers. The rest were mainly jazz and pop, but check out 'Have Yourself A Ball' (Krazy Kat 819), a 20th Century compilation which includes a hitherto unissued take of 'Disc Jockey's Boogie' and the band's cover of Faye Adams's mammoth R&B hit, 'Shake A Hand'. Faye Adams and Savannah Churchill sold well in the pop market and another cover version by Red Foley went Top Ten on the C&W chart. But there was no pop hit for Mike Pedicin on this go-round.

Pedicin signed with RCA-Victor in 1955. The two-year contract was arranged by Pat Vacca, a friend and fan who used his wealth from a construction business to promote Pedicin's interests. For the most part it was the same guys: Pedicin (alto), Buddy LaPata (piano), Sam Cocchia (guitar) Lou DeFrancis (bass) and drummer-vocalist Al Mauro. Other musicians flitted in and out including Robert Sentenari (drums) and Louis 'Ace' Devecchis (piano, trumpet and trombone). Recording dates were supplemented by hand-picked New York sessionmen like Lloyd Trotman and Sam 'The Man' Taylor. All told, however, Pedicin changed musicians infrequently (Cocchia has been with him for forty-nine years), and the famous dictum of Benny Goodman's pianist, 'Once you're a bandleader, you become a prick, automatically', finds no favour in this case.

The first RCA session in February 1955 produced a cover of Buddy Griffin and Claudia Swann's Chess hit, 'I Wanna Hug Ya, Kiss Ya, Squeeze Ya' (Bull Moose Jackson also leapt on that one), and a version of 'Mambo Rock', a Top Twenty hit for Bill Haley who'd recorded it one month earlier. Pedicin doesn't recollect the producers as having much say but affirms: 'We shocked Hugo Winterhalter. He said he'd never heard five men play so loud, but then he'd never done A&R for rock music before.'

Bickley 'Bix' Reichner, who helped write 'Mambo Rock', played a big role in things Pedicin and Haley. Pedicin met him at 20th Century Records, where he was trying to sell some songs, and the two men became firm friends. Reichner had attended the University Of Pennsylvania and sung in Schubert musicals. During the Thirties and Forties, he was a reporter for the city's *Evening Bulletin* and wrote songs in his spare time. His earliest success, 'You Better Go Now' from the revue, *New Faces Of 1936*, was recorded by Billie Holiday and revived by Jeri Southern. In 1938, Tommy Dorsey had a best-seller with Reichner's 'Stop Beatin' Around The Mulberry Bush', which Bill Haley resuscitated in 1952.

Some sources say it was Reichner, then a deejay on radio WPWA, who suggested that the Saddlemen should change their name to the Comets. According to Marshall Lytle, who played in both, the switch was inspired by WPWA's programme director. Either way, 'Stop Beatin' Around The Mulberry Bush' became the very first record by Bill Haley and his newly-christened Comets.

'When I Go A-Dreamin'', another of Reichner's big band success stories, was a hit for Benny Goodman in 1938 and revived by Mike Pedicin on Malvern in 1957. Reichner also penned 'Fable Of The Rose' (another of Benny Goodman's best-sellers), 'Stop, It's Wonderful' (a hit for Orrin Tucker), 'Papa Loves Mambo' (massive sales for Perry Como) and 'Teenage Prayer' (Top Ten for Gale Storm in 1956). He won a *Freedom Foundation Award* for the anti-communist song 'The Red We Want Is The Red We've Got (In The Old Red, White And Blue)'. It was a hit for Ralph Flanagan in 1950. Despite all this, the best was yet to come: nothing in Reichner's catalogue of hepped-up nursery rhymes sparkles quite so much as the sure touch which Elvis brought to 'I Need Your Love Tonight' (Top Five in 1959).

A third session, augmented by Sam 'The Man' Taylor, took place in August 1955. Taylor and Pedicin blow their formidably creative brains out on Reichner's hard-swinging 'You Gotta Go'. The same date produced 'When The Cats Come Marching In'. This time, Haley took a leaf out of Pedicin's sheet music and recorded 'The Saints Rock'n'Roll' the following month. Everyone and his brother habitually annexed traditional songs in the public domain and Haley was no exception. He changed the credits to 'Arr. Haley', thus ensuring there was no free ride into the Top Twenty for

Reichner and Pedicin's adaptation of the New Orleans post-funeral anthem.

Reichner didn't get rich on Mike Pedicin's sales but the band relied on his material throughout their career. In May 1955, they commuted to New York to record a trio of Reichner's songs including 'Jackpot' and a first attempt at 'Large Large House'. A fourth song (not by Reichner) offered some solace to soft-pedalling programmers and ethnic fans. 'The Hot Barcarolle' — perhaps the only example of Venetian Rock — drew from the kind of song delivered by gondoliers ('barca' is Italian for 'boat'). This, of course, is long before it became fashionable to talk of 'roots' or 'world music'.

There's a bit of everything dance-floor in Pedicin's music. The jump blues tendencies meant the bass-player got plenty of opportunities to snap at his stand-up instrument, and there were times when Sam Cocchia's in-the-round finger-picking rivalled Franny Beecher's jazzier solos. The quasi-spiritual nature of Reichner's songs was heightened by arrangements built around Pedicin's wailing alto and lots of shouting and handclapping. Some of the arrangements may seem mundane today, but few sound quite as studio-generated as Bill Haley's Decca hits.

The Reichner–Pedicin formula finally paid off with a reworking of 'Large Large House' which provided Pedicin's first taste of Hot 100 mini-stardom. The flip, 'Hotter Than A Pistol', was written by Joe and Noel Sherman, the Brooklyn-born brothers whose credits include 'Ramblin' Rose', 'Eso Beso', 'Por Favor' and 'To The Ends Of The Earth'. In 1955 they were flush with their first major hits: 'Jukebox Baby' (Top Ten for Perry Como) and 'Graduation Day' (Top Twenty for the Rover Boys). But the Sherman luck didn't rub off on Mike Pedicin.

RCA's New York studio was booked for the penultimate session in May 1956. The songs chosen included Bix Reichner's mock-gospel, 'Save Us Preacher Davis', and 'The Beat', penned by Kal Mann and Bernie Lowe and also recorded by Billy May, one-time trumpet player with Pedicin's major inspiration, Charlie Barnet. 'Teenage Fairy Tales' was written by Frankie Day, a local bass-player with Billy Duke & His Dukes. Day would manage Bobby Rydell for some fourteen years.

Pedicin's final RCA single coupled 'The Hucklebuck' with Frank Pingatore's 'Calypso Rock'. This last sounds very much as if it was written for Bill Haley, but the kiss-curled pioneer never recorded it. Pingatore, Haley's hairdresser from West Chester, Pennsylvania, claimed a Juilliard education. He helped Bill with some of his arrangements and managed some of his publishing companies. At the age of twenty-four he wrote 'Happy Baby' (the flip of 'Dim, Dim The Lights') and another of Haley's Top Twenty hits, 'Two Hound Dogs'. He snuck off to manage the Jodimars (three ex-Comets) and penned most of their songs including 'Clarabella' and 'Well Now Dig This'. But 'Calypso Rock' flopped, as did 'The Hucklebuck', though three years on Chubby Checker would have a vocal hit with the same tune. Pedicin's version was probably inspired by

Paul Williams, a fellow altoist whose record dominated the R&B charts in 1949. Then again, Tommy Dorsey and Frank Sinatra had the pop hits.

After nine singles in two frustrating years, Mike Pedicin's RCA career came to an end. Various items remained in the can including 'Hi-Yo Silver', 'T.D.'s Boogie' and two raw versions of Doc Starkes's 'Rock-A-Bye'. 'Hi-Yo Silver' — the Lone Ranger's battle-cry — was already a blues standard with versions, in one form or another, by Charlie Gonzales, Harold Burrage, Jimmy Rushing and Grant Jones. Pedicin probably took his cue from the 1952 version by the Treniers. He played Vegas with them in 1957.

Tommy Dorsey ('T.D.') delivered the first fully orchestrated arrangement of 'Pinetop's Boogie Woogie' in 1938; his version sold over four million copies for Victor and inspired numerous bandleaders including Pedicin, whose efforts remained unheard until the release of a Bear Family collection in 1993. Ironically, Don Covay would rewrite the tune as 'Pony Time', providing a chart-topper for Chubby Checker in 1961.

The Bear Family anthology also exhumed parts of a live concert at Detroit Stadium. It's a poorly (ahem) miked and fragmentary picture, but listening now it's briefly possible to imagine what the house-rock age must have been like; the nights when a wailing alto and a rhythmic punch were enough to thrill a jumping sweatbox. While the band worked clubs and casinos as far afield as Las Vegas and Canada, they didn't tour and never stayed away from home too long. Each summer for two decades, they were based at the Bay Shores Club in Somers Point, New Jersey. Grace Kelly was fond of dropping by Bay Shores; film stars, socialites and college swells danced there on the concrete floor as the Mike Pedicin Quartet rocked 'Shake A Hand' three times in a row.

Pedicin re-cut 'Shake A Hand' for Cameo in 1957. 'One mike!' he recalls. 'We stood around it, singing into it, doing instrumentals. The mike never moved from the height it was. When I was doing a horn solo, I had to bend down in order to get the mike and sax lined up.'

This time, assisted by a Christmas Day appearance on *American Bandstand*, Pedicin was back in the Hot 100, albeit briefly. Nevertheless, the re-tooled spiritual became a theme vehicle for his jaunty sax riffs and the Cameo disc is still the one for which he's best remembered.

There were problems when it came to collecting off 'Shake A Hand': 'I didn't make any money from it. At least, not directly. The record was big — bigger than I thought it was in those days. We didn't have lawyers to run things. It was a shame. None of the guys like me had a lawyer who'd say "Look, there has to be some money".'

There was nothing else on Cameo, not even a follow-up, but the band continued making records into the Sixties including albums on Apollo. Other discs appeared on Platter, Federal and ABC-Paramount, for whom Reichner and Pedicin drummed up 'Gotta Twist' in 1962.

For the past forty years, Pedicin has lived in the same single brick house in Ardmore, Pennsylvania. A black door knocker in the shape of a musical note is the only thing that distinguishes his house from others in a quiet neighbourhood of business and professional people. He still plays at parties and bar mitzvahs, but people generally come to him — some of them old-time fans who want a band for their daughters' weddings.

Nowadays, it's the Mike Pedicin Trio. Buddy LaPata died in a car accident in 1983 and Lou DeFrancis has lost his eyesight. Jimmy Valerio replaced the malleable voice of Al Mauro in 1978. Bix Reichner, songwriter-in-chief, died a couple of years ago; he was 82.

The Pedicin Trio played at the reunion of Bill Haley's Comets at Philly's Academy of Music in October 1987. Comet Dick Richards turned to writer David Hirschberg: 'He could have been as big as Bill or the others, only he didn't want to leave Philadelphia. If you didn't tour, you didn't get to be a star.'

The Pedicins celebrated their 50th anniversary in June 1990. They have a daughter who lives nearby and a son, Michael Jr, a resident of Penn Wynne. Pedicin the Younger, a reed player himself, leads his own group which recorded for Philadelphia International. It's a neat rock'n'role reversal. Pedicin Jr, musical director at Trump Castle in Atlantic City, favours progressive jazz. His father still digs rock'n'roll. Mike Pedicin slapped a preservation order on his kind of rock'n'roll — the earliest link between dance-band swing and its hybrid, house-rocking heyday.

Liner notes from *Jive Medicin* (Bear Family BCD-15738) 1993.

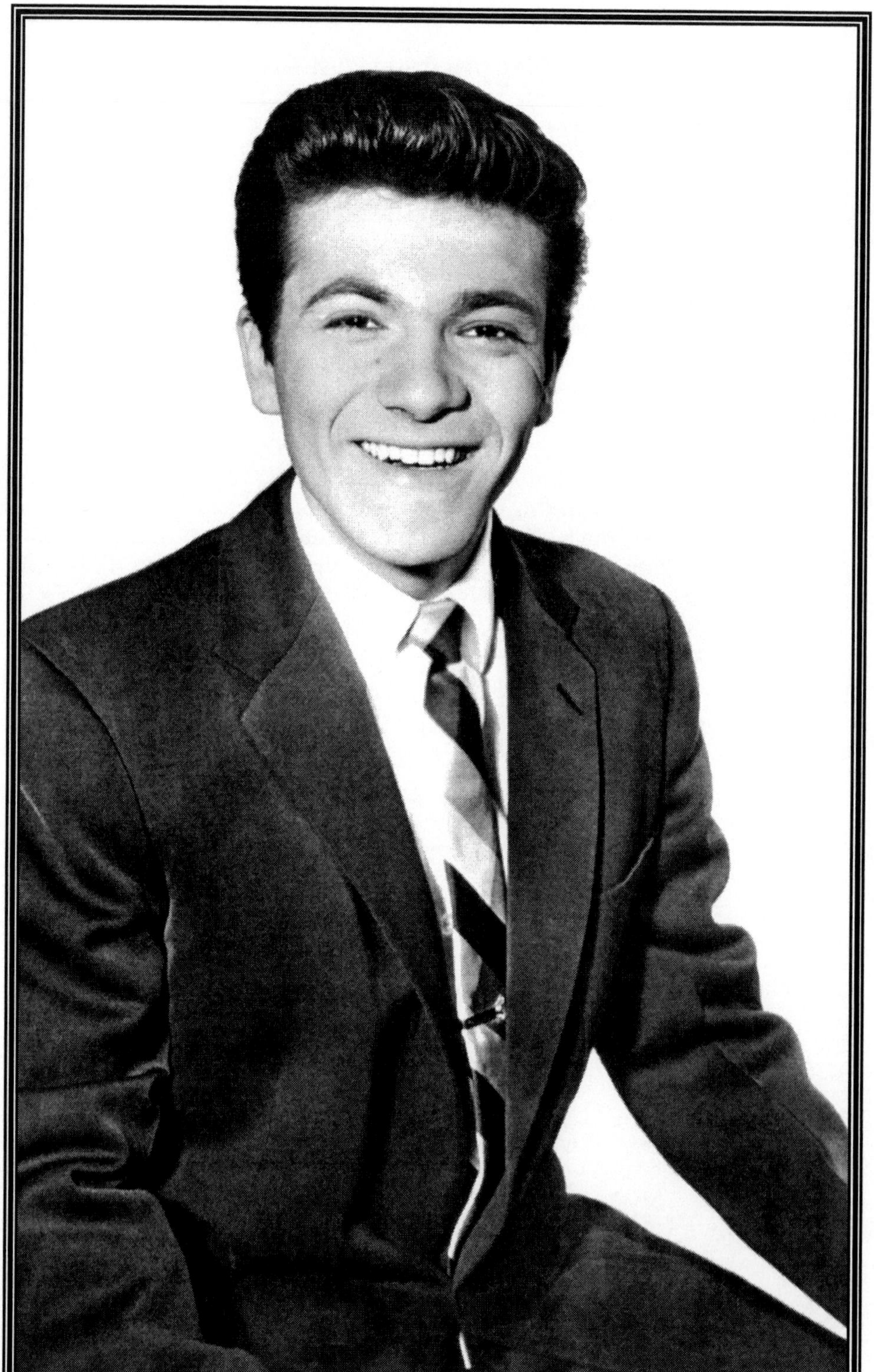

4.10
TOMMY SANDS
The Worryin' Kind

Tommy Sands had been the one to watch. His was the next golden larynx in the long queue of Elvis-inspired singers, and he was the boy considered most likely to survive when the hip-swivelling stopped. Unlike Elvis, a phenomenon of mystified repulsion to many adults, Sands was seen as a neater, U-certificate model; a conservatively-groomed, threat-extracted innocent who grinned when he could have sneered. His biggest hits, which wallowed in teenage ritual and adolescent mooning, reinforced the air of inoffensive soppiness. Alone among early rockers, Sands started out with uninteresting material which got better. By 1959, he was into crude, hard-driving music with a fine rockabilly band. But it couldn't last. Torn between the urge to make decent records and the crushing embrace of showbusiness, Tommy Sands became the lost boy of rock'n'roll, denied glowing references in the history books and long regarded with scepticism even by those who ordinarily liked the music.

Thomas Adrian Sands was born of Scots and Irish ancestry in Chicago's Grant Hospital on 27 August 1937. Benny, his father, was a professional pianist who travelled away from home a good deal. His mother, formerly Grace Lou Dixon, spent some time as a band vocalist including several years with Art Kassel's big band, Kassels In The Air. She'd been raised in Louisiana and frequently took the children, including Sands's half-brother, Edward, to stay with relatives who owned a farm near Greenwood, a few miles from Shreveport. For part of the year, Sands went to school in Chicago, where his father played the hotel lounges. In the winter, when Benny went out on the road, his wife returned to Louisiana with the children. That was how early publicity put it; according to Sands, his parents were always fighting, splitting up and getting back together again.

Tommy was not a blissfully contented child. At Greenwood grade school he was teased for being a 'Yankee'. Brother Ed, eleven years older, couldn't provide the companionship he needed. By the age of seven, he was infatuated with country music. 'Tommy,' his mother recalled, 'haunted the radio the way other kids haunt the icebox. He'd rather listen to radio than eat, sleep or romp around. No sooner would I settle down in another room when he'd be after me to come back. "Mama!" he'd yell. "It's

Jimmie Davis! Mama, it's Harmie Smith! Listen to those guitars."'

Mrs. Sands put a down-payment on a guitar in time for the boy's seventh Christmas: 'It became a part of him, flesh and soul. He taught himself at first because we couldn't afford the instrument and lessons. He played all the time, before school and after, evenings and weekends. We all felt he was getting real clever at it, but none of us realised how clever until we went shopping in Shreveport and he walked into the radio station and got himself an honest-to-goodness job.'

At eight years of age, Sands had toddled into KWKH lugging a guitar as big as himself. Station manager Henry Clay was probably as much amused as impressed, but the child became a twice-weekly afternoon attraction on $2.50 per performance. 'At first,' producer Pop Echols remembered, 'I told the audience not to expect too much, but we were surprised. Tommy cut out with the prettiest rendition of 'Oklahoma Hills' you ever heard.'

Sands took to the South. He spent hours in H.C. (Hard Cash) Wilkerson's J&S Music Store listening to hillbilly records; he joined the Greenwood Methodist Church and stood on an apple crate to preach; he even told classmates that he was born in 'South' Chicago, and that made him a rebel. Back in Chicago, he appeared on WBKB-TV's *Barn Dance*, and *TV Forecast* lived up to its name by predicting that Sands was a star in the process of rising.

Down South, Sands began singing with Harmie Smith, one of his earliest inspirations. Others included Hank Williams and his namesake, Tex; Tommy was obsessed with the latter's 1947 hit, 'Smoke! Smoke! Smoke! (That Cigarette)'. He and Harmie were heard on KWKH, where Sands — now ten or eleven — dressed in a cowboy outfit and sang 'My Mommy Bought Me An Ice-Cream Cone'.

Tillman Franks, who'd played bass with Pop Echols, gave the kid a few tips. Franks also worked on Webb Pierce and would later make a star out of Johnny Horton. It was probably Franks who persuaded Horace Logan, producer of KWKH's famed *Louisiana Hayride*, to give Sands a shot. Logan wasn't too keen: 'I was inclined to class Tommy as one of the "maybes". He was attractive and winning, but many lads of twelve will please a crowd. I definitely felt his talent was in the projection of a song, rather than in any unusual quality of voice. I hesitated at taking on Tommy but, luckily for my reputation as a talent scout, I did put him on the *Hayride*.' Sands made his *Louisiana Hayride* debut on 3 September 1949; he sang 'Candy Kisses', a hit for George Morgan. Nine months later, on his final appearance (27 May 1950) he sang 'Who Shot A Hole In My Sombrero'.

That same year, Mr. and Mrs. Sands were divorced. For a while, Tommy stayed with his father in Chicago before rejoining his mother in Greenwood. Ever ambitious for her youngest son, Mrs. Sands thought Houston might provide a wider audience for his talents, and Tillman Franks agreed to take him. They sought out prominent deejay Biff Collie, who also hosted KPRC-TV's *Hoedown Corner*. Sands appeared in a spot sponsored by Sun-Up Ice Cream.

Houston's Sidney Lanier Junior High School welcomed Sands as a ninth-grade student. There, he pursued an interest in acting as well as singing. 'Crowds liked him,' recalled Horace Logan with the benefit of hindsight, 'but I felt it was more for his personality than his singing talent. As an actor, I knew he'd make it.' Sands played a sensitive adolescent in *The Magic Fallacy* at the Alley Theatre (*'The kid has something on the acting ball'* noted the *Houston Press*). He also appeared in a radio series on KXYZ and alongside Reginald Owen in *Open House*, a play which narrowly missed a Broadway showing.

In 1951, Sands cut his first record for Saul Kahl's Freedom label. When he sang with Biff Collie and the Hoedown Corner Gang, he'd usually concentrate on the songs of Little Jimmy Dickens, and 'Love Pains' *c/w* 'Syrup Soppin' Blues' had their Dickens-ish aspects. Credited to Little Tommy Sands *'The West's Wonder Boy'*, he sang with an assurance and maturity which his teachers attributed to his association with older people in radio drama. But the Houston-based Freedom label was known for its R&B roster and nothing on the hillbilly series sold very well.

By 1952, Sands had been taken under the wing of Colonel Tom Parker's Jamboree Attractions, a successful company which represented Pee Wee King, Jimmie Davis, Mac Wiseman and Eddy Arnold, whose RCA-Victor records had already sold 25 million copies. Parker, who had heard Sands singing at a Houston club, placed him with RCA — a move which raised his profile without shifting too many records. His RCA discs (seven during 1953-55) were pure cornball. He re-recorded 'Love Pains' and covered 'A Dime And A Dollar' from the Paramount picture, *Red Garters*. Guy Mitchell, the knee-slapping star of the film, sold more copies.

1954 was a busy year, and the trade papers reported Sands's affairs in increasingly attentive detail. By June, he was voted 13th *'Most Promising Male Vocalist'* in *Cash Box's* 'Folk & Western' poll. Before the year was out, he'd covered Terry Fell's 'Don't Drop It' (a No. 6 C&W hit for Fell), staged appearances with Biff Collie at Houston high schools (Sands was still a full-time student at Lamar Senior High), and obtained a three-hour show as a deejay on Houston's KNUZ, where he received a visit from Capitol's A&R man, Ken Nelson. Rob Finnis interviewed Nelson in 1970: 'Biff asked me if I would go and talk to Tommy because he was feeling down in the dumps. I said "Sure". So, I went to the station and I spent two hours while he was doing his deejay show, and after that we went to dinner. He took me to a hamburger stand in a beat-up old Ford he had. I listened to his record on Victor and I said to him: "If I were you, I would write to Mr. Sholes and ask him not to record you for at least another two years." He was recording the wrong kind of stuff. He'd cut a real bluegrass — it just wasn't Tommy Sands, it wasn't the right kind of song for him. What I didn't know was that Tommy had that day gotten a letter from Steve *[Sholes]* saying he was off of Victor. Anyway, what happened was, I said to Tommy then: "Tommy, if you get off Victor, and you're still around and you haven't got a record contract in a couple of years, you come to see me and I'll sign you." You can't sell immaturity in a voice,' Nelson concluded. 'The only thing an artist has to sell is their emotions and a kid that young is not emotionally developed. Brenda Lee was the only one able to get through.'

Early in 1955, Sands appeared with Elvis Presley on shows which Biff Collie promoted in Houston. Sands's girlfriend, Betty Moers, recalled leaving Eagles Hall with Sands and Presley, whose first pink Cadillac had been stripped of its hubcaps: 'Elvis was getting popular by then but he wasn't being mobbed by souvenir-hunters. So it's anybody's guess whether they were taken by fans, vandals or plain old thieves.'

A year or so later, Presley put a call through to Sands while the teenaged deejay was hosting *Tommy's Corral* on KCIJ, a Shreveport station which he'd flunked graduation to join. Mindful of Sands's prowess as an actor, Presley promised to try and get him a part in his first picture. Fellow KCIJ deejay, Vera Stierman, was impressed by Sands's ambition: 'The Sandses made no bones about their plan to get to Hollywood as soon as possible. They lived simple, worked hard and saved, saved, saved. Mrs. Sands tried to get Tommy to rest more, but he had the bit between his teeth and he had to keep going. The nights he wasn't making personal appearances, he'd pick extra money doing TV commercials. All the while the dream got bigger and bigger. You could just see him reaching...'

Sands left Shreveport in May 1956. He and his mother moved to an apartment in the Hollywood hills, close to Pasadena where his half-brother and family were living. He auditioned for Cliffie Stone's *Hometown Jamboree*, which went out live on Saturday night over KTLA-TV. Stone, California's gift to C&W, became Sands's manager (Colonel Parker, who didn't get along with Mrs. Sands, had dropped out of that particular picture, though he and Tommy remained friends). Despite Stone's close association with Capitol Records —he recorded there and had acted as A&R consultant since 1946 — Sands was not signed to the label immediately. Nonetheless, he was about to define the phrase 'overnight sensation'.

In December 1956, Sands was invited to New York to audition for the leading role in the *Kraft Theater Hour* production of *The Singin' Idol*, a play by Paul Monash. Teens ordinarily watched Kraft Theater Hour because this NBC-TV series often featured singers in dramatic roles (eg Ferlin Husky and Julius LaRosa). Indeed, the part of up-and-coming rock'n'roller had been offered to Elvis Presley, upon whom the story was loosely based. Presley, however, was now fully committed and Colonel Parker pitched for Sands, who got the job.

When Ken Nelson heard that Sands had landed an hour's primetime TV, he kept his promise and drew up a five-year contract with

Capitol. 'Teenage Crush', the song chosen for Sands's Capitol debut, was written by Joe and Audrey Allison, then in their mid-thirties. Joe Allison was a country deejay at WMAK in Nashville, where he acted as a representative for Cliffie Stone's company, Central Songs. (Three years on, Joe and Audrey would give Jim Reeves's career a lift with 'He'll Have To Go').

On 30 January 1957, Sands sang 'Teenage Crush' in *The Singin' Idol*, and NBC were swamped with eight thousand requests for information and pictures (seven thousand more than they'd ever received before). Released the day after the broadcast, 'Teenage Crush' reached Top Three in both *Billboard* and *Cash Box* (and Kraft probably sold an awful lot of cheese). The song was not an instantly memorable pop masterpiece, nor was Sands's mush-mouthed singing especially attractive — he'd been advised to lose his Southern accent if he wanted to work in films. Nonetheless, Sands wore the magic halo that provoked calf-love in abundance and thousands of teenaged girls gave a sensational boost to a career which had struggled for a dozen years. Within twenty-four hours, he was offered contracts by four major film companies including 20th Century-Fox who bought the rights to *The Singin' Idol*.

The question has to be asked: how could someone who 'played' at being a rock'n'roll singer do so much better than the dozens of truly authentic artists whose telephones rarely rang? Sands himself has no illusions: 'It wasn't because of the song; it was the impact of the TV show. Every girl in America was watching that show just to see what an Elvis Presley was like. And the story happened to be a real tear-jerker. It was an excellent drama, the kind of role that was destined to make whoever played it a star.'

Sessions in March 1957 produced 'Ring-A-Ding-A-Ding' (No. 50) and 'Goin' Steady' (No. 19), which Faron Young had taken to the top of the C&W chart in 1953. On 27 March, Sands sang 'Friendly Persuasion' at the annual *Oscar Awards Ceremony*. His full dress suit impressed the right people and led directly to his 10 April appearance on *This Is Your Life*. The host, Ralph Edwards, had told his director: 'Look, with a kid like Tommy we could reassure millions of parents that rock'n'roll is not nearly as dangerous as they think.'

There was nothing remotely subversive about the first album, *Steady Date With Tommy Sands*, which contained 'Goin' Steady', 'Ring My Phone' (from the Kraft NBC-TV show, *Flesh And Blood*) and ten shrivelled old standards from writers who were born in the previous century. It reached No. 4 on the LP charts, where it stayed for eighteen weeks. Elvis, Ricky Nelson, Pat Boone and Fabian sold more albums than Sands, but no other roughly contemporaneous teen idol came close.

Sands never quite lived up to that first public burst of fame. The 'next Elvis' tag became an instant burden and his new manager, movie executive Ted Wick, lacked Colonel Parker's entrepreneurial acumen. Sands's material was also badly judged. Although Tommy Sands occasionally appears on the writing credits of his records, Ken Nelson, who preferred show tunes to rock'n'roll, generally chose the songs. Much of the time, Nelson had the vision, commitment and spirit which allowed him to supervise rock'n'roll sessions without imposing his own artistic values. For Sands's fourth single, however, he picked 'Let Me Be Loved', the theme song from *The James Dean Story*. It was written by Ray Evans and Jay Livingston, the Tin Pan Alley tunesmiths responsible for 'A Dime And A Dollar' as well as 'Buttons And Bows', Nelson's very first hit back in 1948. That Sands could sing this stuff was without question — his voice was smooth, accurate, versatile and technically accomplished — but it evidently took an occasional twitch of the hips to keep his largely female admirers happy. 'Let Me Be Loved' flopped altogether, and it would not be long before he could walk unmolested in public places.

Sands wrote 'Man, Like Wow!', his fifth single and the best to date. It oozed rock'n'roll toughness, but sold as well as bibles in Baghdad; he had to be seen as well as heard. In late '57, Sands repeated the *Singin' Idol* role in *Sing, Boy, Sing,* filmed by 20th Century Fox who'd already made movies with Elvis and Pat Boone. He played Virgil Walker, an orphan raised in the South by his gospel-preaching grandfather and aunt. Grandad wants Virgil to thump the bible too, but he's lured into the corrupt world of rock'n'roll by a duplicitous manager (none other than Edmond O'Brien, the singing gangster from *The Girl Can't Help It*). The kid's a hit, but when grandpa suffers a heart attack he promises to give up rocking for religion. He's saved from this dreadful dilemma by his aunt, who convinces him that God wants him to sing. Built-in roles for three disc-jockeys (including Biff Collie) increased box-office appeal and the film was well received by *Variety* (*'Tommy is not only a slim and vital juvenile but, what is more unexpected, he is a surprisingly sensitive and sincere young actor'*) and the *Los Angeles Examiner* (*'the kind of movie to make any audience plain happy to have bought tickets'*).

The soundtrack (which reached No. 17 on the LP chart in 1958) lived up to its title with a dozen unexpectedly eclectic songs. Neo-blues (Sands's own 'Your Daddy Wants To Do Right') crackled alongside gospel (Martha Carson's 'Gonna Walk And Talk With My Lord') and pop songs like 'That's All I Want From You'. A hit for the Silva-Tones in 1957, and since revived by legions of soul singers, Sands probably heard the 1955 Top Ten pop hit by Jaye P. Morgan. Lionel Newman, music consultant on *Love Me Tender* and *The Girl Can't Help It*, also included a couple of hoary ballads. There was also 'Soda Pop Pop', a mild rocker written by Darla and Betty Daret. Darla Daret had sung with Bob Wills in 1956 and recorded with Eddie Cochran in 1957.

Sands cut the title track on three occasions. There was a version for the soundtrack with Lionel Newman's orchestra in November 1957 and a faster (unissued) rendition accompanied only by drums. The fully-developed Capitol single was a hit (No. 46 in 1958). The song was written by Sands and Rod McKuen, the actor and best-selling poet who also

4.10 - Tommy Sands

penned the title track for Universal's *Rock, Pretty Baby*, in which he starred.

'Teenage Doll', released while 'Sing, Boy, Sing' was still on the charts, peaked at No. 81. The flipside, 'Hawaiian Rock', was attributed to Jack Hammer, the New Orleans-born ex-paratrooper who got his name on 'Great Balls Of Fire'.

Next up, in what would now be called an attempt to gain some street-credibility, is the Tommy Sands R&B album. *Sandstorm*, recorded over five days in April 1958, demonstrates a real affection for the verities of black popular music. In a recent interview with Stuart Colman, Sands explained the importance of R&B during his high-school years: 'All the kids were switching off the C&W channels and the pop music stations that played 'Oh, My Papa' and stuff like that, and we were looking for something else and we found race music, R&B. We used to go out at lunch and sit in our cars at the back of the school and listen on the sly to the black music. It wasn't accepted in our homes, and you couldn't hear it anywhere else, so we'd get radios and get off in the woods someplace and listen to the R&B stations. Elvis was doing the same thing in Memphis, Jimmy Burton's doing the same thing in Shreveport, and out in Lubbock, Texas, Buddy Holly's doing the same thing. We're all about to come together with these black roots combined with our country & western roots.'

It would be perverse to use any gush-words to describe Sands's particular merger, or to pretend that he could sing as subtly or affectingly as Joe Turner ('Chicken And The Hawk'), Clyde McPhatter ('Such a Night' and 'Honey Love') or the Clovers ('Little Mama' and 'Hey Miss Fannie'), but then who could? He adds an appealing lustre to the backbeat and doesn't sacrifice all the original guts and integrity. More to the point, he was now singing as if he'd never heard of Pat Boone. These songs, like most of the earlier Capitol recordings, feature unidentified session musicians. Although it's not possible to be certain as to who plays on what, Bob Bain (lead guitar) Buck Owens (rhythm guitar) and Merrill Moore (piano) are among the names most commonly cited.

Tommy Sands came closest to perfection in the summer of 1958. By this time he'd met up with the Raiders, a rockabilly band led by Scotty Turner, who played guitar like a virtuoso and wrote material that stimulated Sands's finest instincts. 'Blue Ribbon Baby' and 'The Worryin' Kind', written by Diane Lampert and Scotty Turner (under the pseudonym of Allison Dewar) also feature Turner's matchlessly pure rock'n'roll riffs. His short solos do little more than restate the melody, but they shine with power and authority.

Turner (real name Graham M. Turnbull) was born in Sydney, Nova Scotia on 23 August 1931. He received a track scholarship from Dubuque University in Iowa, where he ran one hundred yards in 9.6 seconds. Some say he hasn't slowed down since, and his story has certainly touched a number of fascinating bases. In 1957, while completing an advanced degree at Texas Tech. in Lubbock, he wrote a clutch of songs with Buddy Holly. The year before, he'd been introduced to fellow student, Hal Goodson, leader of a group which Goodson had formed in high school. The pair quickly formed a new band with Turner on guitar and Leon Bagwell on bass. Renamed the Raiders, they trekked to Norman Petty's studio in Clovis, where they cut a rockabilly single with Goodson on vocals. This emerged on a Hollywood label and the band left Texas for California taking a rhythm guitarist, Eddie Edwards, with them. There, according to Turner, 'we starved until Tommy Sands heard us and then we travelled with him all over the world'.

It was Sands who insisted that the Raiders should get a drummer. Ted Wick hired Hal Blaine, who was playing the Garden Of Allah, a Hollywood jazz lounge, with the Carol Simpson Quartet. A smart Jewish kid who moved out West at fourteen, Blaine was quick to admit his strict jazz background: 'These Texas fellas immediately started training me, and I found I was very fond of this 'country' music — songs like 'My Bucket's Got A Hole In It', songs which I'd never even dreamed existed.' Blaine, a few years older than Sands, doubled as road manager and kept the boys in line.

Sands and the Raiders featured 'The Worryin' Kind' (No. 69 in 1959) on the *Milton Berle Show*. Berle liked the beat so much, he asked the band to play it again while he ad-libbed some lyrics about the show's sponsors.

Fronting hand-picked instrumental wizards like Turner and Blaine, Sands sounded great on anything. Take 'Bigger Than Texas', a Paul Webster–Sammy Fain tune from the flick, *Mardi Gras*, in which Tommy starred with Pat Boone and Gary Crosby. The accompaniment here is pure rockabilly and Sands even succumbs to a hiccup or two. 'Is It Ever Gonna Happen' also has a lot of bite, and there's a real blue-eyed blues feel to 'I Ain't Gettin' Rid Of You'. Both were cut with the Raiders, who had changed their name to the Sharks (according to Hal Blaine: 'It was a name we adopted after playing Hawaii a number of times').

Texan desert blues-rock could have been Sands's new direction, but 'I Ain't Gettin' Rid Of You' didn't catch on. Capitol pulled 'I'll Be Seeing You' off a smoochy album with Nelson Riddle and it bisected the Hot 100 in October 1959. That, in effect, put paid to Sands's rock'n'roll releases, and high-energy tracks like 'Wicked Woman' and 'One Day Later' remained in the vaults, unissued until the release of a Bear Family anthology in 1992. Although Capitol never released 'Wicked Woman', the song got an airing on the other side of the world. When Sands and the Sharks toured Australia, the band took an interest in local artists and played on a number of their records. 'Wicked Woman', written by Hal Blaine, was released on the Teen label by New Zealand rocker, Johnny Devlin. Scotty Turner and Hal Blaine played on the record. (Blaine also wrote, or co-wrote, other songs for Tommy Sands including 'I'm All Shook Up' from the rock'n'roll medley on *Sands At The Sands*.)

When Sands stopped rocking, Scotty Turner and Hal Blaine remained in Hollywood as sessionmen. Turner played on Gene Vincent's *Crazy Beat* album and co-wrote 'If You Want My Lovin'' with John Marascalco. He also worked for Guy Mitchell and Eddie Fisher. In the mid-Sixties, he fetched up at A&M Records, where his tunes got the Baja Marimba Band off the ground. He's written for Wynn Stewart, Dean Martin, Tennessee Ernie Ford and Eddy Arnold. 'Shutters And Boards', a smash hit for Jerry Wallace, was co-written by Turner and his good friend Audie Murphy. He and America's most-decorated war hero also penned 'When The Wind Blows In Chicago' for Roy Clark. After a brief stint as manager of Central Songs, Turner was invited to head Liberty/United Artists' country music department, where he produced Slim Whitman, Del Reeves, Penny DeHaven and fellow guitar maestro, Jimmy Bryant.

Hal Blaine became the Rolls-Royce of drummers with a carefully-kept logbook numbering many thousands of sessions. If you've got any kind of record collection, Blaine's in it somewhere. He's the light touch behind John Denver and the thunder of Phil Spector. Anonymity beckoned for those other Raiders, Leon Bagwell and Eddie Edwards, but Hal Blaine's autobiography provides neat cameos of both men: *'Leon Bagwell was a slap-bass player. A good-looking Texan in the mold of Rock Hudson, he spoke with the most countrified drawl I had ever heard. I knew Leon was green to the business, hailing from Loop, Texas, and having been a dirt farmer for all his nineteen or twenty years. Leon was the tall, silent type, but boy could he slap the shit out of that old upright bass.*

'Eddie Edwards was from San Saba, Texas, famous for its paper-shell pecans. Eddie was the comedian of the group. He was also a great rhythm guitar player, but it took me the longest time to get used to his snuff spitting. Eddie was featured on songs like 'Who Wears Short Shorts'. Audiences loved his antics.

'The guys in the band were just wonderful. They taught me more about the true feel of country music than I could ever have learned in school.'

Sands stayed with Capitol and the tuxedo'd supper-club circuit until his contract expired. He had his first and only British hit with 'The Old Oaken Bucket' (No. 25 in 1960); this cool, acutely-phrased finger-snapper would have been really hip if Bobby Darin had not been among its obvious antecedents. There were more films (eight in all) and a lot more records: on Vista, ABC-Paramount, Liberty, Imperial (Scott Turner producing), Superscope and Brunswick. Following the break-up of his much-publicised marriage to Nancy Sinatra (1960-65), he worked out of Hawaii for twenty years. Hal Blaine again: *'Tommy more or less quit the business. Rumors had it that Frank Sinatra put out the word that Sands was not to work anywhere, but insiders knew it was total hogwash. Tommy called me just prior to his move to Hawaii and told me he didn't really want to work anymore. He wanted to find himself and get back on the right track. He just had to get away, and what better place than Hawaii...'*

There was a nightclub and a clothing business, a second marriage and another divorce. Eventually, promoter Paul Barrett, who'd never forgotten Sands's gospel-shouting entrance in *Sing, Boy, Sing*, brought him to England for a rock'n'roll festival at Brean in 1990. For one so long regarded as an opportunist teen idol, he proved eminently capable of unbuttoning rock'n'roll's raw spirit. 'Y'know,' he told Stuart Colman, 'Capitol could have gotten a lot more out of me if they had let me do what they let Gene Vincent do. When Ken Nelson first heard me, he heard me in the South in a bar in Houston singing the things I sing, rockabilly. It wasn't called rockabilly then, but that's what it was. 'Teenage Crush', 'I'll Be Seeing You' — that kind of middle-of-the-road sound was a sound that I just never really liked. It wasn't really my thing. The thing that I grew up with, what I really felt comfortable doing, was the kind of stuff your kids here found twenty or thirty years later.

Sandstorm was not a big hit, but it's my favourite album. And 'The Worryin' Kind,' the only song I ever did in one take, that's my favourite record. But people over twenty-five thought rock'n'roll was a passing fad. Nobody realised it was the birth of the new American music.'

Today, almost thirty-five years after he made his best records, Tommy Sands deserves a fresh respect for his niche in rock'n'roll's history.

Liner notes for *The Worryin' Kind* (Bear Family BCD-15643) 1992.

Note   Publicity puffs should normally be handled with a lengthy barge-pole, but make an exception for *Tommy Sands — The Complete Life Story* by Eunice Field (Bartholomew House Inc, 1957). It's a lavishly-illustrated and particularly diligent piece of research.

5

DOO-WOP DAYS

5.1
Acappella: Voices In The Night

To judge from fanzines old and new, acappella has a variety of spellings and any number of meanings. Derived from the Italian *capella* (chapel), it was originally applied to Sixteenth Century church music written for voices alone. Nowadays, it's a synonym for almost any unaccompanied music, choral or otherwise. And the *Oxford English Dictionary* provides two spellings; one 'p' or two.

As a recorded form of music, the origins of acappella are hard to determine. In the pre-war gospel field, the absence of instrumentation was normal enough, but secular black vocal groups rarely recorded without any musical accompaniment. The Virginia Four (on Decca in 1940) and the Four Vagabonds (Bluebird) were among the first to have specialised in unadulterated harmony, but the majority — including the Ink Spots and the Mills Brothers — carried a guitarist. Away from the recording studio, acappella was *de rigeur*. Deprived of a more meaningful existence, a degree of self-fulfilment could be realised by every group of blacks to sing on a street-corner. The practice, common through the Thirties and Forties (the Ink Spots began as the 'Percolating Puppies' on an Indianapolis sidewalk), reached epidemic level in the Fifties and thereafter tailed away. Financial success and fleeting recognition were impossible without records, but acappella was not commercially recorded until the early Sixties when, ironically enough, white groups produced some of the finest examples. The Persuasions have since tried to rectify the imbalance, but the best acappella is still that produced around 1964 by white youngsters who idolised the black harmony of childhood favourites — the Orioles, the Five Keys, the Nutmegs.

In New Haven, Connecticut in 1954, the Nutmegs stood around a tape recorder in a church cellar and sang. They couldn't afford instruments and wouldn't have bothered anyway. They always practised without music; doing so helped to ensure perfect harmony. A stack of those practice tapes gathered dust for nigh on ten years and, in the meantime, the Nutmegs were signed to Herald and hit the R&B charts with 'Story Untold' and 'Ship Of Love'. Other records featuring the husky lead voice of Leroy Griffin (plus instrumental accompaniment) were also popular, but the hits stopped coming and Griffin was forced to work in a factory until the day he died.

In 1960, the late Leo Rogers, owner of Bruce, Tip-Top and Forever, located the New Haven tapes and sold them to Irving 'Slim' Rose of New York's legendary Times Square record shop. Slim did not release them immediately but chose his moment carefully. By 1961 pop music was already too complicated for many R&B fans, and reaction in New York and other north-eastern cities was to go back. Way back. While the early Sixties are generally held to mark the end of simple R&B harmony groups, doo-wop put up more than a token resistance. A number of black, Puerto Rican, Italian and Anglo-Saxon groups had an appreciation for earlier forms of R&B which reacted against the excesses of producers like Leiber & Stoller, Luther Dixon and Phil Spector. Progress was halted by sounds like the Capris ('There's A Moon Out Tonight'), the Chimes ('Once In A While'), Little Caesar & The Romans (actually from L.A., with the significantly titled 'Those Oldies But Goodies') and the Devotions ('Rip Van Winkle', who — you may recall — woke up twenty years behind the times). Rock was now aware of its history but the movement, growing fast through 1962 (Don & Juan, the Earls, Ronnie & The Hi-Lites), was all but blotted out by the English Invasion.

Slim Rose released the Nutmegs' 'Let Me Tell You', a decade old practice tape *sans* orchestration, in 1964 — the year in which the Beatles first made the US charts. All the kids who'd been singing those old songs down in the subway (echo at its finest) could make records just like the Nutmegs. Eddie Gries at Relic, Stan Krause (he discovered the Persuasions) at Catamount, and Slim at Times Square were besieged by street-corner groups. Acappella was the order of the day. There were dozens of acappella labels, some with as many as thirty groups. The accent was on the past — Relic, Medieval, Old-Timer — but others included Mellomood, Crimson, Mason, Snowflake, Fellatio (someone had more than a tongue in their cheek), Siamese and Harlequin. *Blues Train* No. 6 (August 1964) carried this report: *'Undoubtedly, the Number One no-music record is the Nutmegs. In fact, it's the Number One heading all the oldies on the latest Danny Stiles hit parade. Stiles plays this and others each night from 11.00 pm to 2.00 am on WNJR.'* Stiles played 'Let Me Tell You' on his *Kat Kingdom* show every night for several weeks. It sold two thousand copies and every kid who bought a copy realised what it meant. They emerged by the hundred. The discs they made were pressed in red, black, orange and transparent pastel-blue, but most of the groups were white. That is to say Spanish, Italian, Puerto Rican. There were not, comparatively speaking, many black acappella groups. Young blacks, who were largely unaffected by 'the English onslaught', had moved on to soul. They didn't want to relive the past (the Nutmegs were a museum piece, but the Temptations were gonna last), and they didn't go for cover versions of their own hits (would you have bought Freddie & The Dreamers if you already had James Ray?).

If blacks in general were unimpressed, white oldies freaks were positively incensed. While increasingly sophisticated production techniques had spawned a short-lived doo-wop revival, the US success of the Beatles *et al* provoked a more extreme reaction. *'New York'*, ran the liner notes to *The Best Of Acappella (Volume Two)*, *'is starving for group sounds due to the mass brainwashing of the public with imported English garbage.'* What then, was being offered in its place? Well, it's difficult to describe the thrilling aural attractions of acappella if you've not heard any — harder still if you're already inured to the Persuasions, who too frequently come across like the Four Tops without a band. First of all, it's important to get the best; bad acappella just has to be the worst music ever recorded. To start, more or less, at the beginning, there's a whole album by the Nutmegs (Relic 5002) containing two tracks with music and the rest without. There's a lot of those natural church cellar sounds, where the echo on 'Down In Mexico', 'You're Crying' and 'Out Of My Heart' enhances already perfect songs beyond belief. At the same time, it's not high fidelity and there are passages where the bass resembles a chest of drawers being dragged across the floor. But, accept these limitations, and you could be touched by the Nutmegs' innocence, sincerity and craftsmanship. You may even find a protest song in 'Why Must We Go To School'.

Anthologies present less of a gamble for the uninitiated, and there are plenty of acappella compilations. Few are so appropriately named as *The Best Of Acappella (Volume One)* (Relic 101), which has two of the Nutmegs' best and a host of famous doo-wop hits performed instead by ephemeral groups from New York and New Jersey. You'll never hear of any again, but this was their moment of glory. The Zircons' 'Lonely Way', *Rolling Stone*'s nomination for the finest acappella single of all time, is absurdly polished. The effects of the acappella craze were rarely felt beyond New York, New Jersey and Philadelphia, and 'Lonely Way' and the Camelots' 'Chain Of Broken Hearts' were just about the only acappella singles to make the North-East's regional best sellers. The Zircons' lead is white but his voice, high, pure, and strong, avoids the graceless vibrato so common in white imitations of R&B. 'Lonely Way' is an old Skyliners' song — you had no chance of making acceptable acappella unless you dug the Skyliners, the Harptones, the Orioles... Acappella discography is riddled with countless versions of 'Pennies From Heaven' and 'Stormy Weather', and no group's repertoire was complete without variations on 'Gloria' or 'Sunday Kind Of Love'. *Volume One* has all of these and more.

Volume Two (Relic 102) has another twenty delicious tracks including 'Ten Commandments Of Love' (the Shadows via the Moonglows), 'It Happened Today' (the Holidays via the Skyliners) and 'Sentimental Reasons' (the Chessmen via Deek Watson of the Ink Spots). Original tunes are scarce; like barbershop quartets, acappella teams recreate a bygone age. The Citadels may have short back and sides, but they're the best singers going. The lead, Dennis Ostrum (tributes to his pristine and rangy voice still appear in the collector mags) and his group soar through 'New Love Tomorrow', 'When I Fall In Love' and a superb version of the Bopchords' 'Woke Up This Morning': *Dang lang lang lang, zoom, zoom,*

zoom, bop, bop, bop'. Believe me, it's catchy. Other volumes are not so hot. The third has more from the Citadels and includes the Quotations who had stab at acappella when they were unable to repeat the success of their Marcels imitation, 'Imagination'. Unfortunately acappella died from an overdose of imagination. By 1966, it had been milked to virtual extinction by a bandwagon of unreal gimmickry. Girl groups, tiny tots with excruciating pre-pubertal voices, lead singers who imitated a muted trumpet in the middle of 'Speedoo', units who'd sung together for less than half an hour. The goodies drowned in a sea of awesome mediocrity.

Since the golden years, good acappella records have been scarce, but the growing passion for older group styles has led to a revival of interest in this, the most basic of musical genres. Here's one more nugget: *Acappela [sic] Session With The Shells* (Candlelite 1000) is pressed on brilliant yellow vinyl and the contents are pure gold. The actual recording, by Wayne Stierle, is excellent; and, for the first time with an acappella disc, you don't have to press the 'High Filter' button. There are seventeen tracks from 'Baby Oh Baby', the group's own big hit of 1960, to the Miracles' 'Ooh, Baby Baby' — a song that positively demanded an acappella reading. And, if you're really zonked, you could do worse than try some of these:

1 *Acappella Showcase Presents By Popular Demand The Chessmen* (Relic 106). Blacks and Latinos on some good performances. Too much soul though.

2 *Acappella Showcase Presents The Velvet Angels* (Relic 5004). Nolan Strong and three of his Diablos on fifteen tracks full of gospel-slanted harmonies.

3 *Acappella Session With The Original Zircons* (Snowflake 1003). Not heard it, but reviews were bad.

4 *New York To L.A., Acappella All The Way* (Acappella 1001). Notable for cuts by the Ad-Libs of 'Boy From New York City' fame.

5 *I Dig Acappella* (Cat-Time 210). Some of Stan Krause's pre-Persuasion discoveries. Nice but not essential.

6 *Cigars, Acappella, Candy* — The Belmonts (Buddah 5123). Italian doo-wop minus Dion. Some overdubbing, but a good try.

7 *Velvet Soul For Lovers Only* — The Five Jades (Relic 107). Highly-rated group with four leads on plenty of original songs.

8 *Philadelphia's Greatest* (Pantomime 2003). This one has also escaped me but 24 tracks sounds like good value.

9 *Acappella Showcase Presents The Universals* (Relic 5006). 1962 practice tapes from the group who hit with 'Again' on Mark-X in 1957. Fine portrait sleeve.

10 *Gospel Music: The Legendary Master Series* — The Soul Stirrers (Imperial 94007). Holy acappella from 1947-48. More hiss than music, but 'Why I Like Roosevelt' and 'His Eye Is On The Sparrow' are still beautiful.

Note   This piece (*Let It Rock*, February 1975) was recycled from *The Rise And Fall Of Acappella* (*Record Mirror*, 4 June 1972). I also recommend the thoroughly informative feature by Lenny Kaye and Ed Ward in *Rolling Stone* (16 April 1970).

Top to bottom: David Lynch *(left)*, Paul Roby *(right)*, Tony Williams, Herb Reed and Zola Taylor.

5.2
THE PLATTERS
The Birth Of The Platters

The Platters, who sold fifty million records to become the most successful black vocal group in the history of rock, were managed, coached and directed by songwriter Buck Ram, a middle-aged lawyer who believed a fusion of R&B and classical music would go straight to the roots of people's emotions. In an era when black music was generally tagged as dirty or subversive, Ram's orchestral arrangements of comforting songs were conspicuous. He and the Platters upended a segregated music world, making it possible to say the words 'doo-wop' and 'London Palladium' in the same breath.

Born in Chicago in 1907, Samuel 'Buck' Ram studied law at the University Of Illinois and was called to the bar in California in 1933. While advocacy would have pleased his parents, Ram was more interested in music, which he wrote and arranged. He quickly became successful at it, working in Chicago and New York with the bands of Duke Ellington, Count Basie and the Dorsey Brothers, and establishing himself with songs like 'Afterglow', 'At Your Beck And Call', 'I'll Be Home For Christmas' and, in 1944, 'Twilight Time' — a monster instrumental hit for the Three Suns. The following year, Columbia Records sent him back to California to write a film score. The contract fell through and Ram suffered a nervous breakdown. By the time he recovered, big bands were virtually obsolete and R&B vocal groups were appearing on the hitherto segregated pop charts.

Remaining in Los Angeles, Ram launched Personality Promotions & Productions with Jean Bennett, a young secretary who came out from Joplin, Missouri to try her luck as a singer but made her name instead as a song-plugger responsible for breaking 'Only You' as a national hit.

' "Personality" was a nice name,' said Ram. 'I felt we were developing personalities. But I didn't know then what "Productions" meant — that was tagged on because it sounded good.' Most agencies rode with the winners while the inexperienced, the strugglers and the losers — those most in need of a lawyer — flocked in Ram's direction. *Cash Box* listed the artists handled by Personality Productions in June 1954: there were several C&W performers (Mary Rose Bruce, Audie Andrews, Jack Tucker) and two R&B acts, Peppy Prince & His Rhythm Lads and the

Platters. Personality's stable, hardly a year old, also included Cpl. Stewart Rose, the Chansonaires and Linda Hayes (who had a No. 2 R&B hit with 'Yes I Know') and would soon incorporate the Colts and the Penguins, who sold a million copies of 'Earth Angel' in 1955. With a group in the Top Ten, Personality Productions was red-hot. Ram couldn't walk down the street without groups popping out of the shrubbery.

Linda Hayes (real name Bertha Williams) introduced Buck Ram to her brother, Tony Williams — the Platters' lead singer and the man who most identifies their music. Samuel Anthony Williams was born in Elizabeth, New Jersey in 1928, the youngest of seven children born to Ed Williams, a preacher, and his wife, Bertha, a church soloist. He sang in the church choir and enlisted in the air force after high school. Stationed in Texas, he was later sent to Guam, Japan and other Pacific islands. In 1953, he joined his sister in L.A. where he worked as a car-washer by day and a singer by night. He also married the secretary of KPOP disc-jockey Hunter Hancock, one of the first to properly harness the power of R&B on radio. It was a move which can't have hurt the Platters' airplay on the West Coast.

The most trustworthy account of the Platters' formation does not involve Buck Ram or Jean Bennett or even Tony Williams. The earliest personnel included Cornel Gunter, Alex and Gaynell Hodge and Joe Jefferson, all of whom attended Jefferson High School. They recruited Herb Reed, a bass singer who came from Kansas City and sang with a Los Angeles version of the famous Wings Over Jordan Choir. Herb usually sang lead, but on their first TV appearance (*Ebony Showcase*) the group was led by Cornel Gunter on a jumping doo-wop arrangement of 'Old Macdonald'. David Lynch, a cab driver from St. Louis and a close neighbour of the Hodges, also flitted in and out. This loose aggregation called themselves the Flamingos and some of them sang background vocals on sessions produced by Ralph Bass, who had worked for Savoy Records bringing Johnny Otis, Esther Phillips and Big Jay McNeely to the label. In 1950, he was hired by King Records' Syd Nathan and put in charge of the Federal subsidiary in Los Angeles. It was here, at a June 1953 session for saxophonist McNeely ('Nervous, Man, Nervous') that Bass introduced the group to Tony Williams. He related the story to Norbert Hess: 'I first met Tony at the amateur show at the Club Alabam. He didn't sound like a blues singer. To me he was a modern Bill Kenny (the Ink Spots' lead singer). He was very nervous and he didn't even win third prize, but he impressed me so much I took him in my office and signed him that night. I told him I couldn't sell singles: "Let me put a quartet with you." I told them: "This is your new lead singer. Do you want to record for us, or don't you?" That's how I did it. I didn't have time to rehearse them, and we did one session and nothing happened with it.'

By September 1953, Cornel Gunter — in later years he preferred to spell his name 'Cornell Gunther' — had left to form the Flairs and the group that recorded the very first Platters session at Radio Recorders

5.2 - The Platters

The Platters appear in The Girl Can't Help It, *1956.*
Left to right: Herb Reed, David Lynch, Tony Williams, Zola Taylor and Paul Roby.

consisted of Tony Williams (lead), David Lynch (second tenor), Alex Hodge (baritone) and Herb Reed (bass). It was Reed, then driving a jitney cab for the Chrysler Corporation, who came up with the group's new name. He and the Hodge brothers were flicking through a stack of records at the Hodges' home on East 56th Street: 'You got the name right there in your hand. We call records "platters".' Linda Hayes claims she too was on the first session. The band included guitarist Jesse Ervin, Clifton Pitts on drums and two members of Johnny Otis's R&B caravan, Devonia Williams (piano) and Mario Delagarde (bass).

The debut single was released on Federal in November 1953. 'Hey Now', a jump tune, featured Herb Reed. Herb was always proud of the fact that he sang lead on the group's first single and couldn't fully conceal his resentment when the stardust fell on Tony Williams, whose tentative vocal is heard upfront on the devotional 'Give Thanks'. This attempt to cash in on the Orioles' 'Crying In The Chapel' sank without a bubble.

A second single was issued in January 1954. Tony Williams sang lead on 'I'll Cry When You're Gone' and 'I Need You All The Time'. There's a wobbliness in the lower register, but a heart-touching quality remains. Once again, the record would have made a bigger splash if he'd dropped it in the bath.

5.2 - The Platters

Buck Ram enters the picture at this stage. When speaking to me, he made it perfectly plain that he had no involvement in the Platters' genesis or their affiliation with Federal: 'We were fabulously lucky. Linda Hayes was having a hit with 'Yes I Know'. Her manager came to me 'cos he didn't know how to handle things. Linda was sensational, but after six weeks her husband wanted to manage her himself. I wasn't gonna stand in her way and, before she left, she said: "My brother Tony really sings great, maybe you can do something for him." I watched Tony sing 'My Buddy' and 'Trees' in a local amateur contest and he was tremendous, but I didn't know what to do with him 'cos he wasn't country, rock'n'roll or race as such. I told him we'd have to organise a group, and he said he'd been singing with a group called the Platters who'd already had a record on Syd Nathan's Federal label but they weren't getting anywhere. They all came up to my tiny office on Western Avenue and, boy, they were terrible, they were just horrible. The harmony was really off and Tony was the only one who sounded any good. They'd been started by Cornel Gunter, but he'd left and the fellows in the office were Tony, David Lynch, Alex Hodge and Herbert Reed. I think Herb saw the dollar signs when Cornel left. He was malicious. He used to stand behind Tony onstage and mutter "Ah, you drunken bastard" and just aggravate him. Tony had this neurotic insecurity and just couldn't take it. We'd rehearse every night spending three or four nights on one song, which really bugged me. We'd play jukebox meeting places and local contests for the race disc-jockey, Hunter Hancock. Always for food — never any money!'

Ralph Bass and Buck Ram agreed to work together. 'I was in my office,' recalled Bass, 'when someone came in and asked for Platters' records. It was Buck Ram and he was interested to see if I planned any further recordings. It turned out he was their manager and vocal coach. I told him I knew of Tony's talent and if he worked on the group I'd do further records.'

By now, Linda Hayes was continuing a solo career. She made some thirty recordings for Hollywood, King, Decca and Buck Ram's Antler label singing jump blues and blues ballads in a strident voice that recalled a bluesier Billie Holiday. Ram replaced her with Zola Taylor, a student at Centennial Senior High School and already a member of Shirley Gunter's group, the Queens. 'She was a cute little kid,' said Buck. 'I decided to put her with the Platters just to smarten the group up. She didn't mind *[leaving the Queens]* 'cos it was all interchangeable anyhow.'

Taylor, a red-haired fourteen year old of Ethiopian, Irish and Choctaw Indian ancestry, had won a Lincoln Theatre talent contest and recorded a solo single at Burbank Studios for RPM Records with members of the Queens (including Blondean Taylor and Rosemary Johnson) backing her up. But there's no overt evidence of her presence at the Platters' next session in March 1954, when the group cut four tunes including 'Roses Of Picardy' with drummer Peppy Prince's Quintet. Although Taylor remembered the session (and emphatically recalled the titles), she told

5.2 - The Platters

Seamus McGarvey that her adolescent voice would carry so loudly the rest of the group would sometimes make her stand well away from the microphone.

Ralph Bass coupled 'Roses Of Picardy' with Buck Ram's 'Beer Barrel Boogie'. Herb Reed sang with some confidence on the jump side, but 'Roses Of Picardy', a World War I ballad, exposed his limitations. It's not easy to lambaste a man who's sung with a Platters ensemble for nigh on fifty years, but even Buck Ram was scathing: 'Herb couldn't sing, see? The only song I got out of him was 'Sixteen Tons', and that took two days 'cos he'd go flat all the time.' (To be fair, the *Cash Box* review was favourable, and Herb sang lead on many more album tracks including a remake of 'Roses Of Picardy' in 1960). The group's fourth single featured 'Love All Night', a Latin jump tune led by David Lynch, and a ballad, 'Tell The World', which showcased Tony Williams's lovely voice to full shimmering effect. Here too is something of the operatic tendency which the Hodge brothers noticed when Williams first auditioned for Ralph Bass. According to Buck Ram, both singles sold some 20,000 copies on the West Coast. Jean Bennett tried to get airplay on New York pop stations, but jocks realised the Federal imprint was reserved for R&B and threw the records in the trash-can as soon as they saw the green and silver label.

In the spring of 1954, Alex Hodge was arrested for selling marijuana and Buck Ram sought a replacement. Al Frazier, who sang with fellow Federal act, the Lamplighters (and, very much later, the Rivingtons), was approached, but he recommended Paul Robi, a chorister and house painter from New Orleans. Frazier told Art Turco that they'd both been members of groups called the Mello-Moods and the Emanons: 'When he joined the Platters, Robi changed his name to Roby. 'Only You' on Federal was the first number he was on. In fact, the Platters' arrangement of 'Only You' was identical to the Emanons on *[the unrecorded]* 'Bewitched, Bothered And Bewildered'. It all came from Roby. He added the missing ingredient. He's a very talented guy.'

Rumours that Buck Ram bought his songs and arrangements from young black writers persist to this day. They started, he said, because he began using pseudonyms. 'Only You' was written by Buck Ram and Ande Rand, an addition which appears on the Mercury label and Federal reissues, though not the first Federal release. '"Ande Rand", that's me as well,' Buck explained. 'I was originally with ASCAP, which was monopolised by Noel Coward, Irving Berlin and all the top writers. New writers like myself couldn't get anywhere because they weren't paying *[full]* royalties on records, and when BMI started I thought: "To heck with ASCAP, 'cos I can make 4¢–6¢ a record with BMI everytime it's played on the air." But I couldn't write for BMI 'cos I was with ASCAP. So I stuck another name, Ande Rand, on there for the BMI things. "Lynn Paul" — that's me too."' *[As was 'Jean Miles' and, as far as I know, 'Jim Williams', the author of 'Beer Barrel Boogie'.]*

The original version of 'Only You' was cut in L.A. on 20 May 1954, but none of the tracks recorded then were deemed suitable for release at the time. It was a chaotic date, with a different lead singer for each song: Tony Williams ('Only You'), Zola Taylor ('Don't Tickle') and Herb Reed ('Humble Bumble Bee"). The lead on Alex Hodge's song, 'You Made Me Cry', sounds exactly like David Lynch; suggestions that it's Hodge himself are probably wide of the mark, even though there's a Platters website which maintains that Hodge wasn't finally expelled until August 1954.

There's one more wrinkle I shouldn't omit: Michel Ruppli's discography points to the fleeting re-emergence of Cornel Gunter as joint lead singer, while Lou Silvani's *Collecting Rare Records* also lists the flamboyant tenor at the same session. Frankly, if he's there at all, he can't be heard.

Ralph Bass said the group arrived two and a half hours late, while Buck Ram told me they'd all had a fit of nerves. 'They were all frightened, and Zola was scared to death,' he said. 'We gave her some wine, but she started throwing up and the record was terrible. I begged Nathan not to release it. I said we'd make another one for free as long as he didn't release that one. He said he'd think about it.'

Zola Taylor has her own twist on events: 'I wasn't feeling too well,' she told McGarvey. 'David and Tony gave me white port and lemon juice wine before we went to the studio: "Zola, you got to have a little buzz to make you feel better." The studio was *[very small]* and it was so hot. 'Only You', that's the one I fainted on. I fainted doing the song. My mother was at the session. She called me a wino, and I haven't drunk white port and lemon juice since.'

Herb Reed also put this experimental session into perspective: 'These were what you'd call dubs. We'd put ideas on tape with the understanding that we'd go back in and do them over the right way. Would you believe that Federal Records released those later on, those horrible demonstration tapes. We didn't know the harmony correctly or anything. When we became successful they released those as recordings. Man, I wanted to strangle them.'

'Only You' contained Tony Williams's now instantly familiar hiccup, 'Uh-ohhhnly you', which first occurred when the car in which the group were singing went over a bump in the road. The attractive aberration was ruined by Herb Reed's background whistling and the performance remained in the vaults until late 1955, when Mercury Records stormed the best-sellers with a fully subtitled re-recording, 'Only You (And You Alone)'.

The internationally famous line-up on that stupendous hit had coalesced in L.A. in September 1954 when Tony Williams, Zola Taylor, David Lynch, Paul Roby and Herb Reed recorded a further four songs for Federal. Second tenor Lynch took most of the honours: 'Shake It Up Mambo' was in line with the current dance craze, but 'Voo-Vee-Ah-Be', popular with today's jivers, was redolent of Slim Gaillard's vouteroonie mating calls and already old fashioned. The group's final Federal single coupled a spirited 'Maggie Doesn't Work Here Anymore' with a ragged duet, 'Take Me Back, Take Me Back'. Lynch was the most anonymous Platter (more so than Roby who became emcee and spokesman), but he continued taking the lead on jump tunes even after the group went to Mercury (eg 'I Wanna' and 'Hula Hop').

At some point in 1954, Linda Hayes recorded 'My Name Ain't Annie' — an 'answer' disc to the Royals/Midnighters' 'Work With Me Annie'. Trumpet-player Gerald Wilson, another of Buck Ram's acts, led the band. The Platters are said to have contributed the strenuous harmony and keener ears than mine point to Zola Taylor's voice in the mix. (There's no vocal group on 'Let's Babalu', the flip of this King release).

In January 1955, the rest of the Platters backed up Linda Hayes (and organist Luis Rivera) on 'Please Have Mercy', and Linda Hayes and Tony Williams on Johnny Otis's jump tune 'Oochi Pachi'. They may have covered 'Oochie Pachie' *[sic]* by RPM's Arthur Lee Maye & The Crowns, but I'm not sure; *Billboard* listed both under *'New R&B releases'* on 19 February 1955. Whatever, the song evidently caused a rift between Buck Ram and Federal's owner, Syd Nathan, who told Ram he wanted to use the Platters to make a record with Linda Hayes. 'Okay,' Ram replied. 'How much you gonna pay 'em?' 'Pay 'em?' said Nathan. 'I'm not gonna pay 'em anything for just oop-oop-a-doopin'.' Ram told him to go ahead: 'Anything to stop him releasing 'Only You'.' Ralph Bass had a slightly different take on the same tale: 'Buck sent Nathan a bill for $100. Syd said: "Well, they're only worth $50. In fact, I can get anyone to do 'doo-wahs' and 'oodle-oohs'. Why should I pay 'em at all? Forget it!" Buck said if he wasn't getting paid, he was going to Mercury.'

The Platters' one year contract with Federal wasn't renewed. Mercury wanted the Penguins so badly, Ram forced them to take the Platters as well: 'It was the Penguins hitting with 'Earth Angel' that really saved me from having to make another version of 'Only You' for Syd Nathan.' The Mercury pact was sealed on 2 March 1955. The group's first session produced the big hit version of 'Only You' but, originally, Mercury were not enthusiastic. 'Bobby Shad was Mercury's A&R man. He put the record out all right, but he kept plugging the Penguins instead. We almost lost 'Only You' 'cos the Hilltoppers copied it and theirs was a hit in lots of places the Platters hadn't reached. Jeannie was on the road with it for almost nine months, taking the record around the disc-jockeys. They'd say: "Here comes the girl with the party records" — 'cos rhythm & blues had a dirty name then. Suddenly, we got an order for five thousand records from Seattle, and when I told Shad he said: "Aw, that's a mistake, it must be the Penguins record." But Mercury was a running company — the minute they smelled a hit they covered all the jocks. Boy, they really knew what to do with the satchel. We soon had a big smash record and what transpired after that was just fantastic. Alan Freed sold Columbia an idea for making a rock picture, *Rock Around The Clock*, and we had the two top songs, 'Only You' and 'The Great Pretender', in it. That's what did it. We had calls from all over the world after that.'

Liner note to *The Platters: The Complete Federal Recordings* (Ace CDCHD-974) 2003.

5.3
Bring Back Those Doo-Wops

When the cutesy biographical retreads of the pop weeklies and teen magazines gave way to *Rolling Stone*, *Crawdaddy* and *Creem*, rock'n'roll was suddenly (or so it seemed) couched in analytical criticism, pompous theories and acrobatic exegetics. Perhaps you thought that this was all a bit overwrought, and yearn for the days before recent converts began writing about rock as if they'd invented it. Doo-wop, left way behind in this cultural shock, is the answer to your problem.

Here's a subject which all the more tangential theorisers leave well alone, seemingly content to place the entire panorama of vocal group harmony into the hands of lovingly attentive record collectors. Such neglect has its drawbacks; as some of you are finding out, we record collectors can be really boring and tedious people, obsessed with the relentless recital of fax'n'info unleavened by wit or sparkle. Ed Engel is another.

Engel is the USA's most indefatigable collector of records by white vocal groups. It's an admission of defeat if he can't draw the watermarks on the Cousins label from memory, and he knows how often Vito & The Salutations changed their shirts. What's missing from his new book, *White And Still Alright* (price $6.95, Box 96, Scarsdale, New York 10583) is some discussion about the music, what it is, where it came from and, above all else, why we ought to listen to it. Published by Rock Culture Books, an explanation of the cultural context is conspicuous by its absence.

Engel has interviewed the components of eight white vocal groups and laid out the results; if you've ever seen a copy of the now-defunct *Yesterday's Memories*, you'll be familiar with the style (or lack of it) and the book format simply permits greater space in which to concentrate on all the indigestible variables which fascinate collectors and bewilder everyone else.

White vocal groups — the sometimes goofy, sometimes beautiful sounds of the Earls, the Regents, the Skyliners — monopolised my own Hot Ten back in 1960-63. By WASP standards, 'white' is a bit of a misnomer, since Rocky Sharpe's spiritual ancestors sprang mostly from lower status minorities. Engel's fact-crammed pages reveal no end of surnames which are hard to spell and impossible to pronounce. Their owners were descended from European immigrants who settled in the

Eastern cities — New York, New Jersey and Philadelphia — where the Orioles and other black groups had left a heritage to which kids of all races could aspire.

The West Coast lacked that tradition, and most white groups from L.A. specialised in soft, pretty, summery sounds without the nutrition of rhythm & blues; these are ignored by Engel, who concentrates on the neo-doowop of the Italian, Hispanic and Polish kids who took to the subways and sidewalks in search of the perfect echo during the early Sixties.

Many of the Puerto Ricans — perhaps, next to blacks the lowest on the social scale — were recruited from street gangs (cf. the original cast of *West Side Story*) and black–Puerto Rican combinations, like Frankie Lymon & The Teenagers, were not uncommon. Of the rest, high-school students abounded, while others enjoyed clerical or technical occupations to which they returned after no more than one or two hit records.

In this respect, white doo-woppers and their black counterparts frequently shared the same destiny. Johnny Maestro of the Crests made it as lead singer with the Brooklyn Bridge, Hank Medress of the Tokens became a successful record producer and Dion told his old friends to sit down while he played guitar and let his hair grow long. The rest now scuffle between daytime jobs and rock'n'roll revival shows.

White doo-wop is not everyone's favourite milkshake, and there was an undeniably wimpy strain to the poetic content of most such records. The subject matter lacked variety, and the words were always slightly desperate. The Excellents' 'Coney Island Baby' is typical: *'You mean so much to me / You're my pretty little lady / I love you tenderly / You're my lucky star / That's what you are / You're my everything / Soon you'll wear my ring'*. Immature attitudes were taken to their logical extremity in a handful of lullabies by the Mystics, the Chevrons and the Elegants — a group with the dubious distinction of failing to follow up a million-selling Number One in 'Little Star' (Engel devotes no fewer than ten pages to these most unfortunate of one hit wonders).

Groups like these appropriated a black singing style while denying the candid language of black groups, rarely expressing love and desire in sexual terms. Lyrics were romantic, magical and puritan, filling the same need which the Osmonds tap today. The many white groups who celebrated fluctuating love affairs in an historical context were more acceptable to the ears of British R&B fans. Tin Pan Alley ballads — 'Once In A While', 'Over The Rainbow', 'Count Every Star', 'Unchained Melody', 'Where Or When', 'Look Homeward Angel' — were superb vehicles for untrained voices, and they were revived manifold by everyone from the Chimes to Vito & The Salutations.

Dusty R&B hits were also resuscitated. The Orioles' repertoire was plundered by the Duprees, the Classics and Dante & The Evergreens, while versions of particularly obscure songs by teenaged whites far out-sold those by black originators. As Showaddywaddy, Darts and Rocky

Sharpe & The Replays have discovered, there simply isn't an easier way to get a hit.

Then, as now, new compositions were pretty derivative, many containing a fierce blast of *déjà vu*: the Sixties movement was summed up by the Earls' 'Remember Then' and, less abstractly, 'Those Oldies But Goodies' by both Little Caesar & The Romans and Nino & The Ebbtides.

Record-buyers were so behind the times that several groups — the Devotions ('Rip Van Winkle'), the Regents ('Barbara-Ann'), the Capris ('There's A Moon Out Tonight') — had disintegrated long before their records began to attract any interest. A 1964 notice in *Billboard* sought the whereabouts of the Devotions to let them know that 'Rip Van Winkle' was up from 57 to 47 with a bullet.

Before writer and researcher Ed Engel began to tip the scales, white doo-wop had its detractors. Few of the records were scarce — a situation which invited a pejorative 'non-collector' tag. Black group enthusiasts were also heard to suggest that it wasn't the real juba; it was 'dork rock', a vulgar caricature of black doo-wop which lacked finesse. This, I think, missed the point: by the early Sixties, mixed groups (Marcels) and black groups (Edsels) were selling large quantities of records with a rampantly commercial sound that exaggerated bass and falsetto roles. The development was temporal and not racial.

Then, there were the lead singers. In Jimmy Beaumont (the Skyliners), Dion DiMucci (the Belmonts), Johnny Maestro (the Crests) and Lenny Cocco (the Chimes), the idiom had the greatest lead vocalists of their generation. Even allowing for a self-conscious lack of humour, these were exceptionally good singers by any standards; mountains of emotion, a tremendous range and a vibrant, inbuilt piquancy were only a few of their virtues. There was a keen edge to their voices, and a purity of tone that escaped many of the black ex-sanctified church singers they idolised. And, despite the increasing segregation of R&B radio playlists, most nationally successful white doo-woppers dented the R&B charts with their first hit; as new and totally unknown artists, R&B stations simply couldn't tell what colour they were.

An unwritten assumption among collectors of vocal group records — hits or not — is that, somehow, they're all good. Engel's in-depth studies of the Jumpin' Tones or the Consorts are of no use to anyone who wants to know how their discs compare to, say, the Earls or the Skyliners. I can't be alone in wanting to know which of the groups I haven't heard are worth seeking out. Surely that's what it's all about — one fan trying to communicate the reasons for his particular enthusiasm to as many people as possible. On this level Engel fails, but — if you're already one of the converted and you have the records to which *White And Still Alright* makes fleeting reference — you'll be delighted with the disclosures in the text. And if you saw *Mean Streets* and left the cinema enthralled, the book has enough photos to recapture something of that milieu. Indeed, each case history (Randy & The Rainbows, the Earls, the Regents, Vito & The

Salutations and the story of the Cousins label) is liberally dotted with label photos and pix of ever-changing personnel.

Since so few doo-wop books can be read as entertainment, you might just as well go for those which strip away the prose and publish the bare essentials. Three impressively huge discographical tomes do exactly that. Albert Leichter's *Discography Of Rhythm & Blues And Rock'n'Roll Circa 1945-64* comes in a 200-page loose-leaf binder. It covers solo artists as well as groups, and the entries are arranged by song-titles ('ABC Boogie' to 'Zup Zup') — useful if you know the song but not who recorded it. Robert D. Ferlingere's *Discography Of Rhythm & Blues And Rock'n'Roll Vocal Groups 1945 To 1965* lists more than 2,600 groups in more than 570 lucid pages. Streets ahead of these and any others I've seen is Fernando L. Gonzalez's well-planned and extremely thorough reference manual, *Disco-File: The Discographical Catalog Of American Rock'n'Roll And Rhythm & Blues Vocal Harmony Groups 1902-1976*, which carries labels, matrices, dates, bootlegs, unissued recordings and all the other minutiae which collectors appreciate.

Note 1   Originally published in *Melody Maker* (18 June 1979).

Note 2   Ferlingere's third edition (1999) is now available in two volumes together with a separately-published index which lists the names of all the group members in both (Effendee Trust, PO Box 1558, Jackson, California 95642).

5.4
CECIL HOLMES
Doo-Wop Survivor

If there's really a growing interest in doo-wop, there also exist arguable misconceptions about its nature; that it was easy to do, that ill-disciplined delinquents were marched up to the microphone in droves, that they were not so much ripped off as deserving of little reward for minuscule skills — in the immortal words of Syd Nathan: 'Pay 'em? I'm not gonna pay 'em for just oop-oop-a-doopin'!' An interview with Cecil Holmes does not crush all these assertions, but he provides the antidote to several myths and he's a lot of fun to talk to, trading easily on a manifestly likeable manner.

Here to represent the Pips' recording interests during their recent London Palladium season with Gladys Knight, Holmes is not a household figure but his name has dotted the business columns of the US trade papers for nigh on two decades and a close encounter looked promising. Ultra cool, one clean dude — cringe-inducing words to describe the current swarm of superflies — they all apply to Cecil Holmes, the forty-one year old Vice President of Casablanca, perhaps the most aggressive of disco record companies. It's a long way from the Brooklyn stoop where Holmes, then a fifteen year old baritone, formed the Cavaliers from amongst high school friends who lived in the Fort Greene housing projects.

It was 1953: Holmes, Lowe Murray, Leroy Randolph, Ron Anderson and Ron Mosely recorded 'Dynaflow' for Tommy Robinson, owner of Harlem's Atlas and Angletone labels. Holmes, who sang lead on this greasy rock'n'roll car song, thought it was the worst record in the world.

The Fi-Tones were formed in 1954 after Mosely had been conscripted. Lloyd Davis and Gene Redd joined Holmes, Murray and Anderson, making the Fi-Tones a better proposition. Their singles, nine of them on Atlas and Angletone, appear together on one of those copiously-annotated albums in the Relic series (5010). It's not a record I would wish to live without, but that says much for my magpie tendencies and little for the quality of the music, which is not readily distinguishable from thousands of other groups in the highly-competitive close harmony style of the mid-Fifties.

The group's strongest support was confined to the North-East —

specifically New Jersey, where vocal harmony appreciation ran deepest. Today, their appeal is restricted to a small band of fanatics whose tastes are determined by a record's scarcity; apart from 'Foolish Dreams' and 'Let's Fall In Love', the Fi-Tones didn't sell too many discs and their somewhat fossilised recordings are consequently prized collectors' items. 'I thought we were pretty good,' said Holmes. 'We admired the Orioles, the Ravens, the Swallows and that was a whole different level, but fundamentally, singing wise, the Fi-Tones did the right things. Gene Redd and Lloyd Davis were *music* people. Lloyd knew music and it wasn't a matter of just guessin' at chords. He'd play the chords for us and direct us. We'd feel for our notes like groups still do today, and we did it properly: we were in tune in other words. We practised for hours at my mother's house and Tommy Robinson was very personal with us, he was really concerned about us. He came to our houses when we rehearsed, and when we got bigger he'd rent studios and never miss a rehearsal.'

'Let's Fall In Love' was played a lot by Alan Freed, the disc-jockey who coined the phrase 'rock'n'roll' and contributed beyond measure to the advancement of black artists by opening up hitherto segregated airwaves. He's been called an out-and-out opportunist, but Holmes's praise is unqualified: 'Freed was the King and our biggest thrill was to work on one of his shows. When Alan played your record, it was a hit. We even went as far as to record one of his numbers — well, I doubt if he really wrote it, but what the heck, Alan was such a beautiful guy.'

Holmes's father, an accountant from British Guyana who helped inaugurate the United Mutual Life Insurance Co, was less than overjoyed with his son's prospects: 'He never cared much for the music profession. He'd say: "That's fine with the groups and stuff, that's fine, but when you gonna get a job?" And he had a point; 'cos it was hard to earn a living. I worked in a grocery store and I'd go out and sing at weekends. If we got a theatre booking for a week or more, I'd quit my job and think: "Well, this is it, I'm going to stardom!" We'd do three weeks at the Howard in Washington or the Royal in Philadelphia, and then we'd come back home and the money would run out and I'd end up in the grocery store again.'

Tommy Robinson — one of the first blacks to operate his own label back in 1951 — continued to release Fi-Tones singles until 1959. However, the group cut their last disc in 1957 for Old Town, an outfit owned by the colourful Hymie Weiss, who was hot with the Fiestas, Billy Bland and the Solitaires, a polished harmony group with a substantial career in neon lights long before Cecil Holmes joined them in 1960.

Few commentators have a benevolent word for Weiss, but Holmes isn't one of them: 'People will say things about Hymie, but he's another guy I love. He treated me like a gentleman and I still admire him. He might have ripped me off, but producers did that in those days. It was accepted for you to produce yourselves but Hymie would sit there with his big cigar and call himself producer. We didn't know anything about publishing, so if we wrote songs we gave them to Hymie. People can sit

Left to right: Gene Redd, Lloyd Davis, Ron Anderson, Cecil Holmes and Lowe Murray.

back and complain about it, but you either got ripped off or you never got in in the first place. He gave us the opportunity to record and I thank him for that, and I thank him for his knowledge, 'cos Hymie was the greatest salesman in the world. I have to say this. If I have a problem today, he's the first person to phone with advice: "Hey, ya did this wrong — don't forget *your* morals now!" '

Holmes toured the East Coast with the Solitaires until 1964, when he formed RMH Productions with Gene Redd, who arranged the music, and Ron Mosely, who took care of the publishing. Holmes promoted the records — a craft he had learned by watching Hymie Weiss and Tommy Robinson, who'd introduced him to a host of top deejays including Hal Jackson, Tommy Smalls and Rocky G. Their first production, by the Soul Sisters, was a big one. Smokey McCallister, who managed these enormous, gut-wailing girls, brought them into RMH's 53rd Street office with a tune he'd written for them, 'I Can't Stand It'. The rhythm track and the girls' voices were laid down at King in Cincinnati (where Redd's father had been house producer), while the horns were dubbed on at Herb Abramson's New York studio. Holmes took the master to Sue's Juggy Murray, whose first wife worked as a secretary for Tommy Robinson.

The Soul Sisters' album, also released on Sue, is one of the finest gospel-like soul sets of all time, but their burning presence on wax did not

5.4 - Cecil Holmes

come over on stage. They appeared on *Ready Steady Go* in November 1964 (*'Fab singing but poor stage act,'* I'd noted in the vernacular of the era). 'That must have been an off-night,' suggested Holmes. 'They were good. They played the Apollo and really tore the joint up.' Cecil also has a startling anecdote about Titus Turner, who wrote the Soul Sisters' 'Soul Food' and other culinary delights: 'He was a flamboyant type of guy and a very fine songwriter. He wrote 'Fever' and all that.' Come again — I thought of similar claims by Otis Blackwell and Joe Tex. 'Yeah, well, I remember Titus telling me how he wrote it one day when it was very hot outside. I don't know if he was jivin' me or not, but a guy like Titus could write a song and, just because he needed some money, he'd come up to a Hymie Weiss or a George Goldner and sell it. I'm sure he was involved in 'Fever'.'

Smokey McCallister also brought in the Jewels, a less hysterical girl group whose 'Opportunity' climbed the middle reaches of the Hot 100 on Dimension in 1964. This was the Washington, DC-based act who recorded for Checker and backed Billy Stewart on 'Reap What You Sow'. But 'Opportunity' was their biggest hit. The attractive, bittersweet sound and a follow-up, 'Smokey Joe' (written by Valerie Simpson and Nick Ashford) were leased to Don Kirshner after Holmes and Mosely gatecrashed his office complaining that they'd tried to get the Soul Sisters on Dimension — it was a lie — but no-one had listened to them and surely Kirshner wouldn't want to miss out on the next big hit from RMH?

Kirshner flipped over the Jewels and Holmes stayed on at Colpix doing promotion work, while Gene Redd eventually went on to great success with Kool & The Gang. Colpix was not a R&B label but Holmes usually managed to get five or six records on the Top Forty playlists of black stations like WWRL. When Kirshner left Colpix, Holmes hooked up with Carl Proctor, national promo man for Mercury, and worked on Clyde McPhatter, Bobby Byrd, Mack Rice — ' 'Mustang Sally' was my big one' — Otis Leavill and Dee Dee Warwick. 'I was making only $150 a month and Carl couldn't get me any more money. There were lots of political things going on at Mercury and I was getting calls to do national promotion for other companies. Eventually, I switched to Cameo, who started me out on $200 a week in 1964.'

Originally owned by Bernie Lowe, Cameo had recorded few exceptional artists, generally churning out mediocre teen-oriented material which profited from regular *Bandstand* exposure. Their reputation as a hit factory with no concern for artistry changed immediately Holmes joined: 'Some Texans had bought the label from Lowe. I was hired on a Monday, and on the Thursday they hired another guy, Neil Bogart, to do pop promotion. We were a team and we became real good friends. I worked on Dee Dee Sharp, ? (Question Mark) & The Mysterians — that was our first gold record — Bunny Sigler, Eddie Holman, the Stairsteps. Terry Knight and Bob Seger were on the pop end, but most of our business was R&B. Then Al Rosenthal, a one-stop owner who'd bought Cameo from the Texans, he upped and sold to Allen Klein in 1967. Klein's a big shot and we thought it would be interesting: y'know, lotsa money and no problems. Well, Klein never came to the office. We'd call him and he'd say: "Don't worry about it." Weeks would go by and there was simply no direction. It was a waste. We were known as a dynamite bunch: if people didn't want me, they wanted Neil.'

Holmes and Bogart accepted an offer from Artie Ripp at Kama Sutra. He'd formed Buddah Records and required management personnel immediately. Within months, Holmes was Vice President — second only to Neil Bogart, an arrangement which led to a five year string of million-sellers (Curtis Mayfield, Isley Brothers, Honey Cone, Edwin Hawkins, Gladys Knight *et al*) and which still persists at Casablanca, where the dynamic duo now dominate the world with disco.

How come Holmes became a successful executive when so many of his fellow doo-woppers are back in the car-wash or dead from drug addiction? 'Number One' — he coats every soft-spoken word with a sincerity print can't convey — 'I think I was very fortunate. I had a guy like Tommy Robinson who looked after me like a son, and I watched everything, even the way he talked on the phone. Number Two, I always realised I wasn't a great singer, I wasn't a talented guy like, say, a Frankie Lymon or a Pookie Hudson. They took it seriously and tried to take it to the top and, unfortunately, there just wasn't room. I was smart enough to realise that.'

Originally published in *Melody Maker* (7 October 1978).

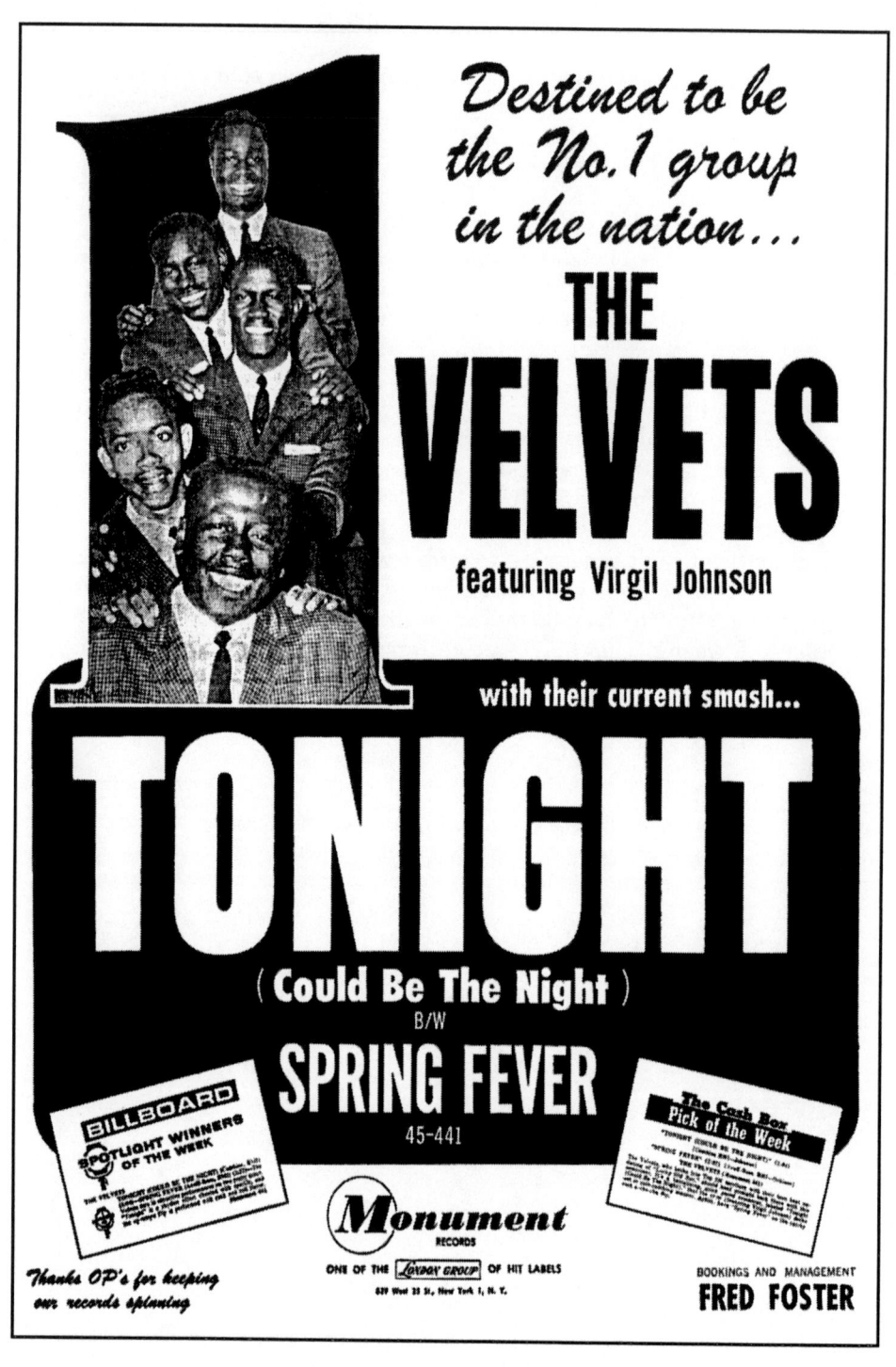

Top to bottom: William Solomon, Virgil Johnson, Robert Thursby, Mark Prince and Clarence Rigsby.

5.5

THE VELVETS
The Complete Velvets

The Velvets didn't conform to any of doo-wop's norms. They hailed not from New York, but from Odessa, where the Texan panhandle meets the rest of the state. In the age of the street-corner amateur, they made records as polished as their patent leather shoes. Lead singer Virgil Johnson, the Velvets' 'Mr. Sheen', didn't overdose when the hits stopped; he had aspirations outside music and never gave up his day job. Weirdest of all, the Velvets barely dabbled in R&B. Like their mentor, Roy Orbison, they sang songs which straddled that increasingly invisible line between country and pop. The Velvets and Roy Orbison shared the same producer in Fred Foster and the same session musicians in Nashville's A-team. In essence, the Velvets dusted Orbie's sombre, *bel canto* agonies with a faint but cheerful shot of proto-soul.

Virgil Johnson, born 29 December 1935 in Cameron, Texas, sang in his church choir. Later, he listened to the Spaniels, the Clovers and the Flamingos. He attended Dunbar High School in nearby Lubbock; researcher Alan Jenkins has pointed to a page in the 1953 Lubbock High School year-book, which refers to the Dunbar exchange assembly and an appearance by a trio which included Virgil Johnson accompanied by the Dunbar Combo. Buddy Holly, who attended Lubbock High from 1953 to 1955, may have seen them.

In the late Fifties, Johnson sang with the Dynatones, a group of fellow students at Bishop College in Marshall, Texas where he studied English. On graduation, he joined the staff at Blackshear Junior High School in Odessa where he taught English to eighth grade pupils.

It was November 1958: according to the brief liner on the Velvets' London EP, Johnson heard two students, Mark Prince and Clarence Rigsby, singing as a duo. He recruited two more students, adding Robert Thursby's first tenor and William Solomon's baritone to Rigsby's tenor and Mark Prince's bass. 'They were very clean-cut kids,' Virgil told me. 'They did not drink and they didn't smoke. Robert was musically inclined. He played trombone and read music and helped a lot with our arrangements. Mark had a brother, Paul Prince, who wrote songs including the song 'Dawn'. Solly *[William Solomon]* was just a wonderful guy, and Clarence was the centre of our joy. We picked on him a lot because he had a sleeping sickness. We were always waking him up. But he was one of the best golfers I've ever seen. Being black, he never had the opportunity to expound on his golfing talents, but he was very good.'

The quintet performed at school sock-hops and campus functions, and they worked up a repertoire which included 'That Lucky Old Sun'. In 1960 they impressed Roy Orbison, who heard them whilst visiting Odessa where he and the Teen Kings had attended Junior College. Flush with the success of his first Top Ten hits, the King of Bug-Eyed Operatics recommended Virgil and pals to Fred Foster, the owner of Monument Records and the producer of 'Only The Lonely', 'Blue Angel' *et al*.

Foster, who grew up on a farm in North Carolina, named the company after the Washington Monument, which he first saw when he arrived in the city on a visit to his sister at the age of seventeen. He took a job as a curb-boy at a fast food drive-in and soon met prominent Washington music men like singer and club owner Billy Strickland and music publisher Ben Adelman. Foster and Strickland wrote songs which Strickland recorded for King Records in 1951. Thereafter, Foster put lyrics to melodies supplied by Adelman; the McGuire Sisters were among the first takers. Adelman, owner of Washington's only recording studio, let Foster supervise a session by Jimmy Dean. The results were sold to 4-Star and Foster was on his way. He promoted records for Mercury and ABC-Paramount. He also worked for J&F Distributors before setting up Monument in 1958.

The company's first release, 'Gotta Travel On' by Jimmy Dean's guitarist, Billy Grammer, was a monster, rising to No. 4 on *Billboard*'s Hot 100 in 1959 and remaining on the chart for twenty weeks. That success financed an office in the Nashville suburb of Hendersonville and a host of fresh hitmakers including Billy Graves, Stan Robinson (the father of the Black Crowes' Chris Robinson) and Dick Flood, whose cover of 'The Three Bells' notched the Top Thirty. Foster, who had successfully merged pop and C&W, could do no wrong. Then came the Big 'O', signed from RCA to Monument because Wesley Rose, Orbison's manager, was struck by Foster's ambition.

One thing Monument didn't have was a black vocal group. Indeed, discounting Grandpa Jones & His Grandchildren, the label didn't have *any* kind of vocal group. 'Monument wanted to come up with a group,' Virgil Johnson recalled. 'We were doing some singing in the Odessa area and Roy Orbison heard us one or two particular times. He called me at work one day and told me who he was, and asked me if I would like to come to Nashville. We drove all the way there. It was Fred Foster's idea to call us the Velvets. In fact, he decided it should be 'The Velvets featuring Virgil Johnson' because there was a group called the Velvets years before. They had a song out called 'I' *[on Red Robin]*. That was a totally different group.' (Parenthetically, Virgil Johnson's Velvets confined themselves to Monument; they had no hand in Velvets' records on Plaid or 20th Century-Fox, and there is no connection with Ronnie Price & The Velvets on Carousel.)

The group's first session, at RCA's Nashville studios, produced four tunes: 'Time And Again', 'That Lucky Old Sun', 'Spring Fever' and 'Tonight (Could Be The Night)'. Roy Orbison had thrilled to Frankie Laine's big-voiced rendition of 'That Lucky Old Sun' when it topped the best-sellers in 1949. This particularly valuable copyright was co-written by Beasley Smith, one of Nashville's premier musical minds. Smith, who also penned 'Beg Your Pardon' and 'Night Train To Memphis', had worked as music director on Nashville's WSM for twenty years.

'That Lucky Old Sun' has always been a black music favourite, with pre-Velvets versions by Sarah Vaughan, Sam Cooke, LaVern Baker, Hot Lips Page and any number of vocal groups. The song got post-Velvets treatment from Ray Charles, Cash McCall, Lou Rawls and Solomon Burke. Some of these were hits in the USA, where the Velvets' debut made no chart noise at all. None of them were hits in Britain, where the Velvets clipped *Record Retailer*'s chart at No. 46 for one week in May 1961.

Beasley Smith's enduring composition was coupled with 'Time And Again', a melodic ballad which Roy Orbison penned with Joe Melson, one of his staunchest co-writers. Melson, from Bonham, Texas, first met Orbison in 1957 but lost touch until '59, when he spotted Orbie's green Cadillac passing by an Odessa drive-in. He'd sung with the Fannin County Boys and the Cavaliers, whose act included nutritious helpings of R&B. He also cut beat ballads, rock'n'roll and ersatz blues for Hickory Records. None of it sold, but he became a wealthy man on the royalties from 'Only The Lonely', 'Blue Angel', 'Crying', 'Running Scared' and the rest.

The Velvets' second release paired Virgil Johnson's song, 'Tonight', with Roy Orbison's 'Spring Fever'. Roy's lyrics (*'bells are ringing, birdies are singing'*) could suggest that collaborators like Melson brought out the best in Roy's songwriting skills. It was 'Tonight' which took off, 'Tonight' which soared up the Hot 100 (ascending to No. 26 in June 1961) and 'Tonight' which now resonates in the memory as a prime-cut oldie but goodie. Who knows, it may even have widened the Nashville path of access for songwriters who were not country at all.

'Tonight' is as perfect as black pop music would get. Johnson may not have had the chops to sing the churchiest soul, but his light, Johnny Mathis-ish tenor sounds just right in Fred Foster's shimmering setting. Charm and innocence leap out of every groove. The foursome behind Johnson actually chant 'doo-wop', but the outstanding production and musicianship — provided by Music City's finest — were light years away from the subway or street-corner. Once again, and for the last time, the Velvets made the British charts; 'Tonight' clocked in at No. 50 for one week in August 1961.

The London EP blurb also referred to appearances with Brook Benton, the Falcons and Ruth Brown, but these were strictly local gigs. According to Virgil, a family man with a steady job outside music, touring was out of the question. The other members of the group were still in high school and none of them enjoyed air travel.

Monument chose two Orbison–Melson songs for the third release. 'Lana', with at least two hooks as big as a barn, was buried on the B-side of 'Laugh', which barely dented the Hot 100 at No. 90. 'We ran into a problem there,' Virgil recalled. 'Part of the country was playing one side, and another part of the country was playing the other side. We should never have put those two songs out together. The record never did happen big here, but 'Lana' was Number One in Japan.' Roy Orbison's own version of 'Lana', released as a single in 1966 after he had moved from Monument to MGM, wasn't a hit, and a cover of the Velvets by George McCannon III on Parkway likewise never dented anyone's consciousness.

Virgil Johnson retains the fondest memories of Fred Foster and Roy Orbison. 'Fred,' he told me, 'was a super individual and always very straight with the Velvets. There was his sincerity and his honesty. Those were the two qualities that he had that a lot of producers did not have. He had produced records in the past, and I think he had some unpleasant experiences earlier as a producer. I think he told himself that he would not let that happen to him and that, in return, he would never get that way. That's why I say he was very, very honest.'

Johnson had similar praise for Roy Orbison. Speaking to Seamus McGarvey, he declared: 'Roy was just a genuine, down-to-earth, talented individual. He would help us and give us pointers. And when we were working on a song he had written, he would try and guide us. He always encouraged us, and he always had time to stop and talk with us. Nowadays, to get to a superstar you have to go through thirty secretaries to find out what city he's in, but Roy was never that way.'

Monument continued putting out Velvets' singles — nine in all — until 1966. Roy Alfred had written a few anthemic songs which tripped off a million tongues (eg 'The Hucklebuck' and 'Rock & Roll Waltz'), but 'The Love Express' attracted few buyers. The group's fifth single, a revival of Shirley & Lee's 'Let The Good Times Roll', went nowhere, though other versions have been hits since then. 'Crying In The Chapel' was next up. This Artie Glenn C&W tune went pop in 1953 (the Orioles) and again in 1965 (Elvis Presley), but few remember the Velvets' Latin slant on it. Two more C&W tunes made up the group's seventh single: Dick Flood, Monument's early hitmaker, wrote 'Here Comes That Song Again', and Jan Crutchfield's 'Nightmare' is unusual material — scarcely a patch on 'In Dreams', though not dissimilar in its subject matter and its resolution without repetition. A complete change of tack ushered in the group's recording of 'If, an operatic ballad in the Roy Hamilton vein. This Tin Pan Alley standard, published in 1934, had been a Number one for Perry Como in 1950.

The Velvets finally bowed out with 'Let The Fool Kiss You', another of Virgil Johnson's songs. And that was that, apart from thirteen tracks which were left in the can. These appeared on a scarce Japanese vinyl collection and have also been liberated by Ace. There's a clutch of Johnson's songs as generic as any early Sixties black pop. Almost all of them have a broadly appealing tunefulness coupled with inventive string arrangements by Anita Kerr or Bill Justis. 'Be Evermine' has a dose of 'yakety sax' from Boots Randolph, and the Coasters-ish 'You Done Me Bad' also deserves special mention — it's the only Velvets song on which Clarence Rigsby sings lead. The versatile Virgil Johnson is out front on every other track.

Charley Pride was still looking for a hit when the Velvets turned to C&W favourites from Boudleaux Bryant, Vic McAlpin (the Acuff–Rose staff writer famed for his contribution to 'Long Gone Lonesome Blues') and Roger Miller, whose own version of 'Husbands And Wives' charted in 1966 (Ray Stevens arranged the Velvets' version).

'Poison Love', a 1951 hit for Johnnie & Jack, is the best of the lot; I doubt if Roy Orbison, as Gothic as he could be, ever came up with a line as chilling as *Your poisoned love has stained the lifeblood in my heart and soul*. This wrist-slasher was written by Elmer Laird, a used car salesman from Houston who never lived to see the royalties. He was stabbed to death during an argument with a customer who refused to pay up.

Monument moved on. Foster signed other black artists including Lloyd Price (whom he'd promoted at ABC-Paramount), Ray Sharpe, Nashville-based Gene Allison and the equally underrated Arthur Alexander. In this respect, Fred Foster was ahead of his time. But the company prospered instead with a substantial roster of groundbreaking country stars, eventually going bust in 1981. 'Something to do with a bank out of Kentucky,' Billy Swan told *Now Dig This*. 'Fred had money in that bank.'

The Velvets went back to a Texas they had never really left. Robert Thursby moved to Hawaii, where he plays clubs with a small band. Mark Prince works in Sherman, Texas and William Solomon lives in Denver, Colorado. Clarence Rigsby won the men's golfing tournament at the Municipal Golf Club in Lubbock, Texas but perished in a car crash in 1978. Virgil Johnson also settled in Lubbock, where he became a deejay on radio KSEL on Sunday nights. He kept on teaching and, in 1993, he retired from his job as principal of Lubbock's Dunbar-Struggs Junior High School, a post he had held for twenty-five years.

Johnson can afford to look back at his moment in the sun without rancour. He's adamant though on the reasons for the group's relatively short chart life: 'You got to realise, thirty-five years ago there were two music markets in the US. You had a black market and you had a white market. We were extremely popular with whites, but we were never extremely popular with blacks. We were black and we didn't sound like it. People didn't know we were a black group. We couldn't tour, and that really hurt us.'

Liner note from *The Complete Velvets* (Ace CDCHD-625) 1996.

5.5 - The Velvets

6

SOUNDS OF THE SWAMPS

6.1
Rockin' On The Bayou

Swamp pop; the glorious rolling sounds of Jivin' Gene, Joe Barry, Cookie & The Cupcakes, Rod Bernard and just about anything that sounds like a classically doomy Louisiana ballad. When the entire school was fixated by Presley's Neapolitan balladry, I'd be monopolising the communal Dansette with 'This Should Go On Forever', 'I'm A Fool To Care', 'Sea Of Love' or 'Breaking Up Is Hard To Do', revelling in the secret loveliness of it all. Where those records actually came from was anybody's guess. Now we know.

Between Port Arthur, Texas in the West and New Orleans, Louisiana in the East, there's four hundred miles of US highway — take a peek at the back of *Another Saturday Night* (Oval 3001) for a handy map. On either side you'll find the townships of South Louisiana; Lake Charles (the home of Goldband and Khourys); Ville Platte (Floyd Soileau's Jin and Swallow labels); Abbeville (where Bobby Charles lives in hermit-like seclusion); New Iberia, which spawned 'The Cajun Twist'; Crowley, where Jay Miller recorded the finest Excello blues; Lafayette (Carol Rachou's La Louisianne Records); swampland's outer extremities like the aptly-named Cut Off (home to Joe Barry)... Thibodeaux, Big Mamou, Sulphur, Opelousas and all the other settlements which spring to life in the songs and stories of rock'n'roll, Cajun or swamp pop style.

Between 1958 and 1962, the US charts were alive with white Louisiana boys — Joe Barry, Jivin' Gene, T.K. Hulin, Warren Storm and Rod Bernard were five of the biggest — and for a brief period these genuinely unaffected singers captivated American record-buyers with a strange, eerie sound that's indigenous to South Louisiana (where it still survives), but now alien to the general mainstream of popular music.

It's been called a number of things — swamp pop, Cajun rock or bayou beat — but the locals have a less expansive phrase: South Louisiana music. 'That's what we call it,' said Johnnie Allan who was here recently, promoting his reactivated 'Promised Land'. 'I guess the only way to describe it is to say that it's the musicians who make the sound different. Those guys, Jivin' Gene, T.K. Hulin, virtually all of them speak French. Their family names are French, and some of them played in French accordion bands just like I did. Consequently, I think we all kept part of this French-Cajun music ingrained in us, you can detect it, something of a Cajun flavour in the song.'

The Cajuns of South-West Louisiana are unique. Banished from Nova Scotia, these French-settler descendants arrived in Louisiana in the 1760s, developing a distinctive and colourful music in virtual isolation. Cajun followers differentiate between a traditional music — played on accordion, fiddle, rhythm guitar and triangle, with vocals in French patois — and a more progressive, but none the less authentic strain which encompasses a marked hillbilly influence and can lead with a fiddle instead of accordion. Steel guitar, bass and drums are heard and, as often as not, English lyrics replace the Cajun dialect.

Joe Falcon, who made the first Cajun records during the late Twenties, is synonymous with traditional Cajun, while most of today's South Louisiana groups play in the 'modern but authentic' style. A third category, pop or Nashville-Cajun might embrace Jimmy Newman or the Kershaw brothers, musicians who strive for national appeal without losing their local identity. Rusty & Doug Kershaw's 'Louisiana Man', a song which boasts over four hundred recordings, is the best-known example. An aural travelogue, it paints a three-minute scenario of local traditions, drying muskrat skins in the sun and web-footed children named Ned or Mack who fish from a pirogue and accompany Papa Jack on his trips to town.

Swamp pop, bayou beat or South Louisiana music was born of many things. In the form that first spilled on to the Hot 100 — Warren Storm's 'Prisoner's Song' dented the best-sellers in 1958 and Rod Bernard's 'This Should Go On Forever' reached the Top Twenty the following year — the influences lay as much in the intensity of early Elvis and the black music of Fats Domino as the French-Cajun style of Joseph Falcon. Western swing and hillbilly — the oil industry along the Gulf Coast attracted many outsiders — had already altered the character of French-Cajun music, particularly in the Thirties when many string bands eliminated the accordion altogether.

And after World War II, country fiddler Harry Choates — not, in fact, a true Cajun — did much to revitalise Cajun music with his recording of 'Jole Blon'. The impact of rock'n'roll was infinitely more drastic: when Arhoolie's Chris Strachwitz stopped at a Lafayette bar in 1960 he heard 'only a band trying to imitate Fats Domino'. Johnnie Allan, Jivin' Gene, Rod Bernard and many of their French-speaking contemporaries had already crossed over.

Domino's clipped vocals and infectious piano triplets were particularly pervasive, but the meandering songs of other New Orleans artists, Guitar Slim ('The Things I Used To Do') and Earl King ('Those Lonely, Lonely Nights') contributed much to the structure: ' 'Those Lonely, Lonely Nights',' explained Dr. John, 'is a classic South Louisiana two-chord — E-flat B-flat — slow ballad.' The same progressions characterise most swamp pop and, although whites enjoyed the most success with this musical hybrid, black artists like Elton Anderson ('The Secret Of Love') and Cookie & The Cupcakes were paradigms of the style.

Jerry Lee Lewis, himself from Ferriday, Louisiana, revived

'Mathilda' and 'Got You On My Mind', two of the Cupcakes' greatest, and the quaintly-named group has always had a strong following among rock'n'roll auction-hunters. Cookie, otherwise Huey Thierry from Jennings, Louisiana, led a loose aggregation of local musicians including Shelton Dunaway, a rich and vibrant singer whose voice oozed swampland soul.

Although tiny, one-man record labels have existed in most South Louisiana towns, aspiring swamp-rockers generally ended up on Mercury, a label which had the muscle to distribute nationwide. Mercury had already proved it could make hits out of Southern music and local producers — Huey Meaux, George Khoury and Floyd Soileau — developed strong ties with the major company. Meaux works mostly in Texas and Mississippi, although he was born in Kaplan, Louisiana and is widely known as 'The Crazy Cajun'.

He first recorded Jivin' Gene in Port Arthur in 1959 and East Texas/South Louisiana sounds have flecked virtually everything he's since produced. A bundle of albums on Meaux's Starflite label (Doug Kershaw, Joey Long, T.K. Hulin, Freddy Fender and the enigmatic Jimmy Donley) reactivated swamp pop a few years back and Meaux has now turned full circle, recently producing Joe Barry and calling Freddy Fender's latest album *Swamp Gold*; it's a deliciously cobwebbed selection of swamp pop favourites, and by far the most exciting stuff Fender's done since 'Wasted Days And Wasted Nights'.

Floyd Soileau, who distributes almost every Cajun label and produces a high percentage of Cajun records on his own, is no less dedicated to what he calls 'South Louisiana rock'n'roll'. Like most Southern record men, he doesn't want to get too big and, if a disc of his begins to attract sales outside Louisiana, he automatically places the master with a major label: Johnnie Allan's 'Lonely Days And Lonely Nights' (MGM), Joe Barry's 'I'm A Fool To Care' (Smash) and Rod Bernard's 'This Should Go On Forever' (Argo) were all Soileau's records, as was Tommy McLain's 1966 million-seller, 'Sweet Dreams' (MSL).

These occasional, unexpected, even accidental breakthroughs into the pop field overshadow a never-ending stream of Cajun and rock'n'roll records for local consumption, some of which exceed sales of 50,000 copies. Soileau carries a vast stock at his record shop in Ville Platte. As an introduction to swamp pop, I can recommend three compilations. Rod Bernard, Lee Martin, Johnnie Allan, Phil Bo and Jivin' Gene can be enjoyed on *A Rockin' Date With South Louisiana Stars* (Jin LP-4002), while Charlie Gillett rounded up his favourite Jin tracks for *Another Saturday Night*, the Oval collection which surprised and enchanted all who heard it. It includes some of the finest singles by Tommy McLain, Belton Richard and Clint West, as well as Johnnie Allan's 'Promised Land'. An album I compiled for Mercury, *The Other Song Of The South: Louisiana Rock'n'Roll"* (Philips 6336 256) — sold no more than 1,500 copies. It includes Jivin' Gene, Cookie & The Cupcakes, Rod Bernard, Phil Phillips and Elton Anderson, and would have featured Joe Barry had the rights to his Mercury hits (on the

Smash subsidiary) not reverted to Jin. Since it contained virtually all the real cream and still managed to crap out — by way of contrast, some of the recent rockabilly anthologies have topped sales of 18,000 — there does not appear to be much scope for further reissues of this kind.

All very distressing, because Mercury have trunk-loads of it — and the Jivin' Gene catalogue ('You've Got A Spell On Me', 'You're Jealous', 'Gini Bon Beni', 'I Cried', 'My Need For Love' et al) is particularly magnificent. Somehow, this material has to be made available to those who want it; bootlegs are not the universal panacea, but then consigning Jivin' Gene's work to mildewed tape-boxes is hardly the answer.

While Mercury had the foresight to purchase masters which attracted heavy local attention, the company often exerted an unwelcome control over their new acquisitions, eviscerating the qualities which made their first records so agreeable. Phil Phillips's story is typical: 'Sea Of Love', his sole contribution to the history of rock, has a relaxed, almost intimate vocal, a rudimentary moaning back-up from the Twilights and all the natural qualities one could wish for. Produced by Eddie Shuler for George Khoury, who leased the master to Mercury, Phillips all but topped the Hot 100 in 1959. Mercury promptly whisked him off to Nashville and recorded him with strings and a female chorus; his next seven singles strove in vain for the elusive simplicity which made 'Sea Of Love' a million-seller. Jivin' Gene escaped the worst excesses, but this depressing pattern was repeated with Joe Barry, Rod Bernard and their black counterparts, including Elton Anderson.

Swamp pop has now been relegated to the backwaters of pop appreciation and the music would appear to have few devotees outside South Louisiana. Many of the stalwarts retired to play in the clubs and bars of Louisiana and East Texas as soon as their Mercury contracts expired, sometimes resisting efforts to persuade them to record for major labels again. Jivin' Gene (back in Port Arthur and no longer recording), T.K. Hulin, Gene Terry (now a policeman) and others are pretty well out of it, including the smaller fry: Phil Bo who works in a Lafayette TV store, Leroy Martin who's a deejay in Thibodeaux and Jerry Starr from New Iberia who's confined to a wheelchair.

Still, Joe Barry has a new LP on ABC/Dot, and the Jin label continues to issue prolific quantities of albums and singles. It's too late to help Jimmy Donley, who killed himself in 1963, but Joe Barry, Jimmy Newman, Johnnie Allan, Rod Bernard, Tommy McLain and others are keeping the music of South Louisiana alive. I think they deserve a wider hearing.

Originally published in *Melody Maker* (17 February 1979).

6.2

ROD BERNARD
Hot Rod

It's been twenty years since Rod Bernard dented the American Top Twenty with 'This Should Go On Forever', the all-time swamp pop classic which hangs in the air over South Louisiana and still remains high on the list of Southern jukebox requests. South Louisiana music also goes on forever, an enclave in which the Fifties sounds of rock'n'roll and triplet blues ballads remain unaltered by the bizarre musical times in which we live. Rod Bernard helps preserve these traditions with a regular stream of albums and singles; he may never make the Top Twenty again, but he's still a big man around Lafayette, Lake Charles and Opelousas where, even today, there's an insatiable demand for new versions of swamp pop favourites by genuine singers with racially undetectable voices. Theirs is not a progressive rock, but it's still a living tradition from which both the new (Eddy Raven) and the near-superannuated (Freddy Fender) draw their strength and inspiration.

'Freddy gives credit to Fats Domino and me for the things that've happened to him,' says Rod, 'but mine wasn't really the first. Bobby Charles had 'On Bended Knee', Earl King had 'Those Lonely, Lonely Nights' and Bobby Page sang 'Loneliness' when I was in high school. A lot of black dudes had the South Louisiana sound way before I did. 'This Should Go On Forever' opened the doors for a lot of local white guys, but plenty of songs opened doors for me.' Bernard, then aged ten, got his start when a local feed and seed store, Dezauche's Red Bird Sweet Potatoes, sponsored a daily radio broadcast over KSLO, Opelousas and encouraged would-be Hank Williamses to bring their guitars along on a Saturday morning. During the early Fifties, 'race music' attracted his attention, and he sang the songs of Fats Domino and B.B. King with a high school band in Winnie, Texas, where Huey Meaux, the local barber, cut his hair and talked about the Cajun-French band he played with on the side.

In 1957, Bernard recorded his first sides for Carl, a label owned by Jake Graffagnino, who ran a music store in Opelousas. Very few people heard either 'Set Me Free' or 'Linda Gail' ($20 minimum bid in the last *Goldmine*) and Rod became a deejay on KSLO, where he hosted *Boogie Time* and gained the nickname 'Hot Rod'.

In 1958, Bernard dropped by the Moonlight Inn to catch Guitar Gable and his singer, King Karl. 'Here comes Hot Rod from KSLO!'

shouted Karl. 'I'm gonna sing him my next record.' The band went straight into 'This Should Go On Forever' and Rod was totally floored: 'It really hit me as being one helluva song, and whenever I saw Karl I'd ask him when it was coming out. He kept saying: "Well, it's comin'," but it never did. Eventually, I went to his home in Opelousas and asked him if I could record it, and he taught me how to sing it.' Bernard cut his version for Floyd Soileau, who'd decided to start a record company and called on Rod because Guitar Gable, who led the other local band, had been snapped up by Jay Miller, who produced him for Excello. Rod and his group, the

Twisters, travelled to Miller's studio in Crowley; it was the only bona fide studio in the area and Miller owned the publishing on 'This Should Go On Forever', which was written by King Karl under his real name, Bernard Jolivette. The Twisters — Marion Presley (piano), Charles Boudreaux (trumpet), Rod's brother Rick Bernard (bass) and Ray Thomasine (drums) — were unaccustomed to studio conditions and the session continued into the early hours of the morning before Jay Miller decided the band could use help from his regular sessionmen, Al Foreman (lead guitar) and Bobby McBride (bass). Around 2.30 am, Rod developed a dreadful nosebleed and sang the final take with a towel around his face: 'We thought we'd got it right,' he laughs, 'but now it's embarrassing to hear how bad the thing was.'

Soileau's brand new Jin label had no distribution to speak of, but Bernard remembered his high school barber-shop and sent a boxful of records to Huey Meaux who ran a French music show on KPAC in Port Arthur: 'Huey got it played all over East Texas, he took a copy to J.P. Richardson, the Big Bopper, at KTRN in Beaumont and he was the first to play it. It took six or seven months to break out and when it got to Houston, the distributors told the major companies about it. All of a sudden we started getting phone calls. Jim Vienneau at MGM called me at home and somebody from Capitol phoned Floyd, who didn't want to lease it. He had dreams of keeping it on his label and turning Jin into the next RCA, but we started getting cover versions on it. Half a dozen came out real quick and we'd have lost the thing unless we leased it to a bigger label. Floyd made a deal with Leonard Chess and it came out on Argo.'

Bernard, the only Cajun boy to make the Top Twenty and probably the best-known exponent of the South Louisiana sound, left his Opelousas deejay job and took to the road, lip-synching his hit on countless TV shows including *American Bandstand*, where somebody objected to the line *'If it's a sin to really love you, then a sinner I will be'*. 'Dick Clark had us re-record it. There were no music tracks then, so Chess arranged for the band to cut a track in Crowley and then they flew the tape up to Chicago, where I put another vocal on it in the Chess studios. They pressed up a few with me singing *'If it's wrong to really love you, then wrong I'll always be'*. We didn't tell anybody about it, and very few people knew we'd even switched it. To think we went through all that trouble 'cos of the word 'sin' — people seem really entertained by that, particularly these days when anything goes.'

Leonard Chess also took first preference on the follow-up, 'You're On My Mind', a song originally recorded by Roy Perkins for Meladee in 1956. Thereafter, Bernard signed a management contract with Bill Hall whose affiliation with Mercury had already led to hits by the Big Bopper and Johnny Preston. Rod has few complaints about the major label, who treated him well ('a $2,500 advance and $100 a side') but failed to promote his records: 'Mercury had so many people like Brook Benton, Dinah Washington and the Platters doing exceptionally well, they didn't need to

6.2 - Rod Bernard

spend money on me or Jivin' Gene. 'One More Chance' (No. 74 in 1959) could have done well if they'd pushed it, but I was just one of the small names at the bottom of the list.'

The Mercury recordings have not stood the test of time. Cut in Nashville with Floyd Cramer, Boots Randolph and the Anita Kerr Singers, these distressingly vacuous teen ballads were never less than faintly ridiculous, though, as Rod remarked, 'they were in the groove with what was happening then: Johnny Tillotson, violins, an' all.' The rocker, 'Let's Get Together Tonight', is the best, while other songs, including 'Give Me Back My Cadillac' and 'Little Mama', remain unissued and unheard.

In 1962, the Mercury contract expired and the services beckoned. Before leaving for the Marine Corps, Bernard recorded a pile of Cajun dance songs down in Beaumont, where Johnny and Edgar Winter played guitar and sax on some of the finest discs he's made to date including 'Colinda', 'Fais-Do-Do', 'Diggy Liggy Lo' and 'Loneliness'. There's probably no better version of 'Colinda' — a Cajun anthem and a Southern hit for Rod — while 'Loneliness' exemplifies the music he sings best. Asked to explain the South Louisiana sound, he denies any special insight but gives the perfect answer when pressed: 'I can sing it, I know how to play it and I know how to write it — but I can't read music and I can't describe it. There's a little flavour of country, the rock'n'roll sound of the Fifties and a little bit of Cajun. It's a combination of all these things, but the changes are identical. If you know four chords, you can play all of 'em. Freddy Fender and I were talking about that not so long ago, and we reached the conclusion that you could sing almost every South Louisiana ballad to the same music track. It's not very original or difficult in that respect.'

Out of the Marine Corps, Rod returned to Louisiana, took further jobs in radio and formed the Shondells with Warren Storm and Skip Stewart. The group appeared on Lafayette's KLFY-TV and built up a following, which led to the well-known *Saturday Hop* album on La Louisianne in 1965. He's also recorded for Teardrop (a cover of Jerry Raines's 'Our Teenage Love'), Copyright — in Huey Meaux's Clinton, Mississippi studio, where children would ruin sessions by throwing pebbles at the tin hut-cum-echo chamber out back — and Arbee, a label he jointly owned with La Louisianne's Carol Rachou. 'Recorded In England', leased from Arbee to Scepter, was a tremendous rocker with brother Rick on the Berry-ish lead guitar: 'I was still a deejay then, and all the songs that were happening had *'Recorded In England'* stamped on 'em. It was a perfect rock'n'roll song and I hoped some English rock group would get hold of it. The only bad thing about it was that no-one ever heard of it.'

Bernard regards the early tours as a mere interruption to his broadcasting career ('when I had to force myself to smile on *Bandstand*, I thought it was time to quit') and the heavy schedule he put in with the Shondells was enough to sour him to life on the road. But he still loves recording and, although he's been writing and producing commercials for KLFY-TV since 1970, he's also managed to cut half a dozen albums for labels like Jin and Crazy Cajun. They're all easily obtained from specialist outlets, and I'd happily recommend any to lovers of swamp pop. *Boogie In Black And White* (Jin 9014) teams Bernard with zydeco king Clifton Chenier; it's a wild and woolly rock'n'roll set with a spontaneity one normally only dreams about: 'We didn't rehearse or anything, just said what key it was and took off wailing. Clifton's from Opelousas, and his name is up there with Fats Domino and Jimmy Reed.' The first album, *Rod Bernard* (Jin 4007), gathers up the Hallway tracks, while the rest — *Country Lovin'* (Jin 9008), *Night Lights And Love Songs* (Jin 9010) and *This Should Go On Forever And Other Bayou Classics* (Crazy Cajun 1086) — are full of those intangibly magical ballads like 'Mathilda', 'Just A Dream' and 'Breaking Up Is Hard To Do'. Here are the molasses-thick laments of Bobby Charles, Jimmy Donley, Gene Thomas, Roy Perkins and the Big Bopper twenty years after they were written and first recorded. Louisiana swamp pop continues to roll along unaffected by the commercial ventures of the world beyond the bayous. Bernard's children (aged twelve and six) may be dazzled by John Travolta, but that's no kind of threat to a music which has remained so completely immune to the Beatles, psychedelia and the rest. Here's to the next twenty years.

Originally published in *Melody Maker* (17 February 1979).

Note   Shane K. Bernard, the twelve year old, grew up to write the highly recommended *Swamp Pop: Cajun And Creole Rhythm & Blues* (University Press of Mississippi, 1996).

6.3
JOHNNIE ALLAN
Cajun And Proud Of It

It's somewhat ironic that Johnnie Allan, who has made so many vivid South Louisiana ballads, should be best known in Britain for 'Promised Land', a tough accordion-tinged rocker which he recorded in 1973 and probably forgot about until Charlie Gillett released it on the Oval label. The record didn't chart — it was a sort-of Metropolitan hit, denting Capitol Radio's Top Ten — but might have done better if Elvis hadn't decided to revive the durable Chuck Berry composition at roughly the same time.

Flyright Records have contracted with Ville Platte label-owner Floyd Soileau to issue a great many Johnnie Allan records and these will provide a good picture of an active musician who spans the complete history of South Louisiana music.

Allan's latest British album, *Good Timin' Man* (Flyright 551) was cut with European audiences in mind. It features a number of much-loved favourites from Charlie Gillett's old *Honky Tonk* radio shows, including Delbert McClinton's 'Victim Of Life's Circumstances' and tunes by Gary Stewart and Dave Edmunds. Allan's next album will be strictly Cajun material, performed in French as well as English.

Coming from the peculiarly shut-off South Louisiana French Catholic enclave, Johnnie Allan is Cajun and proud of it. His grandfather once told him a story about two draft-dodging brothers who escaped execution and eventually settled near Thibodeaux at a dent in the road which came to be known as Brulle de Guillot — hence his real name, John Allen Guillot (pronounced like 'guillotine' without the 'ine'). Was it true? Allan smiles: 'That's what he told me before he died. I'm French on my father's side, while my mother's folks came directly from Spain.'

Born on 10 March 1938 in Rayne, Louisiana — on the main highway between Crowley and Lafayette — Allan spent most of his childhood working the fields near the oil town of Bosco. At six, he spoke no English; his parents spoke nothing but French and therefore he and his brothers and sisters were brought up to do the same. Although his father was a sharecropper, the picture Allan paints is a romantic one, far removed from the memories of the first raggedy-poor rockabilly immortals.

I was about six when I got my first guitar,' he recalls. 'My brother and I would sell garden seeds to the neighbours, and I finally got half the money together. One day my brother and I were out in the fields, and my mommy and daddy came back from Lafayette in the horse and buggy. I went back in and there was the guitar on my bed.'

At thirteen, Allan joined Walter Mouton & The Scott Playboys as a rhythm guitarist. He was surrounded by Cajun music and it's a subject he holds dear. 'I grew up with it, and when I say that I'm referring to the authentic Cajun music which is comprised of accordion — the dominant instrument — an unamplified rhythm guitar and a fiddle. This was the conception in the early Twenties. As time progressed, they added drums, steel guitar and now they've added bass guitar. To be authentic, the accordion has to be in it. My great-uncle, whose name was Joe Falcon, cut the first French song of that type ever recorded. I don't wanna sound like I'm bragging 'cos he's related to me, but Joe Falcon will go down in history. He's the guy that's mentioned in any book about Cajun Louisiana when you talk about French accordion players.' (Falcon, who died in 1965, recorded in New Orleans in 1928. His first disc was 'Allons A Lafayette', and it's said that Cajuns bought several copies so they'd never be without one wherever they were.)

The Scott Playboys did not record and, at fifteen, Allan switched to steel guitar and joined Lawrence Walker, another famed Cajun accordionist (he died of a heart attack several years ago). Allan recalls a session with Walker at Radio KEUN in Eunice, Louisiana. It's just possible that he appears on Walker's finest rocker, 'Allons Rock And Roll' (La Louisianne 8019): he remembers an up-tempo number and the date fits (1957).

Somehow, within the isolation of the fundamentally French culture, Allan heard very little black music until he graduated from high school at eighteen. 'That's when I really got interested in rock'n'roll,' he says. 'Fats Domino was the big thing, and I was also very fortunate to have heard Elvis Presley before he was really popular. He appeared on the *Louisiana Hayride*, which is the only time I ever saw him perform live. He sang 'Heartbreak Hotel', which he was going back to Nashville to record. He really impressed me. It was my senior year in school — I was doing agriculture and the professor took us on a field trip; a visit to the *Hayride* was part of it.'

In 1957, the nucleus of Lawrence Walker's band dropped the French accordion and began to play straight-ahead rock'n'roll. Al Foreman (lead guitar), U.J. Meaux (Huey Meaux's first cousin, who played fiddle with Walker, but now switched to piano), Bhuel Hoffpaur (drums) and Allan (who reverted to rhythm guitar) became the Krazy Kats. They added a tenor sax player, Leroy Castille, and a bass guitarist, Mickey Stutes. Apart from Allan, the band had local stars in Castille — who recorded as 'Lee Castle' — and Foreman, who played lead guitar on Rod

Bernard's 'This Should Go On Forever' and a whole host of Jay Miller's Excello rock and blues sessions.

The Krazy Kats recorded a demo of two songs which Allan had written — 'Lonely Days And Lonely Nights' and 'My Baby's Gone' — at a friend's house in Lafayette and the tape was taken to Floyd Soileau, who liked the material. Since Jay Miller operated the area's only bona fide recording studio in nearby Crowley, Floyd Soileau paid for a session which Miller engineered. Via Huey Meaux, the disc was leased to a major corporation, MGM, in 1959. 'Huey Meaux and I are real good friends,' laughs Allan, 'but I'm the sole writer of 'My Baby's Gone.' If you notice, he stuck his name on it, and that was part of the deal to get on MGM. Nationwide, 'Lonely Days And Lonely Nights' was my best seller, although others have sold more among the Gulf Coast states. I went on a tour from Florida, through Texas, Arizona and into California. It was partly promotional and partly for pay. We stopped off in Houston where I did the Larry Kane TV show. The disc wasn't a monster; it was bubbling under but never did crack the 100 mark.' As his debut disc ran out of momentum, Allan recorded a follow-up in Bill Hall's Beaumont studio with bandsmen from combos led by Jivin' Gene and Gene Terry. Since Hall and Meaux were responsible for placing most local acts with Mercury (Johnny Preston, the Big Bopper and others were doing better than anyone on MGM), they followed suit with Allan's second disc, 'Angel Of Love' c/w 'Letter Of Love'. These sides, mournful and nearly identical, were very close to Jivin' Gene's sound: mouth full of marshmallow and heavy on the Domino pronunciation.

Ever since the Mercury disc, Allan has recorded with his own band. Al Foreman joined Warren Storm in 1960 and was replaced by Hank Redlich, whose brother, Dago, owned the tiny Viking label to which Allan gravitated, mainly as a favour to Hank. Viking treated him very well, but record sales were not spectacular and he obtained a teaching post which was interrupted by army service. 'Your Picture' was getting some reaction in the South, but he couldn't promote it. When he came out of the army after a year at Fort Sill, he returned to teaching and reorganised the Krazy Kats. Lee Castille, who worked with Warren Storm at the Lafayette City printing plant and is now in a mental institution, was replaced by Harry Simoneaux. Generally, all in the band held day jobs; Johnnie taught the 5th grade in Lafayette. But the singles kept coming on Jin, and the Krazy Kats played weekends for six years without stopping: the Green Lantern in Lawtrell on Thursdays and Sundays, the River Club, Mermentau on Fridays and the Jungle Club, Ville Platte on Saturdays. In 1967, Johnnie quit music and returned to college, where he obtained a master's degree. Two years later he was out of the classroom altogether.

Allan is now Vice-Principal of the Acadian Elementary School in Lafayette. On stage he's still Johnnie Allan, but at school he's Mr. John Guillot. He doesn't let one thing interfere with the other, but music remains an industrious sideline. With his unending flow of singles has come seven albums. If you don't have any at all, I'd strongly recommend the second, *Johnnie Allan Sings* (Jin 9002). Apart from 'Somewhere On Skid Row', it doesn't have the songs which Allan identifies as his Gulf Coast best sellers — 'Your Picture' and 'South To Louisiana' — but it does have an abundance of goodies including 'Promised Land', Little Willie John's 'Talk To Me' and two classic Louisiana ballads, 'Secret Of Love' and 'You Got Me Whistling'. (Don't write in to tell me that the last-named comes from the West Coast; thousands of people think it's a Louisiana ballad, and that's what counts.)

South To Louisiana (Jin 4001) has the early near-hits and most of the Viking material, including the title track, which is 'North To Alaska'

6.3 - Johnnie Allan

with different words. *Dedicated To You* (Jin 9006) verges on Nashville easy-listening (and has an Engelbert-type pose from Allan on the front sleeve) but it does contain one top-flight track, a revival of the Jivin' Gene rocker, 'I Cried'. This is so hummable it makes even 'Promised Land' sound dull.

You'll have noticed the breadth of the material's sources — not just Chuck Berry, but Little Willie John, Elton Anderson, Johnny Fuller, Jivin' Gene, Johnny Horton, Jimmy Wilson and Bobby Charles. The best record collections are full of discs by these underrated and largely uninterviewed giants of Southern music. Allan has interpreted songs by these and many more tasteful trendsetters. He has an almost scholarly intuition for choosing the best songs.

'Having played throughout South Louisiana, I've developed a knack of finding out what sort of music the people want to hear,' Allan maintains. 'Every now and then I'll go to Floyd's *[Soileau's]* and go through his enormous stack of records and pick out those I want to record — say Frankie Lowery's 'She's Walking Toward Me.' It's a great song and one that I have to do. Then 'This Life I Live', which was written by Rocket Morgan, who got on a religious kick and went out on the road as a preacher about twelve years ago. And I heard Guitar Junior play 'Family

Rules' at a club on the Texas-Louisiana border, and although his version sold good around Port Arthur and Orange, it never did get into Louisiana. So, I recorded it especially for South Louisiana. 'Love Me All The Way' was taken off a Percy Sledge album, and 'Somewhere On Skid Row' came from a Merle Haggard LP.'

Johnnie Allan's perseverance has paid dividends. He never had what you would call a national hit but, unlike so many of his contemporaries, he's never had to live up to the ballyhoo of *Bandstand* appearances, nor had to adjust to follow-ups which failed to repeat a chart-busting debut disc. He sells about five to six thousand copies of each new album and, although he might not dent the Top Forty, the situation is a happy one for all concerned. The music of South Louisiana is in good hands.

Originally published in *Goldmine* (June 1982).

7

SOULED OUT

7.1
JOHN RICHBOURG
Southern Soul Man

'I guess maybe one of the primary reasons I got started in this business was to try and help black people get a foothold in some kind of way. I realised early on that, things being as they are, this is one of the only things they can do to achieve any degree of prominence. Anyhow, I like R&B and blues — certain types of blues — and then of course there are the financial aspects. I've made a pretty good living at it.'

Producer and disc-jockey John Richbourg may attempt to disguise his humanitarian nature, but a few hours' research into Nashville R&B soon puts the record straight. Known on the air for over two decades as John R, Richbourg is a powerful man in Tennessee and there is no black talent he has failed to help. One-time Excello chief Ernie Young has claimed that the 50,000-watt WLAC is heard in thirty-eight states and that 98% of his sales were achieved from nightly advertising on John R's show. After seventeen years in Tennessee State Penitentiary, there weren't too many people ready to give Johnny Bragg a break — except Richbourg. 'Man, that cat's white but he's got a black soul,' said Bragg. 'He played my last record to death, really tried to get it off the ground.' Unable to obtain airplay in his hometown of Cincinnati, Albert Washington tells *Living Blues*: 'My records get played on WLAC because John R and I have been friends for a long time.' Bobby King, who drives a Lewis cab and describes most of his dealings with record companies as a Mafia-type situation, was grateful for the care, attention and encouragement he had received from Richbourg. John thinks he is quite inept, but he's going to do some more records with him just the same.

Of French Huguenot descent, Richbourg was born in 1910 in Davis Station, a small rural crossroads in South Carolina. He came to R&B via work in radio. 'I really have no R&B background in my earlier days in music. I became involved sorta through the back door. I began radio in New York City doing soap opera work and dramatic work, but I took a vacation down to my home state in 1941 and I auditioned there for a radio station in Charleston and got the job. At that time, I transferred over to announcing at WBMA, and I came to WLAC in Nashville in 1942 and I've been there ever since. Shortly thereafter, I decided to go into the R&B field because nobody was programming to an ethnic audience. At that time it was very difficult to find R&B — race music we called it then — we'd go all over town trying to find three or four R&B records. Naturally, we couldn't play all R&B because we just didn't have the music, but it began to get better and WLAC was one of the first stations in the country to programme to a black audience. I began playing anybody's records I could find — Aladdin, RPM, Aristocrat — this was when Leonard Chess was starting. He was going around in an Oldsmobile selling the records himself. Much later, I began recording R&B as a little experimentation more than anything else.'

Richbourg's experiments involved local singers including Bobby Hebb and Cornell Blakely, and his first production, 'Night Train To Memphis' (Rich 1001) was also Hebb's first record, pre-dating 'Sunny' by ten years. Although he produced other sides by Hebb, a prolific performer with records on FM, Battle, Smash and Boom, none were successful. 'I was just beginning in the field and really didn't know what was happening. Johnny Vincent picked up the records on Rich and distributed them but nothing ever came of them. I had no strength and no real company.' The full-time job with WLAC, which he held down all the while (and where, until recently, he continued as deejay and programme director) was not enough to occupy him. He began Southern Record Distributors in Nashville and then went into training radio announcers: 'I've tried to train black announcers. As you well know, we had a state law which said blacks and whites could not go to school together. I set up a special school and I've trained fifteen to twenty black announcers that are scattered all around.' Ultimately, this venture lost more money than any other and John was forced to look around again.

Fred Foster was anxious to get into the R&B field and asked John to see what he could do with the Sound Stage 7 label. It had been formed as a subsidiary of Monument in April 1963 and had enjoyed some success in the pop market. The first releases, produced in Nashville by Bob Moore, Bill 'Raunchy' Justis and Steve Poncio were uniformly dull and of only marginal interest to R&B fans. The Dixiebelles, who made the Top Twenty with '(Down At) Papa Joe's' (2507) and 'Southtown, USA' (2517) were promoted as a black girl trio, but Justis now admits that this contrived kind of honky-tonky was made by white session singers, while he signed black chicks to perform the stuff on *Caravan Of The Stars* and the like.

Among a lot of evidently white pop acts, only Joe Perkins's novelty 'Little Eefin' Annie' (2511) and Boot Hog Pefferly's version of the Joe Tex calypso, 'I'm Not Going To Work Today' (2513) can be regarded as more than totally unmemorable. When John Richbourg reactivated Sound Stage 7 in 1965, it became a dependable R&B label issuing over a hundred exclusively black 45s inside five years.

Bill Justis continued to produce the odd single (notably Little Hank's revived British mini-hit, 'Mr. Bang Bang Man' (2566)), while Fred Foster looked after the exceedingly great, but nonetheless declining talent of Arthur Alexander. Richbourg was responsible for virtually everything else. 'Fred said he wanted to go R&B with it so I went along all the way. I already had many contacts through my own publishing company, Cape Ann Music, which I had started in 1962 and which I still operate. I signed up an awful lot of artists to my own J.R. Enterprises. I signed the acts, produced them and leased the masters through Sound Stage 7, which Fred actually owned. My first contract with him was for three years and we renewed that for two more. Everything on Sound Stage 7 from 1966 to 1970 was produced by me, and the acts were under contract to my own company.'

While Lost-Nite oldie compilations in Richbourg's name reflect his popularity as one of America's top R&B jocks, he remains unheralded as a soul producer. He doesn't, as far as I'm aware, write songs (although his wife has penned a few), or play an instrument, and producers have to do both (Leiber & Stoller, Spector, Ragavoy, Gamble & Huff, Toussaint) before they can be lauded to the skies as truly creative. It has also been said that he never made a great (ie mind-blowing, earth shattering etc) record, but he produced a helluva lot of good ones and that counts for a lot in my book. He could also be relied upon to produce the kind of music on which R&B opinion is easily united; Sound Stage 7 represented all that was best in Southern soul and Richbourg, as executive producer, made it all a recognisable entity, no matter how diverse the artist's style or background. And they were a pretty varied bunch. Fairly new names (Ella Washington, the Ambassadors, Jimmy Church, Sam Baker) shared the roster with veteran bluesmen (Piney Brown, Fenton Robinson, Little Joe Blue, Ivory Joe Hunter) and popular soul singers (Roscoe Shelton, Arthur Alexander, Lattimore Brown, Joe Simon, Roscoe Robinson).

The soul balladeers were provided with a powerful but intelligently restrained combination of horns and strings fused in an arrangement which invariably featured a biting blues guitar answering one and then the other, or bobbing around beneath both. (Cliff Parman, who usually arranged the strings, deserves some attention; a wizard with strings behind black singers doing C&W songs, his credentials include the superb backdrops behind Joe Henderson on Todd and Little Esther Phillips on Lenox). The songs too, often written by label executive Allen Orange, Roscoe Robinson or country composers, personified another age of soul with very few messages and no stuttered three minutes in praise of hot pants. Just simple, lovely songs. A number of top producers including the fussier Gamble & Huff, latter-day Allen Toussaint and, in particular, Jerry Williams are using these broad devices in much the same way. Richbourg began stitching them all together with a rare and tasteful panache some seven years ago.

Joe Simon, not the most vibrant or dynamic of Sound Stage 7's artists, was by far and away the most popular, with over fifteen hits in the USA — all, apparently, too mellow for English consumption. 'It was a mistake to send Joe to England with a bunch of jazz acts,' reckons Richbourg. 'It did him an awful lot of harm all through Europe, but over here he rapidly approached the stature of Otis Redding.'

My own feelings worked in reverse. *Simon Pure Soul* (Monument LMO-5005) with his first hit, 'A Teenager's Prayer' (2564), is an oft-played old friend. *No Sad Songs* (SMO-5017) and *Simon Sings* (SMO-5026), I dip into less frequently. There are a lot of country songs here, and if they share two things with much modern country it's exquisitely tasteful arrangements without the necessary fire from the vocalist to set them off. The songs of white writers with blues-tinged country roots (Dan Penn, Willie Nelson, Spooner Oldham) fare best from the Simon soft soul treatment, while a true blues standard like 'Sweet Black Angel' is positively alive by comparison. By the time *The Chokin' Kind* (SMO-5030) came out, I had got a bit tired of the increasingly mannered and self-conscious approach. After listening to 'Little Green Apples' and the rest, I filed it away after one play. Strictly reference material only. 'Joe couldn't relate to songs like that. He had an awful time. We'd record it bit by bit, teach him a line and record it, then teach him the next line.'

I guess it had to be done. Stuff like this was Richbourg's insurance against singles like those by Ivory Joe or Piney Brown which didn't even rate a mention in the trade papers.

Getting away from the excesses which attended Simon's

burgeoning popularity and digging back through other Sound Stage 7 singles can be a more profitable experience. Many possess greater depth with far less sentiment and only the tired adjectives 'deep', 'soulful' and 'churchy' can describe the effect of Roscoe Shelton, Ella Washington, or Sir Lattimore Brown's best sides.

Brown has a powerful baritone employed to devastating effect on slow dirges with a smoky, old-fashioned Texas flavour. There are some slight up-tempo things including 'Cruise On Fannie' (2586), an appropriately hoarse sequel to 'Mustang Sally', but 'Nobody Has To Tell Me' (2586), a Dan Penn-arranged ballad of stark simplicity, soon gets the adrenalin going. 'Please, Please, Please' (2598) is also steeped in the church, opening with the now popular soul corn monologue and flowing on over bouncy horn patterns. There's no girl group, Brown takes care of the responsorial shrieks himself.

Much of Lattimore Brown's passion is shared by Ella Washington, whose frighteningly brutal vocal explains why she is 'Starving For Love' (2611). There's no self-pity or little girl innocence in that voice; her tree's been shaken a few times and she clearly can't get enough. 'He Called Me Baby' (2621) is more tender. A Harlan Howard song with a pronounced hook, it was a hit for Ella in 1969. She didn't have another, but the less melodic 'Stop Giving Your Man Away' (2632) and the Bobby Womack tune, 'I Can't Afford To Lose Him' (2665) repeat the technique of pulling out all the stops and wailing to distraction over the chorus.

Sound Stage 7's debt to Atlantic, which shows itself most in the use of choral accompaniment, lends a more professional, more polished sound than is usually heard on Southern R&B records — even though many, according to Monument's general manager, Jack Kirby, were recorded in Memphis 'where we can get the deep blues-type musicians'. Roscoe Shelton is the finest example. Richbourg used Shelton as a foil to Joe Simon, turning this erstwhile, rather drab Excello bluesman into an excellent, harsh, gospel-based singer with all the barely-suppressed energy of Solomon Burke. Indeed, the most apt comparison is to be found in the incredibly satisfying collaborations between Burke and Jerry Wexler in the early Sixties. 'I'm Ready To Love You Now' (2615) opens quietly with cooing girls and distant strings, but builds and builds with Shelton's voice fed through an echo chamber over the crescendos so it's still there ringing after he's dropped back into softer coaxing. 'Tonight's The Night' (2582) is another first-rate production. Shelton begins quietly, talking over an organ hanging by one chord. Then he's hitting you, soaring in and out of the hard-wailing girl chorus, who really pump the record along. 'Roscoe,' says Richbourg, 'was my favourite. We had far more success with Joe, but we tried awfully hard with Roscoe. He was a really great artist in his youth but he had a drinking problem and got a little jammed-up.' Shelton now works as a porter at Nashville's Hubbard Hospital. If you ever come across his album, *Music In His Soul* (Sound Stage 7 SSM-5002), which has a nice selection of Sound Stage 7 singles plus some old Sims masters, do pick it up. It won't do him any good, but you're bound to be moved by his pleading, raw-edged vocals.

When his contract with Monument expired in December 1970, Richbourg produced Joe Simon for Spring. Joe subsequently left for Philadelphia and Gamble & Huff, while Richbourg set up three independent labels — Seventy-7, Luna and Sound Plus — with a wealth of talent on each.

There's Brief Encounter, a sweet soul vocal group produced by Harry Deal in North Carolina; Lee Fields, an organist recorded by Jerry Williams in Norfolk, Virginia; and Azie Mortimer, a torchy female singer who Leiber & Stoller once produced for Big Top. Skip and John Phillips in Memphis send in masters by the Hopson Family, a primitive gospel unit who gargle 'Handwriting On The Wall' (Luna 803) to the intriguing accompaniment of banjo and mandolin. Alvin Cash (& The 100 Dollar Bills) is still leading an anonymous bunch of Chicago sessionmen through their paces on dance tunes like 'Doin' The Creep' (Seventy-7 118) and the blues are served up by Fenton Robinson, who recently hit with 'The Sky Is Crying' (Seventy-7 105) and followed that with the loudest blues album (Seventy-7 2001) I've ever heard. Robinson has never made a bad record but this is not his finest. His vocals are as intense as ever, but the Nashville session men (he doesn't play his own guitar much for some reason) try to drown him out. Charles Smith wails deliciously on the sort of slow, uncluttered soul that could only come out of the South, and his duet with Jeff Cooper, 'My Great Loss (Ashes to Ashes)' (Seventy-7 106), about a recently deceased girl friend, will appeal to death disc cultists everywhere. Finally, Willie Hobbs and Ann Sexton are the best bets for future stardom. Hobbs, with Richbourg and Jackey Beavers producing, has several fine sides including the semi-classically orchestrated Kenny Gamble tune 'You Don't Know What You've Got' (Seventy-7 101) and a version of 'Big Legged Woman' (Seventy-7 119) as spicy as Israel Tolbert's original. Ann Sexton has an aggressive style with a voice higher, but not unlike Ann Peebles, and David Lee's tight horn arrangements suggest that he's listened to a lot of Willie Mitchell lately.

John R has already earned his place in rock'n'roll history; from the gravel-voiced hipster who presented R&B to a huge audience in the Fifties to the producer of emotion-packed deep soul in the Sixties. Some of his latest productions, which lean towards sultry, up-to-the-minute funk, suggest the glory days are far from over.

Note   John wrote and thanked me for the interest in his endeavours and said the above piece (*Let It Rock*, April 1975) was 'the best by far' — but then, I'd never seen another outside the Richmond, Virginia *Times-Dispatch*. He died on 15 February 1986 after a long battle with cancer.

7.2
Blue-Eyed Soul

The phrase 'blue-eyed soul' was coined by Georgie Woods, a black disc-jockey on WDAS in Philadelphia. One of the major personalities in the field, Woods invented the term to categorise the Righteous Brothers whose records were played on R&B radio stations before black disc-jockeys and programme directors realised they were white.

It was not always thus. For most of the Twentieth Century, there was not that much difference between the music of Southern blacks and whites. Forty years of musical miscegenation is described in Tony Russell's *Blacks, Whites And Blues* (Studio Vista, 1970), a groundbreaking essay which took the reader from the mockery of minstrelsy, through the white blues of Jimmie Rodgers and Jimmie Davis, to the western swing of Bob Wills and the boogies of the Delmore Brothers.

Boogie-woogie echoed through the C&W field during the Forties and early Fifties. Those who fared best included Cliffie Stone, Merle Travis, the Maddox Brothers & Rose and Tennessee Ernie Ford, but to single these out is to neglect others as fine. On the pop front, Ella Mae Morse adapted R&B hits with a degree of integrity unrivalled by her very much blander peers. Of the major hillbilly singers, Hank Williams also represented a confluence of country and R&B which presaged rockabilly. Some of Williams's records (notably 'Move It On Over') were covered by black blues-shouters. 'Williams,' said Jim Stewart, the owner of Stax, 'was a soul singer and the R&B people dug him.'

For the few whites who sang black outside the C&W and pop fields, the late Forties were lean times. However, one man, Johnny Otis, became the most convincing and most successful of all such cultural transplants. Known as 'The Godfather of R&B', Otis was born of Greek immigrant parents in Vallejo, California and raised in the integrated neighbourhood of Berkeley. During his teens he adopted the black culture; he married black and lived the rest of his life in the ghetto. Between 1940 and 1945, he played drums with a number of famous black bands and in 1948 opened a R&B nightclub — the Barrelhouse — in the Watts section of Los Angeles.

Otis discovered an amazing number of black artists including Little Esther Phillips, the Robins, Jackie Wilson and Etta James, wrote a clutch of R&B standards ('Every Beat Of My Heart', 'Double Crossing Blues', 'So Fine') and riddled the best-sellers throughout the early Fifties when the Top Fifteen R&B chart just wasn't long enough to accommodate all the many manifestations of his work as bandleader, singer, writer, producer and talent scout. Otis returned to the charts with 'Willie And The Hand Jive' in 1958 and 'Country Girl' in 1969. His total identification with the black community extended into an involvement with civil rights and a semi-autobiographical plea for understanding, *Listen To The Lambs* (Norton, 1968).

Pushing further into the early Fifties, Ray Charles's fusion of blues and gospel was not without its influential white counterparts. The fast, skiffle-like performances of Brother Claude Ely provide the often-overlooked yet pivotal link on which blues and country were moulded into rockabilly. 'Elvis,' remarked Sleepy LaBeef, 'followed Claude Ely from one tent meeting to another.' Ely's King recordings, including 'We're Gonna Move' and 'Ain't No Grave Gonna Hold My Body Down', were at least as important as Sister Rosetta Tharpe's 'Strange Things Happening'. For sheer, berserk excitement they rival anything by black gospel singers. No other white gospeller has come close to matching Ely's venom-drinking abandonment.

Rockabilly, perhaps the most celebrated of all black-influenced white musics, evidently sold well in black locations. The R&B charts, then open to all-comers regardless of race, creed or colour, were a second home to Elvis and Jerry Lee Lewis, while Ronnie Hawkins reached the R&B Top Ten with his cover of Young Jessie's 'Mary Lou'.

'Rockabilly,' wrote Arnold Shaw, *'might be regarded as "blue-eyed soul", save that R&B had not yet moved into its "soul" phase, and the sound of Elvis, Jerry Lee and other white Southerners was a blend, not an imitation.'* When Elvis first appeared on Dewey Phillips's radio show, he was required to authenticate his true colour by assuring listeners that he attended the all-white Humes High School. During his later career, he could still sing soul like a black man: 'Any Day Now', 'It Hurts Me' and 'Stranger In My Own Home Town' contain a passion, a swagger and an intensity more commonly associated with Solomon Burke.

The late Fifties and early Sixties were also boom years for whites who sang black. The Skyliners, the Capris and (initially) the Four Seasons were among the many white vocal groups whose music provided no clue as to the real colour of their skins. Joe Barry, Rod Bernard, T.K. Hulin and other South Louisiana swamp-poppers reigned briefly with a mournful approximation of Fats Domino's blues ballads. Both contingents were successful on the increasingly racist R&B chart; they were new artists and, until they appeared on network television, R&B radio stations simply didn't know they were white.

The social and political undercurrents which eventually surfaced in the 'I'm Black And I'm Proud' movement created a prejudice which consumed black record-buyers. Take, for example, the fate of Bruce Channel, a white Texan whose 'Hey! Baby' was performed in a naturally ragged and bluesy manner. The producer, Major Bill Smith, had been advised how white blues singers should be marketed: 'Huey Meaux came over to me while Bruce is doing a local TV show in Houston: "You got a big one there, you don't even know what you got. I wanna tell you somethin': keep that boy under wraps. Y'know a record called 'I'm A Fool To Care'?" I says: "Sure, it sounds like Fats Domino but they say it's a guy called Joe Barry." Meaux said: "There he sits over there." I look at this dude and he's... white. "Take my advice," said Meaux, "don't you ever put your boy on the Dick Clark show."

Well, I forgot about that episode and I get a telegram from Clark's producer. 'Hey! Baby' is No. 1 Pop and No. 2 R&B. They want Bruce. I get all the neighbours and we gather 'round the TV to watch our star. Clark peels off the Top Ten until... "Here he is, the Number One record in America today, Bruce Channel, bring him on!" Here comes Bruce with his pot belly and his little round white face. Next week, I pick up the *Billboard*; he's still Number One on the Hot 100; I turn to the 'R&B' page and 'Hey! Baby' ain't even on the cotton-pickin' chart! Then it dawned on me what Mr. Meaux had said.' Despite soulful pop hits during the Sixties — 'Going Back To Louisiana', 'Mr. Bus Driver', 'Keep On' — Channel did not make the R&B chart again.

Sixties soul music was forged from an indelible country background. Many of the most important producers had played in country or rockabilly bands, the Memphis and Muscle Shoals sessionmen were usually white and, as often as not, the black vocalist sang C&W songs. 'Just Out Of Reach' (Solomon Burke), 'Dark End Of The Street' (James Carr) and 'Release Me' (Esther Phillips) are country songs performed with a church feeling. C&W guitar licks permeated the finest Southern soul records and Nick Tosches's over-generalisation 'every time you hear an Otis Redding record you're hearing a bunch of white guys' sums up an era in which such cross-pollenisation was both meaningful and enjoyable.

The genre produced a tiny handful of good 'white soul' records (notably sessionmen-turned-singers like Dan Penn or Travis Wammack) but none capable of matching the emotional intensity of the best black artists. Whites generally failed, and failed clumsily: such derivatives as the Young Rascals or the Box Tops did not fully satisfy those who looked for authentic vocal quality, while Janis Joplin's desperation stemmed largely from an inability to sound as convincing as Etta James or Big Mama Thornton.

Other blue-eyed soulmen added little but subtracted plenty from the giants of black music. James Brown played a vital role in shaping the performances of many self-styled pink soul brothers including Len Barry, Steve Colt and Wayne Cochran. An ex-rockabilly of some distinction — he also wrote the million-selling 'Last Kiss' — Cochran won fantastic acceptance in black theatres and night clubs. But his was the type of show which refused to come over on vinyl, and his numerous recordings smacked of strenuous but artificial excitement. James Brown and Little Richard also inspired the work of Mitch Ryder (whose biggest hits segued into Little Richard's songs) and the stuttering urgency of Matt Lucas whose 'I'm Movin' On' reached the charts in 1963. Another ex-rockabilly, Lucas cut several soul records before settling in Canada where he let his hair grow long and played the blues. Mitch Ryder (*aka* William Levise) first sang with a black quartet, the Peps. Later, he broke a kneecap imitating James Brown's stage act. His records with the Detroit Wheels evinced little authenticity in relation to the music he loved, but at least one commentator thought 'What Now My Love' approached the introspective intensity of Ray Charles.

Blue-eyed soul flew off into various lines of descent. There was the uptown smoothness of Len Barry or Ben Aiken, the hard testifying of Jo-Ann Campbell and her husband, Troy Seals, and the tambourine-thumping, Southern Sunday pseudo-soul of Leon Russell, Delaney & Bonnie, Don Nix and their pals. Spare a thought too for Larry Bright, whose 'Mojo Workout' dented the Hot 100 in 1960.

Any really comprehensive collection would also need to include at least one record by Steve Alaimo (with James Brown's band), Tony Joe White, Gene Kennedy ('all my stuff was reviewed in *Billboard*'s R&B section'), the Magnificent Men, Billy Vera, Timi Yuro (who was coached by the black singer-novelist, Sonny Knight), Dr. John, the O'Kaysions, Dallas Frazier and Baby Ray.

A number of these singers came out of the C&W field and recorded soul in search of a pop hit. Some acquired a cult reputation among Carolina 'beach music' fans and dancers in the North of England. A tiny minority, including Johnny Daye ('Marry Me'), Roy Head ('Treat Her Right'), Ronnie Milsap ('Never Had It So Good'), Chris Clark ('Love's Gone Bad') and Jo-Ann & Troy ('I Found A Love, Oh What A Love') managed to hoodwink black record buyers long enough to score a solitary R&B hit. Kenny Jeremiah of the Soul Survivors (who reached Top Five R&B and Pop with 'Expressway To Your Heart') recalled: 'Most people thought we were black, and the reason it sold in the States was because all the black stations picked up on it. And for that reason, the record company *[Crimson]* wouldn't put our picture out.'

Ultimately — for consistency and depth of feeling — the best blue-eyed soul is defined by Lonnie Mack's ballads and virtually everything the Righteous Brothers recorded. Many R&B deejays felt they'd been tricked by the Righteous Brothers' first recordings, particularly 'Little Latin Lupe Lu' and 'My Babe'. WWRL's general manager said of his most acute black disc-jockey: 'You should have seen Rocky G's face drop when he found out they weren't really Negroes!'

When the revelation came, it ceased to matter: Bill Medley told black audiences that 'soul music travelled up the Mississippi 'cos they wouldn't let it on the bus' and they got the feeling he knew what he was singing about. The Righteous Brothers' utterly convincing, melismatic singing was equalled by Lonnie Mack who wailed a soul ballad as gutsily as any black gospel singer. The anguished inflections which stamped his best songs ('Why', 'She Don't Come Here Anymore', 'Where There's A Will There's A Way') had a directness that would have been wholly embarrassing in the hands of almost any other white vocalist, and his gospel screams were an object lesson to the many black singers who eschewed root influences for the sake of broader appeal.

Blue-eyed soul did not travel well and, apart from nods in the direction of Van Morrison, Dusty Springfield and Stevie Winwood, European examples are thin on the ground. Los Pop Tops' 'Oh Lord, Why Lord' reached the R&B Top Forty in 1968, and this Spanish tribute to Martin Luther King brought a lump to the throats of those who heard it. Pete Wingfield, possibly Britain's only real blue-eyed soulster, began *Soulbeat* — the first of the soul fanzines — in 1964. His purist zeal for a distant culture eventually culminated in the incomparably soulful 'Eighteen With A Bullet', a Transatlantic hit in 1975.

While 'black music' lovers regarded the British invasion as an unwelcome irrelevance, it undoubtedly helped lower American resistance to indigenous blues bands — black and white. Paul Butterfield, who frequented Chicago's South Side clubs as a youth, and Charlie Musselwhite, whose background lay in rockabilly, came closest to matching music which black bluesmen had already perfected. J. Geils's tough early albums also made the grade, while John Hammond Jr. and Barry Goldberg (who played piano on Mitch Ryder's 'Sock It To Me Baby') were less successful contenders. During the late Seventies, the Fabulous Thunderbirds and George Thorogood also overcame the prejudice of those who normally sneered at whiteface R&B. Thorogood's singing fooled no-one, but he returned that sheer goggle-eyed, face-quivering senselessness to rock'n'roll and his vehement, all-enveloping quilt of black guitar styles helped make his first albums the best new blues released in at least ten years.

By the Eighties, black entertainment was dominated by disco, a racially homogenous music with new white superstars including Daryl Hall & John Oates. The duo's unprecedented success in the soul charts reflected the tastes of an audience which had consigned real soul — black or white — to the unfashionable pages of history.

Originally published in edited form in *The History Of Rock* (No. 59, 1983).
I have restored the editor's cuts.

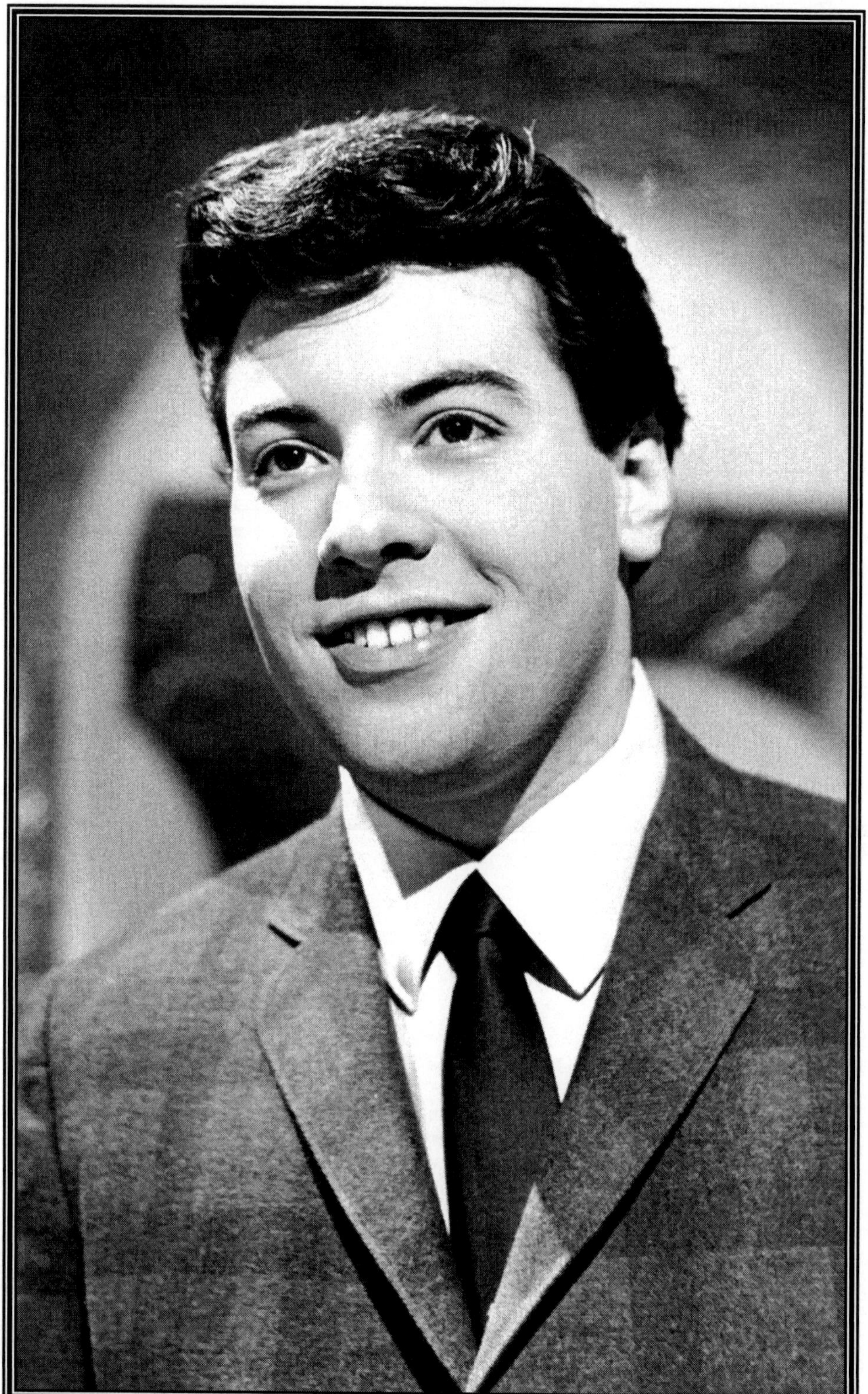

7.3
TONY ORLANDO
The Last Of The Teenage Idols

The Odeon, Kingston-upon-Thames. Or maybe it was the Granada. It's 9.20 pm on 15 February 1962 and Clarence 'Frogman' Henry has just boogied his head off. He's covered in gold lamé and beaming at everyone. Three hits in a row and really pleased with himself. Off he goes, never to be heard of again unless you've been to the Club 444 in New Orleans where, according to the title of his last, unpublicised Roulette album, *Clarence Henry Is Alive And Well And Doing His Thing*.

The theatre stinks of orange peel and everyone is fidgety because it wasn't Clarence Henry they had paid to see. Top of the bill is Bobby Vee, soppy as a cream puff only we don't know that yet. So, before the big moment arrives we've got to sit through another one-hit wonder. Lights out, solitary blue spotlight. The big build-up. No-one ever tuned up on stage in those days.

And here he comes. A dark, swarthy, incredibly good-looking teenager singing 'Stand By Me'. It's only his first number and he's already on his knees with his jacket off. Tony Orlando, the last of the teenage idols and — apart from a handful of vintage rock'n'rollers — one of the very few with any talent. But it's 1962 and talent doesn't count any more, and Orlando doesn't make it for very long because he's none too photogenic. Seen his photos? He's plump and goofy. But in the flesh, the girls are going spare and Bobby Vee is forgotten. The press agree that Orlando stole the show. George Harrison was among those who watched the seventeen year old white kid who rolled around the floor singing new wave soul songs so rarely heard on this side of the Atlantic.

Michael Anthony Orlando Cassavitus was born on 3 April 1944 and grew up in Queens, New York with his Greek-Spanish parents and younger sister. As a boy soprano he sang in the church choir and formed his own group, the Five Gents. There are two tracks by another group, the Milos, on a cheap Mount Vernon album called *Chartbusters*. The sleeve describes Tony as the epitome of rock pop singing but, in fact, it's not him (that Tony Orlando was an Italian doo-wopper from Newark who recorded 'Ding Dong' for Milo Records of Harrison, New Jersey; he was shot to death while working as a security guard).

Orlando Cassavitus ('cassavitus' is Greek for 'house of life') spent three weeks at Aviation High School, but spent his time drawing the marquee of the Paramount Theatre instead of pistons and gaskets. (He told Jack Dey that he'd write Chuck Berry and Jerry Lee Lewis in small print and Tony Orlando in 'big fat letters'). He also approached Aldon Music, the independent production and publishing firm of Don Kirshner and Al Nevins. 'I sat down and played them some songs, Ritchie Valens-style, with my guitar, and Don told me I should work with this girl writer, Carole King, who hadn't had a hit yet. She was eighteen at the time and very heavily into R&B... or what we used to call R&B, which was the Shirelles, the Drifters and all those Leiber & Stoller records. She didn't care for the Valens bag that I was in and asked: "Can you do anything black?" Now, I was into street-corner black music, my guts were in the Spaniels, the Heartbeats, all that stuff, and the only reason I was doing Valens material was because those were the only chords I knew on the guitar.'

Nevins-Kirshner Associates, the architects of Brill Building pop, had discovered a host of young songwriters including Barry Mann, Neil Sedaka, Howie Greenfield and Carole King. To begin with, they employed Orlando as a demo singer and, if for nothing else, he should go down in history as the first man to sing 'Will You Love Me Tomorrow', 'Some Kind Of Wonderful' and 'Take Good Care Of My Baby' — hits for the Shirelles, the Drifters and Bobby Vee. Eventually, Kirshner took Orlando to Epic Records, who accepted his demo of 'Halfway To Paradise', written and arranged by Carole King and Gerry Goffin. This, a Top Forty hit in America, was covered in Britain by Billy Fury. Orlando's second single, 'Bless You', written by Barry Mann and Cynthia Weil (No. 15 in the USA and No. 5 in the UK), was another perfect pop single. 'We thought 'Bless You' was funky,' John Lennon remarked. 'We thought it was funky in those days.'

These productions echoed the symphonic R&B of the Drifters. Goffin and King used rich, cascading strings, Spanish guitars and castanets, punchy stops and starts, tenor saxophone solos and a girl chorus who squealed 'bop shoo bop' in stuck-pig voices. Despite all this, it was Orlando you heard; he was among the first of the blue-eyed soul singers with a voice that could soar and glide around material that didn't always deserve the effort. As well as Al Jolson and Mario Lanza, he had listened closely to contemporary black singers. This much was obvious from the distinctive rasp to his emotional tenor, the scream in the middle of 'Beautiful Dreamer' and the intense treatment he gave to 'Happy Times', an impeccable soul ballad which Goffin & King forgot to give to the Drifters. Orlando testified, spreading monosyllables over half a dozen notes; Caucasians were not meant to sing like that in the early Sixties, yet Orlando out-emoted genuine soulmen including Freddie Scott and the Drifters' Rudy Lewis, who were often emulsified by a welter of Brill Building trademarks. 'Orlando,' wrote Richard Williams, *'is one of the finest of all American pop singers.'* We had to wait until the Righteous

7.3 - Tony Orlando

Brothers teamed with Phil Spector before hearing such a potent sound from white vocalists again.

There were other fine singles on Epic — 'Talkin' About You', 'Chills', 'I'll Be There' — but they didn't brush the charts. Fan magazines, the teen idol's main hope of visibility, lost interest. For the rest of the Sixties, Orlando cut sporadic singles under his own name (Atco, Cameo) and used a variety of pseudonyms for records on United Artists, Diamond, Harbour and A&M. He also accepted a management post at April–Blackwood Music, the publishing arm of CBS, where he played an important role by acquiring publishing rights to material by James Taylor, Laura Nyro and Blood, Sweat & Tears.

By 1970, Orlando was a prosperous publishing executive whose singing career seemed long gone. That year, Hank Medress, former member of the Tokens, sought his opinion on the master of a song he'd produced with Dave Appell, one-time house-rocker and co-author of 'Let's Twist Again'. The new song was called 'Candida'. It was first offered to the black singer, Lenny Welch, who turned it down because his label, Commonwealth United, was about to go bankrupt. Ben E. King also rejected it; he said it sounded like something he would have cut ten years earlier. Orlando thought it was a smash, Top Forty at least. He told Medress to take it to Bell Records, who specialised in disposable pop. Bell didn't like the singer and, remembering that Orlando hummed just like Ben E. King, Medress asked him to overdub his voice on the original backing track. The record was sold to Bell who asked Orlando if they could use his name on the disc. He refused on the grounds that it would be unfair to CBS for whom he still worked. Eventually, Medress chose the name Dawn, after a girl whose father worked in Bell's promotion department. 'Candida' by Dawn reached Number Three and sold a million. The follow-up, 'Knock Three Times', reached Number One and sold three million. Orlando left his publishing post at CBS and put a group together. Telma Hopkins (born Louisville, Kentucky on 28 October 1948) and her cousin, Joyce Vincent (born Detroit on 14 December 1946), accompanied Orlando on records and tours. Both girls were veteran session singers; Telma had told Isaac Hayes to shut his mouth on 'Shaft'. (Telma and Joyce replaced Toni Wine and Ellie Greenwich, who sang on 'Candida' and 'Knock Three Times').

'I Play And Sing', 'What Are You Doing Sunday', 'Tie A Yellow Ribbon Round The Ole Oak Tree' (one of the largest selling singles of all time) and 'Say, Has Anyone Seen My Sweet Gypsy Rose' (all billed as 'Dawn featuring Tony Orlando') were among the trio's Drifters-ish hits for Bell. In 1975, they switched to Elektra scoring with 'He Don't Love You', a revival of Jerry Butler's 1960 hit, 'He Will Break Your Heart'. Orlando's guts were still in early black soul music, and Dawn continued to record the twenty year old hits of Clyde McPhatter, Sam Cooke and the Drifters. In 1977 the group split up and Orlando embarked on a second solo career with Casablanca. Success eluded him this time around but some of his records, including a stab at the Drifters' 'Sweets For My Sweet', were as faithful as those by almost any blue-eyed soul revivalist you could name.

Note This piece fuses two articles: *Tony Orlando: The Last Of The Teenage Idols* (*Record Mirror*, 3 April 1971) and *Before Dawn* (*The History Of Rock* No. 23, 1982). I've also added a quote or two from Orlando's fascinating interview with Jack Dey (*DISCoveries*, April 1989).

7.4
LONNIE MACK
Memphis Wham

The term 'influential' is applied to almost anyone these days, but there's still a case for saying that the massively popular blues-rock guitar genre can be traced way back to the strength, power and emotional passion of Lonnie Mack whose classic Fraternity album, *The Wham Of That Memphis Man*, was the first record to dent a hole in the pocket money of a ten year old Stevie Ray Vaughan.

Mack's convincing distillation of blues, gospel and country also prefigured the roadhouse booze'n'boogie movement, inspiring a fresh generation of Southern country rockers. This familiar 'Hoosier guitar legend' hype isn't what every Lonnie Mack admirer wants to hear though. It doesn't cut much ice with the pre-metal fan who prefers the Sixties Lonnie Mack, the spontaneous purveyor of ratcheting rock'n'roll instrumentals and the untutored singer of blue-eyed soul *in excelsis*. That's the Lonnie Mack for me and, I suspect, the Lonnie Mack which most appeals to you.

Mack was born Lonnie McIntosh on 18 July 1941 in the backwoods of Harrison, Indiana, some twenty miles west of Cincinnati. His mother, who played guitar, and father, a banjo picker, named their son after Lonnie Glosson, a popular harmonica player whose influence greatly exceeded the relatively small number of records he made. The family soon moved to Aurora, where Mack went to school. He got his first guitar — a Lone Ranger model — and sang and played country music with his brother Alvin and sisters Berlis and Audrey. He also listened to the *Grand Ole Opry* and to WCIN, Cincinnati's black station where he first heard T-Bone Walker, whose records combined blues riffs with jazz sophistication. He took instruction from Ralph Trotto, a blind guitarist and gospel singer who lived nearby, and from an uncle who taught him how to play the thumb-and-finger style of Merle Travis. Other influences have included Les Paul, Howard Roberts and Chet Atkins but, apart from his parents, Mack usually cites Trotto as his first important, pre-teen mentor. (Trotto is not, incidentally, the clichéd old black man of earlier articles; the white gospel singer recorded several stirring albums prior to 1990, when he was rendered bedridden and brain-damaged following a collision with a drunken driver.)

7.4 - Lonnie Mack

Elvis Presley turned Mack's head around in 1956. At fifteen, he formed a rockabilly trio and sang 'Blue Suede Shoes' on local television. Two years later, he bought a Gibson Flying V — one of the first — at Glen Hughes Music in Cincinnati and booked his band into honky-tonks and clubs around Indiana, Kentucky and Hamilton, Ohio — where the owner of the Twilight Inn called them 'the Twilighters' and suggested that Lonnie should shorten his surname from McIntosh to Mack. He recruited bass player and vocalist Troy Seals in Hamilton, and his friendship with the blond-haired, Nashville-based country singer continues to this day. Later, in Dayton, Ohio, he worked with drummer Greg Webster and guitarist Robert Ward, founder members of the Ohio Untouchables. Mack told John Berg that he had a sound in his mind and tried all sorts of things, such as putting a fan in front of or behind his amplifier, in attempts to get it. Then he saw Ward perform using a Magnatone amp and 'That was it!' Mack got one too; the guitar playing on his finest soul ballads, and more besides, is directly informed by the distinctive tone which Robert Ward achieved on records by the Ohio Untouchables and the Falcons. 'There's nothing like those old Magnatones,' Mack told *Guitar World*. 'Nothing with that depth.'

These biographical nuts and bolts are now well-known (Ward, who was rediscovered by John Berg in 1989, even opened for Mack at concerts in 1991), but Mack's first recordings are not so well documented. The burly Big Mack and nerdy discographical queries do not go well together, and interviewers have a hard time squeezing details out of this generous but non-committal bear of a man who once spent time in the Cincinnati slammer. Asked if he'd done any pre-'Memphis' recordings, Mack told *Goldmine*: 'Just some real... I wouldn't really call them records. A couple of them were local stuff.' Mack collectors are still hunting for 'Pistol Packin' Mama', allegedly the first 45 he played on. Dobbs, the semi-mythical label, was owned by a woman who ran a jukebox supply service to small towns in rural Ohio and cut 'custom' records for local artists.

By strange coincidence, a group called the Twilighters recorded 'To Love In Vain' *c/w* 'Beginning Of Love' for Fraternity Records in 1961, but these are white doo-woppish sides without much R&B nutrition. They don't appear to have anything to do with Lonnie Mack's Twilighters.

Lonnie Mack also had a number of local imitators including the Earl Klugh-related Clarence Klugh *aka* Big Red of the Comancheros. He watched Robert Ward up in Dayton and named his Hamilton, Ohio-based label, Flying V Records, after the fabled instrument which Mack has always played.

Mack may not have figured on sessions for King Records until the Sixties were well under way (his guitar work crops up on singles by Hank Ballard, James Brown and Freddy King) but he was asked to help out at Fraternity, another of Cincinnati's independent companies. Even 'Memphis', recorded in 1962 at King Records' Studios, was allegedly laid down at the close of someone else's spare session time. Mack's Twilighters had been hired to back the Charmaines, and when Fraternity's black girl group had finished there was still twenty minutes left on the studio clock. Piano-playing buddy Dumpy Rice has claimed credit for pointing out the instrumental potential of Chuck Berry's 'Memphis Tennessee' (a Berry B-side which wasn't a hit in the USA) and Mack has said he began playing it as an instrumental one night when Rice didn't show up. Whatever, it was producer and local bandleader Carl Edmondson who drew the tune's commercial possibilities to the attention of Fraternity's owner, Harry Carlson. According to Mack, latter-day session engineer Gene Lawson played drums on it — a duty he reprised on Alligator's 'Long Way From

Memphis' some twenty-two years later.

Mack forgot all about 'Memphis' and went on the road with Troy Seals. They were in Minneapolis when one of the Fendermen told him the record had got four stars in *Billboard*. Later in Miami, where Seals was backing wife-to-be Jo-Ann Campbell, someone else told Mack he had a hit on his hands. By the time the record peaked at No. 5 (rubbing shoulders with Rolf Harris and Kyu Sakamoto), Mack was back in Cincinnati cutting a follow-up and an album with his regular unit including Irv Russotto and Marv Lieberman (saxophones), Truman Fields (keyboards), Wayne Bullock (bass) and Ron Grayson (drums).

'Wham!' (No. 24 in 1963) was another powerhouse manic assault on which Mack employed Ward's old trick of feeding the notes into an ancient Magnatone amp to deliver a distinctive ringing vibrato from his '58 Flying V with its customised Bigsby tailpiece or 'whammy-bar'. It isn't just a guitar record; the amplifier which boosts that plangent, thick-textured tone, takes equal billing. It's like an extra instrument — as important to the sound of Lonnie Mack as the echo chamber was to Duane Eddy.

Though much has rightly been written about Mack's guitar-playing, his very best singing is no less distinctive. I doubt if another white vocalist has ever got quite as close to deep black soul. Indeed, there are black soul singers of frenzied rank falsity compared to Mack; so much so you feel like telling them to sit down, offering a cuppa and asking them what the matter is. When white singers get close, it usually takes two or more — the Righteous Brothers obviously, or the aforementioned Jo-Ann & Troy who managed to hoodwink black record buyers long enough to score a solitary R&B hit.

Mack's third Fraternity single, 'Where There's A Will There's A Way', a faithful revival of a Vee-Jay record by the Five Blind Boys of Mississippi, could well have been a massive R&B hit, but the political undercurrents leading to the 'I'm Black & I'm Proud' movement created a bigotry which consumed black deejays. 'It came closer to hitting for me than any other vocal I ever cut,' Mack told Ben Sandmel in 1984. 'It never made the major pop markets but in the South and Midwest it was real big. And everybody thought I was black. We were working in Birmingham, Alabama, and the black station there was playing it to death, and they wanted me to come by. The deejays are saying: "Today we'll be interviewing the man, Mr. Lonnie Mack, with his big hit record, and blah, blah." So I went to the station and introduced myself and the guy takes one look and says: "Baby, you the wrong colour".' Other stations also dropped Mack from the playlist when they discovered he wasn't black. White radio preferred the other side, 'Baby What's Wrong'; this stomping cover of Jimmy Reed nudged into the Hot 100 for one week in November 1963. ('Where There's A Will' bubbled under for six weeks reaching No. 113).

Both sides of the first three Fraternity singles were included on

The Wham Of That Memphis Man along with 'The Bounce' (an instrumental of the Olympics' Top Forty hit, which Mack used to sing onstage), Martha Carson's 'Satisfied' (a 1951 pure gospel tune which struck a chord with rockabilly singers like Elvis and Sleepy LaBeef) and two Mack originals including the first, titanically soulful version of 'Why'. This rough-hewn ballad has the extremes of tenderness and barely-controlled power seldom heard this side of a Solomon Burke record. And then there's a gut-wailing scream of the kind ordinarily confined to hard gospel quartets led by Archie Brownlee or the Rev. Julius Cheeks. The fact that 'Why' was never issued as a single has not stopped it becoming, for many, the Mack performance to treasure. 'I've been raised up with blues,' he told Jim Delehunt in 1967. 'Once you get interested in soul music, it's hard to get interested in anything else. I've always enjoyed the real heavy R&B stuff.'

As befits an album of enduring brilliance, *The Wham Of That Memphis Man* has been around the block a few times: issued in the UK on President, re-mixed by Elektra, revised on Alligator etc. In 1999, Ace put it out with additional tracks including a slew of irrepressible instrumentals like 'Gee Baby' (a hitherto unissued homage to the fat, horn-driven sound of New Orleans), 'Chicken Pickin'' (so good that Fraternity issued it twice), 'Tension' (both sides of this 'Wham!'-motifed burner), 'The Freeze' (an atypical, minus-Magnatone take on Fenton Robinson's Duke recording, also known as 'Soul Express' and 'Jam And Butter') and a couple of venerable Bobby Bland songs on which the guitarist is complemented by a potent horn section. There are pleasant interludes in the shape of the Charmaines' Dixie Cups-ish slant on Huey Smith and a blues-drained version of a Beatles tune (well... even Link Wray felt obliged to record 'Please Please Me').

Mack cut instrumentals in order to please Fraternity boss, Harry Carlson. It wasn't what he did onstage where he sang soul stuff; Otis Redding, Sam & Dave, even underground classics like Bobby Parker's 'Watch Your Step'. (Heavy-duty Mack collectors circulate a tape of Lonnie at Cincinnati's Wintergarden Club in 1962-63; he sings 'Gee Baby', 'There Is Something On Your Mind', 'Watch Your Step' and Jimmy Reed's 'You're Something Else'). Mack's smouldering vocals have customised many other fine soul songs including Hank Ballard's 'I'll Keep You Happy' and Johnnie Morisette's 'Dorothy (On My Mind)'. 'Say Something Nice To Me' was written by Ray Pennington, another Cincinnati-based artist who cross-fertilised rockabilly, R&B and country. Pennington wrote many a reflective soul ballad as well as country classics like 'Three Hearts In A Tangle', recorded by Roy Drusky and James Brown. 'Farther On Up The Road' attests, once again, to the very considerable influence exerted by Bobby Bland's Duke recordings and the solo shows off Mack's contact-high technique to perfection. 'Oh, I Apologize' (originally by Barrett Strong) is like stumbling on one of the Ohio Untouchables' stark, haunting soul-mantras for the very first time. It stands proud next to almost anything

7.4 - Lonnie Mack

by Robert Ward or Wilson Pickett.

Apart from a percolating remake of 'Honky Tonk', there were no more hits. 'Lonnie On The Move', an instrumental version of 'Turn On Your Love Light', bubbled under the Hot 100 at No. 117. 'I've Had It' could only manage No. 128 for one week in 1964. In the memorable words of John Morthland: *'It was the era of satin pants and histrionic stage shows, and all the superior chops in the world couldn't hide the fact that chubby, country Mack probably had more in common with Kentucky truck drivers than he did with the new rock audience'.*

Despite periods of self-imposed obscurity, Mack has rarely stopped making records. Apart from little-known singles on small Cincinnati labels (AMG, Jewel and a Lonnie Mack-arranged record by the Voices Of Canaan on CLM), he cut three albums for Elektra, a bluegrass set with Rusty York on QCA (1973), a Troy Seals-produced single for Roulette (1975), two somewhat pastoral albums for Capitol (1977), a country-rock album with an eight-piece band, South, in 1980 (it wasn't commercially issued and I'm going to thank Ian Wallis for my copy) and a strong Muscle Shoals set of rock'n'boogie for Epic (1988). This one contained 'Too Rock For Country, Too Country For Rock And Roll', a wonderful collaboration which linked the *Grand Ole Opry* and Bobby Bland in one graceful but hard-driving swoop of a song.

Albums for Alligator have emphasised the link between Mack's fast, intense fluid style of the Sixties and the blues-rock of Duane Allman, Johnny Winter and Stevie Ray Vaughan, who co-produced Mack's Alligator debut, *Strike Like Lightning*. These are all very listenable, often thrilling hybrids of blues, gospel and country, but, to be perfectly blunt about it, they don't contain anything quite as riveting as 'Where There's A Will' or the original version of 'Why'. Now heading for sixty, Lonnie Mack remains one of the finest exponents of roadhouse boogie. But there was a time — and it's well worth repeating — when he was also the greatest of blue-eyed soul singers who packed a wham instrumentally as well as vocally.

Liner note for *Memphis Wham!* (Ace CDCHD-713) 1999.

7.5
ROY C
That Shotgun Wedding Man

Roy Charles Hammond *aka* Roy C is a singer apart, the loose marble of soul music whose brilliant, self-mocking, bittersweet songs lift today's black music out of its processed, packaged, communal rut. Thirty-five years around the backwaters of New York R&B have produced a singer-songwriter whose every inflection proclaims a mastery of his craft and an emotional integrity which is rare, even by the standards with which soul music is usually judged.

Real soul fans know all this. They're fully aware that Roy C isn't a one-hit wonder, but up there with the best-loved black musicians on the planet. For Peter Guralnick (*Sweet Soul Music*) Roy C's records are among those You Should Not Be Without But Might Never Find. *Goldmine*'s Cub Koda called him 'a soulman with a capital 'S', a singer who continues to release real soul-sounding records oblivious to current trends in funk and dance'. *Voices From The Shadows*, the luxurious deep soul magazine, is also aware that his music has never sounded more moving or necessary than it does today; the magazine regularly awards its single or album of the issue to Roy C's latest.

The object of all this admiration was born in Newington, Georgia in 1939, the son of an impoverished railway worker who ensured that all ten of his children attended church. Roy — who would shorten his name to avoid confusion with Ray Charles and Roy Hamilton — sang in the Baptist choir at the age of nine. Despite a temporarily crippling disease during adolescence, he tried boxing in downtown workout joints and once sparred with Hurricane Jackson, a heavyweight who would fight Floyd Patterson. 'It was rough,' he recalled, 'especially the training. After running the beaches every morning, I thought there must be an easier way to earn a living.'

By the late Fifties, Roy's major inspirations, like countless aspiring black singers of the day, were Sam Cooke and Clyde McPhatter. Roy sang lead tenor with the Genies, a group of transplanted Southerners formed by utility vocalist, Claude Johnson. All five teenagers — Bill Gaines (second tenor), Alexander 'Buddy' Faison (baritone) and Fred Jones (bass) completed the personnel — rehearsed Johnson's songs on the boardwalk at Long Beach, Long Island. 'Every night we'd go and sing

7.5 - Roy C

there,' Roy told me. 'All through that summer *[1958]*. Bobby Shad came over and listened and gave us his business card with *'Mercury Records: A&R'* printed on it. We went in *[Bell Sound Studio]* and recorded two songs including 'Who's That Knockin' ', which Claude had written. When it came out, we were all surprised 'cos Bobby had put it on his own label, Shad, and we were expecting it to come out on Mercury.'

'Who's That Knockin' ', a catchy rush job awash with vocal gimmicks and instrumental discord, was recorded in June 1958 and released eight months later. It sold 300,000 copies in the East, spending six weeks on *Billboard*'s Hot 100 and peaking at No. 71 in the spring of 1959. The group played the chitlin' circuit and went on a thirty-day tour with Sam Cooke and Eugene Church. But it didn't last. Bill Gaines was the first to go. He fell for a girl in the audience at the Apollo Theatre and split there and then, taking his baggy-trousered stage uniform with him. Roy was conscripted into the army, serving his time in West Germany. Claude Johnson became half of Don & Juan (famous for that stirring proto-soul ballad, 'What's Your Name') while Buddy Faison drove a truck, eventually replacing Don's original partner. Jayotis Washington, tenor with the Persuasions, thought of becoming a member just before they disbanded. 'They were hell of a group,' he told *Bim Bam Boom*. ' 'Who's That Knockin' ' was completely different from what they really did. Most of the songs they could do were standards like 'Moonlight In Vermont'.'

There are corners of Geniedom which lamplight has not fully illuminated. One group recorded 'No More Knockin' ' *c/w* 'On The Edge Of Town' for Hollywood — a United Telefilm Company — in 1959. Claude Johnson told Seamus McGarvey that this was a bogus unit who took over the name. But the writer credits (Hammond-Johnson-Gaines) point inexorably to the earlier personnel. Whatever, in 1960 Roy Hammond adopted fresh singers — likely members included Estelle Williams and Haskell Cleveland — and took them to Morty Craft's Warwick label, another United Telefilm affiliation. 'There Goes That Train', with its woo-woo harmony and 'slapped jelly' drumming, was the best of their three Warwick singles (all recorded, according to Roy, after he had left the army and returned to New York). Though they stood out in a crowded field, this second edition vanished almost as quickly as their hit-worthy predecessors.

Roy told the *New Musical Express* that he spent his off-duty hours in Germany listening to British pop music on Radio Luxembourg and honing his songwriting skills. One of his songs, 'Shotgun Wedding', had a hook as big as all outdoors. He recorded the tune at Broadway Studios in New York City and pressed a thousand copies on his own label (Hammond 001). 'I didn't attempt to sell 'em. I'd just send them to radio stations hoping someone would hear it and want to distribute it.' After thumbs-down from Decca and Mercury, the record fetched up on Black Hawk, a subsidiary of Bill Seabrook's tiny, New York-based independent, Jameco Records.

'Shotgun Wedding's ricochet sound effects quickly resolve into the kind of seamless pop R&B that Sam Cooke made between losing religion and espousing black pride. Roy's voice bore a close resemblance to Sam's and he wasn't ashamed to admit it: 'With each song I try to have a different style of singing, and there's often nowhere to go but to follow someone else. There's a whole lot of Sam Cooke in 'Shotgun Wedding'.'

The record was not a monster in the US, where deejays were reluctant to give airplay to any kind of immoral message. Nonetheless, it sold 70,000 copies and spent nine weeks on *Billboard*'s R&B chart, rising to No. 14 in December 1965. (That same year saw a string of Sam Cooke's posthumous hits and a welcome gaggle of his soundalikes — James Phelps, Bobby Harris, the Ovations — all over the R&B chart).

In London, 'Shotgun Wedding' found a receptive audience among mods and Afro-Caribbeans. Island Records' Guy Stevens told *Melody Maker*: 'Demand built up slowly over the months as clubs went on playing it. The Cue Club in Paddington gave it exceptional play, and the Ram Jam Club in Brixton adopted it as a signature tune.' Also popularised by pirate radio, 'Shotgun Wedding' reached No. 6 in 1966. Island Records, founded by Chris Blackwell who distributed Jamaican dance records from the back of his blue Mini Cooper, was finally on its way after three years without a hit. (Ember Records shared in this good fortune. They issued an album, *That Shotgun Wedding Man*, containing sides which Roy had cut with the Genies on Warwick. The company also re-issued an old Genies single, 'Twistin' Pneumonia' — a Dadaistic combination inspired by Huey Smith's 'Rocking Pneumonia And The Boogie Woogie Flu').

Roy toured Britain in the summer of 1966. He arrived on 1 June (on the same flight as Billy Bowen's fake Ink Spots) and stayed for six weeks, appearing at clubs and dancehalls from Bromley to Burnley. He thought he might settle in England. 'It's so congenial,' he told the *NME*. 'The cats dig my stuff better here than in the States.' In truth, it wasn't a mould-breaking visit. At Oxford Street's Tiles (3 June) he opened and closed with 'Shotgun Wedding'. He also sang 'There Is Something On Your Mind', the Everlys' 'When Will I Be Loved' (which he finally recorded for Three Gems in 1983), 'My Girl' and a trio of Sam Cooke favourites, 'Bring It On Home To Me', 'It's Got The Whole World Shakin'' and 'Frankie And Johnny'. He used a hand microphone, but suffered from first-night nerves and remained static throughout. The glitzy performing end of the business was evidently not Roy's forte. Peter Stringfellow, the table-dancing entrepreneur, recalled Roy's appearance at his first club, the Mojo in Sheffield: 'He could only sing 'Shotgun Wedding', and I swear he sang it six times — he was terrible. But the place was packed. They loved it.'

There were no takers for other Black Hawk/Jameco material ('The Wedding Is Over', 'My Mother Is Your Mother's Sister', 'Dance Girl') and, back in the USA, he signed with Bert Berns's Shout Records for a sombre item, 'Gone Gone' — a dead ringer for Arthur Alexander. He also leased two attractive, 'Shotgun Wedding'-ish sides to Smash Records and they were issued under the pseudonym of Little Frankie in November 1966.

After a two-year gap, Roy formed his own company, Alaga ('I saw the name on a syrup jar') and made up for lost time by issuing singles almost as quickly as he changed shirts. His band, including James Hines on guitar, Freddy Zieke (tenor sax) and Willie Grant (drums) recorded at New York's Ultrasonic Studios, but confounded geographical expectations by trading shrill and elaborate Northern arrangements for warm, loping soul romps redolent of Muscle Shoals or Memphis. Roy always wrote proper songs without a 'sock it to me' in sight. Some of them, particularly those he leased to Mercury Records, actually garnered a share of the black audience. 'Divorce Court', 'I Found A Man In My Bed', 'Merry Black Christmas', 'Got To Get Enough Of Your Sweet Love Stuff' (No. 45 R&B in 1971), 'I'm Gonna Love Somebody Else's Woman', 'I Caught You In The Act', the mega-soulful 'She Kept On Walkin' ', 'Don't Blame The Man' (No. 56 R&B in 1973), 'Loneliness Had Got A Hold On Me' (No. 48 R&B in 1974) and 'Love Me 'Til Tomorrow Comes' (No.46 R&B in 1975) were among the best of his unusually adult, often desolate fantasies.

As ever, airplay was a problem: 'Well, sex is the most important thing in our lives, but people don't face up to it and the public are often kicking against my records. 'Got To Get Enough' got plays on WWRL, but ministers raised hell with the station. One didn't like the bit about adultery. He was a Moslem with a show of his own and he broadcast a thirty minute sermon on the evils of that record. I thought he was crazy. After all, it's the truth, a lot of people are doing it. I write about life's realities. I don't care for ordinary love songs. I write what I think and hope it won't offend too many people.'

The early Seventies were reasonably good to Roy. As well as his minor R&B chart entries, he produced Mark IV, a sweet soul quartet who reached the same best-sellers with 'Honey I Still Love You' (No. 13 in 1972) and two lesser hits. Jonathan King's UK label reissued 'Shotgun Wedding' and it was a British hit (No. 8) all over again. (It was also a hit for Rod Stewart, another Sam Cooke admirer, in 1993.) There was a second British jaunt on which Roy sang his quirky Alaga/Mercury hits. The *Melody Maker*'s David Milton found Roy's honesty refreshing, but thought he must have been dropped on his head as a baby or molested as an adolescent in the ballgame crowd. But despite his Mercury albums, *Sex And Soul* and *More Sex And Soul*, Roy had other interests. Some of his songs, including 'Feel The Pain', 'We're On The Road To Hell' and 'Open Letter To The President' (*'South Africa? New York ain't no better'*) were politicised statements making Roy C a militant long before the growth of rap.

In the Eighties, Roy set up Three Gems and now has the advantage of owning his recent catalogue which includes releases by Dennis Edwards and former Shout labelmate, Bobby Harris. His Three Gems tracks are superb examples of graceful, insinuating soul. Assisted by loyal guitarist and fellow arranger, James Hines, Roy achieves a synthesis comparable to that of the truly great soul singers. The overall tautness of the band, probably John Adams (organ), Paul Henegan (tenor), Jeff Silberschlag and Laurie Frink (trumpets), Frederick Bush (bass) and Earl Williams (drums), displays a real awareness of form achieving all that soul freaks could wish for.

The singing is subtle and hugely authoritative. Roy has made a singularly successful effort to nurture his own voice and style. Falsetto whoops and recitations have become trademarks. He combines the vocal filigree of an Al Green ('Love Me 'Til Tomorrow Comes') with a hoarse churchiness ('Pick Up The Pieces') or a reggae-ish playfulness ('Rock Me All Night'). When he lurches from 'If I Could Love You Forever' into 'I Stand Accused', he practically shreds the competition — Isaac Hayes, Al Wilson, Toussaint McCall, Inez & Charlie Foxx, even Jerry Butler.

Roy's own songs are as pungent as ever, perhaps more so. They underline his resistance to formula and a capacity to surprise. 'Peepin' Through The Window' is a creepy psychodrama brimming with knee-buckling, jaw-slackening moments. And 'She's Gone (She Took The TV And Telephone)' is a towering, all-time gem. Was there ever a finer distillation of soul so desolate and yet so funny? It's one of those pain-wracked confessionals that resonates in the memory for a whole slew of reasons. There's the cheesiest, nerve-jangling strings ever heard on a soul disc. And Roy's conversation with the bank teller is almost cinematic; that note of resignation, that clammy little 'mmm, mm, mm', is one of the great footnotes in pop R&B on a par with Shang's falsetto singing on Maurice Williams's 'Stay', or Bunker Hill's scream in Part Two of 'Hide And Go Seek'.

Roy C reaffirms one's faith in soul music as an enduring form. He is a singer and songwriter of timeless gifts and his kind of soul is something today's black music can never have enough of.

Note   This essay began life as 'That Shotgun Wedding Man' in *Let It Rock* (March 1973) and ended up as a liner note for a Sequel CD (NEM-764) that wasn't released. It should have come out in 1996.

INDEX OF PEOPLE'S NAMES

Abernathy, Marion 165
Abramson, Herb 136, 275
Ace, Johnny 101, 123, 180
Acuff, Roy 38, 46, 82, 196
Adams, Carl 216, 229-230, 231
Adams, Faye 237
Adams, John 332
Adams, Johnny 190
Adelman, Ben 23, 32, 206, 280
Ad-Libs 258
Agee, Ray 167, 168
Ahbez, Eden 89
Aiken, Ben 314
Alaimo, Steve 314
Alexander, Arthur
   283, 307, 308, 330
Alexis, Bobby 115
Alfred, Roy 282
Ali, Bardu 140, 143
Allan, Johnnie 287, 288, 289,
   290, **297-302**
Allen, Annisteen 169, 171
Allen, Bill 'Hoss' 125-6, 227
Allen, Jesse 118
Allen, Lee 119, 165
Allen, Marie 150
Allen, Milton 212
Allen, Steve 232
Allison, Gene 283
Allison, Jerry 28, 30
Allison, Joe & Audrey 247
Allman, Duane 326
Allsup, Tommy 62, 79
Ambassadors 308
Ames Brothers 176
Anderson, Elton 288, 289, 301
Anderson, John 141, 157
Anderson, Ron 273
Andrews, Audie 261
Animals 54, 57
Anka, Paul 70
Anthony, Ray 147
Appell, Dave 198, 235, 236,
   237, 319
Arch, Cleotis 114
Arden, Don 54, 57, 161, 163
Armstead, William 87
Armstrong, Lil 227
Armstrong, Louis 118
Arnaudon, Jean-Claude 126
Arnold, Eddy 29, 76, 196, 213,
   245, 251

Arnold, Jerry 61
Ashford & Simpson 276
Asman, James 84
Atkins, Chet 46, 76, 216, 321
Atkins, Jim
   (& The Pinetoppers) 39
Austin, Sil 165, 201
Autry, Gene 38, 122
Avalon, Frankie 91
Aznavour, Charles 24
Baby Ray 148, 314
Bacher, Flip 24
Bad Boys 218, 233
Bagby, Doc 198
Bagwell, Leon 250, 251
Bailes, Walter 49
Bailey, DeFord 46
Bain, Bob 249
Baja Marimba Band 251
Baker, LaVern 107, 130, 281
Baker, Mickey 'Guitar' 120
Baker, Sam 308
Baker, Tommy 59, 61
Balk, Harry 201, 202, 203
Ball, Noel 38-9
Ballard, Hank 107, 108, 323, 325
Ballard, Jimmy 172
Ballen, Ivin 196, 237
Bare, Bobby 42
Barker, Delbert 78
Barnet, Charlie 236, 239
Barrett, Paul 252
Barrix, Billy 232
Barry, Joe 192, 287, 289, 290,
   312, 313
Barry, Len 313, 314
Bartholomew, Dave
   109, 117, 118, 119
Basie, Count 117, 122, 147, 154,
   261
Bass, Ralph 76, 78, 108, 141,
   146, 262, 264,
   265, 266, 267
Baugh, Smokey Joe 57
Bazelle, Shelton 230
Beal, Eddie 68
Beard, Dean 190
Beatles 55, 58, 97, 180, 192, 193,
   218, 256, 257, 296, 325
Beaumont, Jimmy 271
Beavers, Clyde 42
Beavers, Jackey 310

Beck, Jeff 220, 222
Beck, Jim 76
Bee, Molly 131
Beecher, Franny 239
Belew Twins 85
Bell, Freddie (& The Bell Boys)
   198, 235
Bell, William 132
Belmont, Maurice 236, 237
Belmonts *[post-Dion]* 271
Belvin, Jesse
   77, 109, 145, 158, 175
Benjamin, Bennie 219
Bennett, Jean 67, 68, 70, 261,
   262, 265, 267
Benson, Al 141
Benton, Brook 93, 97, 281, 293
Berg, John 323
Berger, Bettye 127
Berle, Milton 250
Berlin, Irving 136, 265
Bernard, Rick 293, 295
Bernard, Rod 114, 287, 288,
   289, 290, **291-6**,
   298-9, 312
Berns, Bert 330
Berry, Chuck 54, 79, 150, 181,
   194, 295, 297,
   301, 318, 323
Berry, Richard
   108, 109, 154, 155, 158, 167
   See also Pharaohs
Bertram, Bob **89-92**
Bertram, Karen Ann 90
Betty & Dupree 109
Big Bopper
   20, 89, 102, 293, 296, 300
Biggs, Bill 61
Big John's Untouchables 71
Big Maybelle 161, 186
Big Red 323
Big Rivers 96
Big Tiny 114
Bihari Brothers
   108, 109, 154, 156, 180
Bihari, Joe 154
Bihari, Jules 154
Bihari, Saul 109
Binnick, Bernie 207
Bissell, Shelton 230
Black, Bill (Combo)
   61, 62, 76, 85-6

Index of People's Names

Black Crowes 280
Blackman, Thelma 95
Blackwell, Bumps
    158, 177, 178, 179, 180
Blackwell, Chris 330
Blackwell, Otis 276
Blaine, Hal 250-1
Blaine, Jerry 68
Blair, John 82, 84, 85
Blake, Tommy 231, 233
Blakely, Cornell 306
Bland, Billy 274
Bland, Bobby 62, 109, 116, 123,
    124, 125, 156,
    325, 326
Blesh, Rudi 135
Blivens, Cliff 144
Blockbusters 68, 69, 70, 156
Blood, Sweat & Tears 156
Blue, Little Joe 308
Blue Caps – *See* Vincent, Gene
Blues Kings 233
Bo, Eddie 118
Bo, Phil 289, 290
Boatman, Tooter 191
Bobby & The Temps 219, 220
Bogart, Neil 276, 277
Boland, Tate 38
Bond, Eddie 37
Bongiovi, Tony 98
Booker, James 119
Boone, Dick 124
Boone, Pat 130, 131, 208, 213,
    247, 248, 249, 250
Boone, Wild Bill 146
Bopchords 257
Boudreaux, Charles 293
Bowen, Billy 330
Box Tops 313
Bradley, Harold 84, 129
Bradley, Owen 53, 54, 57, 84
Bradshaw, Tiny 27
Bragg, Johnny 305
Brando, Marlon 64
Brant, Bobby – *See* Poe, Bobby
Brawley, Joe 94
Brennan, Cody
    (& The Temptations) 219-220
Brewer, Teresa 32, 130, 131, 219
Brief Encounter 310
Briggs, Billy 227
Bright, Larry 314
Brinkley, Jay 78
British Walkers 218, 220
Britt, Elton 101
Broadwater, Eleanor 227
Brooks, Elkie 57
Brooks, Gene 137
Brothers 230
Broven, John 117

Brown, Buster 192
Brown, Charles 127, 128, 129,
    152, 169, 180
Brown, Ellwood 220, 221
Brown, Gatemouth 21, 23, 101,
    114, **121-6**,
    226
Brown, Ike 147
Brown, J.W. 185
Brown, James 97, 120, 121,
    173, 313, 314,
    323, 325
Brown, James 'Widemouth' 121
Brown, Lattimore 308, 309
Brown, Nappy 158, 161, 173
Brown, Piney 114, 308
Brown, Roy
    118, 137, 154, 169, 173
Brown, Ruth 23, 84, 107, 281
Brown, Shuler 212
Brownlee, Archie 325
Broza, Stan Lee 236
Bruce, Mary Rose 261
Bryant, Boudleaux 283
Bryant, Jimmy 251
Bryant, Willie 144
Bubis, Alan 211
Bubis, Alvin 211, 212
Buchanan, Roy
    97, 121, 208, 209, **215-223**,
    227, 231, 232, 233
Buddy & Claudia 238
Bullock, Wayne 324
Buntin, Billy 82, 83, 85
Burgess, Sonny 156
Burgess, Wilma 29
Burke, Solomon
    97, 127, 131, 158, 162, 281,
    309, 312, 313, 325
Burley, Dan
    (& His Skiffle Boys) 135
Burnette, Dorsey 102
Burnette, Johnny 102, 133, 172
Burns, Hal 46
Burns, Sonny 18, 20, 41
Burrage, Harold 240
Burris, J.C. 138
Burton, Dorian 130
Burton, James 57, 216, 222,
    226, 227, 229,
    249
Burton, John 73
Bush, Frederick 332
Butler, Billy 203
Butler, Carl & Pearl 72
Butler, Jerry 319, 332
Butterfield, Paul 315
Byrd, Bobby 276
Byrnes, Edd 87
C, Roy **327-332**

Cadaly, Joseph 140-1
Cadets 109
Cadillacs 77
Caldwell, Len 96
Callas, Dimitri 218
Calloway, Cab 101, 139
Camelots 257
Cameron, Ray 57
Campbell, Archie 46
Campbell, Choker 147
Campbell, George 190, 191
Campbell, Jo-Ann 314, 324
Campi, Ray 79, **101-4**
Canard, Pete 141
Cann, Gloria 161
Cann, John P. 161
Canned Heat 113, 115
Cannon, Freddy 219, 220, 232
Canon Girls 68
Cantrall, Bobby 203
Capehart, Jerry 212
Capris 256, 271, 312
Caraway, Bobby 104
Caraway, Terry 104
Cardwell, Jack 138
Carlisle, Jumpin' Bill 84, 104
Carlisles 47, 75
Carlson, Harry 323, 325
Carman, Jenks 'Tex' 89
Carr, James 313
Carr, Leroy 129
Carrigan, Jerry 30
Carrol, Marvin 23, 24
Carroll, Johnny **81-8**, 190
Carroll, Ted 20
Carson, Don (& The Casuals) 89
Carson, Martha 248, 325
Carson, Mindy 131
Carter, Anita 46
Carter, Fred
    29, 30, 216, 226, 229
Carter, Goree 125
Carter Family 134
Cash, Alvin 310
Cash, Johnny 42, 84
Castille, Leroy 298, 300
Castle, Lee 298, 300
Castle, Roy 21
Casuals 191
Catlett, Big Sid 170
Cavaliers *[Cecil Holmes]* 273
Cavaliers *[Joe Melson]* 281
Cavello, Jimmy
    (& The House Rockers) 235
Cedrone, Danny 235
Cell Block Seven 85
Chaney, Lon 229
Channel, Bruce
    189, 192, 194, 233, 312-3
Chansonaires 262

334

Index of People's Names

Chaparrals 75, 191
Chapman, Grady 158
Charles, Bobby
   226, 287, 291, 296, 301
Charles, Ray
   79, 94, 127, 130, 148, 150,
   206, 281, 312, 314, 327
Charlie & Ray 161
Charmaines 323, 325
Charms 82
   See also Williams, Otis
Chartbusters 97, 98
Checker, Chubby 239, 240
Cheeks, Rev. Julius 325
Cheers 102
Chenier, Clifton 296
Cherry, Don 154
Chesnut, Jerry 30
Chess, Leonard
   96, 109, 110, 111, 226, 227,
   229, 293, 306
Chess, Marshall 111
Chessmen 257, 258
Chevrons 270
Chimes 256, 270, 271
Chipmunks 232
Choates, Harry 288
Choralettes 96
Christie, Gaylon 75
Chudd, Lew 120
Church, Eugene 329
Church, Jimmy 308
Churchill, Savannah 237
Citadels 257, 258
Clanton, Jimmy 180
Clapton, Eric 115, 191, 222
Clark, Chris 314
Clark, Dick
   180, 191, 216, 229, 293
Clark, Dudley 23
Clark, Hestor 22
Clark, Paul 23
Clark, Roy **21-5**, 32, 93, 99,
   126, 206, 251
Clark, Sanford 92, 179
Classics 270
Clay, Henry 244
Clayton, Buck 173
Clement, Jack 66, 114
Clements, Shorty 153
Cleveland, Haskell 329
Cline, Patsy 23, 29, 206, 221
Clovers 82, 154, 227, 249, 279
Coasters
   151, 155, 156, 158, 233, 283
Coates, Don (& The Bon Aires)
                              85
Cobb, Arnett 129, 140
Cobb, Kenny 77
Cocco, Lenny 271

Cochran, Eddie 212, 213, 248
Cochran, Wayne 193, 313
Coe, Jamie (& The Gigolos) 202
Coffey, Breathless Dan 56, 162
Cohen, Leon 130
Cohen, Paul 83, 84
Cohn, Dude 83
Cohn, Nik 188
Cole, Darnell 147
Cole, Nat 'King'
   89, 93, 148, 180
Coleman, Bee 46
Coleman, Brother Dutch 46, 48
Coleman, Cornelius 120
Coleman, Ornette 192
Coleman, Trudy 192
Collette, Buddy 141
Collie, Biff 244-5, 246, 248
Collins, Albert **113-6**, 121, 125
Colman, Stuart 231, 249, 252
Colt, Steve 313
Colts 68, 262
Comancheros 323
Commodores 116
Como, Perry
   92, 212, 238, 239, 282
Connor, Chris 173
Consorts 271
Cook, Little Joe 163
Cook, Sam 237, 239
Cooke, Sam
   281, 319, 327, 329, 330, 331
Cookie & The Cupcakes
   148, 287, 288-9
Cooley, Pete Gabriel 154
Cooper, Cathy 140
Cooper, Dolly 156
Cooper, Jeff 310
Coots, J. Fred 226
Copas, Cowboy 40
Copeland, Johnny 190
Copland, Edward 228
Cotton, Billy 196
Cousins 90, 92
Covay, Don 240
Coward, Noel 265
Craft, Morty 329
Craig, Jimmy 102
Craig, Ken 91, 92
Cramer, Floyd 33, 295
Crandall, Eddie 28
Crawford, Sugar Boy 118
Crayton, Pee Wee 154
Creedence Clearwater Revival 35
Crests 271
Crickets *[post-Holly]* 30
Criss, Sonny 140
Crosby, Bing 172
Crosby, Gary 250
Crutchfield, Jan 282

Cuoghi, Joe 61
Curtis, Mac 59, **75-9**, 191
Curtis, Sonny 28, 30
Customs 212
Daffan, Ted 127
Daily, Pappy 18, 20, 67
Dale, Larry 133
Dalton, Danny 91
Dandridge, Dorothy 177-8
Daniels, Charlie 133, 218
Daniels, Leroy 145
Danny & The Juniors 219
Dante & The Evergreens 270
Daret, Betty & Darla 248
Darin, Bobby 150, 158, 251
Darnell, Larry 176
Darrell, Johnny 30
Darts 270
Dave & Sugar 214
David, Dwight 147
Davis, Benny 226
Davis, Billy 110
Davis, Clifford 195
Davis, Dale 34
Davis, Eddie 'Lockjaw' 171
Davis, Jimmie
   127, 244, 245, 311
Davis, Judge 114
Davis, Link 102
Davis, Lloyd 273, 274
Davis, Maxwell 108, 151, 178
Davis Jr, Sammy 213
Davis, Sheriff Tex 206
Dawn 319
Dawson, Jim 152
Dawson, Ronnie 75
Day, Frankie 198, 239
Day, Jackie 150, 151
Daye, Johnny 314
Deal, Harry 310
Dean, David 115
Dean, Eddie 89
Dean, James 64
Dean, Jimmy 23, 32, 206, 280
Dean, Wally 133
Dean & Jean 163
Dean & Marc 230
Debonaires 154
DeFrancis, Lou 236, 237, 241
DeHaven, Penny 251
Delagarde, Mario 263
Delaney & Bonnie 314
Delehunt, Jim 325
Delmore Brothers
   47, 102, 104, 121, 311
Denny, Jim 28, 42
Denton, Mickey 202
Denver, John 251
Denver's Soundmasters, Danny
                              221-2

Index of People's Names

Derby, A.D. 212
DeVecchis, Ace 237
DeVille Sisters 179
Devil's Sons 221
Devlin, Johnny 250
DeVorzon, Barry 69
Devotions 256, 271
Dewar, Allison 249
DeWitt, Earl 147
Dexter, Al 102
Dey, Jack 318
Diamonds 120
Dickens, Little Jimmy 125, 245
Diddley, Bo 227
Dillon, Matt 43
DiMucci, Dion – *See* Dion
Dinning, Ace 191
Dion (& The Belmonts) 270, 271
Dixiebelles 306
Dixie Cups 325
Dixon, Floyd 129, 173
Dixon, Grace 243
Dixon, Helene 130
Dixon, Luther 256
Dixon, Willie 232
Dodd, Bonnie 40
Dodds, Dar 66
Doggett, Bill
   115, 147, 148, 171, 203
Dolan, Jimmie 18
Dolls 114
Dolphin, John 151, 154
Domino, Fats
   24, 59, 61, 79, 86, 93, 94,
   96, 97, 117, 118, 119, 120,
   148, 173, 192, 288, 291,
   296, 298, 300, 312, 313
Dominoes 27, 48, 150, 154
Don & Dewey 179
Don & Juan 202, 256, 329
Donley, Jimmy 289, 290, 296
Doonican, Val 21, 25, 218
Dope & Skillet 145
Dorsey, Jimmy 261
Dorsey, Lee 163
Dorsey, Tommy
   172, 238, 240, 261
Doucette, Stan 221
Douglas, Jerry 49
Douglas, Steve 158
Douglas, Walter 158
Downing, Big Al
   21, **93-9**, 169, 220
Downing, Don 21, 93, 94
Downing, Walter 94
Doyle, Buddy 18
Doyle, Gene 18
Doyle, Ira 18
Dr. John 288, 314
Drake, Jay 203

Drake, Pete 42
Draper, Rusty 84
Drifters 219, 318, 319, 320
Drusky, Roy 325
Dryden, Spencer 216
Dubas, Johnny 96, 97
Duconge, Wendell 119
Dudley, Dave 213
Duke, Billy (& The Dukes)
   198, 235, 239
Dunaway, Shelton 289
Duncan, Jimmy 125
Duncan, Johnny 33
Dunlop, Boyd 147
Dunn, John 38, 39
Dunn, William 75
Dupree, Champion Jack 133, 138
Duprees 270
Durham, Hal 50
Duvall, Huelyn 191
Dybvig's Royalaires, Bruce 146
Dylan, Bob 77
Dynatones 279
Earls 256, 269, 271
Echols, Gene 82
Echols, Pop 244
Eckstine, Billy 147, 169, 172
Eddie & Dutch 232
Eddy, Duane 157, 201, 219, 324
Edmondson, Carl 323
Edmunds, Dave 55, 297
Edsels 271
Edson, Estelle 165
Edwards, Dave 89, 91
Edwards, Dennis 331
Edwards, Eddie 250, 251
Edwards, Ralph 247
Egan, Willie 139
Elbert, Donnie 163
Eldorados 83
Elegants 270
Ellington, Duke 117, 129, 261
Ellis, Martha 40
Ellis, Ray 131
Ellis, Wilbert 136, 137
Ely, Brother Claude
   45, 46, 48, 312
Emanons 265
Emerson, Bill 86
Emerson, Wild Bill 201
Emmons, Bobby 61
Engel, Ed 269, 270, 271
Epstein, Brian 193
Erskine, Les 171
Ertegun, Ahmet 130, 136
Ervin, Jesse 263
Escott, Colin 46, 48, 61
Esquerita 96, 163
Esquire Boys 235
Evans, Gene 28

Evans, Jimmy 137
Evans, Margie 152
Evans, Ray 248
Everett, Todd 216
Everly Brothers 29, 192, 330
Ewing, Jesse 'Streamline350
   141
Excellents 270
Fabian 247
Fabulous Thunderbirds 315
Fain, Sammy 250
Fairburn, Werly 231
Faison, Buddy 327, 329
Falcon, Joe 288, 298
Falcons 281, 323
Fannin County Boys 281
Fardon, Don 33
Feathers, Charlie 63
Feld, Irvin 171
Fell, Terry 245
Fender, Freddy 99, 289, 291, 295
Fendermen 323
Ferguson, Gary 126
Ferguson, H-Bomb 137
Ferlingere, Robert 272
Fields, Frank 119
Fields, Lee 310
Fields, Truman 324
Fiestas 274
Finfer, Harry 193
Finnis, Rob 130, 245
Fireballs 27, 29
Fisher, Eddie 251
Fi-Tones 273, 274
Fitzgerald, Ella 29, 117, 172
Five Americans 233
Five Blind Boys Of Mississippi
   324
Five Finks 91
Five Gents 317
Five Jades 258
Five Jets 233
Five Keys 147, 255
Five Satins 181
Five Smith Brothers 195
Five Stars 85
Flairs 68, 69, 154, 155, 262
Flames 109
Flamingo, Johnny 175
Flamingos 279
Flanagan, Ralph 238
Flatt, Lester, & Earl Scruggs 28
Flood, Dick 280, 282
Flowers, Phil 220
Foley, Red 32, 64, 237
Fontaine, Eddie 173
Fontana, D.J. 76
Ford, Tennessee Ernie
   45, 46, 47, 48, 196, 251, 311
Foreman, Al 293, 298, 300

336

Index of People's Names

Foster, Fred   279, 280, 281, 282, 283, 306, 307
Four Fellows   129
Four Freshmen   108
Four Men Of Rhythm   237
Four Seasons   312
Four Sharps   236, 237
Four Skins   221
Four Tops   257
Four Vagabonds   255
Fourmost *[US Group]*   221
Fowler, T.J.   203
Fox, Pete   154, 156
Foxx, Inez & Charlie   332
Francis, Connie   35
Francis, Panama   171
Franklin, Aretha   107
Franks, Tillman   244
Fraternity Brothers   69
Frazier, Al   265
Frazier, Dallas   314
Fred, John   233
Freddie & The Dreamers   256
Freed, Alan   24, 77, 119, 127, 180, 227, 267, 274
Freed, Mort   173
Freeman, Art & Dottie   91
Freeman, Ernie   157, 179, 180
Frink, Laurie   332
Fritz, Joe   115
Frizzell, Lefty   18, 28, 75, 76, 102
Fry, Carl   59, 61
Fuller, Blind Boy   45, 215
Fuller, Johnny   301
Fulson, Lowell   151, 152, 167
Fuqua, Harvey   109, 110, 158, 232
Fury, Billy   318
G, Rocky   275, 314
Gable, Guitar   291, 292
Gaillard, Slim   266
Gaines, Bill   327, 329
Galbraith, Jimmy   76, 77
Galbraith, Kenneth   76, 77
Gallo, Frank   109
Gamble & Huff   307, 308, 310
Gangwisch, Kathy   22
Garland, Hank   33, 69, 216
Garrison, Glen   72
Gaston, Henry 'Shang'   332
Gay, Connie   23
Gaye, Barbie   77
Gaye, Marvin   116
Geils, J.   315
Genies   327, 330
Gentrys   233
Gibbs, Georgia   108
Gibson, Don   127
Gibson, Johnny   202

Gideon, Vince   97
Gillespie, Dizzy   140, 176
Gillett, Charlie   89, 107, 136, 188, 289, 297
Gilley, Mickey   97, 214
Gilmer, Jimmy (& The Fireballs)   27
  See also Fireballs
Glass, Melvin   143
Glasser, Dick   229
Glenister, Derek   63
Glenn, Artie   86
Glosson, Lonnie   17, 103, 211, 321
Glover, Henry   42, 171
Godfrey, Arthur   32
Goffin, Gerry   318
Goldberg, Barry   315
Goldman, Jack – *See* Tiger, J.G.
Goldner, George   68, 276
Goldsboro, Bobby   30
Gomez, Juvie   86
Gonzales, Charlie   240
Gonzalez, Fernando   272
Good, Jack   185
Goodman, Benny   235, 238
Goodman, Nat   120
Goodson, Hal   250
Gordon, Jim   216
Gordon, Loy   133
Gordon, Robert   205, 209
Gordon, Rosco   85, 158, 173, 176
Gordy, Berry   110
Gordy, Gwen   110
Gore, Charlie   40
Gottehrer, Richard   209
Gowans, Sammy   221
Gracie, Charlie   **195-9**, 229, 235, 236, 237
Graffagnino, Jake   291
Grammer, Billy   32, 280
Grant, Willie   331
Graves, Billy   280
Grayson, Ron   324
Green, Al   332
Green, Cal   121
Green, Irv   67, 69
Greenfield, Howie   318
Greenwich, Ellie   319
Greer, Big John   133, 165
Gregg, Bobby (& His Friends)   209, 220
Gries, Eddie   256
Griffin, Buddy   238
Griffin, Leroy   255
Griggs, Bill   28
Grimes, Tiny   237
Grissim, John   188
Guess, Don   28
Guitar Junior   301

Guitar Slim   115, 116, 121, 125, 156, 225, 288
Gunter, Cornel   154, 262, 264, 266
Gunter, Shirley   264
Guralnick, Peter   188, 327
Hagans, Buddy   177
Haggard, Merle   99, 216, 302
Haley, Bill (& His Comets)   40, 201, 235, 238, 239, 241
Haley, Bill (& The Saddlemen)   196, 198, 236
Hall, Bill   114, 115, 116, 293, 300
Hall, Daryl, & John Oates   315
Hall, Ronnie   82
Hall, Roy   186
Hall, Tom T.   99
Hallyday, Johnny   72
Halsey, Jim   21, 25, 95, 126
Hamilton IV, George   77
Hamilton, Roy   161, 282, 327
Hammer, Jack   249
Hammond Jr, John   315
Hampton, Lionel   133, 140, 145
Hancock, Hunter   140, 146, 150, 262, 264
Hardesty, Herb   **117-120**
Hardiman, Leonard   143, 147, 148
Harlem Hotshots   169
Harman, Buddy   33, 69
Harptones   257
Harris, Bob   135-6, 137
Harris, Bobby   330, 331
Harris, Cecil   147
Harris, Dimples   68
Harris, Emmylou   49
Harris, Kent   25
Harris, Peppermint   233
Harris, Plunky   153
Harris, Porkie   146
Harris, Puddler   231
Harris, Rolf   324
Harris, Thurston   157, 167
Harris, Wynonie   121, 133, 137, 170
Harrison, George   55, 317
Hatcher, Ray   198
Haven, Don (& The Hi-Fis)   235
Hawes, Hampton   140
Hawkins, Dale   215, 216, 217, 218, **225-233**
Hawkins Sr, Delmar   225
Hawkins, Edwin   277
Hawkins, Erskine   176, 180, 219
Hawkins, Jennell   152
Hawkins, Jerry   216, 225, 226
Hawkins, Martin   38, 48
Hawkins, Ronnie (& The Hawks)   156, 218, 226, 229, 231, 232, 312

Index of People's Names

Hawkins, Screamin' Jay
   77, 89, 154, 157, **161-4**, 198
Hayden, Geoff 151
Hayes, Henry 114
Hayes, Isaac 132, 319, 332
Hayes, Linda
   69, 262, 263, 264, 267
Haymes, Joe 227
Haywood, Leon 150, 151
Hazlewood, Lee 179
Head, Roy 314
Heap, Jimmy 102, 103
Heartbeats 216, 231, 318
Hebb, Bobby 306
Helms, Don 39, 40
Henderson, Herbert 114
Henderson, Joe 308
Henderson, Luther 196
Hendon, R.D. 18
Hendrix, Jimi 215, 221
Henegan, Paul 332
Hennen, Bill 82, 83, 86
Henry, Clarence 'Frogman' 173, 317
Henry, Earl 30
Henry, Shifty 167
Herrera, Little Julian 175, 216
Herring, Cliff
   76, 78, 86, 94, 191, 192
Herring, Jesse 150
Hess, Bennie 20
Hess, Norbert 151, 262
Hi-Boys 220
Hicks, Johnny 86
Higgins, Chuck 139, 146, 178
Hill, Bunker 208, 332
Hill, Don 167
Hill, Henry 102
Hill, Raymond 143
Hilltoppers 267
Hi-Los 108
Hines, Earl 131, 139
Hines, James 331, 332
Hinton, Joe 191
Hirschberg, David 241
Hobbs, Willie 190, 310
Hodge, Alex
   262, 263, 264, 265, 266
Hodge, Gaynell 262, 265
Hodge, Sam 97
Hoedown Corner Gang 245
Hoffpaur, Bhuel 298
Hogg, Smokey 107, 131
Hogsed, Roy 89
Holden, Lorenzo 140
Holden, Ron 175
Holiday, Billie 107, 238, 264
Holidays 257
Holiness Singers 49

Holland, Roscoe 151
Holly, Buddy (& The Crickets)
   27, 28, 29, 71, 79, 249, 250, 279
Hollyhawks 28
Hollywood Blue Jays 154
Holman, Eddie 276
Holmes, Cecil **273-7**
Holmes, Chib 96, 97
Holmes, Wade 32
Honey Cone 277
Hooker, Earl 115
Hooker, John Lee
   27, 31, 54, 113, 162
Hopkins, Herman 114
Hopkins, Lightnin'
   27, 107, 114, 125, 133, 227
Hopkins, Linda 109
Hopkins, Telma 319
Hopson Family 310
Horn, Bob 198
Horton, Johnny
   104, 231, 244, 301
Horton, Shorty 206, 221
Hot Rocks 83, 85
Houston, David 29, 78
Houston, Joe 146
Howard, Bobby 208, 218, 220
Howard, Harlan 309
Howard, Jack 40, 198
Howard, Paul 230
Howlin' Wolf 192, 225, 227
Hua Paka 181
Hudson, Bill 77
Hudson, Pookie 277
Hudson, Rock 251
Huff, Jimmy 145
Huge, Hoyt 122
Huggy Boy 177
Hughes, Jimmy 115
Hulbert, Snooky 171
Hulin, T.K. 287, 289, 290, 312
Humes, Helen 165
Humperdinck, Engelbert 301
Humphries, Maylon 228, 229
Hunter, Ernie 18
Hunter, Ivory Joe **127-132**, 308
Hunter, Lee 131
Hunters 156
Husky, Ferlin 83, 246
Hutton, Ina Ray 227
Ink Spots 255, 257, 262, 330
Inman, Autry 42
Innis, Louis 39, 40, 78
Innocenti, Frank 38, 39
Inocencio, Tim 177
Irby, Jerry 42
Isle, Jimmy 72
Isley Brothers 277
Ives, Burl 72

Jackson, Bull Moose
   165, **169-174**, 238
Jackson, Eugene 146
Jackson, Hal 275
Jackson, Hurricane 327
Jackson, Monroe 64
Jackson, Stonewall 72
Jackson, Tommy 39
Jackson, Wanda
   21, 25, 95, 97, 98, 107
Jackson, Willis 'Gator Tail' 173
Jacquet, Illinois 129, 140
James, Etta
   107-111, 154, 167, 311, 313
James, Harry 148
James, Joni 219
James, Sonny 76, 83, 132, 190
Janes, Roland 61
Jano, Johnny 133
Jarmusch, Jim 164
Jay, Bobby 216
Jaye, Jerry **59-62**
Jefferson Airplane 216
Jefferson, Blind Lemon 130, 153
Jefferson, Joe 262
Jenkins, Alan 279
Jennings, Waylon 111, 194
Jeremiah, Kenny 314
Jessie, Dwayne 153
Jessie, Lenis 154
Jessie, Young 139, **153-9**, 312
Jewels 68, 276
Jill & Ray 193
Jivin' Gene 287, 288, 289, 290, 295, 300, 301
Jo-Ann & Troy 314, 324
Jodimars 239
John, Little Willie
   43, 147, 156, 161, 202, 300, 301
Johnnie & Jack 283
Johnny & The Hurricanes **201-4**
Johnson, Bill 114
Johnson, Bob 77
Johnson, Byron 72
Johnson, Claude 327, 329
Johnson, Don 108
Johnson, Harold 171
Johnson, Lil 227
Johnson, Lonnie 134, 225
Johnson, Rosemary 264
Johnson, Virgil
   279, 280, 281, 282, 283
Johnson, Wendell 148
Johnston, Diane 77
Johnston, Don 77, 78
Jolly-Jax 148
Jolson, Al 318
Jon & Robin 233
Jones, Al 217, 226

Index of People's Names

Jones, Fred 327
Jones, George 17, 18, 20, 37, 42, 79, 104, 132
Jones, Grandpa 23, 280
Jones, Grant 240
Jones, Little Sonny 120
Jones, Philly Joe 137
Jones, Sonny 217, 226
Joplin, Janis 114, 313
Jordan, Louis 27, 101, 114, 121, 122, 129, 148, 235
Jordan, Taft 130
Jordanaires 53, 78
Joy, Benny **63-73**
Judy & Johnny 88
Jumping Jax 221
Jumpin' Tones 271
Justis, Bill 283, 306
Kahl, Saul 245
Kalin Twins 220
Kane, Larry 300
Kassel, Art 243
Kassels In The Air 243
Kay, Jack 42
Kaye, Tony 202
Keitel, Harvey 164
Keleman, Steve 229
Kelley, Fred 202
Kelly, Bob 78
Kelly, Grace 240
Kennedy, Gene 314
Kenny, Bill 262
Kerr, Anita 283, 295
Kershaw, Doug 288, 289
Kershaw, Rusty 288
Kessel, Barney 216
Khoury, George 289, 290
Kilgore, Jerry 198
Kilgore, Merle 216, 230
Kindred, Zell 167
King, Albert 113, 115
King, B.B. 23, 82, 85, 94, 113, 116, 117, 127, 129, 150, 151, 156, 196, 197, 211, 216, 236, 291
King, Ben E. 319
King, Bobby 305
King, Carole 318
King, Clyde 198
King, Earl 232, 288, 291
King, Freddy 115, 219, 323
King, J.D. 177
King, Jewel 118
King, Jonathan 331
King, Martin Luther 315
King, Pee Wee 245
King, Sid 88, 104
King, Tom 202

King Curtis 165
King Karl 291-2
Kirby, Jack 309
Kirby, Larry 71
Kirkland, Frank 226
Kirshner, Don 276, 318
Klein, Allen 277
Klugh, Clarence 323
Klugh, Earl 323
Knight, Baker **211-4**
Knight, Gladys (& The Pips) 273, 277
Knight, Sonny 158, **175-181**, 213, 314
Knight, Terry 276
Knox, Buddy 27, 29, 30, 156
Koda, Cub 226, 327
Kool & The Gang 276
Kopa, Eddie 96
Krause, Stan 256, 258
Krazy Kats 298, 299, 300
Kristofferson, Kris 214
Krupa, Gene 147
Kuf-Linx 191
Kuhn, Joe 237
LaBeef, Sleepy 104, 312, 325
Laboe, Art 179, 180
Ladd, Phil 96
Laine, Frankie 147, 175, 176, 181, 196, 281
Laird, Elmer 283
Lampert, Diane 249
Lamplighters 265
Lands, Smokey 147
Lane, Glenn 212
Lanham, Bill 47, 49
Lanza, Mario 318
LaPata, Buddy 237, 241
Larkin, Billy 181
LaRosa, Julius 246
LaRue, Lash 38
Law, Don 47
Lawrence, Bill 89, 90, 91, 92
Lawrence, Freddy 90, 91
Lawrence, Sonny 90, 91
Lawrence Brothers Combo 90, 91
Lawson, Gene 323
Lay, Rodney (& The Wild West) 21, 93, 99
Leadbelly 45
Leavill, Otis 276
Lee, Brenda 55, 71, 161, 203, 246
Lee, David 310
Lee, Jackie 198
Lee, Peggy 167
Legendary Stardust Cowboy 190
Leiber & Stoller 109, 154, 155, 156-7, 172, 176, 233, 256, 307, 310, 318

Leichter, Albert 272
Lennon, John 208, 318
Leroy & Skillet 145
Lesley, Alis 216
Lewis, Billy 97
Lewis, Bobby 164
Lewis, Charlene 90
Lewis, Doc 18
Lewis, Francis 227
Lewis, Frank 146
Lewis, Hugh X. 71, 72
Lewis, Jerry Lee 46, 58, 59, 61, 93, 94, 99, 133, **185-8**, 214, 221, 288, 312, 317
Lewis, Linda 90
Lewis, Margaret 230, 233
Lewis, Myra 185
Lewis, Pete 108, 215
Lewis, Rose 230, 233
Lewis, Rudy 318
Lewis, Smiley 118
Lewis, Stan 225, 226, 227
Lewis, Wally 92
Lewis Sisters 230, 233
Lieberman, Marv 324
Liggins, Jimmy 167
Liggins, Joe 129, 152, 158
Lindsey, Judy 87
Little Caesar & The Romans 256, 271
Little Eva 107
Little Frankie 331
Little Hank 306
Little Richard 40, 78, 93, 94, 102, 109, 123, 147, 173, 178, 313, 314
Little Walter 216
Little Walter Jr. 151
Livingston, Jay 248
Lloyd, Jimmie 40, 42
Locklin, Hank 17
Logan, Horace 244, 245
Logsdon, Jimmie 40, 42
Lomax, John A. 128
Lone Ranger 240, 321
Long, Gillis W. 233
Long, Jerry 158
Long, Joey 289
Lord, Bobby 64
Loss, Joe 56
Los Top Pops 315
Loudermilk, John D. 33
Louvin Brothers 46
Lowe, Bernie 198, 239, 276
Lowe, Jim 102
Lowe, Jim (DJ) 94
Lowery, Frankie 301
Lubinsky, Herman 138, 141
Lucas, Matt 133, 314

339

Index of People's Names

Lucky, Rocky 150
Luke, Robin 89, 91, 92
Lulubelle & Scotty 198
Luman, Bob 29, 216, 226, 229
Lunceford, Jimmy 114, 145
Luper, Luther 167
Lyles, Dave 25
Lymon, Frankie
   (& The Teenagers) 270, 277
Lynch, David
   262, 263, 264, 265, 266, 267
Lytle, Marshall 238
Mack, Bill 75
Mack, Ira 202
Mack, Lonnie 21, 314-5, **321-6**
Mack, Warner 72
Macleod, Iain 185
Macon, Uncle Dave 46
Maddox, Johnny 102
Maddox Brothers & Rose
   75, 84, 103, 311
Maestro, Johnny (& the Crests/
   Brooklyn Bridge) 270, 271
Magic Sam 115
Magnificent Men 314
Magnificents 96
Malone, Bill 30
Maloy, Vince 133
Mammarella, Tony
   191, 198, 207
Mandina, Tommy 226, 228
Mangano, John 70
Mann, Barry 318
Mann, Bill 171
Mann, Kal 198, 239
Maphis, Joe 89
Marascalco, John 251
Marcels 258, 271
Marchan, Bobby 148
Marcus Brothers 230
Mar-Keys 115
Mark IV 232, 331
Markley, Bob 180
Marsh, Billy 203
Martin, Benny 41
Martin, Bobbi 72
Martin, Dean 211, 251
Martin, Grady 31, 33, 84
Martin, James 228
Martin, Janis 107
Martin, Lee 289, 290
Martinez, Ramon 151
Mascari, Eddie 232
Matassa, Cosimo 96, 109, 118
Mathis, Dean 'Pee Wee'
   43, 230
   See also Mathis Brothers
Mathis, Johnny 281
Mathis, Marc 230
Mathis Brothers 230

Matthews, Little Arthur 145
Mattice, Butch 202, 204
Maughn, Dicky 221
Mauro, Al 237, 241
May, Billy 239
Maye, Arthur Lee
   (& The Crowns) 267
Mayfield, Curtis 277
Mayfield, Percy 167
Mayhand, Ernest 145
McAffe, Royce 86
McAlpin, Vic 283
McBride, Bobby 293
McCall, Bill 18, 23, 32
McCall, Cash 281
McCall, Darrell 72
McCall, Toussaint 332
McCallister, Smokey 275, 276
McCannon III, George 282
McClinton, Delbert
   189, 192, 194, 297
McCoy Boys 102
McCracklin, Jimmy 97, 124
McCullough, John 68
McCurn, George 180
McGarvey, Seamus
   265, 266, 282, 329
McGee Brothers 45
McGhee, Brownie
   133, 135, 136, 137, 138
McGhee, Howard 140
McGhee, Stick **133-8**
McGowan, James 129
McGriff, Edna 131, 177
McGriff, Jimmy 115, 116
McGuire Sisters 130, 280
McKuen, Rod 248-9
McLain, Tommy 289, 290
McLean, Ernest 119
McLemore, Ed 86
McLollie, Oscar 233
McNeely, Big Jay
   139-152, 167, 262
McNeely, Bob 139, 141, 143,
   146, 148, 151
McNeely Jr, Dillard
   139, 143, 147, 148, 151
McNeil, Walter 115
McPhatter, Clyde
   109, 249, 276, 319, 327
McVea, Jack 123, 140
Mead, Larry 179
Meard, Jimmy 171
Meaux, Huey
   114, 289, 291, 293, 295,
   299, 300, 313
Meaux, U.J. 298
Medley, Bill 314
Medlicott, Sir Frank 185
Medress, Hank 270, 319

Mellin, Robert 237
Mello-Moods 265
Melson, Joe 281, 282
Menard, Paul 81
Merseybeats 173
Mesner, Eddie 176-7, 178
Micahnik, Irving 201, 202, 203
Midnighters 107, 108, 267
Mighty Clouds Of Joy 208
Migil Five 55
Milburn, Amos 173, 178
Milburn Jr, Amos
   190, 192-3, 194
Miles, Jean 265
Miller, Dave 137
Miller, Frankie 18, 41
Miller, Glenn 141, 235
Miller, Jay 287, 292-3, 299
Miller, Jody 99
Miller, Roger 283
Miller, Steve 156
Millinder, Lucky 169-171
Mills Brothers 255
Mills, T.M. 76
Milos 317
Milsap, Ronnie 314
Milton, David 331
Milton, Roy 129, 158, 167
Mimms, Garnet 93, 97
Miracles 258
Mitchell, Abbye 107
Mitchell, Frank 114
Mitchell, Guy 245, 251
Mitchell, Jean 107
Mitchell, Sinx 30
Mitchell, Willie 310
Moers, Betty 246
Moffat, Tom 92
Monash, Paul 246
Monestier, Jean-Marie 126
Monk, Thelonius 177
Monroe, Bill 23
Monroe, Charlie 48
Monroe, Vaughn 172
Montana, Vince 199
Montana Slim 101
Montgomery, Bob **27-30**
Montgomery, Marvin 86, 193
Montrell, Roy 118
Mooney, Bob 47, 48, 49
Moonglows
   77, 109, 147, 231, 232, 257
Moore, Bob (& The Temps)
   69, 219, 220, 233, 306
Moore, Harvey 218
Moore, Lattie 18, **37-43**
Moore, Merrill 249
Moore, Scotty 76, 85-6, 216
Moore, Willie 135
Moore's Three Blazers, Johnny
   129

Index of People's Names

Morgan, Dorinda 178, 179
Morgan, Frank 154
Morgan, George 56, 72, 244
Morgan, Hite 178, 179, 180
Morgan, Jaye P. 248
Morgan, Rocket 301
Morgan, Tom 25
Morisette, Johnnie 325
Morrison, Van 315
Morse, Ella Mae 311
Morthland, John 326
Mortimer, Azie 310
Morton, Shadow 27
Moseley, Ron 273, 275, 276
Moss, Wayne 57
Mountbatten, Lady Iris 163
Mouse & The Traps 233
Mouton, Walter 298
Muddy Waters
    94, 109, 125, 176, 178, 233
Mullican, Moon 114, 172
Murphy, Audie 251
Murphy, Chuck 173
Murphy, Florine 48-9, 50
Murphy, Jimmy **45-50**
Murray, Anne 19, 48
Murray, Juggy 275
Murray, Lowe 273
Musselwhite, Charlie 315
Musso, Vinny 146
Mystics 270
Nader, Richard 204
Nashville Teens 54, 55, 57
Nathan, Syd
    39, 40, 42, 43, 76, 108, 120,
    129, 147, 171, 172, 192, 262,
    264, 266, 267, 273
Neal, Dixie 206
Neal, Jack 206
Nelson, Carl 24
Nelson, Jimmy 115
Nelson, Ken
    86-7, 245-6, 248, 252
Nelson, Ricky
    92, 211, 212-3, 226, 231, 247
Nelson, Walter 120
Nelson, Willie 308
Nevins, Al 318
Newbeats 43, 230
Newcombe, Jim 72
New Creations 152
Newman, David 'Fathead' 153
Newman, Jimmy 'C' 288, 290
Newman, Lionel 248
Newsome, Jimmy 125
Nichols, Roy 216
Nightcaps 78, 133
Nino & The Ebbtides 271
Nix, Don 314
Noack, Eddie **17-20**, 41, 48

Nobles, Gene 227
Nolen, Jimmy 215, 216
Norman, Gene 154
Norris, Charlie 167
Nunn, Bobby 140
Nutmegs 255, 256, 257
Nyro, Laura 319
Oak Ridge Boys 25
Obrecht, Jas 220
O'Brien, Edmond 248
O'Brien, Jimmie 141, 144
O'Bryant, Jimmy
    See O'Brien, Jimmie
Ohio Untouchables 323, 325
O'Kaysions 314
Okie Dokie 123
Oldham, Spooner 308
Olenn, Johnny 68
Oliver, Tommy 216
Olympics 325
Opsasnick, Mark 217, 220
O'Quin, Gene 18, 41
Orange, Allen 308
Orbison, Roy
    192, 279, 280, 281, 282
Orbits 201, 202
Orioles 255, 257, 263, 270, 274,
    282
Orlando, Tony 192, **317-320**
Orrell, David 78, 191, 192
Osborn, Joe 230
Osborne, Jimmy 38
Osmonds 270
Ostrum, Dennis 257
Other Two 54
Otis, Clyde 97
Otis, Johnny
    107-8, 139, 140, 145, 165,
    175, 216, 262, 263, 267, 311
Otis, Phyliss 108
Otis, Shuggie 108
Outcasts 221
Outsiders 221
Ovations 330
Owen, Grady 86
Owen, Reginald 245
Owens, Buck 95, 104, 249
Owens, Don 24
Owens, Doodle 191
Owens, Judy 217-8
Page, Bobby 291
Page, Frank 'Gatemouth' 27
Page, Hot Lips 281
Page, Jimmy 222
Page, Patti 137
Pahinui, Gabby 89
Palmer, Earl 109, 117, 119
Palomino Ranch Gang 205
Palumbo, Frank 236
Pan, Pot & Skillet 145

Paris, Johnny 201-4
Parker, Bobby 325
Parker, Charlie 140, 144, 201
Parker, Colonel Tom
    28, 67, 245, 246, 247
Parker, Junior 123, 124, 178
Parliaments 202
Parman, Cliff 308
Parrish, Avery 218
Pastels 150
Patterson, Floyd 327
Paul, Les 321
Paul, Lynn 265
Paul & Paula 189, 193
Paulsen, Kenny 216, 230, 232
Peaches 107
Pearlman, Bernie 76
Peck, Bill 68, 76, 77
Pedicin, Mike **235-241**
Pedicin Jr, Mike 241
Peebles, Ann 310
Pefferly, Boot Hog 306
Penguins 152, 262, 267
Penn, Dan 308, 309, 313
Pennington, Ray 42, 325
Peps 314
Percolating Puppies 255
Pere Ubu 133
Perkins, Carl
    19, **53-8**, 59, 63, 72, 103
Perkins, Joe 306
Perkins, Roy 293, 296
Persuasions 255, 256, 257, 329
Peters & Lee 30
Peterson, Carl 143
Peterson, Ray 213
Petty, Norman 27, 28, 29, 250
Pharaohs 216
Phelps, James 330
Phillips, Bobby 39
Phillips, Dewey 312
Phillips, John 310
Phillips, (Little) Esther
    97, 262, 308, 311, 313
Phillips, Marvin 145
Phillips, Phil 289, 290
Phillips, Sam 29, 64-5, 69, 86, 94
Phillips, Skip 310
Phipps, Ernest 49
Piano Red 75, 76
Pic & Bill 189, 190
Pickett, Wilson 326
Pierce, Don 40-1
Pierce, Jim 72
Pierce, Webb 28, 42, 56, 72, 244
Pingatore, Frank 239
Pitts, Clifton 263
Pitts, Jack 89
Platters 67, 69, 72-3, 156, 208,
    213, **261-8**, 293

341

Index of People's Names

Playboys 235
Plebs 57
Poe, Bobby (& The Poe-Kats)
    93, 94, 95, 96, 97, 99
Polk, Bob 94
Pompilli, Rudy 201
Poncio, Steve 306
Poovey, Joe 88
Porter, Jake 158
Poss, Barry 49, 50
Post, Leon 229
Presley, Elvis
    19, 28, 39, 40, 46, 47, 63,
    64, 67, 69, 71, 76, 81, 83,
    85, 91, 94, 101, 102, 103,
    127, 132, 156, 163, 187, 203,
    206, 208, 212, 213, 216, 221,
    238, 243, 246, 247, 248, 249,
    282, 287, 288, 297, 298, 312,
    322, 325
Presley, Marion 293
Preston, Johnny 114, 293, 300
Price, Alan 57
Price, Big Walter 115
Price, Joe 77
Price, Lloyd 118, 158, 283
Price, Ray 221
Price, Ronnie (& The Velvets)
    280
Pride, Charley 93, 111, 283
Prima, Louis 197, 236
Prince, Barbara 158-9
Prince, Graham 196
Prince, Mark 279, 283
Prince, Paul 279
Prince, Peppy 261, 264
Proctor, Carl 276
Professor Longhair 118, 148
Pryor, Cactus 104
Prysock, Red 165
Pullen, Whitey 133
Pullum, Joe 131
Purse, Ernest 171
Pyle, Pete 39
Queens 264
? & The Mysterians 276
Quinn, Bill 18
Quinn, Lance 98
Quotations 57, 258
Rachou, Carol 287, 295
Ragavoy, Jerry 307
Raging Storms 96
Raiders 249, 250, 251
Raines, Jerry 295
Rainwater, Marvin
    23-4, **31-5**, 206, 208
Rainwater, Ray 24, 35
Ram, Buck 67-8, 69, 70, 156,
    261-2, 264-7
Ram, Michael 70

Ramey, Gene 137
Ramsey, Yvonne 122
Rand, Ande 265
Rand, Johnny 141
Randazzo, Teddy 77
Randolph, Big Jim 76
Randolph, Boots 69, 283, 295
Randolph, Eugene 130
Randolph, Leroy 273
Randy & The Rainbows 271
Raney, Wayne
    47, 49, 171, 172, 211
Raven, Eddy 291
Ravens 274
Rawls, Lou 281
Ray, David 190
Ray, James 256
Ray, Johnnie 127, 147, 148, 196
Redd, Gene 273, 274, 275, 276
Redd, Vi 140
Redding, Otis 111, 308, 313, 325
Redlich, Dago 300
Redlich, Hank 300
Red River Dave 198
Reed, Herb
    262, 263, 264, 265, 266
Reed, Howard 86
Reed, Jerry 37, 42
Reed, Jimmy 79, 162, 192, 206,
    296, 324, 325
Reeves, Del 30, 251
Reeves, Glenn 133
Reeves, Jim 29, 58, 247
Regents 269, 271
Reichner, Bix 238-9, 240, 241
Rene, Leon 144
Revere, Paul (& The Raiders) 231
Reynolds, Debbie 72
Rice, Dumpy 323
Rice, Mack 276
Rich, Charlie 72
Richard, Belton 289
Richard, Cliff 29
Richards, Dick 241
Richards, Earl 30
Richards, Keith 115
Richards, Sue 214
Richardson, J.P.
    See Big Bopper
Richbourg, John **305-310**
Rick & The Keens 189
Riddle, Nelson 250
Riddles, Leslie 135
Ridgley, Tommy 148
Righteous Brothers
    311, 314, 318-9, 324
Rigsby, Clarence 279, 283
Ripp, Artie 277
Ritter, Tex 82, 101
Rivera, Luis 267

Rivers, Johnny 72
Rivingtons 148, 157, 265
Rizzo, Frank 236
Robbins, Marty 28, 72, 96, 104
Robbins, Mel 'Pig' 42, 69
Roberts, Howard 321
Robertson, Robbie 218
Robey, Don 109, 114, 122-3,
    123-5, 191
Robins 140, 155, 167, 311
Robins, Jimmy 168
Robinson, Chris 280
Robinson, Fenton
    114, 308, 310, 325
Robinson, Floyd 41
Robinson, Roscoe 308
Robinson, Stan 280
Robinson, Tommy
    273, 274, 275, 277
Roby, Paul 265, 266, 267
Rodgers, Jimmie
    19, 46, 49, 102, 134, 137,
    190, 311
Rodney & The Blazers 21
Rogers, Jesse 198
Rogers, Junior 158
Rogers, Kenny 111
Rogers, Lelan 96, 97, 98
Rogers, Leo 255
Rogers, Roy 122, 146
Rogers, Shorty 213
Rollins, Sonny 201
Rondells 194
Ronnie & The Hi-Lites 256
Ronson, Dave 25
Ronstadt, Linda 190
Roppolo, Nick 226, 230
Rose, Cpl. Stewart 262
Rose, Fred 40, 206
Rose, Slim 256
Rose, Wesley 280
Rosenthal, Al 276-7
Roses 29
Rothbard, Bernie 197-8
Round Robin 213
Roush, Sonley 193, 194
Rover Boys 239
Rowe, Dick 55
Royals 267
Royaltones 202
Rupe, Art 178, 179
Ruppli, Michel 266
Rush, Ray 29
Rushing, Jimmy 240
Russell, Leon 314
Russell, Tony 311
Russotto, Irv 324
Ryan, Buck 23
Rydell, Bobby 91, 198, 239
Ryder, Mitch 313-4, 315

342

Index of People's Names

Sahm, Doug 192, 194
Sakamoto, Kyu 324
Salem, Jay 82, 83, 85
Sam & Dave 325
Sanderson, David 202
Sandmel, Ben 324
Sands, Benny 243
Sands, Tommy **243-252**
Sandusky, Vernon
    21, 93, 94, 95, 96, 97, 98-9
Savas, Mike 68
Savich, Bo 202, 204
Savile, Jimmy 203
Scarborough, Estel Lee 47
Scheflin, Alan 218
Scott, Freddie 318
Scott, Jack 219
Scott, Ray 40, 68
Scott, Shirley 152
Scudder, Gene 228
Seabrook, Bill 329
Seals, Troy 314, 322, 324, 326
Sears, Big Al 119
Secrets 220
Sedaka, Neil 318
Seeds Of Freedom 158
Seger, Bob 156, 276
Sellers, Pappy 85
Sentenari, Robert 237
September, Anthony 198
Seven Stars Quartette 48
Sexton, Ann 310
Shad, Bob 267, 329
Shadows [*doo-wop group*] 257
Shadows [*UK group*] 201
Shannon, Del 202
Sharks 250
Sharp, Dee Dee 198, 236, 276
Sharpe, Ray 88, 283
Sharpe, Rocky 269, 270
Sharps 157
Shaw, Arnold 172, 312
Shaw, Artie 114
Shearing, George 147
Sheeley, Sharon 212
Shell, Jim 77
Shells 258
Shelton, Roscoe 308, 309
Shepard, Roy 47
Sherman, Joe & Noel 239
Sherrill, Billy 78
Shirelles 318
Shirley & Lee 118, 282
Shirley, Everett 144, 151
Shirley, Ted 141, 144, 167
Sholes, Steve 46, 208, 245-6
Shondells 295
Short Brothers 103
Showaddywaddy 270
Shuler, Eddie 290

Shurman, Dick 229
Sigler, Bunny 198, 276
Silberschlag, Jeff 332
Silbersdorf, Karl 232
Sill, Lester 157
Silvani, Lou 266
Silva-Tones 248
Simmons, Bill 76, 77
Simon, Freddie 167
Simon, Joe 29, 308, 310
Simon, Paul 111
Simone, Nina 127, 163
Simoneaux, Harry 300
Simpson, Carol (Quartet) 250
Simpson, Valerie 276
Sims, Snake 167
Sinatra, Frank
    110, 117, 161, 213, 237,
    240, 251
Sinatra, Nancy 251
Singer, Hal 120, 176
Singleton, Shelby
    66, 69, 99, 192, 193
Sinks, Earl 30
Sizemore, Asher 45
Skaggs, Ricky 43, 49
Skinner, Jimmie
    17, 18, 38, 41, 46, 47, 48,
    49, 104
Skyliners
    257, 269, 271, 312
Slades 102
Sledge, Percy 302
Smalls, Tommy 275
Smith, Arthur 197
Smith, Beasley 281
Smith, Bessie 134
Smith, Bobby 180
Smith, Carl 45, 72
Smith, Charles 310
Smith, George 151, 167
Smith, Harmie 244
Smith, Huey 'Piano'
    161, 325, 330
Smith, Jimmy 152
Smith, Joe 178
Smith, Major Bill
    78, **189-194**, 312-3
Smith, Paul 47
Smith, Preacher
    (& The Deacons) 85
Smith, Ray 72
Smith, Rodney 71
Smith, Warren 84
Snow, Hank
    17, 19, 38, 46, 64, 83, 84,
    101, 104, 214
Snowden, Gene 102, 104
Soileau, Floyd
    287, 289, 292, 293, 297,
    299, 301

Solitaires 274, 275
Solomon, William 279, 283
Sonics 151
Sonny & Cher 88
Sons Of The Pioneers 198
Soul Sisters 275-6
Soul Stirrers 259
Soul Survivors 314
South 326
Southern, Jeri 238
Sovine, Red 39, 72
Spaniels 279, 318
Spector, Phil 251, 256, 307, 319
Spic & Spann 96
Spiders 118
Spinners [*Johnny Carroll*] 86
Spivey, Victoria 227
Spottswood, Richard 45, 49
Spriggs, Walter 68, 69
Springfield, Dusty 315
St. John, Barry 57
Stacy, Clyde 96
Staczek, Don 202
Stairsteps 276
Stampley, Joe 213
Stamps, Roy Armstead 87
Stamps Quartet 87
Standish, Tony 129, 130
Stanley, Joe (& The Saxtons)
    218, 220
Stanzel, Prinze 'Candy' 141
Stapleton, Buck 157
Starkes, Doc 240
Starnes, Jack 18
Starr, Blaze 221
Starr, Jerry 290
Starr, Kay 38, 147, 179
Starr, Ray 42
Starr, Ringo 98
Starr, Sid (& The Escorts) 133
Steinberg, Irwin 192
Stevens, Connie 87
Stevens, Guy 330
Stevens, Ray 283
Stevenson, Bobby 24
Stewart, Billy 276
Stewart, Gary 297
Stewart, Jim 311
Stewart, Rod 331
Stewart, Skip 295
Stewart, Wynn 251
Stierle, Wayne 258
Stierman, Vera 246
Stiles, Danny 256
Stone, Cliffie 246, 247, 311
Stone, Pappy Dave 28
Stone, Rocky 43
Stop, Dicky 232
Storm, Gale 238
Storm, Warren
    287, 288, 295, 300

Index of People's Names

Stover, Smokey 19
Strachwitz, Chris 288
Straight-Jackets 191, 192, 194
Streetser, William 141
Strickland, Billy 280
Stringfellow, Peter 330
Strong, Barrett 325
Strong, Nolan
 (& The Diablos) 258
Stubbs, Levi 93
Stutes, Mickey 298
Sullivan, Bob 226
Sullivan, Carolyn 192
Sullivan, Ed 110
Sullivan, Gene 96
Sullivan, Niki 28
Sullivan, Phil 18
Summers, Gene 190
Superlites 158
Sutton, Glenn 79
Swallows 180, 274
Swan, Billy 283
Swann, Claudia 238
Swinging Blue Jeans 54
T, Booker 115, 116
Talley, John 29
Tampa Red 227
Tanner, Bob 102
Taylor, Big John
 64, 66, 67-8, 69, 70-1
Taylor, Blondean 264
Taylor, James 319
Taylor, Kingsize 54
Taylor, Little Johnny
 148, 150, 168
Taylor, Sam 'The Man'
 119, 171, 237, 238
Taylor, Ted 173
Taylor, Zola 264, 266, 267
Team-Mates 191
Tempest, Roy 163
Temple, Johnnie 49
Temptations 256
Terry, Gene 290, 300
Terry, Sonny 133, 137, 138
Tesluk, Paul 201, 202, 204
Tex, Joe 276, 306
Texas Moonlighters 82-3
Tharpe, Sister Rosetta 227, 312
Theard, Sam 135
Thomas, Duke 147
Thomas, Gene 296
Thomasine, Ray 293
Thompson, Beverley 154
Thompson, Fred 151
Thompson, Hank 25, 206
Thompson, Joe 61
Thompson, Lucky 169
Thompson, Sir Charles 176
Thompson, Sue 29

Thompson, William 76
Thornton, Big Mama
 123, 152, 313
Thorogood, George 138, 315
Three Dots And A Dash 145
Three Peppers 237
Three Suns 261
Thursby, Robert 279, 283
Tiger, J.G. 83, 84, 85
Tillis, Mel 29, 71, 72
Tillotson, Johnny 42, 295
Tilton Sisters 91, 92
Toderice, Nat 212
Tokens 270, 319
Tolbert, Israel 310
Tomsco, George 29
Toombs, Rudolph 136
Toops, Richard 232
Topping, Ray
 20, 48, 93, 113, 115, 117, 158
Torok, Mitchell 53, 54
Torres, Johnny 146, 147
Tosches, Nick 313
Toussaint, Allen
 109, 119, 307, 308
Townshend, Pete 205
Tractors 43
Trammell, Bobby Lee 59
Trammell, Sonny
 226, 227-8, 230
Travis, Merle
 47, 76, 77, 102, 311, 321
Travolta, John 296
Trenier, Claude 165
Treniers 133, 167, 195, 199,
 235, 236, 240
Trent, Buck 25
Trotman, Lloyd 237
Trotto, Ralph 321
Tubb, Ernest 18, 24, 32, 38, 40,
 64, 82, 102, 114
Tucker, Bob 62
Tucker, Jack 261
Tucker, Orrin 238
Tucker, Tommy 56, 57
Tuminello, Anthony 226, 227
Turco, Art 265
Turner, Al 40
Turner, Big Joe
 82, 84, 130, 147, 157, 165,
 196, 236, 249
Turner, Ike 85
Turner, Scotty 249-251
Turner, Titus 163, 276
Turner, Zeb 39
Turner, Zeke 39
Twilighters 322, 323
Twitty, Conway
 37, 59, 69, 99, 214, 226
Tyler, Alvin 119

Tyler, T. 169
Tyrones 235
Uncalled Four 221
Uniques 233
Universals 259
Upsetters 123
Vacca, Pat 237
Vale, Jerry 130
Valens, Ritchie 318
Valerio, Jimmy 241
Van Story, Marcus 133
Vaughan, Sarah
 148, 172, 219, 281
Vaughan, Stevie Ray 321, 326
Vee, Bobby 69, 317, 318
Velvet, Jimmy 208
Velvet Angels 258
Velvets **279-283**
Vera, Billy 314
Vernon, Ray 23, 31, 206, 208
Versatiles 24
Vestine, Henry 113
Vickery, Mack 201, 232
Vienneau, Jim 35, 293
Vincent, Gene (& The Blue Caps)
 56-7, 78, 81, 86, 87, 88, 102,
 180, 206, 229, 251, 252
Vincent, Johnny 306
Vincent, Joyce 319
Virginia Four 255
Vito & The Salutations
 269, 270, 271
Vizell, Shelton 230
Voices Of Canaan 326
Waganfeald, Eddie 203
Wagoner, Porter 121
Wainwright, Bob 177
Waits, Tom 117
Walker, David 208
Walker, Frank 32
Walker, Johnny 147
Walker, Junior 165
Walker, Lawrence 298
Walker, T-Bone
 114, 123, 125, 165, 167, 321
Walker, Wayne 42
Wallace, Billy 48
Wallace, Jerry 213, 251
Waller, Fats 131
Walls, Van 137
Wammack, Travis 313
Wang, Wayne 164
Ward, Billy 150
 See also Dominoes
Ward, Robert 323, 326
Warner, Little Sonny
 148, 150, 167
Warren, Earle 68
Warring, Mike 173
Warwick, Dee Dee 276

Index of People's Names

Washington, Albert 305
Washington, Charles 114
Washington, Dinah
   97, 107, 176, 293
Washington, Ella 308, 309
Washington, Jayotis 329
Washington Monuments 221
Watson, Deek 257
Watson, Gene (& The Rockets)
   66, 67
Watson, Johnny 'Guitar'
   108, 109, 121, 154, 167, 178
Watts, Michael 205, 218
Wayne, Tom 79
Webb, Charlie 85
Webb, Mark 42
Webster, Freddie 169
Webster, Greg 322
Webster, Paul 250
Weil, Cynthia 318
Weinstein, Bill 212
Weiser, Ronny 79, 87, 102-3
Weiss, George 219
Weiss, Hymie 274-5, 276
Welborn, Larry 28
Welch, Lenny 319
Welding, Pete 115
Wenzlaff, Dutch 232
West, Clint 289
West, Marvin 24
Westberry, Kent 71
Western Cherokees 18
Wexler, Jerry 111, 127, 130,
   131, 229, 309
Wheeler, Kay 85
Wheeler, Onie 47
White, Cliff 161, 163
White, Tony Joe 314
Whiteman, Paul 196
Whitman, Slim 20, 82, 251
Wick, Ted 247, 250
Wilburn Brothers 28
Wiley, Pee Wee 167
Wiley, Rudolph 114
Wilkerson, H.C. 244
Wilkin, Marijohn 42, 71
Willett, Slim 103
Williams, Atla 137
Williams, Blind Boy 136
Williams, Clarence 131
Williams, Devonia 'Lady Dee'
   108, 109, 263
Williams, Dick 208
Williams, Don 25
Williams, Earl 332
Williams, Estelle 329
Williams, Hank
   18, 23, 24, 28, 32, 38, 39,
   40, 42, 43, 46, 49, 64, 75,
   94, 102, 111, 125, 196, 206,
   211, 244, 291, 311

Williams Jr, Hank 211, 214
Williams, J. Mayo 136
Williams, Jerry 158, 308, 310
Williams, Jim 265
Williams, Jody 229
Williams, Joe 154
Williams, Larry
   40, 161, 162, 164, 229
Williams, Maurice 332
Williams, Otis 43, 59
   See also Charms
Williams, Paul 240
Williams, Richard 30, 318
Williams, Tex 244
Williams, Tony
   262, 263, 264, 265, 266, 267
Williamson, Sonny Boy 227
Willis, Chuck 130
Wills, Bob 17, 18, 75, 76, 94,
   102, 122, 190, 206,
   248, 311
Wills, Johnnie Lee 19
Wilson, Al 332
Wilson, Dale 64, 66, 67
Wilson, Eddie 40
Wilson, Gerald 68, 267
Wilson, J. Frank 189, 193-4
Wilson, Jackie 72, 233, 311
Wilson, Jimmy 301
Wilson, Rocky 148, 150
Winding, Kai 203
Wine, Toni 319
Wingfield, Pete 315
Wings Over Jordan Choir 262
Winter, Edgar 295
Winter, Johnny 295, 326
Winterhalter, Hugo 238
Winwood, Stevie 315
Wiseman, Mac 245
Witherspoon, Jimmy 167
Wizdom 159
Womack, Bobby 309
Wood, Randy 91, 92, 179
Wood, Tommy 19
Woods, Georgie 311
Woodson, Buddy 147
Woodward, Mickey 32
Wray, Doug 23, 206, 208
Wray, Link
   23, 24, **205-9**, 220, 221, 325
Wray, Lucky
   (& The Ranchhands) 23, 206
Wray, Vernon
   See Vernon, Ray
Wright, Arthur 151
Wright, Jimmy 165
Wright, O.V. 115
Wright, Steve 190
Wynette, Tammy 25, 132
Wynn, Big Jim
   108, 139, 143, **165-8**

Yelvington, Malcolm 133
York, Rusty 49, 326
Yorko, Dave 201, 202, 204
Young, Faron 56, 84, 247
Young, Lester 107
Young, Reggie 61
Young Ernie 305
Young Jessie
   See Jessie, Young
Young Rascals 313
Yuro, Timi 180, 314
Zappa, Frank 121, 156
Zeiger, Hal 150
Zieke, Freddy 331
Zircons 257, 258
Zito, Tom 222

INDEX OF SONGS & ALBUM TITLES

■ = LP Title

100,000 Women Can't Be Wrong 40
ABC Boogie 272
A Brand New Case Of Love 39
■ *Acappella Session With The Shells* 258
■ *Acappella Session With The Original Zircons* 258
■ *Acappella Showcase Presents By Popular Demand The Chessmen* 258
■ *Acappella Showcase Presents The Universals* 259
■ *Acappella Showcase Presents The Velvet Angels* 258
Ace Of Spades 24
A Dime And A Dollar 245, 248
After A While 29
Afterglow 261
After Hours 176, 218-9, 221
After Sundown 53, 54
Again 259
A House, A Car And A Wedding Ring 232
Ain't No Grave Gonna Hold My Body Down 312
Ain't That A Shame 119
Ain't That Dandy 123
Ain't That Lovin' You Baby 206
Albino Stallion 24
All About My Girl 116
All By Myself 119
All I Could Do Was Cry 110
All I Want Is You 93, 97
All My Love Belongs To You 171, 173
Allons A Lafayette 298
Allons Rock And Roll 298
All The Time 104
Almost Persuaded 78
A Love I'll Never Win 55
Am I The One 219
Angel Of Love 300
Another Place, Another Time 30
■ *Another Saturday Night* 287, 289
Any Day Now 312
■ *A Rockin' Date With South Louisiana Stars* 289
Artie's Jump 141
A Taste Of The Blues 29
A Tear Fell 127, 130
A Teenager's Prayer 308
■ *At Home With Screamin' Jay Hawkins* 163
A Time And A Place For Everything 72
At Last 107

At My Front Door – *See* Crazy Little Mama
Atomic Energy 123
At Your Beck And Call 261
Baby, Baby 229
Baby Come Back 178
Baby, I'll Soon Be Gone 39
Baby It's Love 28
Baby Let's Play House 70
Baby Oh Baby 258
Baby One More Chance 221
Baby What's Wrong 324
Back In Baby's Arms 29
Back To School Blues 232
Badly Bent 43
Ballad Of Donna And Peggy Sue, The 102
Ballin' Keen 104
Bandstand Doll 86
Barbara-Ann 271
Beachcomber 202
Be A Playboy 138
Beat, The 239
Beatin' And Blowin' 120
Beatnik Fly 202, 203
Beautiful Dreamer 318
Be-Baba-Leba 165
Be-Bop-A-Lula 227
Be-Bop Country Boy 158
Be-Bop Grandma 131
Be Careful Of Stones That You Throw 40
Been So Long 150
Beer Barrel Boogie 265
Beer Drinkin' Blues 19
Be Evermine 283
Beginning Of Love 323
Beg Your Pardon 281
Behind Closed Doors 30
Bell Bottom Blue Jeans 150
Benson's Groove 141
■ *Best Of Acappella (Vol. 1)* 257
■ *Best Of Acappella (Vol. 2)* 257
■ *Best Of Acappella (Vol. 3)* 258
■ *Best Of Denver With Roy Buchanan* 222
Bewitched, Bothered And Bewildered 265
Big Bad Blues 55
Big Beat, The 119
Big Chief 158
Big Fat Mamas Are Back In Style Again 172
Bigger Than Texas 250
■ *Big Jay Meets The Penguins* 152
■ *Big Jay Rides Again* 145

Index of Songs & Album Titles

Big Jay's Hop 147
Big Jay Shuffle, The 152
Big Legged Woman 310
Big Mama Blues 46
Big Old Ugly Fool 72
Big Ten-Inch Record 172
Billy Boy 91
Birds Of A Feather Fly Together 71
B.J. The D.J. 72
Black Gal, What Makes Your Head So Hard 131
Black Leather Rebel 87
Black Olives 218
Bless You 318
Blow Big Jay 144
Blow, Blow, Blow 145
Blue And Brokenhearted 137
Blue Angel 280, 281
Blue Barrelhouse 137
Bluejean Heart 78
Blue Monday 119
Blue Moon Of Kentucky 19
Blue Ribbon Baby 249
Blues At Sunrise 129
Blues Before Sunrise 129
■ *Blues Consolidated* 109
Blue Suede Shoes 53, 55, 227, 322
Bonaparte's Retreat 206
■ *Boogie In Black And White* 296
Boogie In Front 144
Boogie Woogie Nighthawk 121
Boogie Woogie Teenage Girl 233
Boo Hoo 31
Bop Boogie To The Blues 211
Boss 91
Bottle By Bottle 37
Bounce, The 325
Bourbon Street Jump 143
Boy Meets Girl 233
Boy From New York City, The 258
Braggin' 219
Bread And Butter 230
Breaking Up Is Hard To Do 287, 296
Breathless 186
Bringing In The Sheaves 203
Bring It On Home To Me 330
Bring My Cadillac Back 211, 212
Brown Eyed Handsome Man 61
■ *Buch & The Snake Stretchers* 222
Buffalo Soldiers 98
Bulldog 29
■ *Bullshot* 209
But I Do 96
But Officer 177, 179
Buttercup 216
Butterfly 196, 198
Button Nose 69
Buttons And Bows 248
By The Light Of The Silvery Moon 109
Cajun 220

Cajun Doll 42
Cajun Twist 287
Calamity 145
Caldonia 21, 233
California Hop 141
Call The Zoo 72
Calypso Rock 239
Candida 319
Candy Kisses 244
Catastrophe 145
Caterpillar 102
■ *CBS Rockabilly Classics* 45
Chain Of Broken Hearts 257
Chantilly Lace 89
■ *Chartbusters* 317
Chatterbox 115
Cherokee Boogie 172
Cherry Smash 141
Chicken And The Hawk 249
Chicken Pickin' 325
Chicken Twist 120
Chills 319
■ *Chokin' Kind, The* 308
Chowbay 221
■ *Cigars, Acappella, Candy* 258
Cincinnati Fireball 172
Cisco's 151
City Lights 131
Claire de Lune 206
Clarabella 239
■ *Clarence Henry Is Alive And Well And Doing His Thing* 317
Class Cutter 232
Class Of '59 216
Cleveland, Ohio Blues 171
Clothes Line 25
Colinda 295
Come Back Jack 192
Come On, Let's Stroll 230
Come What May 109
Concrete Jungle 99
Coney Island Baby 270
Confessin' The Blues 180
Confidential 178-9
Convicted 233
Cookin' Catfish 116
Cool Blood 141
Cool Off Baby 232
■ *Cool Sound Of Albert Collins, The* 115
Cops And Robbers 25
Cornbread 176
Cornbread Row 98
Corrine, Corrina 30, 84
Cottage For Sale 59
Count Every Star 270
■ *Country Bluegrass Favorites* 49
Country Boy's Dream 58
Country Girl 312
■ *Country Lovin'* 296
Cowboy Boots 213

348

Index of Songs & Album Titles

Crash The Party 68, 69
■ *Crazy Beat* 251
Crazy Crazy Lovin' 83, 84, 85
Crazy Little Mama [At My Front Door] 83
Crossfire 201, 202, 203, 204
Cross Ties 230
Cruise On Fannie 309
Cry 192
Cry Baby 97
Crying 281
Crying Guitar 91
Crying In The Chapel 86, 263, 282
Cute Little Girls 233
■ *Dance Album* 54
Dance Girl 330
Dance Her By Me 78
Dance Me Daddy 31, 34
Dance With Me Henry 108
Danny Boy 206
Dark End Of The Street 313
Dawn 279
Deacon Rides Again 145
Deacon's Express 145
Deacon's Groove 141
Deacon's Hop 141, 143, 151
Deac's Blowout 144
Dead 192
Dearest Darling 192
Dear Wonderful God 177, 179
Dedicated To You 178, 179, 180
■ *Dedicated To You* 301
Deep In The Night 109
■ *Deep In The Night* 111
Defrost 114
Diamond Ring 138
Diggy Liggy Lo 295
Dim, Dim The Lights 239
Ding Dong 317
Disc Jockey's Boogie 237
Divorce Court 331
Dixie Doodle 207
Dixie Fried 53, 55, 57
Dobro Daddio From Del Rio 104
Doin' The Creep 310
Doin' The Susie-Q 226-7
Do It Again A Little Bit Slower 233
Dolores 19
Don't 156, 209
Don't Ask Me Why 171
Don't Blame The Man 331
Don't Drop It 245
Don't Lose Your Cool 115
Don't The Girls All Get
    Prettier At Closing Time 214
Don't Tickle 266
Don't Trade Your Love For Gold 18
Don't Trade The Old For A New 37, 40
Don't Treat Me This Way 229
Don't You Just Know It 161
Dorothy (On My Mind) 325

Double Crossing Blues 311
Double Crossing Liquor 138
Down At Hayden's 156
(Down At) Papa Joe's 306
Down In Mexico 257
Down On The Farm 21, 93, 94, 95, 169
■ *Down South In The Bayou Country* 121
Down Yonder 202, 203
Drank Up All The Wine 136, 137
Dribble Twist 96
Drinkin' Wine Spo-Dee-O-Dee 133, 135-6, 138
Drivin' Nails In My Coffin 37, 42
Drummer Boy Rock 66
Drunk Again 42
Dyin' Flu 115
Dynaflow 273
Early In The Morning 79
Earth Angel 262, 267
Ee-Bobaliba 165
Eighteen With A Bullet 315
Electricity 46, 49
Empty Arms 131, 132
Endlessly 151
Eso Beso 239
■ *Especially For You* 35
■ *Etta James Rocks The House* 110
Everlovin' 91
Every Beat Of My Heart 311
Expressway To Your Heart 314
Fable Of The Rose 238
Fabulous 195
Fais-Do-Do 295
■ *Family Gospel Album* 49
Family Rules 301-2
Fare Thee Well, Deacon Jones 172
Farther On Up The Road 151, 325
Fatback 24
Fat Man, The 119
■ *Fats On Fire* 97
Feel The Pain 331
■ *Festival Of American Songs* 69
Fever 147, 178, 276
First Love 229
Five Minutes More 91
Flip, Flop And Fly 198
Flying Home 140
Flyin' Saucers Rock'n'Roll 40
Foolish Dreams 274
Fool That I Am 107
For A Little While 53, 54
For You My Love 133
Four Letter Word 226
Four Walls 191
Frankie And Johnny 109, 330
Free At Last 151
Freeze, The 114, 325
Friendly Persuasion 247
■ *From Harlem To Camden* 152
Frosty 113, 114
Frosty The Snowman 195

Index of Songs & Album Titles

Funny How Time Slips Away 189
Gamblin' Man 31
Gatemouth Boogie 123
Gate's Tune 125
Gee Baby 325
Georgia Slop 97
Georgia Town 180
■ *Getaway With Fats* 97
Get Your Mind Out Of The Gutter 138
Ghost Of A Chance 180
Gingercake 144
Gini Bon Beni 290
Girl I'm Gonna Marry, The 97
Give Me Back My Cadillac 295
Give Thanks 263
Gloria 257
Glory Train 213
Going Back To Cleveland 172
Going Back To Louisiana 194, 313
Going Back To Santa Fe 131
Going To The River 59, 119
Goin' Steady 247
Gone Gone 330
Gone, Gone, Gone 53
Gonna Find Me A Bluebird 32
Gonna Walk And Talk With My Lord 248
Good Golly Miss Molly 35, 94
Good Morning Judge 39
Good Rockin' Daddy 109
Good Rockin' Tonight 205
■ *Good Timin' Man* 297
Goof, The 146
Goosebumps 78
■ *Gospel Music: The Legendary Master Series* 259
Gossip, Gossip, Gossip 71
Got Another Baby 206
Gotta Find A Way 99
Gotta Find My Foxhole Dream 89
Gotta Go Get My Baby 32
Gotta Rock 34
Gotta Travel On 280
Gotta Twist 240
Got To Get Enough
    Of Your Sweet Love Stuff 331
Got You On My Mind 289
Graduation Day 239
Grandaddy's Rockin' 76
Grandma's House 216
Grandpa Said Let's Susie-Q 227
Great Balls Of Fire 186, 249
Great Pretender, The 268
Green Door 94
Green Onions 115
Guess Who 129
Guitar Boogie Shuffle 21
Gypsy Man 30
Half A Loaf Of Bread 48
Half-Breed 32, 33
Half-Hearted Love 76

Halfway To Paradise 318
Handwriting On The Wall 310
Happy Baby 239
Happy Happy Birthday Baby 95, 239
Happy Times 318
Happy Vacation 198
Harlem Susie Kue 227
Harmonica Rock 114
Have Blues Will Travel 17
Have Yourself A Ball 237
Hawaiian Rock 249
Head Happy With Wine 138
Heartbeat 29
Heartbreak Hill 96, 97
Heartbreak Hotel 298
Hearts Of Stone 82, 83
Heaven 231
Heaven All Around Me 42
Heaven Came Down To Earth 130
Heavenly Father 177
He Called Me Baby 309
He Don't Love You 319
He'll Have To Go 247
Hello Josephine 61
    See also My Girl Josephine
Help Me Find My Baby 53, 54
Here Comes Henry 156
Here Comes That Song Again 282
(Here I Am) Drunk Again 37
Here's To You Darlin' 62
He's Always The Same 49
He Will Break Your Heart 319
Hey! Baby *[Bruce Channel]* 189, 192, 194, 312-3
Hey Baby *[Bill Lawrence]* 90-1
Hey Bossman 72
Hey, Good Lookin' 208
Hey Henry 109
Hey High School Baby 66, 67, 69
Hey Joe 215
Hey Miss Fannie 249
Hey Now 263
Hey Paula 189, 193, 194
Hide And Go Seek 208, 332
Hideaway Heart 38
High School Blues 232
High School Confidential 186
High Voltage 203
Hi-Heel Sneakers 56, 163
His Eye Is On The Sparrow 259
■ *Hits That Jumped* 230
Hi-Yo Silver 240
Hobo Boogie 144
Holding Back The Tears 72
■ *Holly In The Hills* 28
Home James 72
Hometown Jamboree 145
Hong Kong 164
Honey 30
Honey Don't 79

Index of Songs & Album Titles

Honeydripper, The 171
Honey I Still Love You 331
Honey Love 249
■ *Honkers & Screamers* 141
Honky Tonk 326
Honky Tonk Blues 40
Honky Tonk Hardwood Floor 231
Honky Tonk Heaven 37
Hoppin' With Hunter 144
Hot Barcarolle, The 239
Hot Dog *[Owens]* 104
Hot Dog *[Presley]* 156
Hot And Cold 23, 31
Hot Rock 84
Hotter Than A Pistol 239
Hound Dog 187, 195
House Of Blue Lights 30
House Warmin' Boogie 136, 137
How Important Can It Be 219
How Low Can You Feel 104
Hub Cap 49
Hucklebuck, The 239, 282
Hula Hop 267
Humble Bumble Bee 266
Husbands And Wives 283
I 280
I Ain't Gettin' Rid Of You 250
I Ain't No Fool 99
I Almost Lost My Mind 127, 129, 130
I Can't Afford To Lose Him 309
I Can't Help It 56
I Can't Stand It 275
I Caught You In The Act 331
■ *Ice Pickin'* 116
I Cried 290, 301
I Didn't Mean To Be Mean 102
■ *I Dig Acappella* 258
I Dig You Baby 34
I Don't Want To Be Lonely Tonight 214
I'd Rather Go Blind 107
I Dreamed About Mama Last Night 40
If 282
I Feel Jesus 49
If I Can't Have You 110
If I Could Love You Forever 332
If I Had Me A Woman 76, 77
If I Had Our Love To Live Over 96, 97
If It Ain't On The Menu 20
I Found A Love, Oh What A Love 314
I Found A Man In My Bed 331
I Found A New Love 96
I Found You 218, 220
If The Good Lord's Willing
  And The Creek Don't Rise 37, 42
If You Really Want Me To, I'll Go 194
If You Want My Lovin' 251
If You Want This Love 180
I Get That Feeling 151
I Got A Feeling 212-3
I Got A Wife 232

I Got A Woman 57
I Gotta Go Get My Baby 32
I Had A Love 154
I Hope You're Satisfied 109
I Know Who Threw
  The Whiskey In The Well 171
I'll Always Love You 67
I'll Be Gentle 77, 78
I'll Be Glad When You're Dead,
  You Rascal You 135
I'll Be Holding On 98
I'll Be Home For Christmas 261
I'll Be Seeing You 250, 252
I'll Be There 319
I'll Cry When You're Gone 263
I'll Get Along Somehow 176
I'll Keep You Happy 325
I'll Never Leave You, Baby 130
I Long To Hear Hank Sing The Blues 47
I Love You Because 58
I Love You Madly 161
I Love You, Yes I Do 171, 173
I'm A Fool 109
I'm A Fool To Care 192, 287, 289, 313
Imagination 258
I'm All Shook Up 250
I'm A Lovin' Man 158
I'm Black And I'm Proud 312, 324
I'm Doubtful Of Your Love 66
I'm Gonna Bid My Blues Goodbye 101
I'm Gonna Love Somebody Else's Woman 331
I'm Gonna Move 69
I'm Gonna Tell You Something 40
I'm Gonna Walk Out Of Your Life 97
I'm In Love Again 119
I'm Just Nobody 93
I'm Left, You're Right, She's Gone 216
I'm Looking For A Mustard Patch 47
I'm Movin' On 314
I'm Not Broke But I'm Badly Bent 40, 43
I'm Not Going To Work Today 306
■ *Imperial Rockabillies (Vol. 2)* 90
I'm Ready To Love You Now 309
I'm The Wolfman 213
I'm Walkin' 119
Indian Burial Ground 33
Indian Reservation 33
In Dreams 282
I Need A Whole Lotta You 72
I Need You 213
I Need You All The Time 263
I Need Your Love So Bad 180
I Need Your Love Tonight 238
I Need You So 129
I Never Picked Cotton 25
Insect Ball 145
In Study Hall 66
In The Jailhouse Now 137
I Play And Sing 319
I Put A Spell On You 161, 163, 164

Index of Songs & Album Titles

I Sez Baby 206
Is It Ever Gonna Happen 250
Isle Of Capri 198
I Smell A Rat 156
I Stand Accused 332
It Ain't Me 102
I Take A Trip To The Moon 216
It Happened Today 257
It Hurts Me 312
It'll Be My First Time 216
It May Sound Silly 130
It Must Be Love 96
It Must Be Wonderful 120
I Told You So 42
It's A Sin 132
It's Four In The Morning 30
It's Got The Whole World Shakin' 330
It's Music She Says 206
It's So Easy 29
Ittie Bittie Everything 66, 69
I've Got My Eyes On You 227
I've Had It 326
I Wanna 267
I Wanna Be Loved 213
I Wanna Go Country 59
I Wanna Hug Ya, Kiss Ya, Squeeze Ya 238
I Wanna Thank Your Folks 180
I Wanna Waltz 95
I Want A Bowlegged Woman 172
I Want To Love You 233
I Wouldn't Have You 53, 54
Jackpot 239
Jack The Ripper 209
Jam, The 220
■ *Jam, The* 209
Jam And Butter 325
Jambalaya 56
■ *James Brown Presents His Band And 5 More Great Artists* 120
Jay's Frantic 144
■ *Jay's Loose On Sunset* 152
Jay's Rock 147
Jealous Heart 129
Jesus Is Coming To Reign 49
Jesus Is My Only Friend 48
J.H. Boogie 21
Jivin' Jean 98
John Henry 56
■ *Johnnie Allan Sings* 300
Johnny Carroll Rock 87
John The Baptist 48
Jole Blon 288
Jukebox Baby 239
Juke Box Johnnie 40
Juke Joint Johnnie/Johnny 37, 38, 39, 40, 43
Jungle Juice 138
Junie Flip 144
Just A Dream 296
Just A Little Bit Of Everything 120
Just Around The Corner 96

Just Before Dawn 125
Just Crazy 146
Justice Blues 20
Just Out Of Reach 313
Just Relax 211, 212
K&H Boogie 144
Kaw-Liga 201
Keep A-Walkin' 179
Keep On 233, 313
Kiss Me 66
Knock On Wood 151
Knock Three Times 319
Ko Ko Mo 162
Kool Aide 115
La-Do-Dada 230, 231
Lana 282
Land Of A Thousand Dances 151
Land Of Make Believe, The 96, 97
Large Large House 235, 239
Last Kiss 189, 193, 313
Laugh 282
Lawdy Miss Clawdy 118
Leaping Guitar 191
Left Overs 116
Legend Of Joe Haney, The 49
Let 'Er Roll 104
Let Me Be Loved 248
Let Me Tell You 256
Let My Baby Be 57
Let's Babalu 267
Let's Do It 137
Let's Fall In Love 274
Let's Get Together Tonight 295
Let's Have A Party 95
Let's Split 144
Let's Twist Again 221, 237, 319
Let The Fool Kiss You 282
Let The Four Winds Blow 61
Letter Of Love 300
Let The Good Times Roll 282
Life's Valley 67
Like Long Hair 231
Linda Gail 291
Little Black Train 48
Little David 48
Little Eefin' Annie 306
Little Girl Don't Cry 171
Little Green Apples 308
Little Latin Lupe Lu 314
Little Mama 249, 295
Little Miss Linda 78
Little Pig 230, 231
Little Red Book 67, 68
Little Star 270
■ *Live At Cisco's* 144, 151
Liza Jane 230, 232
Loneliness 291, 295
Loneliness Had A Hold On Me 331
Lonely Boy 70
Lonely Days And Lonely Nights 289, 299

Index of Songs & Album Titles

Lonely Heart 55
Lonely Nights 232
Lonely Way 257
Lonesome Man Blues 40
Lonesome Town 213
Long Black Veil 62
Long Gone Lonesome Blues 283
Long Tall Sally 95, 194
Long Way From Memphis 323
Lonnie On The Move 326
Look Homeward Angel 270
Loretta 216, 217
Louise 49
Louisiana Man 288
Love All Night 265
Love-A, Love-A, Love-A 212
Love Express, The 282
Love Me All The Way 302
Love Me Do 192
Love Me 'Til Tomorrow Comes 331, 332
Love Of My Man, The 107
Love Pains 245
Love, Please Don't Let Me Down 127
Love's A Hurting Game 131
Love's A Job 62
Love's Gone Bad 314
Lovesick Blues 179
Love's Made A Fool Of You 28
Lovin' Bug 216
Lucille 195
Lula Belle 157, 158
Mad Mad World 226
Madness 180
Maggie Doesn't Work Here Anymore 267
Majesty Of Love, The 32
Major Label Blues 104
Make Me Feel A Little Good 158
■ *Make The World Go Away* 181
Make With The Shake 232
■ *Makin' Music* 21
Malagueña 221
Mama Of My Song 57, 58
Mambo Rock 238
Man Eater 141
Man, Like Wow! 248
Margie *[Fats Domino]* 119
Margie *[Young Jessie]* 157
Marie 56
Marine's Rock 91
Marita 114
Married Troubles 38
Marry Me 314
Mary Ann 206
Mary Is Fine 123
Mary Lou 153, 156, 219, 312
Mary, Oh Mary 97
Matchbox 55
Mathilda 289, 296
Maybe 86
May The Bird Of Paradise
    Fly Up Your Nose 125

Mean Mean Man 21, 95
Mean Woman Blues 56
Medley Of Soul 93, 98
Memphis Gal 171
Memphis Tennessee 323-4
Merry Black Christmas 331
■ *MGM Rockabilly Collection (Vol. 2)* 31, 125
Midnight 202
Midnight Dreams 144
Midnight Lace 99
Mighty Good 213
Milk Cow Blues 19
■ *Million Dollar Quartet, The* 127
Mine Again 37
Miss Bobby Sox 68
Miss Lucy 96
Misty Blue 29
Mojo Workout 314
Moments 152
Money Fever 138
Money Honey 95, 201
Money Money 66, 69
Monkeyshine, The 57, 58
Moonlight In Vermont 329
Moose On The Loose 171
■ *More Sex And Soul* 331
Move It On Over 18, 311
Movie Magg 55
Mr. Bang Bang Man 306
Mr. Blues 23, 24, 31, 33, 34
Mr. Bus Driver 233, 313
Mr. Hurt Walked In 97
Mr. Jones 98, 99
Mrs. Merguitory's Daughter 229
Mule Train Stomp 219
Mulholland Drive 191
Mumbles Blues 164
■ *Music City Soul* 98
■ *Music In His Soul* 309
Mustang Sally 276, 309
My Babe 216, 231, 232, 314
My Baby Don't Love No-One But Me 48
My Baby's Gone 299
My Blue Heaven 119
My Boy Lollipop 77
My Brand Of Blues 31, 32
My Bucket's Got A Hole In It 250
My Buddy 264
My Country Cousin 158
My Feet's On Solid Ground 47, 48
My Girl *[Robin Luke]* 91, 92
My Girl *[Temptations]* 330
My Girl Josephine 59, 61, 62
    See also Hello Josephine
My Great Loss (Ashes To Ashes) 310
My Little Rose 137
My Love For You 150
My Love Is Real 32
My Mommy Bought Me
    An Ice Cream Cone 244

Index of Songs & Album Titles

My Mother Is Your Mother's Sister 330
My Name Ain't Annie 267
My Need For Love 290
My Rockin' Baby 66
My Screamin' Screamin' Mimi 102
Mystery Train 216
My Time Is Expensive 123
My Two-Timing Woman 101
My Wife The Dancer 232
My Wish Came True 132
My Woman 131
Nature Boy 89
Nervous, Man, Nervous 262
Never Be Anyone Else But You 213
Never Had It So Good 314
New Love Tomorrow 257
New York Hey Hey 71
■ *New York To L.A., Acappella All The Way* 258
■ *Night Lights And Love Songs* 296
Nightmare 282
Night Owl Man 64
Night Ride 145
Night Train 152
Night Train To Memphis 281, 306
Nobody Has To Tell Me 309
No More Knockin' 329
No More, No More, No More 64
No-One Else 96
North To Alaska 300
■ *No Sad Songs* 308
Nosey Joe 172, 173
No Sin In Rhythm 196
Not My Kind Of People 72
Nothing But Soul 141
Not Too Long Ago 233
Oh Babe 94
Oh, I Apologize 325
Oh Lord, Why Lord 315
Oh My Papa 249
■ *Oh! Suzy Q* 226, 231
Oh, What A Face 137
Oh Yeah 212
Okie Dokie Stomp 123, 125
Oklahoma Hills 33, 244
Old Barn Dance 101
Old Black Joe 187
Old Macdonald 262
Old Oaken Bucket, The 251
Old Spinning Wheel, The 56
On Bended Knee 291
Once In A While 256, 270
One Day Later 250
One Dozen Roses 72, 233
One More Chance 150, 295
One Night Stands 211
One Of The Ruins That Oliver Cromwell Knocked About A Bit 144
One Of These Days 57, 58
One Potato, Two Potato 237
Only The Lonely 280, 281

Only Woman, The 72
Only You 67, 261, 265-6, 268
On The Edge Of Town 329
Oochie Pachie 267
Oochi Pachi 267
Ooh, Baby Baby 258
Open Letter To The President 331
Open The Door Richard 140
Opportunity 276
■ *Other Song Of The South, The* 289
Our Teenage Love 295
Out Of Control 37, 42
Out Of My Heart 257
Over The Rainbow 270
Pachuko Hop 178
Pale Dry Boogie 123
Paleface Indian, The 33
Papa Loves Mambo 238
Park Boulevard Blues 221
Part Time Love 168
Party Doll 27
Patent Leather Boots 101
Peace Of Mind 86
Peanuts 189
Peepin' Through The Window 332
Pennies From Heaven 257
Penthouse Serenade 146
Peter Gunn 221
■ *Philadelphia's Greatest* 258
Piano Nellie 96
Pick Up The Pieces 332
Pigalle Lover 138
Pinetop's Boogie Woogie 240
Pistol Packin' Mama 323
Play It Cool 102
Please Have Mercy 267
Please Mr. Mayor 22, 24
Please Please Me 325
Please, Please, Please 309
Poison Love 283
Pony Time 240
Poor Boy 202
Poor Folks 163
Poor Little Fool 212
Poor Little Heart 211-2
Poor Little Rich Boy 91
Poor Me 119
Por Favor 239
Potato Peeler 220
Pretty Little Girl 212
Pretty Mama 104
Pretty Mama Blues 129
Pretty Please 219
Prison Cell Blues 130
Prisoner's Song 288
Promised Land 287, 289, 297, 300, 301
Psycho 19
Pull Down The Blinds 40
Pushover 107
Pyramid Club 18

Index of Songs & Album Titles

Quit Your Triflin' 102
Raindrops In A River 18
Ramblin' Heart 46
Ramblin' Rose 239
Raunchy 86
Rawhide 209
Real Crazy Cool 144
Reap What You Sow 276
Reconsider Me 230
Recorded In England 295
Red River Rock 201, 202
Red We Want Is The Red We've Got, The (In The Old Red, White And Blue) 238
Reelin' And Rockin' 97, 212
Release Me 23, 97, 313
Remember Then 271
Remember You're Mine 208
Restless 55
Reveille Rock 202
Revival 203
Riff Runner 150
Right By My Side 213
Ring-A-Ding-A-Ding 247
Ring My Phone 247
Rip It Up 94
Rip Van Winkle 256, 271
Riverboat Blues 49
Roadhouse Boogie 144
Robber 208
■ *Rockabilly 1958* 92
■ *Rockabilly Kings* 78
Rock-A-Bye 240
Rock & Roll Ruby 84
Rock & Roll Waltz 282
■ *Rockaphilly* 198
Rock Around The Clock 235
Rock Candy 147
Rockin' By Myself 221
Rocking Goose 203
Rocking Pneumonia And The Boogie Woogie Flu 330
Rocking Redwing 158
Rockin' Is Our Bizness 199
Rockin' Maybelle 85
■ *Rockin' Rollin' Rainwater* 31
Rock It 104
Rock, Maggie, Rock 24
Rock Me All Night 332
Rock'n'Roll Boogie 94
■ *Rock'n'Roll Heaven* 99
Rock'n'Roll Record Gal 94
Rock, Pretty Baby 249
Rock The Joint 195
■ *Rod Bernard* 296
Rollin' To The Jukebox Rock 66, 68
Roll With Me Henry *[The Wallflower]* 107-8, 167
Rootie Tootie 18
Roses Of Picardy 264, 265
■ *Roulette Rock'n'Roll Collection* 201

Rubberlegs 167
Ruby Baby 219
Ruby, Don't Take Your Love To Town 30
Rumble 205, 209
Run Come See 87
Run Red Run 158
Running Bear 158
Running Scared 281
Rye Whiskey 101
Sad, Bad, Glad 138
Sadie Green 169
Sad Story 145
Saga Of The Beatles, The 204
Saints, The 96
    See also When The Saints Go Marching In
Saints Rock'n'Roll, The 238
Salt Peanuts 176
Salvation 201, 203
■ *San Antonio Ballbuster* 123
San Antonio Rose 56, 150
■ *Sands At The Sands* 250
Sandstorm 201
■ *Sandstorm* 249, 252
Santa Fe, The 130
Satisfied 325
■ *Saturday Hop* 295
Save Us Preacher Davis 239
Saving My Love 180
Say, Has Anyone Seen My Sweet Gypsy Rose 319
Say So 78
Say Something Nice To Me 325
Say What You Mean 196
Say When 55
School Bus Love Affair 91
Scrumptious Baby 102
Sea Of Love 287, 290
Searchin' 156, 233
Secret Of Love, The 288, 300
See You Later Alligator 226
See You Soon Baboon 226, 227
Sentimental Reasons 257
Set Me Free 291
■ *Sex And Soul* 331
Sexy Ways 83
Shaft 319
Shake A Hand 235, 237, 240
Shake It Up Mambo 266
Shake, Rattle And Roll 157
Shake The Hand Of A Fool 220
Shanty Boat Blues 49
Share Your Love With Me 62
Sheba 201
She Cried For Me 71
She Don't Come Here Anymore 315
She Kept On Walkin' 331
She Loved Everybody But Me 72
Sherry's Lips 29
She's Gone *[McGhee]* 137

355

Index of Songs & Album Titles

She's Gone *[Rainwater]* 31
She's Gone (She Took The TV
　　　　　And Telephone) 332
She's Mine 133
She's The One 97
She Still Thinks I Care 43
She's Walking Toward Me 301
She Wants To Rock 154, 156
Ship Of Love 255
Shooty Booty 131
Shoppin' For Clothes 25
Short Shorts 251
Short Walk 178, 179, 180
Shotgun Boogie 46
Shotgun Wedding 329-330, 331
Shout 163
Shuffle, The 219
Shuffle In The Gravel 156-7
Shutters And Boards 251
Sick And Tired 119, 206
Signifying Monkey, The 57
■ *Simon Pure Soul* 308
■ *Simon Sings* 308
Since I Met You Baby 127, 130-1, 132
Since I Met You Jesus 130
Sing, Boy, Sing 249
■ *Sing, Boy, Sing* 248
Six To Eight 138
Sixteen Tons 47, 265
Sixteen Tons Rock'n'Roll 47
■ *Sixteen Tons Rock'n'Roll* 45
Skinny Minnie Shimmy 40
Sky Is Crying, The 310
Sleep In Job 138
Smoke! Smoke! Smoke! (That Cigarette) 244
Smokey Joe 276
Snag 209
Sneaky Pete 171
Sno Cone 113
Snowbird 19, 48
Sock It To Me Baby 315
Soda Pop 133
Soda Pop Pop 248
So Fine 311
So Lonely 216
So Long 119
So Many Memories 96
Somebody Else's Heart 72
Somebody Help Me 78
Someday, One Day 216
Some Kind Of Wonderful 318
Something's Got A Hold On Me 110
Somewhere On Skid Row 300, 302
So Much Trouble 138
Son Of Hickory Holler's Tramp, The 30
So Tough 191
Soul Express 325
Soul Food 276
South To Louisiana 300
■ *South To Louisiana* 300

Southern Menu 136
Southtown, USA 306
Speedoo 258
Spin The Bottle 66, 67
Spo-Dee-O-Dee 135
Spoonful 110
Spring Fever 281
Squat, The 150
Stackolee 128, 203
Stand By Me 317
Starving For Love 309
State Street 180
Stay 332
■ *Steady Date With Tommy Sands* 247
Steady With Betty 66, 67
Steel Guitar Rag 103
Sticks And Stones 24
Stingy Thing 83
Stop Beatin' Around The Mulberry Bush 238
Stop Giving Your Man Away 309
Stop, It's Wonderful 238
Stop The Wedding 110
Stop Truckin' And Susie-Q 227
Stormy Weather 257
Story Behind The Story, The 99
Story Of My Life, The 96
Story Untold 255
Stranger In My Own Home Town 312
Strange Things Happening 312
■ *Strike Like Lightning* 326
Strollin' Blues 91
Such A Night 249
Sugar 86
Sugar Baby 85, 86
Sugaree 49
Summer (The First Time) 30
Summertime 125
Summertime Blues 212
Sunday Kind Of Love 257
Sundown And Sorrow 42
Sunny 306
Sunshine 30
Superman 230
Susie Darlin' 91, 92
Susie-Q 216, 217, 225, 226-9, 231, 232
Swag, The 209
■ *Swamp Gold* 289
Sweet Black Angel 308
Sweet Dreams 215, 289
Sweeter Than You 213
Sweetie Pie 233
Sweets For My Sweet 320
Swing, Daddy, Swing 226
Switchblade 209
Syrup Soppin' Blues 245
Take Good Care Of My Baby 318
Take It Away Lucky 18, 20
Take Me Back, Take Me Back 267
Take My Heart 231
Take The Ring Off Your Finger 72

Index of Songs & Album Titles

Take What He's Got 107
Takin' A Chance 212
Talk About A Party 21, 25
Talkin' About You 319
Talking Slim Blues 115, 116
Talk To Me 300
Tallahassee Lassie 232
T.D.'s Boogie 240
Teacher Gimme Back 158
Tears In The Eyes Of A Potato 49
Tears Of Joy 109
Teasin' 219
Teenage Crush 247, 252
Teenage Cutie 206
Teenage Doll 249
Teenage Dolly 233
Teenage Fairy Tales 239
Teenage Hop 145
Teenage Party 180
Teenage Prayer 238
Teen Queen Of The Week 220
Tell Him No 230
Tell Me Why 163
Tell The World 265
Ten Commandments Of Love 257
Tennessee Houn' Dog Yodel 32
Tennessee Waltz 206
Tennessee Waltz Blues 137
Tension 325
■ *Texabilly* 88
That Ain't Nothin' But Right 77
That First Guitar Of Mine 46
That'll Be The Day 28
That Lucky Old Sun 280, 281
That's All I Want From You 248
That's All Right 19, 39
That's Enough For Me 157
■ *That Shotgun Wedding Man* 330
That's My Desire 176
Thaw-Out 115
There Goes That Train 329
There Is Something On Your Mind
 148, 150, 167, 325, 330
There's A Moon Out Tonight 256, 271
■ *There's A Party Goin' On* 25
■ *There's Good Rockin' Tonite* 209
These Hands 19
They're Not Worth The Paper 40
Things I Used To Do, The 115, 288
Think It Over 29
This Life I Live 301
This Should Go On Forever 287, 288, 289,
 291, 292-3, 299
■ *This Should Go On Forever
 And Other Bayou Classics* 296
Those Lonely, Lonely Nights 288, 291
Those Oldies But Goodies 256, 271
Thought Of Losing You, The 104
Three Bells, The 280
Three Hearts In A Tangle 42, 325

Tie A Yellow Ribbon
 Round The Ole Oak Tree 319
Tijuana 206
Time And Again 281
Tiny Praying Hands 62
Tips Of My Fingers 25
To Love In Vain 323
Tondolayo 144
Tonight (Could Be The Night) 281
Tonight's The Night 309
Too Hot To Handle 18, 41
Too Old To Cut The Mustard 47
Too Rock For Country,
 Too Country For Rock And Roll 326
Tornado 230
Torquay 29
To The Ends Of The Earth 239
Touchdown 72
Touch Me (I'll Be Your Fool Once More) 99
Tough Lover 109
Treat Her Right 314
Trees 264
■ *Tribute To Shorty Horton* 208, 222
Trophy Run 219, 233
Troubles, Troubles, Troubles 151
■ *Truckin' With Albert Collins* 115
Trying To Get To You 84
Tumblin' Tumbleweed 99
Turn Around 55
Turn On Your Love Light 326
Twenty Feet Of Muddy Water 190
Twilight Time 261
Twin Exhaust 220
Twistin' Pneumonia 330
Two Hound Dogs 239
Two Of A Kind 29
Unchained Melody 270
Under A Mexico Moon 40
Unhappy Woman Blues 144
Valley Of Tears 96
Valley Of The Moon 33
■ *Velvet Soul For Lovers Only* 258
Victim Of Life's Circumstances 297
Voo-Vee-Ah-Be 266
Wailin' And Sailin' 138
Wake Me Up Sweet Jesus 47, 48
Wake Up Baby 192
Wallflower, The – *See* Roll With Me Henry
Wanderin' Eyes 195, 199
Wasted Days And Wasted Nights 289
Watch My Signals 169
Watch Your Step 325
We Belong Together 208
We'd Destroy Each Other 72
Wedding Is Over, The 330
Wee Wee Hours 137
We Got Love 78
Welcome Home 30
Welcome Home Elvis 89
Well Now Dig This 239

357

Index of Songs & Album Titles

We're Gonna Move 312
We're In Love 109
We're On The Road To Hell 331
Western Union 233
Wham! 324, 325
Whammy, The 161, 162, 163
■ *Wham Of That Memphis Man, The* 321, 325
What Are You Doing Sunday 319
What'd I Say 56, 186
What Kind Of Man Are You 151
What'll I Do 76
What Now My Love 314
What's Your Name 329
What You Want 78
When 220
When I Fall In Love 257
When I Go A-Dreamin' 238
When My Blue Moon Turns To Gold Again 96
When The Cats Come Marching In 238
When The Saints Go Marching In 203
    See also Saints, The
When The Wind Blows In Chicago 251
When Two Ends Meet 104
When Will I Be Loved 330
Where Or When 270
Where There's A Will There's A Way
    315, 324, 326
■ *Where Will I Shelter My Sheep Tonight?* 49
Whiskers 218
Whiskey, Women And Loaded Dice 137
Who Do You Love 232
Whole Lot Of Shakin' Going On 61, 186
Whole Lotta Woman 31, 33, 34, 35
Who Shot A Hole In My Sombrero 244
Who's That Knockin' 329
Who Threw The Whiskey In The Well 171
Why 315, 325, 326
Why Baby Why 20
Why Cry 83
Why Did You Have To Go And
    Leave Me Lonesome Blues 31, 34
Why Did You Lie To Me 41
Why Doncha Be My Girl 97
Why Don't You Haul Off And Love Me
    171, 172
Why I Like Roosevelt 259
Why Must We Go To School 257
Wicked Woman 250
Wild Guy 219
Wild Wig 141
Wild Wild Women 84, 85
Wild, Wild World 226, 231
Wild Wild Young Men 84
Wildwood Boogie 237
Will You Love Me Tomorrow 318
Willie And The Hand Jive 312
Willie The Cool Cat 144
Wind Me Up 29
Wine 29
Wine, Wine, Wine 78, 133

Wishing 28
Without A Love 150, 151
With Pen In Hand 30
Woke Up This Morning 257
W-O-M-A-N 109
Wonder Of You, The 213
Work With Me Annie 107, 267
Worried Mind 127
Worryin' Kind, The 249, 250, 252
Worthless And Lowdown 179
Wrong Door, The 157
Yeah Yeah 232
Yeah Yeah Yeah 98
Yes I Know 262, 264
Yes, I'm Loving You 96
Yes, I Want You 131
Yes Master 89
Yesterday 136
Yesterday When I Was Young 25
You Ain't Treatin' Me Right 77
You Are The Only One 213
You Better Get Ready 49
You Better Go Now 238
You Can't Stop Me From Dreaming 91
You Done Me Bad 283
You Don't Have To Go 151
You Don't Know What You've Got 310
You Got Me (Where You Want Me) 109
You Got Me Whistling 300
You Got Money 123
You Gotta Go 238
You Made Me Cry 266
You Never Miss Your Water 97
Young Blood 156
Young Jessie Bossa Nova 158
Your Daddy Wants To Do Right 248
Your Picture 300
You're A Bundle Of Love 69
You're Crying 257
You're Jealous 290
You're My Special Baby 77
You're On My Mind 293
You're Something Else 325
You're The One 78, 192
Your Picture 300
Your True Love 79
You Two-Timed Me One Time Too Often 83
You've Got A Spell On Me 290
You Win Again 56, 188
Zup Zup 272

INDEX OF FILMS & SHOWS

All Gold Oldies Show 161
American Bandstand 69, 102, 191, 198, 199, 229, 240, 276, 293, 295, 302, 313
American Hot Wax 164
American Song Festival 89
Arthur Godfrey's Talent Scouts 32
Autumn's On Adams 177
Barn Dance 244
Battle Of The Blues 137
Battle Of The Saxes 146
Beat Room 57
Be My Guest 58
Best Unknown Guitarist In The World, The 222
Big D Jamboree 75, 76, 78, 83, 86
Big Town, The 43
Bingo Long 153
Boogie Time 291
Caister Rock'n'Roll Festival 152
Caravan Of The Stars 306
Car Wash 153
Christmas Shower Of Stars 77
Cotton Club Revue 226
Curse Of The Coffin, The 162
Destination Moon 77
Dinner Bell Show 46
Ebony Showcase 262
Ed Sullivan Show 110
Flesh And Blood 247
For Richer Or Poorer 43
Girl Can't Help It, The 68, 248
Godzilla 85
Grand Ole Opry 38, 45, 46, 50, 82, 121, 127, 132, 321, 326
Happy Hal Burns Show 46
Hee Haw 22, 25
Hemsby Rock'n'Roll Festival 43
Hoedown Corner 245
Hometown Jamboree 246
Honky Tonk 297
Horn & Hardart Children's Hour 236
James Dean Story, The 248
Joe Loss Pop Show 56
Jukebox Doubles 203
Juke Box Jury 132
Kat Kingdom 256
Larry Kane Show 300
Louisiana Hayride 85, 216, 226, 229, 230, 244, 298
Love Me Tender 248
Loving You 102
Magic Fallacy, The 245
Mardi Gras 250

Mean Streets 271
Metro Magazine All-Star Jazz Concert 173
Mid-Day Merry-Go-Round 47
Midnight Shift 150
Mid-Western Jamboree 38
Milton Berle Show 250
Monterey Jazz Festival 127, 132
Mystery Train 164
National Folk Festival 50
New Faces Of 1936 238
Oklahoma Bandstand 216, 231
Old Grey Whistle Test 117
Open House 245
Oscar Awards Ceremony 247
Ozark Jubilee 32, 34, 64
Paul Whiteman Teen Show 196
Perry Como Show 92
Pop Inn 193
R&B Jamboree 158
R&B Show '64 57
Ready Steady Go 54, 56, 276
Red Garters 245
Rock All Night 68
Rock & Roll Revival 204
Rock, Baby, Rock It 81, 84, 86
Rock, Pretty Baby 249
Roots Of Rock'n'Roll 120
Saturday Club 54, 56, 57
Scott Joplin Story, The 153
Sincerely The Blues 173
Sing, Boy, Sing 248, 252
Sing Country 93
Singin' Idol, The 246, 247
Smoke 164
Soap 89
Stars From Blackpool 195
Starsky And Hutch 117
Stranger Than Paradise 164
Tennessee Song Bag 33
Thank Your Lucky Stars 162
This Is Your Life 247
Tommy's Corral 246
Top Gear 56, 57
Top Ten Revue 147
Town And Country Time 23
United Artists Dance Party 43
West Side Story 270

ILLUSTRATIONS & PHOTO CREDITS

Main cover photo: Big Jay McNeely (© 1984 Paul Harris).

Photo strip on cover *(left to right, starting on back cover)*: Big Al Downing (author's collection); Tommy Sands (courtesy Bear Family Records); Big Jim Wynn (courtesy Showtime Music Archives (Toronto)); Platters (courtesy George R. White); Jerry Lee Lewis (© 1978 Paul Harris); Screamin' Jay Hawkins (© 1965 Brian Smith); Link Wray (courtesy George R. White); Rod Bernard (courtesy George R. White/Jin Records).

Ad on page 36 courtesy author's collection; ad on page 278 courtesy Tony Watson.

Photo credits: page 16 from author's collection/courtesy Look Records; pages 22 and 322 courtesy Showtime Music Archives (Toronto)/Capitol Records; page 26 ©1979 Graham Barker; page 33 from author's collection/courtesy Marvin Rainwater Friendship Club; pages 34, 74, 77, 90, 177 and 210 from author's collection; page 41 courtesy Lattie Moore/Ian Wallis; page 44 courtesy Bear Family Records/Colin Escott; page 52 courtesy Brian Smith/Columbia Records; page 56 ©1964 Brian Smith; page 60 courtesy Showtime Music Archives (Toronto)/Colin Escott/Bill Cantrell; pages 65 and 80 courtesy of *Now Dig This*; pages 95 and 228 courtesy Showtime Music Archives (Toronto)/Colin Escott; page 98 ©1997 Paul Harris; page 100 from author's collection/courtesy Rollin' Rock Records; pages 103, 170, 242, 260 and 307 courtesy Showtime Music Archives (Toronto); page 106 courtesy Showtime Music Archives (Toronto)/Modern Records; page 112 from author's collection/courtesy Alligator Records (photo by Herb Nichols); page 116 ©1987 Paul Harris; page 118 ©1981 Paul Harris; page 122 ©1995 Paul Harris; page 124 ©1989 Brian Smith; page 128 courtesy Brian Smith/ABC-TV; page 131 courtesy George R. White; page 134 courtesy Showtime Music Archives (Toronto)/Atlantic Records; page 142 ©1984 Paul Harris; pages 149, 155 and 157 ©1983 Paul Harris; page 160 ©1965 Brian Smith; page 166 ©1976 Norbert Hess, Berlin; page 184 courtesy Ian Wallis; page 186 ©1978 Paul Harris; page 190 courtesy Michael H. Price Archive, Pasadena Beach; page 197 from author's collection/courtesy Decca Records; page 200 courtesy Showtime Music Archives (Toronto)/London Records; page 207 ©1996 Brian Smith; page 217 ©1972 Sandy Fenner/courtesy Bob Embrey; page 224 courtesy George R. White/Chess Records; page 234 courtesy Bear Family Records; page 263 courtesy Brian Smith/20th Century Fox Pictures; page 275 courtesy Showtime Music Archives (Toronto) and Atlas/Angletone Records; page 292 from author's collection/courtesy Rod Bernard; page 294 ©1979 Paul Harris; page 299 from author's collection/courtesy Jin Records; page 301 ©1986 Paul Harris; page 316 from author's collection/courtesy ABC-TV; page 328 from author's collection/courtesy Ember Records.

OTHER TITLES FROM MUSIC MENTOR BOOKS

(35 Years of) British Hit EPs
George R. White
ISBN 0-9519888-1-6 *(pbk, 256 pages)* 2001   RRP £16.99

At last, a chart book dedicated to British hit EPs! Includes a history of the format, an artist-by-artist listing of every 7-inch EP hit from 1955 to 1989 (with full track details for each record), analyses of chart performance, and — for the first time ever — the official UK EP charts reproduced in their entirety. Profusely illustrated with *over 600* sleeve shots. A collector's dream!

Long Distance Information: Chuck Berry's Recorded Legacy
Fred Rothwell
ISBN 0-9519888-2-4 *(pbk, 352 pages)* 2001   RRP £18.99

Detailed analysis of every recording Chuck Berry has ever made. Includes an overview of his life and career, his influences, the stories behind his most famous compositions, full session details, listings of all his key US/UK vinyl and CD releases (including track details), TV and film appearances, and much, much more. Over 100 illustrations including label shots, vintage ads and previously unpublished photos.

On The Road
Dave Nicolson
ISBN 0-9519888-4-0 *(pbk, 256 pages)* 2002   RRP £16.99

Gary 'US' Bonds, Pat Boone, Freddy Cannon, Crickets Jerry Allison, Sonny Curtis and Joe B. Mauldin, Bo Diddley, Dion, Fats Domino, Duane Eddy, Frankie Ford, Charlie Gracie, Brian Hyland, Marv Johnson, Ben E. King, Brenda Lee, Little Eva, Chris Montez, Johnny Moore (Drifters), Gene Pitney, Johnny Preston, Tommy Roe, Del Shannon, Edwin Starr, Johnny Tillotson and Bobby Vee tell the fascinating stories of their careers as hitmakers and beyond. Over 150 illustrations.

Elvis & Buddy — Linked Lives
Alan Mann
ISBN 0-9519888-5-9 *(pbk, 160 pages)* 2002   RRP £12.99

The achievements of Elvis Presley and Buddy Holly have been extensively documented, but until now little if anything has been known about the many ways in which their lives were interconnected. For the first time anywhere, rock & roll expert Alan Mann, author of *The A–Z Of Buddy Holly*, takes a detailed look at each artist's early years, comparing their backgrounds and influences, chronicling all their meetings and examining the many amazing parallels in their lives, careers and tragic deaths. Over 50 illustrations including many rare/previously unpublished.

American Rock'n'Roll – The UK Tours 1956-72
Ian Wallis
ISBN 0-9519888-6-7 *(pbk, 424 pages)* 2003   RRP £21.99

The first-ever detailed overview of every visit to these shores by American (and Canadian!) rock'n'rollers. Includes full tour itineraries, supporting acts, show reports, TV appearances and other items of interest. Illustrated with vintage ads, original tour programmes and atmospheric live shots. A fascinating and nostalgic insight into a bygone era.

Elvis: A Musical Inventory 1939-55
Richard Boussiron
ISBN 0-9519888-7-5 *(pbk, 264 pages)* 2004   RRP £17.99

An extraordinarily detailed listing of the King's earliest musical influences – songs he learned at school, spirituals he sang at church, numbers he performed on the radio, etc. The product of over 30 years' original research including interviews with a host of people who knew him including his teacher, church ministers and neighbours. And, for the first time anywhere, complete details of all the historic Sun sessions — taken directly from the personal files of Marion Keisker. A 'must have' for anyone with an interest in early Elvis.

**Music Mentor books
are available from all good bookshops
or by mail order from:**

Music Mentor Books
69 Station Road
Upper Poppleton
YORK YO26 6PZ
England

Telephone/Fax: 01904 330308
International Telephone/Fax: +44 1904 330308
email: music.mentor@ntlworld.com
website: http://musicmentor0.tripod.com